jQuery UI in Action

jQuery UI in Action

TJ VANTOLL

MANNING

Shelter Island

For online information and ordering of this and other Manning books, please visit
www.manning.com. The publisher offers discounts on this book when ordered in quantity.
For more information, please contact

> Special Sales Department
> Manning Publications Co.
> 20 Baldwin Road
> PO Box 761
> Shelter Island, NY 11964
> Email: orders@manning.com

Manning Publications Co.
20 Baldwin Road
Shelter Island, NY 11964

Development editor:	Sean Dennis
Technical development editor:	Teresa Burger
Copyeditor:	Teresa Wilson
Proofreader:	Elizabeth Martin
Typesetter:	Gordan Salinovic
Cover designer:	Marija Tudor

ISBN 9781617291937
Printed in the United States of America
1 2 3 4 5 6 7 8 9 10 – EBM – 19 18 17 16 15 14

brief contents

contents

12 Under the hood of jQuery UI 287

foreword

jQuery has taken the web development community by storm. It has done this by building an API that is approachable for designers and new developers while simultaneously providing the power and extensibility desired by the most advanced and experienced developers. jQuery is easy to learn, easy to extend, and paves over browser differences, making it the go-to choice for millions of developers.

jQuery UI takes the same philosophies used to build jQuery and applies them to various aspects of UI creation. Building elegant interfaces with powerful, customizable widgets should be just as easy as showing and hiding elements. jQuery UI delivers on this promise while addressing often ignored issues such as accessibility and extensibility.

jQuery UI has built a solid base over the past seven years and the number of users is growing steadily. But the web is evolving at a rapid pace and new JavaScript libraries and UI toolkits are popping up left and right. Choosing the right tools for your next project can be quite daunting. *jQuery UI in Action* shows how to leverage jQuery UI to quickly build an application or just add an extra touch of interaction on an existing page.

This book will serve as a fantastic resource for anyone interested in getting started with jQuery UI. As always, TJ has done a great job of walking through tasks in detail and pointing out potential pitfalls. TJ's dedication and desire to help others has been an invaluable asset, not just to jQuery UI, but to the web development community as a whole. I'm sure you'll feel the same way after reading this book.

SCOTT GONZÁLEZ
PROJECT LEAD, JQUERY UI

preface

In 2013 Manning contacted me about writing a book on jQuery UI. Because I had been an enthusiastic user of the library for five years, and had been a member of the jQuery team for approximately two years, I had a lot of experience and knowledge that I wanted to share with the world. I said Yes!

From the start, I made it clear that I wanted to take a different tack with this book: rather than reprinting the library's API documentation in a book, which is something I think far too many tech books do, I wanted to write about how to use the jQuery UI components in real-world usage scenarios and applications. I also wanted to tackle the tough questions for jQuery UI users. Why should you use the jQuery UI datepicker instead of the native date picker included in HTML5? How do you use jQuery UI on mobile devices, especially in low bandwidth situations?

From start to finish the book took about a year and a half to complete, and although it was an exhausting amount of work, I'm extremely happy with the result. jQuery UI is a stable library that helps you write robust, accessible, and cross-browser friendly web applications today. This book represents my attempt to share the knowledge I've gained from building countless projects with jQuery UI, and from working as a member of the jQuery team. I hope you enjoy it.

acknowledgments

I never thought that I would be writing one of these … I feel like I'm at the Oscars or something. Although I hate to list specific names, as it will force me to exclude people I should thank and it'll be totally awkward the next time I see them, I'll do it anyway … otherwise this section would be kind of boring.

I'll start with Scott González, who brought me into the jQuery project, walked me through countless jQuery concepts, and has always been around to help with any problem I run into. In addition to helping me with all things jQuery UI over the last few years, Scott also contributed the foreword to this book.

Next I'll thank Jörn Zaefferer, whose expertise has made me a better developer during my time with jQuery UI. I asked Jörn to perform the technical review of this book because I felt he was the most qualified person for the job (he is the original author of a good chunk of the jQuery UI source), and I wasn't disappointed. The book is unquestionably better because of Jörn.

The entire jQuery UI team has either directly or indirectly helped make this book a reality, so I'd also like to thank Kris Borchers, Felix Nagel, Corey Frang, Mike Sherov, Rafael Xavier, and Alexander Schmitz.

The people at Manning have been great through the long and arduous process of writing a technical book. My development editor, Sean Dennis, not only provided great feedback throughout, but also took care of managing the various tedious processes involved in writing and publishing a book. Robin de Jongh was the one who asked me to write this book and was a great guy to talk to throughout the process. Without him there would be no book.

The following peer reviewers also provided invaluable insights, reading the manuscript a number of times during its development and I'd like to acknowledge them here: Linda Carver, A. Krishna Chaitanya, Alain Couniot, Jürgen De Commer, Dave Corun, Cole Davisson, Mark Elston, Peter Empen, Ed Griebel, Al Scherer, Natalia Stavisky, Philip Taffet, and Gregor Zurowski.

But without question, the lion's share of thanks goes to my beautiful and talented significant other, Trish. In addition to providing desperately needed moral support throughout the harrowing journey that was the writing of this book, Trish also helped shape the structure and flow of the chapters with her own development expertise (as well as her brutally honest criticism). And because she has a wizard-like ability to bend CSS to her will, she *may* even have had her hand in the book's examples directly.

Thank you, Trisha. I love you.

about this book

jQuery UI in Action's primary purpose is to teach you how to use the jQuery UI library to build rich, user-friendly web applications. The book starts with the basics of creating and modifying widgets, and moves on to a series of complex examples, such as building widgets from scratch, optimizing your applications for production, and even building a complete flight-search application.

This book assumes that you have basic knowledge of CSS, JavaScript, and jQuery. If you're not an expert don't despair—when intermediate- and advanced-level concepts are brought up, they're explained. If you're finding yourself a bit overwhelmed, appendix A discusses resources for getting up to speed. On the flip side, if you're an expert don't despair either. You'll build a number of real-world examples and discuss advanced aspects of the library throughout the book.

Roadmap

This book is organized into three parts.

Part 1 provides an introduction to jQuery UI. Chapter 1 introduces the library itself, with an explanation of what is in the library, what the library does well, and what it doesn't do well. Chapter 2 explains the ins and outs of widgets, the core building blocks of jQuery UI.

Part 2 walks through the core components of jQuery UI, starting with its widgets. Chapter 3 introduces the five jQuery UI form widgets, uses them to build a complete form, and compares the widgets to their HTML5 counterparts. Chapter 4 discusses the three jQuery UI layout widgets and the four utility widgets. Chapter 5 introduces the five interaction widgets, and uses them to build a series of real-world interfaces, as well as a few games. Chapter 6 contains a thorough discussion of the jQuery UI effects and chapter 7 explains everything about jQuery UI themes.

Part 3 builds upon the core knowledge taught in part 2 to show a series of advanced topics. Chapter 8 shows how to build your own widgets from scratch, using the same mechanism jQuery UI uses. Chapter 9 shows how to customize the behavior of any widget using widget extensions. Chapter 10 teaches how to prepare a jQuery UI application for production usage, including applying several performance optimizations. Chapter 11 builds upon all this knowledge to explain how to build a complete flight-search application. And finally, chapter 12 looks under the hood of the library, to show the tools that jQuery UI uses to make jQuery UI work.

There are 6 appendixes. Appendix A covers the best ways to learn jQuery. How jQuery UI tests its own widgets (jQuery UI tests jQuery UI!) is the focus of appendix B. Appendix C focuses on using jQuery UI with Backbone. Appendix D is about globalization. Ways to contribute to jQuery UI are explained in appendix E, and polyfilling HTML5 with jQuery UI is touched on in appendix F.

Code conventions

jQuery in Action provides copious examples that show how you can make use of each of the topics covered. Source code in listings or in text appears in a `fixed-width font like this` to separate it from ordinary text. In addition, class and method names, object properties, and other code-related terms and content in text are presented using the same `fixed-width font`.

Code annotations accompany many of the listings, highlighting important concepts. In some cases, numbered cueballs link to additional explanations that follow the listing.

Getting the source code

You can access the source code for all examples in the book from the publisher's website at www.manning.com/jQueryinAction. All source code for the project is also hosted at GitHub, a commercial Git hosting firm, at https://github.com/tjvantoll/jquery-ui-in-action-demos. We will maintain the current URL via the publisher's website. The source is maintained by chapter, so, for example, you can download /source-code/ch06 and you will have a full copy of the source code up to that point in the book.

Author Online

Purchase of *jQuery UI in Action* includes free access to a private web forum run by Manning Publications where you can make comments about the book, ask technical questions, and receive help from the author and from other users. To access the forum and subscribe to it, point your web browser to www.manning.com/jQueryUIinAction. This page provides information on how to get on the forum once you're registered, what kind of help is available, and the rules of conduct on the forum.

Manning's commitment to our readers is to provide a venue where a meaningful dialog between individual readers and between readers and the author can take place. It's not a commitment to any specific amount of participation on the part of the author, whose contribution to the AO forum remains voluntary (and unpaid). We suggest you try asking the author some challenging questions lest his interest stray!

The Author Online forum and the archives of previous discussions will be accessible from the publisher's website as long as the book is in print.

About the author

 TJ VanToll is a developer advocate for Telerik and a jQuery team member. He has over a decade of web development experience—specializing in performance and the mobile web. TJ speaks about his research and experiences at conferences around the world, and has written for publications such as Smashing Magazine, HTML5 Rocks, and MSDN Magazine.

about the cover illustration

The figure on the cover of *jQuery UI in Action* is captioned a "Man from Imotski, Croatia." The illustration is taken from the reproduction, published in 2006, of a nineteenth-century collection of costumes and ethnographic descriptions entitled *Dalmatia* by Professor Frane Carrara (1812–1854), an archaeologist and historian, and the first director of the Museum of Antiquity in Split, Croatia. The illustrations were obtained from a helpful librarian at the Ethnographic Museum (formerly the Museum of Antiquity), itself situated in the Roman core of the medieval center of Split: the ruins of Emperor Diocletian's retirement palace from around AD 304. The book includes finely colored illustrations of figures from different regions of Dalmatia, accompanied by descriptions of the costumes and of everyday life.

Imotski is a small town situated on the northern side of the Biokovo massif in the Dalmatian hinterland, close to the border of Croatia with Bosnia-Herzogovina. The man on the cover is wearing an embroidered vest over a white linen shirt and white woolen trousers, a suede jacket is thrown over his shoulder, and he is carrying a musket. The rich and colorful embroidery on his costume is typical for this region of Croatia.

Dress codes have changed since the nineteenth century, and the diversity by region, so rich at the time, has faded away. It is now hard to tell apart the inhabitants of different continents, let alone different towns or regions. Perhaps we have traded cultural diversity for a more varied personal life—certainly for a more varied and fast-paced technological life.

At a time when it is hard to tell one computer book from another, Manning celebrates the inventiveness and initiative of the computer business with book covers based on the rich diversity of regional life of two centuries ago, brought back to life by illustrations from collections such as this one.

Part 1

Meet jQuery UI

These first two chapters serve as an introduction to jQuery UI. As you'll learn in chapter 1, jQuery UI is a collection of plugins and utilities that build on jQuery, supported by the jQuery Foundation. You can count on them to be officially supported and maintained throughout the life of your application.

In chapter 1 you'll learn about the library itself—what's in it, who maintains it, what it does well, and even what it doesn't do well.

In chapter 2 you'll build on that knowledge to learn the ins and outs of widgets, the core building blocks of jQuery UI. The focus here is on three mechanisms the widget factory provides for customization: options, methods, and events. Options are configurable properties of widgets, methods let you perform actions on widgets, and events let you to respond to changes on the widgets.

What you learn about the library, and about the jQuery UI widgets, will give you the foundation you need to build more complex interfaces in part 2.

Introducing jQuery UI

This chapter covers

- What jQuery UI includes
- Whether jQuery UI is for you
- How to get started using the library

Let's take a trip back to early 2006. The term AJAX had been coined, the second beta of Internet Explorer 7 was released, and John Resig announced a small library he called jQuery. jQuery would soon become wildly popular, thanks in part to how easy it was to extend its core functionality through plugins.

Months passed, and thousands of plugins were created by the jQuery community. Although the abundance of plugins provided variety, they were scattered around the internet, had inconsistent APIs, and often had little or no documentation. Because of these problems, the jQuery team wanted to provide an official set of plugins in a centralized location. In September 2007 they created a new library with these plugins—jQuery UI.

From a high level, jQuery UI was, and still is, a collection of plugins and utilities that build on jQuery. But dig deeper and you find a set of consistent, well-documented, themeable building blocks to help you create everything from small websites to highly complex web applications.

Unlike jQuery plugins, the plugins and utilities in jQuery UI are supported by the jQuery Foundation. You can count on them to be officially supported and maintained throughout the life of your application.

The stability and ease of use of jQuery UI led to continuous growth in the library's popularity. The library is now used in 19% of the top 10,000 sites on the web, and has been incorporated into WordPress core and Drupal.

In this book you'll learn how to use the pieces of jQuery UI to create powerful and interactive websites and applications. In this chapter you'll start by taking a thorough look at what the jQuery UI library is, why you'd want to use it, and how to download the library and get it up and running. Let's get started!

Who is this book for?

This book assumes that you have basic knowledge of CSS, JavaScript, and jQuery. If you're not an expert don't despair—when intermediate- and advanced-level concepts are brought up, they're explained. If you're finding yourself a bit overwhelmed, appendix A discusses resources for getting up to speed. On the flip side, if you're an expert don't despair either. We'll build a number of real-world examples and discuss advanced aspects of the library throughout the book.

1.1   What is in jQuery UI?

The plugins and utilities in jQuery UI are divided into four categories—widgets, interactions, effects, and utilities (the structure of the library is presented in figure 1.1):

- *Widgets* are jQuery plugins used to create UI elements such as datepickers and menus. As of version 1.11, the library has 12 widgets, shown in figure 1.2. The widgets in jQuery UI adhere to the library's CSS framework, and therefore have a consistent look and feel. We'll cover the jQuery UI widgets in chapters 2, 3, and 4 and the CSS framework in chapter 7.
- *Interactions* are jQuery plugins that give the user the ability to interact with DOM elements. The draggable interaction allows users to drag elements around the screen, and the sortable interaction allows users to sort items in a list. We'll cover interactions in chapter 5.
- *Effects* are a full suite of custom animations and transitions for DOM elements. They're built on the animations provided in jQuery Core, and enhance a number of Core's methods such as `show()` and `hide()`. We'll cover effects in chapter 6.
- *Utilities* are a set of modular tools the library uses internally. The widget factory is the mechanism all jQuery UI widgets are built with; we'll cover it in chapters 8 and 9. The position utility provides an easy and precise means of positioning elements on the screen. We'll cover position and the rest of the utilities in jQuery UI in chapter 12.

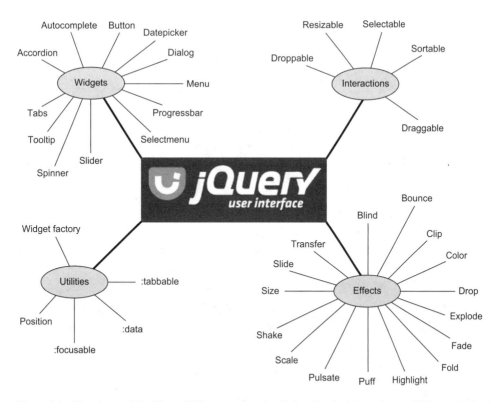

Figure 1.1 The pieces of the jQuery UI library, categorized into widgets, interactions, utilities, and effects

The pieces of jQuery UI work well together, but they were also designed with modularity in mind. Although the widget factory and position utility are heavily used in the library, they're also standalone plugins that can be used outside of jQuery UI; their only dependency is jQuery Core.

Now that we've seen what jQuery UI includes, let's see what jQuery UI can be used for, and how it might be a good fit for your next project.

Who is jQuery UI?

Development on jQuery UI (as well as all jQuery projects) is coordinated by the jQuery Foundation—a nonprofit association funded by community contributions of time and money.

The jQuery UI team is a group of eight individuals (I am one of them) scattered throughout the world. I became enthralled with jQuery UI after I discovered the amazing number of things the library could do with a small amount of code. I started submitting bug fixes and documentation and haven't looked back.

I hope you become as excited about the library as I am. The jQuery UI project is primarily community and volunteer driven, and there's always plenty to do!

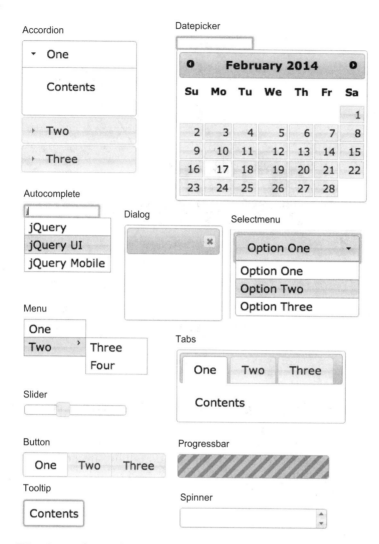

Figure 1.2 An example of all 12 jQuery UI widgets. Because of the jQuery UI CSS framework, each widget has a consistent look.

1.2   *The benefits of using jQuery UI*

Any website or application that uses jQuery almost certainly has a use for jQuery UI. jQuery Core is powerful, but it's a small library that doesn't do everything you need to build modern web applications. If you've been frustrated by searching the internet and piecing together jQuery plugins, then jQuery UI provides an appealing alternative. Let's look at the advantages of using the library.

1.2.1 *Cohesive and consistent APIs*

Because jQuery plugins have different authors, they often have wildly inconsistent APIs. jQuery UI has also faced this problem. The jQuery UI library started as a collection of popular plugins by numerous authors with a variety of programming styles. This resulted in years of refactoring to present a consistent API to end users.

Throughout the process, common patterns emerged and were abstracted into utilities like the widget factory.

Because jQuery UI provides consistent APIs, users can move from one part of the library to another without constantly needing to refer to online documentation.

1.2.2 Comprehensive browser support

When using jQuery UI, you can feel confident that your code works in all major browsers. As of version 1.11, jQuery UI supports Internet Explorer versions 7 and up, as well as the latest two versions of Chrome, Firefox, Safari, and Opera. With jQuery UI, you write your code once and it runs everywhere.

> **NOTE** Internet Explorer 6 support was dropped in version 1.10 of jQuery UI due to low global usage. If you still need Internet Explorer 6 support, you can use version 1.9 of jQuery UI.

1.2.3 Open source and free to use

Everything in jQuery UI is open source. The library's source files are publicly available at https://github.com/jquery/jquery-ui. Not only are the source files open source but the project's home page and API documentation are as well (see https://github.com/jquery/jqueryui.com and https://github.com/jquery/api.jqueryui.com, respectively).

All development is done in the open, and the community is encouraged to participate. If you find a bug in the library, you can submit a patch for it. If you're confused by the documentation, you can ask for clarification. If you find a typo, you can submit a patch that fixes it. The development of all jQuery projects is community driven, and contributions are always welcome. For more information on contributing to jQuery, see appendix E.

jQuery UI is also free. The use of jQuery UI (and all jQuery projects) is under the terms of the MIT license. All jQuery projects are free to use in any project (including commercial ones), as long as the copyright headers are preserved.

1.2.4 Thorough documentation

One of the major pain points with jQuery plugins is the difficulty of finding up-to-date and accurate documentation. All pieces of jQuery UI are thoroughly and consistently documented at http://api.jqueryui.com/. By default, the APIs for the latest version are shown, but previous versions are available as well. For example, http://api.jqueryui.com/1.10/ shows the APIs for 1.10 and http://api.jqueryui.com/1.9/ shows the APIs for 1.9.

1.2.5 Powerful theming mechanism

Another challenge of working with plugins is creating a consistent look. Although some plugins provide a way to theme the elements they create, the conventions used are often wildly different. jQuery UI solves this with a CSS framework that all its widgets use; therefore, all widgets look the same out of the box, but you still have the flexibility to create your own custom look and feel.

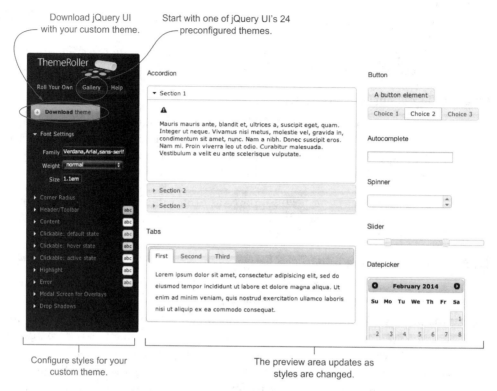

Download jQuery UI with your custom theme.

Start with one of jQuery UI's 24 preconfigured themes.

Configure styles for your custom theme.

The preview area updates as styles are changed.

Figure 1.3   Using jQuery UI ThemeRoller, you can configure a custom theme by playing with CSS properties and seeing their effect on the jQuery UI widgets live.

To make this process easier, the jQuery UI ThemeRoller allows you to visually play with the widgets' displays and generate a CSS file with your theme. Not a designer? No worries. jQuery UI also provides 24 themes you can use or build on top of. ThemeRoller is available at http://jqueryui.com/themeroller/ and is shown in figure 1.3.

1.2.6   *Emphasis on accessibility*

Accessibility is an important consideration when building anything for the web, but making even simple applications accessible to all audiences can be a difficult task. Documentation is scarce, screen readers can be tricky to test on, and specifications such as Accessible Rich Internet Applications (ARIA) can be complex and difficult to understand.

All jQuery UI widgets are designed with accessibility in mind. You can add widgets to your site and feel confident that everyone can use them. The jQuery UI widgets are keyboard accessible, use ARIA roles appropriately, and use proper markup to optimize user experiences on screen readers.

NOTE ARIA is a technical specification published by the World Wide Web Consortium (W3C). It aims to improve the accessibility of web pages—specifically pages with dynamic content and UI components. It specifies a number of HTML attributes that can be applied to elements to help assistive technologies such as screen readers interpret web pages.

1.2.7 Stable and maintenance friendly

Because jQuery UI is maintained by the jQuery Foundation, the library is updated as new versions of jQuery Core and browsers are released. Although using the latest version of the library is encouraged, the jQuery UI team realizes the difficulty of upgrading large and complex applications.

Therefore, two versions of the library are maintained simultaneously. Fixes made to the latest stable release can be incorporated in the previous legacy release. APIs are never removed from the library without being deprecated for a full major release.

To help with upgrading, a detailed guide is published with each major release of the library. The upgrade guide for 1.11 is at http://jqueryui.com/upgrade-guide/1.11/, and the upgrade guide for 1.10 is at http://jqueryui.com/upgrade-guide/1.10/.

A changelog, listing every change—including bug fixes—made to the library in that release, is also produced. The changelog for 1.11.0 is at http://jqueryui.com/changelog/1.11.0/, and the changelog for 1.10.4 is at http://jqueryui.com/changelog/1.10.4.

Now that you know why you'd want to use jQuery UI, let's discuss why you might not want to use the library.

1.3 The limitations of jQuery UI

Although jQuery UI solves a lot of problems, it doesn't solve everyone's. The library receives two main complaints: it doesn't have enough widgets, and it's not optimized for mobile. Let's deal with each of these.

1.3.1 Lack of widgets

As of version 1.11, jQuery UI has 12 widgets. Although these widgets are in the library because they solve common UI problems, 12 widgets certainly don't solve every UI problem that even a small company encounters.

Fortunately, you can use jQuery UI alongside community and commercially written jQuery plugins. Many third-party plugins use portions of jQuery UI, such as the widget factory and the CSS framework, to provide a consistent API and a consistent theme.

If you can't find a widget to meet your needs, it's easy to build your own with jQuery UI. We'll discuss how to build custom widgets using the widget factory in chapter 8.

Finally, all jQuery UI widgets are built with extensibility in mind. You can make subtle alterations to the library's widgets or build completely new widgets on top of them easily. We'll discuss extending jQuery UI widgets in chapter 9.

1.3.2 *jQuery UI and mobile devices*

The other major complaint about jQuery UI is that the library isn't optimized for mobile devices. The primary issues cited are the lack of touch-event support, the display of the widgets, and the size of the library. Let's tackle each of these individually:

- *Touch-event support*—As of version 1.11, jQuery UI doesn't natively support touch events. By default, some widgets and interactions don't work on mobile browsers such as iOS Safari or Chrome for Android. But a workaround is available until true support for touch events comes in a future release. We'll discuss the issues with touch events, how to get jQuery UI to work with them, and future plans for true support when we discuss interactions in chapter 5.

- *Display of widgets*—The look and feel of jQuery UI widgets are more suited for desktop browsers than mobile ones. To address this, the jQuery UI team is working with the jQuery Mobile team to build widgets that look good on all screen sizes. In the meantime, because all jQuery UI widgets conform to the jQuery UI CSS framework, it's easy to adjust the display of all widgets to meet your needs. We'll discuss the jQuery UI CSS framework, along with specific mobile considerations, in chapter 7.

- *Size of the library*—File size is important for any client-side library, especially on mobile devices where connection speed can be limited and latency is frequently high. jQuery UI is a large library with many components, and the full library is a lot to download. But jQuery UI is modularly written, so it's easy to create a build with only the pieces of the library that you need. Although creating a custom build is important for any site or application, it's vital if you're targeting mobile devices. We'll discuss custom builds in chapter 10.

If you're building a site or application that *solely* targets mobile devices, you should consider a mobile-centric framework like jQuery Mobile. But if you're building for desktop and mobile, you can still get all the benefits of jQuery UI with a few tweaks to optimize the mobile experience, which we'll discuss throughout the book.

Now that we've looked at the advantages and limitations of jQuery UI, let's look at how to use it.

---

jQuery UI vs. jQuery Mobile

jQuery Mobile is a UI framework that creates experiences that work on all devices. Like jQuery UI, jQuery Mobile is a series of widgets and utilities built on jQuery Core. In fact, jQuery Mobile includes the jQuery UI widget factory and uses it to create all its widgets.

Because of the similarity in the two frameworks, the teams are working to merge the common pieces of the projects. The end goal is a single set of widgets that work on any device. As a first step, jQuery Mobile's 1.4 release included the jQuery UI tabs widget. This collaboration continuously improves the mobile device support in jQuery UI.

1.4   Getting started with the library

You can get a copy of jQuery UI two ways: download the library from http://jqueryui.com/ or retrieve the files from a content delivery network (CDN). You'll learn about each of these options, but first you need to decide what version of the library to use.

1.4.1   Versions of the library

In this book we'll cover *version 1.11* of jQuery UI. The final position in the version number (1.11.*1*, 1.11.*2*, and so on) is reserved for bug fix releases. Because breaking changes are never introduced in bug fix releases, you can use any release in the 1.11 series with the examples in this book. The code examples explicitly use 1.11.0, but the latest bug fix release in the 1.11 series is recommended.

> ### What's new in jQuery UI 1.11?
>
> The two main features of jQuery UI 1.11 are a new widget, selectmenu, and complete Asynchronous Module Definition (AMD) support to use for dependency management.
>
> Selectmenu is an accessible, customizable, and themeable replacement for the native `<select>` element. You'll learn how to use selectmenu, as well as the other widgets jQuery UI provides for building forms, in chapter 3.
>
> AMD allows you to create highly customized builds of jQuery UI so that users download only the portion of the library that they need. We'll look at AMD when we discuss custom builds and preparing the library for production in chapter 10.

1.4.2   Downloading from the jQuery UI website

The first of the two options is downloading the library from http://jqueryui.com. There you'll find the download section shown in figure 1.4.

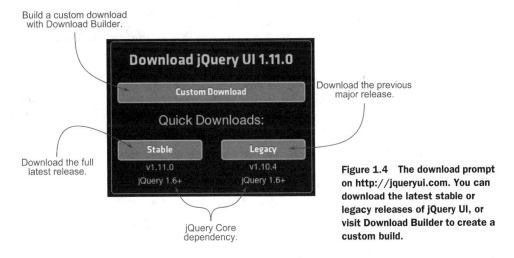

Figure 1.4   The download prompt on http://jqueryui.com. You can download the latest stable or legacy releases of jQuery UI, or visit Download Builder to create a custom build.

Let's look at each element of the download prompt:

- *Build a custom download with Download Builder*—The Custom Download button links to the jQuery UI Download Builder. Download Builder allows you to create a custom build that includes only the portions of the library that you need. This is ideal for production, as you want users to download only the portions of the library they need. For development, it's convenient to have the entire library available, and therefore you won't build a custom download for now. You'll build a production version of the library in chapter 10.

- *Download the latest release*—The quick downloads are links to zip files containing all the files in the library. The Stable button links to a zip file with the files for the latest released version.

- *Download the previous major release*—The Legacy button links to a zip file with all the library's files, but for the previous major version of the library (recall that two versions are maintained simultaneously).

- *jQuery Core dependency*—To aid users in upgrading, jQuery UI maintains compatibility with multiple versions of jQuery Core. Both versions 1.10.x and 1.11.x can be used with any version of jQuery Core 1.6 or higher.

The zip files downloaded using the Stable or Legacy buttons contain every file you need, including all dependencies. Although it's helpful to have all these files when preparing an application for production, it can be overwhelming when getting started. There's an easier way to get the library up and running.

1.4.3   *Downloading from CDNs*

A content delivery network (CDN) is a network of servers designed to serve files to users. Using a CDN moves the responsibility of hosting files from your own servers to a series of external ones. The jQuery Foundation, Google, and Microsoft all provide CDNs that host jQuery Core as well as jQuery UI. You can find documentation and a full listing of the libraries each host provides at the following URLs:

- *jQuery*—http://code.jquery.com/
- *Google*—https://developers.google.com/speed/libraries/devguide
- *Microsoft*—http://www.asp.net/ajaxlibrary/cdn.ashx

Because a CDN doesn't require you to host your own version of jQuery and jQuery UI, it's perfect for demos and experimentation. You'll use CDN versions of the library throughout this book. Next, you'll learn how to take these files from a CDN and get them on a web page.

1.5   *The first example*

You've seen how to download jQuery UI. Now let's see how you can use it. You need to build an HTML page that includes jQuery Core, jQuery UI's CSS, and jQuery UI's JavaScript.

All examples in this book use the same boilerplate HTML using jQuery's CDN (http://code.jquery.com) to download all jQuery files. The boilerplate is shown in the following listing.

Listing 1.1 Boilerplate for examples

> An HTML5 doctype. jQuery Core and UI only support standards mode. This doctype puts all browsers in standards mode.

```
<!doctype html>
<html lang="en">
<head>
    <meta charset="utf-8">
    <title>First Demo</title>
    <link rel="stylesheet"
href="http://code.jquery.com/ui/1.11.0/themes/smoothness/jquery-ui.css">
</head>
<body>
    <!-- Your HTML here -->

    <script src="http://code.jquery.com/jquery-1.11.1.js"></script>
    <script src="http://code.jquery.com/ui/1.11.0/jquery-ui.js"></script>

    <!-- Your JavaScript here -->
</body>
</html>
```

> Import version 1.11.0 of jQuery UI's style sheet from jQuery's CDN.

> Import version 1.11.1 of jQuery Core from jQuery's CDN.

> Import version 1.11.0 of jQuery UI's JavaScript from jQuery's CDN.

The placement of the style sheet and scripts is important. Style sheets are placed in the <head> of the document so that HTML elements in the <body> are styled as they're rendered. When style sheets are placed after elements in the <body>, the user may experience a flash of unstyled content (FOUC). In this case, elements are rendered without styling, and subsequently enhanced after the style sheet is downloaded and parsed by the browser.

Conversely, scripts are placed last in the <body>, after any HTML the page needs. This is done for two reasons. First, if something were to go wrong with the download, parsing, or execution of the script, or if the user had JavaScript disabled, the content of the web page would still be available to the user. Second, because the scripts are at the end of the page, any JavaScript you write doesn't depend on whether the DOM is ready.

The examples in this book assume that the boilerplate shown in listing 1.1 is in place, and the <!-Your HTML here --> and <!-Your JavaScript here --> comments indicate where you insert content. Here's an example of a jQuery UI datepicker:

```
<input id="datepicker">
<script>
    $( "#datepicker" ).datepicker();
</script>
```

Waiting for the DOM to be ready

Historically, `<script>` tags have been placed in the `<head>` of HTML documents. When the browser executes these scripts, the `<body>` isn't rendered. Therefore, scripts need to wait for the browser's `DOMContentLoaded` event before they can access DOM elements. jQuery Core provides a shorthand for doing this:

```
$(function() {
    // The DOM is now ready.
});
```

When scripts are placed at the end of the document (before `</body>`), the wrapping `$(function() {} )` is no longer necessary.

The following listing shows the example after the datepicker code has been inserted into the boilerplate.

Listing 1.2　First example: building a datepicker

```
<!doctype html>
<html lang="en">
<head>
    <meta charset="utf-8">
    <title>First Demo</title>
    <link rel="stylesheet" href="http://code.jquery.com/ui/1.11.0/themes/
      smoothness/jquery-ui.css">
</head>
<body>
    <input id="datepicker">

    <script src="http://code.jquery.com/jquery-1.11.1.js"></script>
    <script src="http://code.jquery.com/ui/1.11.0/jquery-ui.js"></script>

    <script>
        $( "#datepicker" ).datepicker();
    </script>
</body>
</html>
```

Save this text as a .html file, and open it in a browser. Give the input focus, and you see the datepicker shown in figure 1.5.

That's it. With one line of HTML and one line of JavaScript, you have a fully functional datepicker!

The full source code for the examples presented throughout this book is available for download at https://github.com/tjvantoll/jquery-ui-in-action-demos. You don't have to keep

Figure 1.5　The first example. A jQuery UI datepicker opens when the `<input>` receives focus.

track of the boilerplate in your head. The datepicker code can be found at chapter01/ 01-building-a-datepicker.html.

But there's an even easier way to play with jQuery UI—without having to leave your browser.

---

jQuery coding standards

You can write an expression such as $("#datepicker") in JavaScript in several ways: $('#datepicker'), $("#datepicker"), or $('#datepicker'). jQuery UI as well all jQuery projects consistently follow jQuery's JavaScript style guide (http:// contribute.jquery.org/style-guide/js/).

For consistency, this book adheres to the conventions in this guide. Notable conventions include using double quotes for strings ("jQuery" and not 'jQuery') and the liberal use of spacing—$("#datepicker") and not $("#datepicker"). These are jQuery's internal conventions and not requirements of projects using jQuery. If you prefer single quotes then use them. The most important thing is to be consistent in your own usage; don't use single quotes in one function and double quotes in the next.

1.6 Using an online testing tool

Online testing tools allow you to write HTML, CSS, and JavaScript in the browser and preview the results live. You can also save examples and get a unique URL you can save or share with others. You'll use these tools to set up your boilerplate and save it in a bookmark.

JS Bin (http://jsbin.com/), jsFiddle (http://jsfiddle.net), and CodePen (http:// codepen.io/) are examples of these services. Although the core functionality of each service is roughly the same, each has unique features, and you can play with them to see which you like best. Let's look at how to run your datepicker example in jsFiddle.

Visit http://jsfiddle.net. The pertinent portions of the UI are shown in figure 1.6.

Figure 1.6 jsFiddle is an online testing tool that you can use to run jQuery UI code. You place HTML, CSS, and JavaScript in their appropriate panes, and click the Run button to see the results.

First, you need to make jQuery and jQuery UI available as external resources. The URLs you want to use are

- http://code.jquery.com/ui/1.11.0/themes/smoothness/jquery-ui.css
- http://code.jquery.com/jquery-1.11.1.js
- http://code.jquery.com/ui/1.11.0/jquery-ui.js

You can copy and paste these URLs from http://code.jquery.com if you want to avoid typos or to play with other versions. After you add the resources, save the fiddle. This saves the current state and gives you a unique URL you can bookmark so you don't have to enter the external resources again. After this setup, you can enter HTML, JavaScript, and CSS. Then, run the example, and the result displays in the Result pane.

Because the datepicker is one line of HTML and one line of JavaScript, to run the example in jsFiddle you place those lines in the appropriate panes and run the fiddle. The result is shown in figure 1.7.

> **NOTE** You can view this example live at http://jsfiddle.net/tj_vantoll/ Eda2W/. If you append /show to the end of a jsFiddle URL (for instance, http://jsfiddle.net/tj_vantoll/Eda2W/show/), you can view the example outside of the jsFiddle UI—it's the equivalent of looking at just the Result pane. Finally, if you create a jsFiddle account, you can use http://jsfiddle.net/ draft/ to view the result of last example you ran. Because the draft URL is short (and bookmarkable), it's handy for testing on mobile devices.

jsFiddle handles the boilerplate for you so you can concentrate on jQuery UI, making it a convenient option for playing with the examples provided throughout this book.

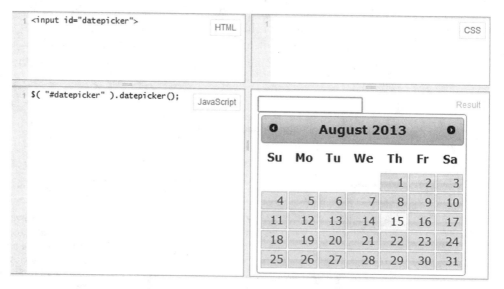

Figure 1.7   The datepicker example running in jsFiddle. The jsFiddle interface takes the HTML in the HTML pane and the JavaScript in the JavaScript pane, runs them, and displays the results in the Result pane.

1.7 Summary

jQuery UI is a collection of widgets, effects, interactions, and utilities to help you build powerful websites and applications. jQuery UI is known for its stable, cohesive APIs, excellent browser support, and comprehensive documentation.

You can download jQuery UI from http://jqueryui.com or from a CDN. You can test jQuery UI locally or use an online testing tool such as JS Bin, jsFiddle, or Code-Pen. You saw how easy it is to build powerful UI elements by creating a datepicker with one line of HTML and one line of JavaScript.

In the next chapters, you'll explore the functionality that the jQuery UI library provides. You'll start in chapter 2 with a deeper look at the core components of jQuery UI: widgets.

Enhancing UIs with widgets

A widget, as explained in chapter 1, is a reusable UI component. The 12 UI widgets in jQuery UI help solve the most common UI problems that web developers run into. In chapters 3–5, you'll look at each widget specifically, but first, you'll learn how widgets in jQuery UI work, and how to customize their behavior.

The widgets in jQuery UI are created with the widget factory: a mechanism for creating powerful, feature-rich jQuery plugins. Because all widgets go through a single factory, after you learn how one works, you'll have a good idea of how they all work. In this chapter we'll focus on three mechanisms the widget factory provides for customization: options, methods, and events. Options are configurable properties of widgets, methods let you perform actions on the widget, and events let you respond to changes on the widget.

To begin, let's see how to create widgets.

2.1 Creating widgets

At their core, jQuery UI widgets are jQuery plugins with added functionality to make them customizable, extensible, and themeable. Whereas most jQuery plugins run once and are done, widget plugins remember the elements they're associated with. You can then customize the widget with options, control it with methods, and respond to changes on the widget with events.

How do you create widgets? Because widgets are also jQuery plugins, the syntax to create them should look familiar. You saw the syntax when you created a datepicker in chapter 1. Let's look at that example in more detail:

```
<input id="datepicker">
<script>
    $( "#datepicker" ).datepicker();
</script>
```

The DOM element that is converted to a datepicker.

Selects the <input> element by its id, and converts it to a widget using the datepicker plugin method.

This example shows the easiest way to create a widget: selecting DOM elements using jQuery and calling the widget's plugin method. You can even create widgets on multiple elements at once. This example creates two datepickers:

```
<input>
<input>
<script>
    $( "input" ).datepicker();
</script>
```

Because all jQuery UI widgets are also plugins, the same syntax of selecting elements and calling the plugin can be used to create any of them. Here is how you can create a dialog widget:

```
<div id="dialog">jQuery UI Rocks!</div>
<script>
    $( "#dialog" ).dialog();
</script>
```

Run this example, and you see the dialog shown in figure 2.1.

> **NOTE** If you're getting an error that "$ is not defined" or "Object has no method 'dialog'," you aren't including jQuery and jQuery UI's JavaScript files. For details on including jQuery and jQuery UI's scripts in these examples, refer to section 1.5.

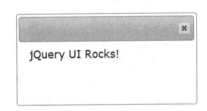

Figure 2.1 A jQuery UI dialog widget created using the `dialog()` plugin.

Like most jQuery plugins, jQuery UI widget plugins return a jQuery object. The plugin can then be chained with other jQuery method calls. The following code creates a dialog and uses jQuery Core's `css()` method to change the text color to red:

```
<div id="dialog">jQuery UI Rocks!</div>
<script>
    $( "#dialog" )
        .dialog()
        .css("color", "red" );
</script>
```

The ability to build a datepicker or dialog in a few lines of code is powerful, but chances are you're going to need more custom behavior than the default widget provides, such as a title or a different width.

jQuery UI widgets have options to provide this customization. Let's take a look at how to use them.

Dynamically creating widgets

In addition to selecting elements on the DOM, you can also dynamically create elements and convert them to widgets. The following uses jQuery to create a new `<input>` element and convert it to a datepicker widget:

```
$( "<input>" ).datepicker();
```

Because the newly created element isn't on the DOM, you need to add it for the widget to be visible. The following creates a new element, converts it to a datepicker, and appends it to the `<body>`:

```
$( "<input>" ).datepicker().appendTo( "body" );
```

The dialog widget is unique because it automatically appends its element to the DOM upon creation. Therefore, to display a new dialog you can create a new `<div>` and call `dialog()`; it displays automatically:

```
$( "<div>" ).dialog();
```

2.2   Customizing widgets with options

Options are customizable properties of widgets. All options have default values that are used when no options are explicitly passed. Recall how you instantiated the dialog in section 2.1:

```
$( "#dialog" ).dialog();
```

No options are specified, so the default set is used. Let's customize these defaults to build something practical. Suppose you need to display a notification to the user after a long-running task, such as uploading a series of files, completes.

The following code creates a new `<div>` and converts it to a dialog with the `title` and `buttons` options set:

```
$( "<div>Your files have been successfully uploaded.</div>" ).dialog({
    buttons: {
        "OK": function() {}
    },
    title: "Success"
});
```

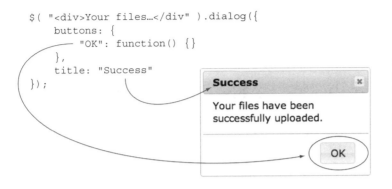

```
$( "<div>Your files...</div" ).dialog({
    buttons: {
        "OK": function() {}
    },
    title: "Success"
});
```

Figure 2.2   A jQuery UI dialog used to display a success message. The `title` option determines the text in the title bar, and the `buttons` option creates an OK button.

This dialog is shown in figure 2.2. As this demonstrates, you can specify options by passing them to the plugin as a JavaScript object.

What other options can you set? The jQuery UI API documentation lists every option available for each widget. Figure 2.3 shows a screenshot of the dialog widget's options taken from its online documentation at http://api.jqueryui.com/dialog/. In this section we'll look at only a few of these options to demonstrate how widget options work. We'll take a more thorough look at the dialog widget and its options in chapter 4.

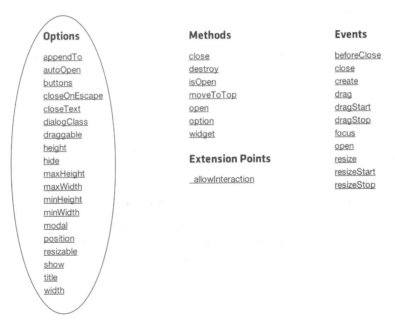

Figure 2.3   The dialog widget's documentation at http://api.jqueryui.com/dialog/. The oval highlights the dialog's 19 configurable options. Each option is a link that takes you to more detailed information.

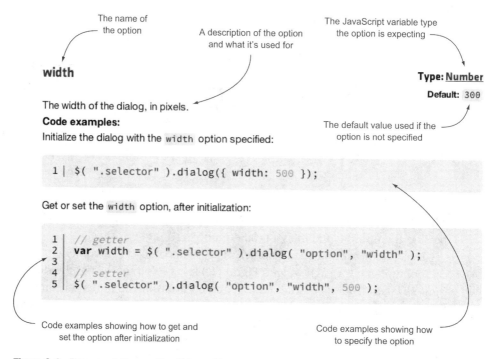

Figure 2.4   Documentation on the dialog widget's width option from http://api.jqueryui.com/dialog/#option-width. The documentation gives a description of the option, lists its JavaScript type, its default value, and gives some examples of how to use it.

Each link listed in figure 2.3 takes you to a section with documentation on the individual option, method, or event. Figure 2.4 shows the documentation for the width option.

Note the following points:

- The default value of the width option is 300; this is why all your dialogs have been 300 pixels wide to this point.
- The option can be retrieved or changed using the option() method. You'll learn how methods work, including the option() method, in the next section.

TIP   All options and their default values are accessible at $.ui.[widget-Name].prototype.options, for example, $.ui.dialog.prototype.options. You can change these values to alter the defaults that jQuery UI sets. If you were to run $.ui.dialog.prototype.options.width = 500, any new dialog instances would default to a width of 500 pixels rather than 300. Existing dialog instances wouldn't be affected.

Let's add one more option to your notification dialog. Recall that the example uses a dialog to notify users that their files have finished uploading. Assuming that uploading is a process that could take a while, the user may have moved on to other tasks in the interface and the default dialog position—the center of the screen—might be an annoyance. To mitigate this, you can change the position of the dialog with its posi-tion option. The following code shows the dialog on the bottom-left corner of the screen:

```
$( "<div>Your files have been successfully uploaded.</div>" ).dialog({
    buttons: {
        "OK": function() {}
    },
    title: "Success",
    position: {
        my: "left bottom",
        at: "left bottom"
    }
});
```

You'll look at the position option more thoroughly in chapter 12, but you can see that it reads like a normal English sentence: position my *left bottom* at the *left bottom* (of the window).

Experimenting with effects as options

Recall that effects—a suite of animations and transitions for DOM elements—are a major component of the jQuery UI library. Although you won't learn about effects until chapter 6, you can get a preview of the power they provide using dialog's show and hide options.

The dialogs you've looked at fade in and fade out when they're shown and hidden. You can change that using the show and hide options. The following code opens a dialog with the fade effect and closes with a puff effect:

```
$( "<div>" ).dialog({ show: "fade", hide: "puff" });
```

The show and hide options also accept an object for added configuration. This dialog slowly explodes when it's closed:

```
$( "#dialog" ).dialog({
    hide: {
        effect: "explode",
        duration: 2000
    }
});
```

Try playing with the following effects to see what jQuery UI makes possible. You'll take a thorough look at these effects in chapter 6.

- blind
- bounce
- clip
- drop
- explode
- fade
- fold
- highlight
- puff
- pulsate
- scale
- shake
- size
- slide

You now have a functioning notification dialog positioned in the corner of the screen. But you still have a major problem with this example: the OK button doesn't close the dialog. How can you fix that?

Although options let you customize a widget on creation, they don't allow you to change the widget afterwards. You can't use an option to close the dialog. You need to use another feature of jQuery UI widgets: methods.

2.3   *Modifying widgets with methods*

All widget actions after initialization happen as method calls. Methods query the current state of the widget as well as alter it. Options let you set a dialog's initial `height`, `width`, and `title`; methods let you change those values, open a dialog, close it, and destroy it.

In this section you'll look at how widget methods are invoked through their plug-ins. Then, you'll see how to get and set the values of options using the `option()` method.

As with options, the jQuery UI API documentation lists every method available for each widget. Figure 2.5 shows the methods available for the dialog widget. We won't be covering each method the dialog widget has. We'll specifically look at `close()`, `isOpen()`, `open()`, and `option()`.

Let's start by looking at how methods are invoked.

2.3.1   *Invoking methods*

You can invoke a widget method in many ways, but the easiest—and the one the API documentation uses—is to invoke the method through the widget's plugin. The following alters your notification dialog to call the dialog's `close()` method when the OK

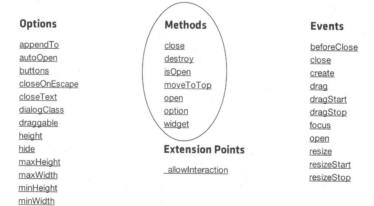

Options

appendTo
autoOpen
buttons
closeOnEscape
closeText
dialogClass
draggable
height
hide
maxHeight
maxWidth
minHeight
minWidth
modal
position
resizable
show
title
width

Methods

close
destroy
isOpen
moveToTop
open
option
widget

Extension Points

allowInteraction

Events

beforeClose
close
create
drag
dragStart
dragStop
focus
open
resize
resizeStart
resizeStop

Figure 2.5   The dialog widget's API documentation with an oval highlighting the widget's seven methods. Each method name is a link to a section with more thorough documentation.

button is clicked. Be aware that the syntax can be confusing initially, so don't be alarmed if you don't understand this; we'll go over what's happening in detail.

```
$( "<div>Your files have been successfully uploaded.</div>" ).dialog({
    buttons: {
        "OK": function() {                        Attaches a click event
            $( this ).dialog( "close" );      ❶   handler to the OK button
        }
    },
    ...
});
```

Invokes the close() method ❷

The dialog's `buttons` option works by associating button labels with a function to run when the button is clicked. The function declared at ❶ runs when the OK button is clicked. The context of the `click` handler, `this`, is set to the dialog's DOM element. You use that reference to invoke the `close()` method ❷.

When you pass the name of the method to the plugin as a string, the method is invoked. This can be confusing as JavaScript methods are typically invoked using `()`, that is, `dialog.close()` rather than `dialog( "close" )`. Why would the jQuery UI widgets use this convention?

- *Convenience*—A true `close` function is associated with the widget that you can retrieve and invoke using `()`, but it requires multiple lines of code to retrieve the instance and invoke the method. You'll look briefly at accessing the widget's instance later in this chapter, and then you'll dig deep into instances in chapters 8 and 12.

- *Ability to affect multiple elements*—jQuery's plugin syntax allows methods to be invoked on multiple elements at the same time. The following code converts two `<div>` elements to dialog widgets, and then opens them both. (The `autoOpen` option prevents the dialogs from automatically opening. We'll discuss the option in more detail momentarily.)

```
<div>A</div>
<div>B</div>
<script>
    $( "div" )
        .dialog({ autoOpen: false })
        .dialog( "open" );
</script>
```

- *Chainability*—Methods that alter a widget's state return the original jQuery object so the call can be chained. Consider the following:

```
<div id="dialog">jQuery UI Rocks!</div>
<script>
    $( "#dialog" )
        .dialog({ autoOpen: false })
        .dialog( "open" )
        .css( "color", "orange" );
</script>
```

Invokes the jQuery Core css() method to change the color of the dialog's text

Initializes the dialog widget on the `<div>`

Opens the dialog with the open() method

The close() and open() methods return the same jQuery object containing the <div>, making it possible to chain the calls with other widget methods—and even jQuery Core methods.

The close() and open() methods are examples of methods that change the widget. The other type of method returns information about the widget. Consider dialog's isOpen() method:

```
<div id="dialog">jQuery UI Rocks!</div>
<script>
    $( "#dialog" )
        .dialog()
        .dialog( "isOpen" );
</script>
```

Returns true as dialogs are opened by default

Methods that return information about the widget can't be chained because they don't return jQuery objects. The following results in a JavaScript error because the JavaScript interpreter attempts to call dialog() on true:

```
$( "#dialog" )
    .dialog()
    .dialog( "isOpen" )
    .dialog( "open" );
```

Returns the Boolean true

Throws a TypeError because you can't call dialog() on true

You can determine a method's return type, and whether the method is chainable, by looking at the API documentation. Figure 2.6 compares the API documentation of the isOpen() and open() methods. The open() method is chainable because it returns a jQuery object; the isOpen() method isn't.

NOTE Were you confused by the "plugin only" text for the open() method's return type in figure 2.6? This indicates that a jQuery object is returned only when the method is invoked through the plugin, for example dialog("open"). When open() is invoked on an instance, nothing is returned. You'll learn about instances shortly.

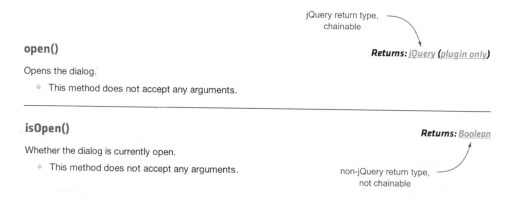

jQuery return type, chainable

open()

Opens the dialog.

- This method does not accept any arguments.

Returns: jQuery (plugin only)

isOpen()

Whether the dialog is currently open.

- This method does not accept any arguments.

Returns: Boolean

non-jQuery return type, not chainable

Figure 2.6 Comparison of the open() and isOpen() dialog methods. The open() method is chainable because it returns a jQuery object; the isOpen() isn't because it returns a Boolean.

The methods you've looked at—open(), close(), and isOpen()—are specific to the dialog widget. Although all widgets have unique methods, several methods are common to all widgets. We'll look at the most common of these, option(), in the next section.

> ### Options vs. the option() method
>
> The difference between options and the option() method can be confusing. Options are configurable widget properties. For example, the dialog widget has height, width, and title options. You use the option() method to get and set the value of these options.
>
> To clarify the difference, whenever methods are referenced in this book they're always suffixed with a set of parentheses. Therefore, close() refers to the widget's close method, option() to the widget's option method, and so forth. The same convention is also followed in the jQuery UI online documentation.

2.3.2 *Using option() to modify widgets*

Widget options can be set on initialization by passing an object to the widget's plugin. This initializes a dialog with a height of 200:

```
$( "#dialog" ).dialog({ height: 200 });
```

The option() method allows you to do two things *after* the widget has been initialized: retrieve the value of options (the getter) and set the value of options (the setter).

To get a specific option, pass its name as a string to the plugin as the second argument. The following returns the value of the height option:

```
$( "#dialog" )
    .dialog({ height: 200 })
    .dialog( "option", "height" );      ⟵ Returns 200
```

To get the values of all the options, call option() with no parameters. It returns an object with the options as key value pairs:

```
$( "#dialog" )
    .dialog()
    .dialog( "option" );
```

To invoke the setter version of option(), pass the name of the option as a second argument, and the value of the option as a third argument. The following sets the dialog's height option to 500:

```
$( "#dialog" )
    .dialog()
    .dialog( "option", "height", 500 );
```

You can pass an object as the second argument to set multiple options at once. The following sets the dialog's height option to 500 and its width option to 500:

```
$( "#dialog" )
    .dialog()
    .dialog( "option", {
        height: 500,
        width: 500
    });
```

The setter form of option() returns a jQuery object, which has two powerful effects: it allows the setter to be applied to multiple elements, and it allows the setter to be chained with other jQuery method calls. The following code creates two dialogs, sets both their heights to 500 pixels, and then changes their text color to red:

```
<div class="redDialog">One</div>
<div class="redDialog">Two</div>
<script>
    $( ".redDialog" )
        .dialog()
        .dialog( "option", "height", 500 )
        .css( "color", "red" );
</script>
```

Sets the height of both dialogs to 500 pixels

Selects both <div> elements

Converts both <div> elements to dialog widgets

Changes the color of both dialogs to red

Because the setter form of option() returns the original jQuery object, the css() call changes the color of both <div> elements.

Changing options is a common task when dealing with jQuery UI widgets, so it's important to understand the syntax of the option() method. Let's look at an example of how changing options can be useful.

2.3.3 Using dialogs to edit lists

A common web interface is a list of items that are editable. The dialog widget provides a convenient means to edit these lists, as it allows you to pop up a form without forcing the user to navigate to another page. It's easier to see this type of interface visually. Figure 2.7 shows a UI with a list of profiles that you'll build. This list has one requirement: the first and last names of all users who aren't admins can be edited.

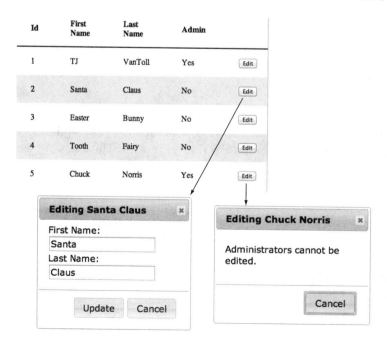

Figure 2.7   An editable list of users. Administrators such as Chuck Norris can't be edited, but regular users such as Santa Claus can be.

Let's look at how to build this list, starting with the HTML shown here:

```
<table>
    <thead>...</thead>
    <tbody>
        <tr>
            <td>1</td>
            <td>TJ</td>
            <td>VanToll</td>
            <td>Yes</td>
            <td>
                <button>Edit</button>
            </td>
        </tr>
        ...
    </tbody>
</table>

<div id="dialog">
    <form>
        <label for="firstName">First Name:</label>
        <input type="text" id="firstName">

        <label for="lastName">Last Name:</label>
        <input type="text" id="lastName">
    </form>
    <p>Administrators cannot be edited.</p>
</div>
```

❶ Displays only for
administrators

> **NOTE**   Some code is omitted to conserve space. You can view the full source in
> the book's code samples or online at http://jsfiddle.net/tj_vantoll/tAp93/.

As you can see, the list itself is an HTML <table>. The editing form is also simple,
although it does contain a note that should only display for admin users ❶. To see
how you enforce this, let's look at the JavaScript code for this example, shown in the
following listing. Although the code is long, we'll go over each piece individually.

Listing 2.1   Building an editable list

```
$( "#dialog" ).dialog({
    autoOpen: false,
    buttons: {
        Update: function() {
            var firstName = $( "#firstName" ).val(),
                lastName = $( "#lastName" ).val(),
                row = $( this ).data( "editingRow" );

            row.find( "td" ).eq( 1 ).text( firstName );
            row.find( "td" ).eq( 2 ).text( lastName );
            $( this ).dialog( "close" ); #2
        },
        Cancel: function() {
            $( this ).dialog( "close" );
        }
    }
```

❶ Doesn't automatically
open the dialog

Updates the table with
the updated names

❷ Closes the
dialog

```
});

$( "table" ).on( "click", "button", function() {          ◄─┐   Attaches a click handler
    var row = $( this ).parents( "tr" ),                   ❸   for all buttons
        firstName = row.find( "td" ).eq( 1 ).text(),
        lastName = row.find( "td" ).eq( 2 ).text(),
        admin = row.find( "td" ).eq( 3 ).text() === "Yes";
    $( "#firstName" ).val( firstName );                    ❹   Fills the first and
    $( "#lastName" ).val( lastName );                          last name <input>
                                                               elements
    $( "#dialog" )
        .dialog( "option", {                               ❻   Changes the
            title: "Editing " + firstName + " " + lastName,    dialog's CSS
            dialogClass: admin ? "admin" : ""     ◄─┘          class name
        })
        .data( "editingRow", row )                     ◄─┐   Stores the row currently
        .dialog( "open" );     ◄─┐                      ❼   being edited
});                             │
                               ❽   Calls the dialog's
                                   open() method
```

Changes the dialog's title ❺ *(points to the `.dialog( "option"` line)*

The first thing you do is convert the `<div id="dialog">` element to a dialog widget. Normally, dialogs automatically open when created; but here you don't want this because the editing dialog shouldn't display until the Edit buttons are clicked. Set the option that controls this behavior, `autoOpen`, to `false` ❶.

Next, you create Update and Cancel buttons on the dialog with the `buttons` option. Both call the `close()` method ❷ to close the dialog in their `click` handlers. The `update()` method does a little logic to update the list first. We'll get back to how that works.

After the dialog is created, you attach an event handler to the `<table>` that listens for clicks on all `<button>` elements ❸. Inside the handler, you set the first and last name `<input>` values based on the person being edited ❹. Then, you call the dialog's `option()` method to change two options: `title` and `dialogClass`.

The title change is simple—you build a string with the user's first and last name ❺. The `dialogClass` option, which controls a CSS class name that's applied to the dialog, is trickier. Here, you add an `admin-dialog` class name only if the user is an admin ❻. This gives you a CSS hook to show and hide elements based on whether the user being edited is an admin. This example uses the following CSS to hide the dialog's `<p>` for regular users and hide the editing form and update buttons for admin users:

```
.ui-dialog p { display: none; }
.admin-dialog p { display: block; }
.admin-dialog form { display: none; }
.admin-dialog button:first-child { display: none; }
```

You use jQuery Core's `data()` method to store a reference to the `<tr>` being edited ❼. The Update button's `click` handler uses this reference to determine which row's information to update after changes are made. You call dialog's `open()` method to display the dialog to the user ❽.

In this example, you used the `option()` method to change its title and class name before displaying it. You were able to use a single dialog that you could reuse even though many different users were being edited.

You've now looked at how to customize widgets with options and how to control them with methods. Next, you'll see how you can respond to widget changes with events.

Retrieving instances with the instance() method

When you initialize a widget on a DOM element, jQuery UI builds a JavaScript object that represents the widget and stores it on the element using jQuery Core's `data()` method. This object is known as the *instance* of the widget.

The instance is how jQuery UI remembers that a given element has a widget initialized on it. If you try to call dialog's `close()` method on an element that isn't a dialog widget, you receive an error:

```
$( "#does-not-exist" ).dialog( "close" );
> Error: cannot call methods on dialog prior to initialization;
attempted to call method 'close'
```

You can retrieve the widget's instance at any time using the `instance()` method. Assuming there's an element with an `id` of `"dialog"`, the following code assigns the instance to a variable:

```
var instance = $( "#dialog" ).dialog( "instance" );
```

The `instance()` method is the only method you can call on an uninitialized element. For example, `$( "#not-a-dialog" ).dialog( "close" )` throws an error, but `$( "#not-a-dialog" ).dialog( "instance" )` returns `undefined`.

The instance contains all options and methods associated with the widget. You can use it to invoke methods using the more traditional JavaScript `()` operator:

```
instance.open();
instance.close();
```

Feel free to explore what's in the widget's instance and what you can do with it. We'll take a thorough look when we dig into advanced widget factory topics in chapters 8, 9, and 12.

2.4 Responding to widget changes with events

All widgets trigger events that allow you to respond to changes in the widget's state. Suppose you need to display a message to the user whenever a dialog is closed. Dialog's `close()` *method* closes a dialog, but it doesn't let you know when a dialog has been closed. The close *event*, however, is triggered every time a dialog is closed, regardless of whether it's closed by a script or a user action such as clicking the Close button.

You can subscribe to events in two ways: event handlers and callbacks. First, we'll look at how each works and the differences between them. Then, we'll look at the parameters passed to the event and what you can do with them.

2.4.1 Subscribing to widget events

To subscribe to widget events as event handlers, you use one of the event listening functions in jQuery Core, such as `on()`. The following code listens for the dialog's create event:

```
<div id="dialog"></div>
<script>
    $( "#dialog" )
        .on( "dialogcreate", function() {
            console.log( "Dialog was created" );
        })
        .dialog();
</script>
```

Selects the `<div>` → `$( "#dialog" )`

Attaches a create event listener on the `<div>`

Converts the `<div>` to a dialog widget

> **TIP** This and subsequent examples log to the console in the browser's built-in developer tools. The F12 key opens the developer tools in Internet Explorer, and Ctrl + Shift + I (Command + Shift + I on OS X) opens the developer tools in Firefox, Chrome, and Safari. You can view the output of these examples there. Refer to appendix A for more details on using the browser's developer tools.

The create event fires when the dialog is created with `dialog()`; this invokes the event handler and the `console.log()`. The create event is the only event all widgets have. A full list of available events is in the API documentation. Figure 2.8 shows the list of events for the dialog widget. As with options and methods, we'll cover a few events to show how they work.

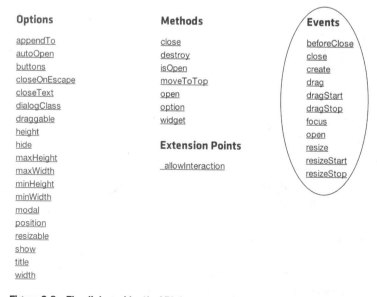

Options

appendTo
autoOpen
buttons
closeOnEscape
closeText
dialogClass
draggable
height
hide
maxHeight
maxWidth
minHeight
minWidth
modal
position
resizable
show
title
width

Methods

close
destroy
isOpen
moveToTop
open
option
widget

Extension Points

allowInteraction

Events

beforeClose
close
create
drag
dragStart
dragStop
focus
open
resize
resizeStart
resizeStop

Figure 2.8 The dialog widget's API documentation with an oval highlighting the widget's eleven events. Each event name is a link to a section with additional documentation.

Like native DOM events such as change, click, and focus, you can attach multiple handlers for any widget event. This example attaches two listeners for the create event, triggering two console.log() calls:

```
<div id="dialog"></div>
<script>
    $( "#dialog" )
        .on( "dialogcreate", function() {
            console.log( "First listener" );
        })
        .on( "dialogcreate", function() {
            console.log( "Second listener" );
        })
        .dialog();
</script>
```

Each widget has a prefix it prepends to all event names to avoid naming conflicts. This is why the previous examples listen for dialogcreate rather than create. Without prefixes, a create event would fire not only dialog creates but also menu, tab, and all other widget creates.

Although the default prefix is the widget's name (as for dialog), some widgets use a different value. These exceptions are

- draggable ➡ drag
- droppable ➡ drop
- slider ➡ slide
- resizable ➡ resize
- sortable ➡ sort
- spinner ➡ spin

If you're unsure, the prefixes are stored on each widget's prototype object. For example, $.ui.dialog.prototype.widgetEventPrefix == "dialog" and $.ui.draggable.prototype.widgetEventPrefix == "drag". These prefix discrepancies are a known source of confusion, and the project is moving toward using widgetName:eventName ("dialog:create", "draggable:create", and so on) for all event names in a future release.

You need the event prefixes when binding event handlers with on(), but all widgets also support passing a callback function to the widget as an option. Like the create event handlers, the callback is called when the dialog is created. The following code uses a callback function for the create event:

```
<div id="dialog"></div>
<script>
    $( "#dialog" ).dialog({
        create: function() {
            alert( "Dialog was created" );
        }
    });
</script>
```

Invokes when the dialog is created

For the most part, event handlers and callbacks can be used interchangeably, but they have a few important differences.

2.4.2   *Event handlers vs. callbacks*

Let's look at an example that uses both an event handler and a callback. Recall that callbacks are passed as options and event handlers are attached using on().

```
<div id="dialog"></div>
<script>
    $( "#dialog" )
        .on( "dialogcreate", function() {
            // I am an event handler
        })
        .dialog({
            create: function() {
                // I am a callback option
            }
        });
</script>
```

Both functions are invoked when the dialog is created. What's the difference between them?

The first is the value of this. When using callbacks, this is always set to the widget's DOM element. This is convenient if you need to make changes to the DOM element in the handler. The following code changes a dialog's text to red when it's created:

```
<div id="dialog">jQuery UI Rocks!</div>
<script>
    $( "#dialog" ).dialog({
        create: function() {
            $( this ).css( "color", "red" );
        }
    });
</script>
```

When using event handlers, this is set to the element the listener is attached to. Therefore, if you attach an event handler to a widget's element, it works exactly like a callback. In the following code, this is set to the dialog <div>:

```
$( "#dialog" ).on( "dialogcreate", function() {
    $( this ).css( "color", "red" );
}).dialog();
```

However, if you try to run this same example with an event handler attached to the document, it does not work:

```
$( document ).on( "dialogcreate", function() {
    $( this ).css( "color", "red" );
});
$( "#dialog" ).dialog();
```

This code does successfully create a dialog, and the event handler is invoked, but this is set to the document object—which you cannot set CSS properties on. Therefore the dialog's text does not change to red. This example also showcases the second difference between callbacks and event handlers: event handlers bubble up the DOM the same way native DOM events do. Unlike callbacks, you can attach a single event handler on a parent element to operate on multiple widget instances. The following listing counts the number of dialogs created and displays it on the page.

Listing 2.2 Counting the number of dialogs created

```
<button>Make Dialog</button>
<p>Dialogs created: <span id="count">0</span></p>

<script>
    var dialogs = 0;
    $( document ).on( "dialogcreate", function() {
        dialogs++;
        $( "#count" ).text( dialogs );
    });
    $( "button" ).on( "click", function() {
        $( "<div>" ).dialog();
    });
</script>
```

❶ Listens for a dialog being created

❷ Updates the text of the `<span>` with the new count

❸ Creates a new dialog

This example starts by attaching a `dialogcreate` event handler to the `document` ❶. You then attach a `click` event handler to the example's button. Every time the button is clicked, you create a new `<div>` and immediately initialize a dialog widget on it ❸. This new dialog triggers a `create` event, which bubbles to each of its parent elements until it reaches the `document` itself. This triggers the `dialogcreate` event handler, which increments a counter and outputs the count in the example's `<span>` ❷. Although this example uses a single event in a single widget, all widget events can be used in this fashion. You can use `$( document ).on( "menuselect", function() {} )` to listen for `select` events on all menu widget instances.

You have two different ways to handle events in jQuery UI, but which do you use, event handlers or callback functions? In general, callbacks are easier to use because you specify them alongside the widget's options. But if you need functionality to run for multiple widgets—as the previous example did—you need to use an event handler.

Now that you've seen how to subscribe to events, let's look at the information passed to the events and what you can do with it.

2.4.3 *Event parameters*

All widget events, regardless of whether they're handled as callback options or event handlers, have two parameters: `event` and `ui`. The following code shows the values passed to dialog's `create` event:

```
<div id="dialog">jQuery UI Rocks!</div>
<script>
    $( "#dialog" ).dialog({
        create: function( event, ui ) {
            console.log( event );
            console.log( ui );
```

```
        }
    });
</script>
```
This logs the following:
```
jQuery.Event {type: "dialogcreate", target: div#dialog…}
Object {}
```

The event parameter contains a populated jQuery Event object, and the ui parameter contains an empty object. Let's look at each of these in more detail, starting with event.

> **NOTE** Event parameters are named event and ui by convention only; you can name them whatever you'd like. But because all online documentation of events utilizes this naming convention, it's worth adhering to.

The two most useful properties on the Event object are type and target, which tell you the name of the event and the DOM element the event occurred on, respectively. The object also has a method you may recognize from native DOM events: preventDefault().

> **NOTE** A full list of the properties and methods on the Event object and what they do can be found at http://api.jquery.com/category/events/event-object/.

For native DOM events, preventDefault() does as its name implies: prevents the default action the browser normally takes. Consider the following code:

```
<a href="http://jqueryui.com">jQuery UI</a>
<script>
    $( "a" ).on( "click", function( event ) {
        event.preventDefault();
    });
</script>
```

If you clicked the link, the browser wouldn't go to http://jqueryui.com because of the preventDefault() call.

Like native DOM events, certain widget events can also be prevented using prevent-Default(). Suppose users must first accept a terms-of-use agreement before they can access an application. To display the terms to the user, you use the dialog shown in figure 2.9.

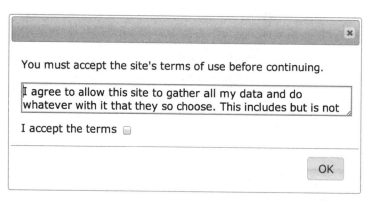

**Figure 2.9
A terms-of-use dialog.
The user must accept
the terms before being
allowed to close the
dialog.**

The following listing shows the abbreviated source used to build this dialog. You can view the full source at http://jsfiddle.net/tj_vantoll/KW3aw/.

Listing 2.3 Building a terms-of-use dialog

```
$( "#dialog" ).dialog({
    buttons: {
        OK: function() {
            $( this ).dialog( "close" );            ①  Invokes the
        }                                               close() method
    },                                   ③ Prevents the dialog from closing
    beforeClose: function( event, ui ) {             ② Sees if the terms
        if ( !$( "#terms" ).prop( "checked" ) ) {       are not checked
            event.preventDefault();
            $( "[for=terms]" ).addClass( "ui-state-error-text" );
        }                                ④ Adds an error class name
    }                                       to the terms' <label>
});
```

The approach used here may seem odd at first. Your OK button's `click` handler blindly invokes `close()` without first checking whether the terms have been accepted ①.

This is because the enforcing is done in a `beforeClose` callback, specified below the buttons. In the callback, you first determine whether the terms' check box is checked ②. If it's not, you call the event's `preventDefault()` method to stop the dialog from closing ③. To tell the user why the dialog didn't close, you add an `ui-state-error-text` class name to the check box's `<label>` element ④.

> **NOTE** The `ui-state-error-text` class name is part of jQuery UI's CSS framework, which we'll cover in chapter 7.

Why would you use the `beforeClose` event instead of putting the logic in the OK button's `click` handler? The `beforeClose` event is triggered regardless of how the dialog is closed. It runs when the user clicks the dialog's OK button *or* its close icon (in the header). This flexibility makes it the preferred means for handling this type of logic.

Although some events can be canceled using `preventDefault()`, most can't. Events that can be canceled are marked as such in the API documentation. The documentation for dialog's `beforeClose` event (http://api.jqueryui.com/dialog/#event-beforeClose) notes that "If canceled, the dialog will not close."

That covers the `event` argument, but what about `ui`, the second argument?

The `ui` argument is an object that contains properties that may be useful in event handlers and callbacks. An object is always passed for the second argument. For events that don't need additional properties, such as the `beforeClose` event you looked at, an empty object is passed.

Each property provided in the `ui` object is listed in the jQuery UI API documentation. The documentation for dialog's `drag` event is shown in figure 2.10.

drag(event, ui)   *Type:* `dialogdrag`

Triggered while the dialog is being dragged.

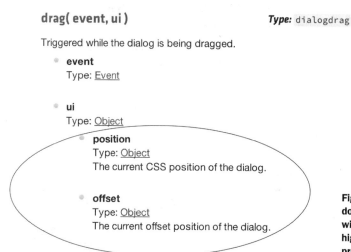

      event
      Type: Event

      ui
      Type: Object
          position
          Type: Object
          The current CSS position of the dialog.

          offset
          Type: Object
          The current offset position of the dialog.

Figure 2.10   API documentation for the dialog widget's `drag` event. The oval highlights the properties provided in the `ui` argument.

As you can see, the `drag` event is passed the `position` and `offset` coordinates of the dialog. The `position` property gives the coordinates of the dialog relative to its offset parent, and the `offset` property gives the coordinates of the dialog relative to the document itself.

> **NOTE**   If you don't understand the difference between position and offset, don't worry. It's a confusing topic, and the point of this section is to show how information is passed to widget events. But if you're curious, check out http://api.jquery.com/position/ and http://api.jquery.com/offset/.

To use these properties, consider the following example. The `option()` method is used to display the current coordinates of the dialog as its title:

```
$( "<div>" ).dialog({
    drag: function( event, ui ) {
        $( this ).dialog( "option", "title",
            ui.offset.top + " x " + ui.offset.left );
    }
});
```

You'll see how the properties in the `ui` object are useful as you look at examples throughout the book.

What about extension points?

In addition to options, methods, and events, you may have noticed a fourth option on the API documentation screenshots in this section: extension points. All methods in the jQuery UI widgets are extensible using the widget factory. You can override any existing method and optionally invoke the original method using `_super()`. The jQuery UI team is documenting methods intended for overriding in extensions as extension points.

The following code shows what is possible with extension points. It extends the dialog widget's `_title()` method so that it appends a prefix to the title used:

```
$.widget( "ui.dialog", $.ui.dialog, {
    _title: function( title ) {
        title.text( "Prefix: " + this.options.title );
    }
});
```

Don't worry if you don't understand this syntax or these concepts. We'll go over this and a number of other advanced widget concepts in chapters 8, 9, and 12.

2.5 Summary

Widgets are jQuery plugins with added functionality to handle customization, theming, and more. Because all jQuery UI widgets are built using the widget factory, they have a consistent API for configuration.

Options allow widgets to be configured on initialization. Each option has a default value that can be overridden. Methods let you retrieve information about a widget and change its state after initialization. Some methods, such as `option()`, are common to all widgets. Events let you respond to changes made to the widgets. You can handle events with either event handlers or callback options. Event handlers use event bubbling to operate on multiple widgets, and callback options always have `this` set to the widget's DOM element.

Now that you've seen what widgets are and how they work, you're going to dig into the individual widgets in jQuery UI. You'll start by using a collection of these widgets to build a common, yet tricky, requirement of many web applications: a contact form.

Part 2

jQuery UI Core

Now that you have the basics, it's time to take a comprehensive look at the components of jQuery UI: twelve jQuery UI widgets (chapters 3–4), five jQuery UI interactions (chapter 5), numerous jQuery UI effects (chapter 6), and the jQuery UI CSS framework (chapter 7).

You'll see how each component works, as well as how to apply that knowledge in real-world applications. Your first challenge will be building a sample form so patients can make a medical appointment.

The knowledge you gain in part 2 will prepare you for part 3, where you'll dig into the more complex parts of jQuery UI, as well as prepare your applications for production.

Building complex web forms with jQuery UI

This chapter covers

- Using the jQuery UI form widgets
- Building an enhanced contact form
- Comparing the jQuery UI widgets to their HTML5 counterparts

Building forms with native HTML is difficult; a limited number of controls offers a limited set of functionality. In this chapter we'll look at how the five form widgets of jQuery UI—autocomplete, button, datepicker, selectmenu, and spinner—enhance these native HTML elements and make it easy to build nontrivial forms.

To learn about the widgets and what they do, you'll build a sample form, one that patients can use to make appointments at a local doctor's office. No one likes visiting the doctor, and your job is to make the appointment process as easy as possible for the user.

You'll explore new elements that appeared on the web with HTML5, many with functionality similar to the jQuery UI form widgets. We'll compare and contrast the

43

HTML5 elements with the jQuery UI widgets and discuss which make sense for you to use today.

Let's get started by looking at the form you'll build.

3.1 *The challenges of building modern web forms*

Let's assume you're a small web development company and you get an email from a US-based doctor's office. They want to add a form to their website that allows patients to request office appointments, and they want you to do it. They list the following requirements:

- Collect the name of the user's insurance company. The office has a database of insurance companies the user should be allowed to filter and select.
- Collect the language the patient speaks—English or Spanish.
- Let the patient select a doctor or nurse. The doctors and nurses should be separated into distinct groups.
- Collect the appointment date from the patient. The office isn't open on weekends, and Dr. Smith doesn't work on Tuesdays. The date should be localized for English and Spanish speakers.
- Collect the number of days the user has been sick. Don't let the user pick invalid values like negative numbers.
- All controls in the form should match the current website's black-and-white color scheme.
- The form should work in all browsers.

Although this list is long, it's not an uncommon list of requirements for a modern web form. As more and more of our daily interactions move to the web, the forms that developers are expected to build are increasingly complex. Think how you'd build a form to meet these requirements.

Without any libraries, you're limited to the native HTML controls—<input>, <button>, <select>, and <textarea>. Although you can build forms that collect this data with native HTML, those forms tend to be neither user friendly nor developer friendly.

> **NOTE** The list of form controls is now slightly larger due to increasing HTML5 form support in some browsers. We'll discuss how HTML5 impacts your form development in the last section of this chapter.

One of your criteria is to allow the user to select an appointment date. This raises a few questions. How do you let the user know what format the date should be in? How do you confirm that the user picked a valid date? No developer wants to write code that manually checks for leap years or number of days in a month. No user wants to try different values to determine which one is correct.

Another frustrating issue with HTML elements is that it's difficult to alter their display. HTML form controls weren't created with styling or themeability in mind; it's impossible to perform some customizations, such as changing the height of a

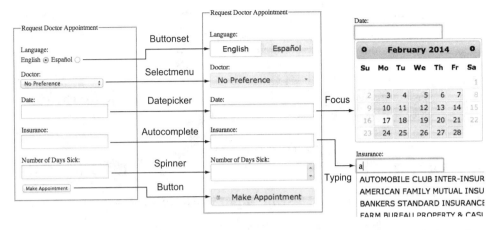

Figure 3.1   Converting form controls into a jQuery UI widget gives them a consistent look. It also makes the controls more usable. When users give focus to the Date input, they see a datepicker. When users enter text into the Insurance input, they see potential options in a menu.

`<select>` element, the size of a radio button, or anything about the `<option>` elements of a `<select>`.

The jQuery UI form widgets alleviate these concerns by providing powerful and customizable controls. The widgets have an attractive appearance and have CSS hooks to customize the display to your desire. Figure 3.1 shows the appointment form built with jQuery UI.

On the left side of figure 3.1 is the form without enhancement—rather dull and uninspiring. In the middle is the form after the controls are converted to widgets. The set of controls has a consistent look and feel that you can use with any of the jQuery UI themes. The user interacts with friendlier controls—a calendar to select a date from and an autocomplete list that filters companies as the user types, shown on the right side.

We'll spend the next several chapters looking at how to build this form with the jQuery UI widgets. Let's start the journey with a widget that helps users search and filter through values: autocomplete.

TIP   If you'd like to follow along, you can view the final version of this example at http://jsfiddle.net/tj_vantoll/Dt8pW/.

Styling form controls

All browsers allow some level of control over the display of form elements, but few styles can be consistently applied. Firefox and Internet Explorer let you change the color of a `<select>`, but Chrome and Safari don't. Internet Explorer allows you to change the height of a `<select>`, but other browsers don't.

(continued)

Furthermore, browsers have specific styling hooks to customize the display of individual form elements. The pseudo-element `::-ms-check` can be used to change the `height`, `width`, `color`, and `background` of check boxes and radio buttons in Internet Explorer 10 and 11. A full list of these styling hooks and how they work can be found at http://tjvantoll.com/2013/04/15/list-of-pseudo-elements-to-style-form-controls/.

Because of the differences in styling forms across browsers, it's highly recommended to test the display of any form customizations in as many browsers as possible. jQuery UI removes much of this guesswork by providing widgets that look great and are consistent across browsers.

3.2   *Autocomplete: suggesting input options to users*

Autocompletion is a pattern that all web users are familiar with. When you type a phrase in your search engine, it suggests results; when you compose an email, your mail client suggests recipients. Although this pattern is commonplace, implementing it on the web is nontrivial. The jQuery UI autocomplete widget provides a powerful means of associating an input field with a series of suggested values.

You'll use the autocomplete widget to tackle the first of your requirements: collecting the name of the user's insurance company.

Why do you build this as an autocomplete and not a `<select>`? Large drop-down menus can overwhelm users and make it difficult to find the value they're looking for. Have you ever been frustrated by sifting through a country drop-down menu with 300+ options?

Also, when using a `<select>` you need to retrieve *all* values from the database before displaying the form. This is a potentially expensive operation on the server and delays the time when the user sees the form.

By using an autocomplete, you let the user filter values by typing. The autocomplete widget also gives you flexibility; you can still load all data on page load, but you can also defer loading it until it's needed—and only load values that match what the user typed. Let's discuss each approach.

Setting up a PHP server

A few examples in this section include PHP to show how the autocomplete widget interacts with server-side code. To run these examples on your own computer, you must set up a PHP server. Don't feel compelled to do this. The PHP code is thoroughly explained, so you don't have to go through the hassle unless you want to tinker with the examples.

If you do, the easiest way to run PHP is to download and install a preconfigured PHP server, such as the following:

- *WAMP*—http://www.wampserver.com/ (Windows)
- *MAMP*—http://www.mamp.info/ (Mac)

Alternatively, you can download PHP directly from http://php.net/ and start a new server from the command line. For more information on this option, see http://php.net/manual/en/features.commandline.webserver.php.

3.2.1 Using local data

The easiest way to use the autocomplete widget is with local data—which means that the options are available to JavaScript directly, without needing to contact a remote server. To drive the autocomplete widget with local data, pass an array for the `source` option. The following is an example of an autocomplete that uses local data:

```
<input id="autocomplete">
<script>
    $( "#autocomplete" ).autocomplete({
        source: [ "Alligator", "Ant", "Anteater", "Ape", "Armadillo" ]
    });
</script>
```

The five options specified in the `source` option are suggested to the user in a menu as the user types. Figure 3.2 shows what happens when the user types an `a`, and then selects the first option with the mouse.

In your appointment example, the list of insurance companies you need is stored in a server-side database. In this case, to use a local array you load that data to a JavaScript array. How you implement this depends on the type of database and server-side environment you're using. The following shows a sample PHP structure:

```
<? $companies = array( "One", "Two", "Three" ); ?>
<? $companies_json = json_encode( $companies ); ?>
<script>
    $( "#autocomplete" ).autocomplete({
        source: <? echo $companies_json; ?>
    });
</script>
```

Converts the PHP array to JSON format.

Creates a PHP array with hardcoded values. In a more realistic environment, this would retrieve the values from a server-side database.

Uses the JSON data as the source option.

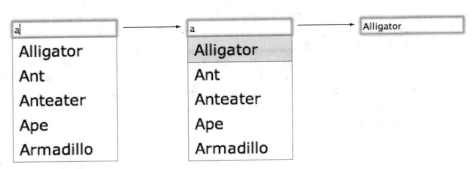

Figure 3.2   How the autocomplete widget displays suggestions to the user. Here the user selects "Alligator" with the mouse, and the input is filled with the user's selection.

This gives you the autocomplete behavior you're looking for. Although the local form of the `source` option is convenient, you have to load all options before the form is displayed and store them in JavaScript. This is fine if you have a few dozen or a few hundred options; however, when you have thousands or tens of thousands of options, managing this data in the browser becomes problematic, and often leads to a slow experience for users. To handle large datasets, let's look at how to load data from a remote source.

Associating options with codes

Often back-end structures need to associate a code with each option in an autocomplete. For example, a back end might require the code "UK" instead of the label "United Kingdom". For this scenario, the `source` option accepts an array of objects with `label` and `value` properties. The following shows an autocomplete that displays country names and maps them to country codes on selection:

```
<input id="autocomplete">
<script>
    $( "#autocomplete" ).autocomplete({
        source: [
                { label: "United Kingdom (UK)", value: "UK" },
                { label: "United States of America (USA)", value: "USA" }
        ]
    });
</script>
```

When the user selects an option, the value is entered in the text box rather than the label. This is shown in this figure.

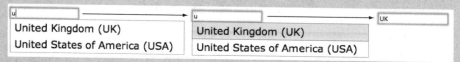

When labels and values are used, the user sees the labels, but the values are placed in the input after selection. Here, the user selects the "United Kingdom (UK)" label, and its corresponding value—"UK"—is placed in the input.

Notice that in this example you include the value of each option within its label ("United Kingdom (UK)" instead of "United Kingdom"). There are a couple reasons for doing this. First, it allows the user to type either labels or values to see autocomplete options. In the country example, this means the user can type "un" or "us" to see the United States. Second, including the value in the label makes it less surprising when the value ends up in the input after selection. For instance, the user could be surprised by their "Switzerland" selection changing to "CHE", whereas they would likely understand the change after selecting "Switzerland (CHE)".

We'll look at a real-world example of how to use codes when we build a flight search application in chapter 11.

3.2.2　*Loading from a remote source*

Loading data from a remote data source provides a quick way for users to filter though large datasets. To show how the autocomplete widget can load remote data, let's look at an example:

```
<input id="autocomplete">
<script>
    $( "#autocomplete" ).autocomplete({
        source: "/path/to/server"
    });
</script>
```

To use remote data, pass a string instead of an array.

Note that the source option is a string rather than an array. This string is a URL where you send AJAX requests to retrieve matched options as the user types. In this example, the autocomplete widget makes GET AJAX requests to /path/to/server after the user types into the <input>.

The autocomplete widget doesn't filter results when using a remote source; rather, the request made to the server includes a term request parameter containing the characters the user typed, allowing the server to filter suggestions. This workflow is shown in figure 3.3.

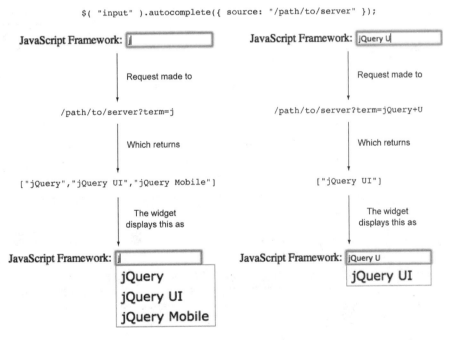

Figure 3.3 When using a remote source, the autocomplete widget sends the typed value as a term request parameter, and the server returns the filtered options. On the left, the user types "j", the widget sends a request to the server with a query string of "term=j", the server responds with an array containing three matches, and the widget displays them in a menu. On the right, the user has continued to type, and the new term ("jQuery U") is sent to the server. The server responds with a single match, which the widget displays.

The remote server must return a JSON-encoded array. As when using local data, the array can contain strings or objects with `label` and `value` properties. jQuery UI doesn't provide server-side implementations to filter the options based on user-typed terms, but most server-side environments provide an easy means to compare strings and encode data to JSON. A sample PHP implementation is shown in the following listing.

Listing 3.1 Filtering autocomplete options in PHP

```php
<?
$term = $_GET[ "term" ];
$companies = array( #B
    "AUTOMOBILE CLUB INTER-INSURANCE EXCHANGE",
    "AMERICAN FAMILY MUTUAL INSURANCE COMPANY",
    "BANKERS STANDARD INSURANCE COMPANY",
    ...
);

$result = array();
foreach ($companies as $company) {
    if ( strpos( strtoupper($company), strtoupper($term) )
        !== false ) {
        array_push( $result, $company );
    }
}
echo json_encode( $result );
?>
```

Retrieves the user-typed term from the request parameter.

A hardcoded array of all potential options. In a more realistic example, this data would be stored in a server-side database.

Loops over all company names.

If the company name contains the search term, adds it to the array that's returned.

Determines whether the company name contains the search term. Both words are uppercase, so the test is case insensitive.

JSON-encodes the resulting array, and outputs it.

Don't worry about the PHP details in this listing; it's offered as a sample because it's infeasible to list the numerous server-side environments that exist. The point is that the server-side code—regardless of what language or framework it uses—needs to take the request parameter `term`, identify the options that match it, and return the valid options as JSON. If the data for the autocomplete is stored in a database, this filtering can be done at the database level.

Cross-domain AJAX requests

By default the browser denies any AJAX request to another domain. For instance, requests to http://example2.com from http://example.com will be blocked. This is per the browser's same origin policy, which prevents malicious sites from grabbing sensitive information from other sites and executing actions on their behalf.

Cross-domain access to web assets and APIs has recently been made available through a specification known as cross-origin resource sharing (CORS).

For information on CORS, see http://www.w3.org/TR/cors/.

Because remote data is loaded as the user types, you no longer have to load the entire database on page load. Nevertheless, loading remote data could create a large demand on the server receiving the requests. You can mitigate this with the `delay` and `minLength` options.

The `delay` option determines the number of milliseconds between when the user types and when a search is done. The default value is `300`; changing the `delay` to `0` makes sense for local data when you have a small number of potential options. The following code shows this:

```
<input id="autocomplete">
<script>
    $( "#autocomplete" ).autocomplete({
        source: [ "Alligator", "Ant", "Anteater", "Ape", "Armadillo" ],
        delay: 0
    });
</script>
```

Conversely, increasing the `delay` makes sense if you're using remote data and you're concerned about the load on the server. The following example waits a full second before performing a request:

```
<input id="autocomplete">
<script>
    $( "#autocomplete" ).autocomplete({
        source: "/path/to/server",
            delay: 1000
    });
</script>
```

One second is a long time for a user to wait before seeing results. Try not to go over 500 milliseconds unless you need to. Another option to reduce server load is to set a `minLength`.

The `minLength` option determines the minimum number of characters the user must type before a search is performed. The default value of `1` is fine for most cases, but can be increased when a single character can match a large number of values—or if server load is a concern. The following requires the user to type two characters before a search is done:

```
<input id="autocomplete">
<script>
    $( "#autocomplete" ).autocomplete({
        source: "/path/to/server",
        minLength: 2
    });
</script>
```

Let's use this knowledge for your insurance carrier autocomplete. Because your requirements stated there were a large number of insurance companies, you use a `minLength` of 2 as shown in the previous example. But you leave the default `delay` in place, as you aren't concerned about server load.

Your final implementation of the company autocomplete is shown in the next listing.

Listing 3.2   Final implementation of the insurance company autocomplete

```
################# index.html ####################
<input id="autocomplete">
<script>
    $( "#autocomplete" ).autocomplete({
        source: "search.php",
        minLength: 2
    });
</script>

################# search.php ####################
<?
$term = $_GET[ "term" ];
$companies = array(
    "AUTOMOBILE CLUB INTER-INSURANCE EXCHANGE",
    "AMERICAN FAMILY MUTUAL INSURANCE COMPANY",
    "BANKERS STANDARD INSURANCE COMPANY",
    ...
);

$result = array();
foreach ($companies as $company) {
    if ( strpos( strtoupper($company), strtoupper($term) )
      !== false ) {
        array_push( $result, $company );
    }
}

echo json_encode( $result );?>
```

This is the version of the insurance carrier autocomplete you'll use in your example. But before we finish with the autocomplete widget, we need to discuss one more scenario: integrating with services that you don't control.

3.2.3   Using autocomplete with third-party services and APIs

In your appointment form, the insurance company lookup was done on your own servers. You were free to tailor the returned data to match your expected format, but often this isn't the case. Applications need to integrate with third-party APIs that don't return simple arrays or data in convenient label-value pairs.

To make it possible to integrate with these services, the source option has a variation that accepts a callback function. The function is called after each character the user types and determines which options should display. To show how the source callback function works, let's look at an example that uses local data before moving on to a third-party call.

All autocompletes you've seen to this point have matched terms anywhere in the options. For example, "a" matches "ant", but it also matches "cat". You can use a callback function to alter the widget so that it matches only at the beginning. This is shown in the following code.

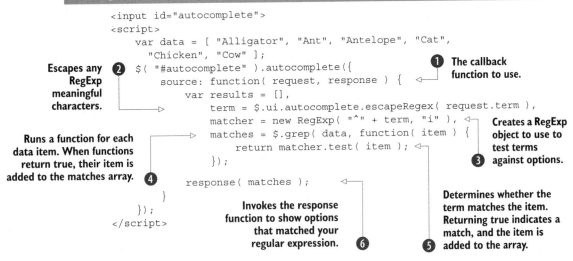

Listing 3.3 Autocompletes that only match at the beginning

```
<input id="autocomplete">
<script>
    var data = [ "Alligator", "Ant", "Antelope", "Cat",
        "Chicken", "Cow" ];
    $( "#autocomplete" ).autocomplete({
        source: function( request, response ) {
            var results = [],
                term = $.ui.autocomplete.escapeRegex( request.term ),
                matcher = new RegExp( "^" + term, "i" ),
                matches = $.grep( data, function( item ) {
                    return matcher.test( item );
                });
            response( matches );
        }
    });
</script>
```

❷ Escapes any RegExp meaningful characters.

❶ The callback function to use.

❸ Creates a RegExp object to use to test terms against options.

❹ Runs a function for each data item. When functions return true, their item is added to the matches array.

❻ Invokes the response function to show options that matched your regular expression.

❺ Determines whether the term matches the item. Returning true indicates a match, and the item is added to the array.

The callback function you use for source receives two arguments ❶. The first, request, is an object that has a single term property. The term has the string that's currently in the <input>. The second, response, is a function that needs to be called with an array of options that should be displayed. With a callback function, determining which options match the term is your responsibility.

To do so, you first escape any RegExp meaningful characters from the term the user typed (request.term) ❷. If you didn't escape it, the user's term would be interpreted as a regular expression. (The "." character would match all options!)

Next, you create the regular expression you'll use to compare the term against the options ❸. The "^" character tells the RegExp to match characters only at the start of the strings. This makes "a" match "ant" but not "cat". The second argument, "i", tells the RegExp to perform a case-insensitive match. For example, both "a" and "A" match "Ant".

After this, you loop over each potential option in the data array using $.grep() ❹. You pass to $.grep() the array to filter and a function that's invoked for each item in the array. For each item, if the function returns true, it's added to the array returned by $.grep(); otherwise, it's not. In your case, you use the RegExp you created earlier to determine whether the term matches each option ❺.

Now the matches array contains only the options that match the user-typed term based on your criteria. The final step is to invoke the source callback's response argument with the array of matched options you have built ❻. This displays the options to the user.

The callback function gives you complete control over what options the user sees. You can adapt the example to make the autocomplete case sensitive, display an option regardless of what the user typed, and more.

Although this approach uses local data, it's easy to adapt to hit third-party services. To show this, let's use GitHub's JSON API to build an autocomplete for the names of all public Git repositories. If you look at the API's documentation (http://developer .github.com/v3/search/#search-repositories), you'll see that a ton of information is returned. How can you sift through all this to get the repository names? An implementation of this is shown in the following listing.

Listing 3.4 An autocomplete of jQuery Git repositories on GitHub

```
$( "#autocomplete" ).autocomplete({
    minLength: 2,
    source: function( request, response ) {                           ① Loads data
        $.getJSON( "https://api.github.com/search/repositories",          using an
            { q: request.term + " in:name" })                            AJAX call
            .then( function( data ) {
                var matches = $.map( data.items, function( repo ) {   ◁
                    return repo.full_name;
                });
                response( matches );
            });                                        Aggregates the full
    }                                                   names of each
});                                                   matched repository  ③
```

Attaches a function to run when the call completes ②

NOTE You can view this example at http://jsfiddle.net/tj_vantoll/jck37/.

The code here is similar to the previous example. The main difference is that you start the `source` callback function by asynchronously loading data using `$.getJSON()`. The GitHub search API takes the keyword to search with as a `"q"` request parameter ①. The rest of the search string, `"in:name"`, is known as a *qualifier*—which is a GitHub-specific syntax for restricting a search. By default the GitHub search matches repositories based on their names, descriptions, and more. The `"in:name"` qualifier tells GitHub to match on names only.

TIP You can read more about GitHub search qualifiers, including a full list of the qualifiers available, at https://help.github.com/articles/searching-repositories.

Next, you use the `then()` method to attach a function to run when the `$.getJSON()` call completes ②. Inside that function, you need to aggregate the data GitHub returned into something that autocomplete can use. A simplified version of the data returned by GitHub is

```
{
  items: [
    { name: "jquery", full_name: "jquery/jquery", ... },
    { name: "jquery-ui", full_name: "jquery/jquery-ui", ... },
    ...
  ]
}
```

You loop over the items array ❸, and place each repository's full_name into a matches array. Then you pass the matches array to the response function to show the list. The callback option gives you flexibility. You could push repo.full_name + " (Forks: " + repo.forks + ")" into the matches array to display the number of forks a repository has alongside its name.

Between local data, remote data, and third-party services, the autocomplete widget gives you the ability to create autocompletes with almost any source of data. Now that you've explored autocompletes, and built the insurance company autocomplete you need for your appointment form, you're going to shift focus to how you can improve the form's buttons.

The autocorrect attribute

Many mobile OSes have a mechanism known as *autocorrection* that automatically corrects misspelled words as you type. Although occasionally helpful, autocorrection is almost never helpful in autocomplete inputs, where you have a predefined list of options. You can turn autocorrection off on any <input> by setting its autocorrect attribute to "off"—for instance, <input autocorrect="off">.

So that you don't have to explicitly include this attribute on all autocomplete <input> elements, you can use the following autocomplete extension that adds the attribute automatically:

```
$.widget( "ui.autocomplete", $.ui.autocomplete, {
    _create: function() {
        this._super();
        this.element.attr( "autocorrect", "off" );
    }
});
```

You'll learn how this works when you look at widget extensions in chapter 9. Some mobile browsers also automatically capitalize the first letter of every <input>. You can turn this behavior off by setting the <input> element's autocapitalize attribute to "off"—that is, <input autocapitalize="off">. This is helpful on fields where it makes no sense to capitalize the first letter, such as email addresses and usernames.

3.3 *Button: enhancing native buttons, inputs, and links*

Although HTML has plenty of button controls, it's difficult to change their display to match the rest of your application, and it's nontrivial to perform common actions such as adding icons or grouping buttons.

The jQuery UI button widgets provide a means to convert native buttons to themeable and customizable controls. You'll use the button widget to fulfill your second requirement: collecting the language the patient speaks.

This requirement is easy to meet with a set of radio buttons or a <select>, so why use radio buttons? In general, when you have a small number of options, radio button controls are preferred as the user can see all options at once. When you have many options or space is limited, a drop-down menu is preferred.

Why can't you meet this requirement by creating HTML radio buttons? Keep in mind that you have to build controls that match the current site's color scheme—and radio buttons are nearly impossible to style.

Luckily, the jQuery UI button widgets can turn `<button>`, `<input type= "button|checkbox|image|radio|reset|submit">`, and `<a>` elements into controls that are styleable and themeable. To show the effect of the widget, the following converts each supported element to a button widget:

```
<button>button</button>
<input type="button" value="button">
<input type="reset" value="reset">
<input type="submit" value="submit">

<label for="checkbox">checkbox</label>
<input type="checkbox" id="checkbox">
<label for="radio">radio</label>
<input type="radio" id="radio">

<a href="http://jqueryui.com">a</a>

<script>
    $( "button, input, a" ).button();
</script>
```

Check boxes and radio buttons must be associated with a `<label>`. We'll look at this momentarily.

Figure 3.4 shows the display before and after the conversion.

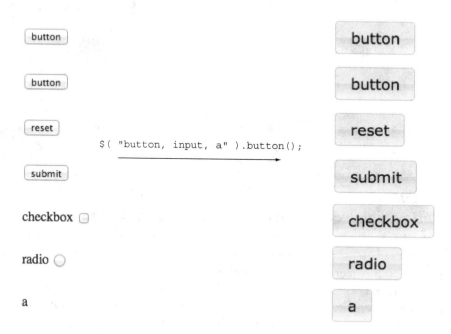

Figure 3.4 The button widget creates a consistent and themeable control from buttons, checkboxes, radio buttons, and links. Here, each of these controls is converted in a single call.

In figure 3.4 you can see how easy it is to use the button widget to create a consistent and decent-looking display for button controls. Now you need to create the radio buttons to collect the user's language.

> **TIP** jQuery UI does a bit of magic to make radio buttons and check boxes styleable. The visual controls—the "checkbox" and "radio" buttons in figure 3.4—are those inputs' `<label>` elements. jQuery UI styles the `<label>` elements and hides the check box/radio buttons in a manner that leaves them available to assistive technologies, such as screen readers. You'll dig into this technique in more detail in chapter 8 when you build a custom widget that uses the same behavior.

Note from the previous example that check box and radio button controls required a `<label>` before the button widget was instantiated on them:

```
<label for="checkbox">checkbox</label>
<input type="checkbox" id="checkbox">
<label for="radio">radio</label>
<input type="radio" id="radio">
```

The `for` attribute of the label must match the `id` attribute of the form control. This is a requirement for form building as it helps assistive devices such as screen readers connect the `<input>` element to its associated `<label>`. It also allows you to click the label to toggle check boxes and select radio buttons. Figure 3.5 shows this behavior.

Why does the button widget force you to provide the `<label>` elements instead of generating them for you? All the jQuery UI widgets are built with accessibility and graceful degradation in mind. If JavaScript were to fail on this page, the user—as well as assistive devices—would still have a usable form with semantic controls. If all goes well, the button widget enhances the markup to something prettier.

```
<label for="checkbox">checkbox</label>
<input type="checkbox" id="checkbox">
```

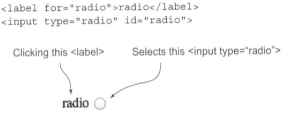

Figure 3.5 **The importance of associating `<label>` elements with `<input>` elements: clicking the labels toggles check boxes and selects radios. This increases the clickable area of these small controls, which is especially important on mobile devices, where fingers can easily miss small targets.**

Also remember that one of your requirements is to make sure the form works in all browsers. By using semantic HTML, you ensure that the form works everywhere, even in browsers that jQuery and jQuery UI no longer support.

Here's the code you use to build the language control:

```
<label for="language-en">English</label>
<input type="radio" id="language-en" name="language" value="" checked>
<label for="language-es">Español</label>
<input type="radio" id="language-es" name="language" value="es">
<script>
    $( "input" ).button();
</script>
```

This produces the buttons shown in figure 3.6.

Although these controls look much better than the native radio buttons, you can do better. jQuery UI also includes a buttonset widget designed to logically and visually group button controls. To create buttonsets, call the buttonset plugin on the parent element of button controls.

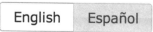

Figure 3.6 Two radio buttons that have become jQuery UI button widgets. The English `<input>` has a `checked` attribute, and therefore appears as the selected button.

The following example switches your language control to use a buttonset:

```
<span id="buttonset">
    <label for="language-en">English</label>
    <input type="radio" id="language-en" name="language" value="" checked>
    <label for="language-es">Español</label>
    <input type="radio" id="language-es" name="language" value="es">
</span>
<script>
    $( "#buttonset" ).buttonset();
</script>
```

The updated display of the radio buttons is shown in figure 3.7.

The buttonset widget provides this visual association between the buttons, and the underlying button widgets ensure the browser's native keyboard controls are preserved. The space bar can still be used to toggle check boxes, and the arrow keys can still be used to toggle the selected radio button.

Figure 3.7 When the parent element of button controls—in this case two radio buttons—is converted into a buttonset, the widget automatically applies the CSS necessary to group the buttons together.

> **NOTE** The buttonset widget isn't limited to radio buttons; it can group any element that can be converted to a button widget.

This concludes your language control for this form, but you have one last customization to make with the button widget. To create a consistent form display, let's also convert the form's Submit button to a button widget, using the following HTML and JavaScript:

```
<button>Make Appointment</button>
<script>
    $( "button" ).button();
</script>
```

To add customization, let's use the button's icons option to display a small icon next to the button. The icons option takes an object with two optional properties—primary and secondary. The primary icon displays on the left side of the button, and the secondary icon displays on the right. The values of these two properties must match one of the 173 jQuery UI icon class names listed at http://api.jqueryui.com/theming/icons/. The following code adds a calendar icon to your Submit button:

```
<button>Make Appointment</button>
<script>
    $( "button" ).button({
        icons: {
            primary: "ui-icon-calendar"
        }
    });
</script>
```

We'll continue to discuss the button in examples throughout this book. Next, let's look at the jQuery UI replacement for native drop-down menus: selectmenu.

Why are there so many HTML button controls?

The HTML specification originally contained only four button types.

- `<input type="reset">`—Resets a form to its original state
- `<input type="submit">`—Submits a form
- `<input type="button">`—Buttons that aren't used to submit forms
- `<input type="image">`—An image to act as a control to submit forms

Unfortunately, `<input>` elements can't contain child elements, and that limits what you can do with them. Thus, `<button>` elements (which can contain children) were created.

`<button>` elements can have a type of reset, submit, or button. The default type is submit. Because images can be added as children of `<button>` elements, a `<button type="image">` is not needed.

The original `<input>`-based buttons have never been deprecated or removed from the HTML specification, meaning you have two sets of controls with overlapping functionality. Because `<button>` is more powerful, its use is preferred.

3.4 *Selectmenu: enhancing native <select> elements*

`<select>` elements are one of the most difficult elements to customize in HTML. Almost no CSS properties work across browsers, and it's impossible to style or position their associated `<option>` elements.

The selectmenu widget solves these problems by replacing the `<select>` element with a customizable and themeable control that retains the accessibility and behavior of the original element. You'll use the selectmenu widget to meet the third of your requirements: allowing the user to select a doctor or nurse.

The selectmenu widget works by converting `<select>` elements as shown in the following example:

```
<style>
    select { width: 200px; }
</style>
<select id="selectmenu">
    <option>One</option>
    <option selected>Two</option>
    <option>Three</option>
</select>
<script>
    $( "#selectmenu" ).selectmenu();
</script>
```

Makes the selectmenu 200 pixels wide

Determines which option to select by default

Per your requirements, the options should be grouped into doctor and nurse categories. The native `<select>` element allows this behavior by grouping `<option>` elements within `<optgroup>` tags.

Although `<optgroup>` elements are implemented in all major browsers, they suffer the same difficulties with styling and customization that the `<select>` and `<option>` elements do. Fortunately, the selectmenu widget handles `<optgroup>` elements without any extra configuration; you call the selectmenu plugin after selecting the appropriate `<select>` element. This is shown in the following example:

```
<style>
    select { width: 200px; }
</style>
<label for="doctor">Doctor:</label>
<select id="doctor" name="doctor">
    <option>No Preference</option>
    <optgroup label="Doctors">
        <option>Adams</option>
        <option>Crowley</option>
        <option>Smith</option>
        <option>VanToll</option>
    </optgroup>
    <optgroup label="Nurses">
        <option>Davis</option>
        <option>Johnson</option>
        <option>Jones</option>
        <option>White</option>
    </optgroup>
</select>
<script>
    $( "select" ).selectmenu();
</script>
```

❶ Makes the rendered selectmenu 200 pixels

Determines the heading displayed for the group of options

Calls the selectmenu plugin

Note that in each example you assign an explicit width to `<select>` elements ❶. The selectmenu widget requires this width be set to determine the width of the rendered control.

Why can't the widget figure out an appropriate width on its own? By default, native `<select>` elements are set to a width of auto, where auto resolves to the width of the longest option in the menu. Although it's desirable to replicate this behavior, it's impossible to get the width of an `<option>` element in JavaScript; you must manually set an explicit width on `<select>` elements when using the widget.

TIP You can also set the width of a selectmenu using its width option.

Figure 3.8 shows the effect of transforming your doctor `<select>` into a selectmenu in Google Chrome.

You've seen that the selectmenu widget is an easy and powerful replacement for the native `<select>` element. Next, we'll look at the most complex and powerful form widget in jQuery UI: datepicker.

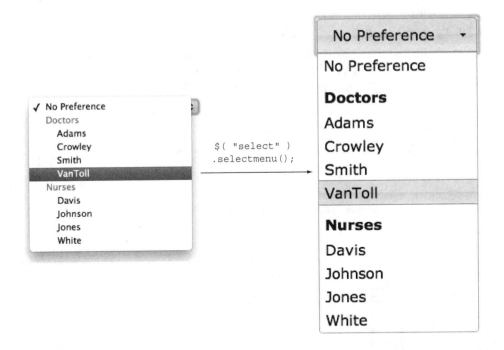

Figure 3.8 The effect of transforming a `<select>` with `<optgroup>` elements into a selectmenu widget in Google Chrome on OS X

3.5 *Datepicker: selecting dates from a pop-up calendar*

Dates are common pieces of data that forms collect. It *should* be easy to collect a date from a user on the web, but that has a number of nontrivial challenges. What format do you need the date in? How do you handle the number of days in a month? Leap years?

These problems frustrate users and programmers alike. Have you ever input a date in a form and been frustrated when you discovered the month needed a leading zero, or used dashes (-) instead of slashes (/)?

In your case, you need to collect an appointment date from the patient. You have to ensure that the user isn't allowed to pick weekends, or Tuesdays if the user wants to see Dr. Smith. Finally, you have to display the calendar in multiple locales.

You saw how to create datepickers in chapter 1 (calling the datepicker plugin on an `<input>`). For your appointment datepicker, you start with

```
<label for="date">Date:</label>
<input type="text" name="date" id="date">
<script>
    $( "input" ).datepicker();
</script>
```

To enforce the available days, you need to use the `beforeShowDay` option. The option takes a function that's called once for each individual day before it's displayed. If December is about to be shown, the `beforeShowDay` function is invoked 31 times—once for each day. The function is passed a date and must return an array with three values:

- A Boolean that determines whether the day should be enabled
- An optional string to use as a CSS class name for the day's cell
- An optional string to use as a tooltip for the day's cell

The following code disables Christmas with a custom display:

```
<style>
    .ui-datepicker .ui-christmas span {
        color: red;
        background: green;
    }
</style>
<label for="date">Date:</label>
<input type="text" name="date" id="date">
<script>
    $( "input" ).datepicker({
        beforeShowDay: function( date ) {
            if ( date.getDate() == 25 && date.getMonth() == 11 ) {
                return [ false, "ui-christmas", "Christmas!" ];
            }
            return [ true ];
        }
    });
</script>
```

In JavaScript, months and days (of the week) are zero-based, but days of the month are one-based. Therefore, 11 is equivalent to December.

Enables all other days.

Disables Christmas and adds a custom class name and tooltip.

For your use case of disabling weekends, the datepicker widget provides a utility function: `$.datepicker.noWeekends()`. The following code uses this function:

```
<label for="date">Date:</label>
<input type="text" name="date" id="date">
<script>
    $( "input" ).datepicker({
        beforeShowDay: $.datepicker.noWeekends
    });
</script>
```

But you also need to disable Tuesdays when Dr. Smith is selected. Let's create a function to handle this

```
                                    0 is Sunday, I is Monday, and so on in
                                    a system when days are zero-based.

  If Smith,
enables the day   function checkDate( date ) {
  only if it's a      var isWeekday = date.getDay() > 0 && date.getDay() < 6;  ◄──
 weekday AND         if ( $( "#doctor" ).val() === "Smith" ) {  ◄──
 not Tuesday.           return [ isWeekday && date.getDay() != 2 ];
                     } else {
                                             Gets the value of the
 If not Smith,          return [ isWeekday ];       doctor <select>,
enables the day      }                            and sees if Dr. Smith
if it's a weekday.  };                                  was selected.
```

then, use this function as the `beforeShowDay` function:

```
$( "input" ).datepicker({
    beforeShowDay: checkDate
});
```

This creates the behavior you desire, but there's one issue: if the user manually types in a date or changes the doctor, the form could be submitted with an invalid value. You need to validate that the user selected a correct date on submission, and datepicker has the tools to do that.

> **TIP** You can also use the `minDate` and `maxDate` options to customize which dates are available. In your appointment example, a `minDate` of 0 would prevent users from selecting dates in the past; a `minDate` of 2 would force the user to pick an appointment at least two days into the future. For details on the data types these options accept, see http://api.jqueryui.com/datepicker/#option-minDate and http://api.jqueryui.com/datepicker/#option-maxDate.

Datepicker and options

Datepicker is the most customizable widget of jQuery UI, with a daunting 50 options. Don't worry about knowing all them, or even a small fraction of them. Most are for specific use cases that you'll likely never need. In fact, it's quite common to have datepickers in production that don't set any options at all. The following figure shows common options you may want to experiment with.

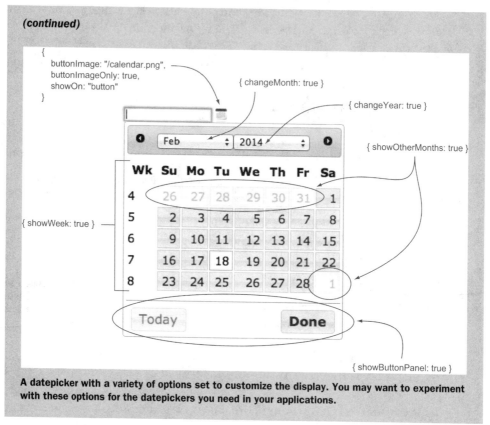

A datepicker with a variety of options set to customize the display. You may want to experiment with these options for the datepickers you need in your applications.

3.5.1 Parsing and formatting dates

Although JavaScript has a native `Date` object built in, it doesn't tackle one common problem: converting `Date` objects to strings and strings to `Date` objects. This is a tricky problem when you consider the solution has to handle leap years, the number of days in each month, and the many formats in which dates can be displayed.

For your appointment field you need to determine whether the string in the `<input>` represents a valid date. To do this, you use two of datepicker's utility functions to convert dates to strings and vice versa—`$.datepicker.formatDate()` and `$.datepicker.parseDate()`.

> **NOTE**   Utility functions can be invoked without being tied to an instance of the widget. You don't have to create a datepicker to use `$.datepicker.formatDate()` and `$.datepicker.parseDate()`; you just call them.

The first parameter each of these functions takes is a string that specifies the format of the date. Here are the common ones:

- *d*—Day of the month with no leading zeros
- *dd*—Day of the month, always two digits

- *D*—Short day name (Mon, Tue, Wed)
- *DD*—Long day name (Monday, Tuesday, Wednesday)
- *o*—Day number of the year (no leading zeros)
- *oo*—Day number of the year (always three digits)
- *m*—Month of the year with no leading zeros
- *mm*—Month of the year, always two digits
- *M*—Short month name (Jan, Feb, Mar)
- *MM*—Long month name (January, February, March)
- *y*—Two-digit year
- *yy*—Four-digit year

NOTE These same formats can be passed to the `dateFormat` option to configure the format of the user-selected date in its associated `<input>`.

Let's start with `$.datepicker.formatDate`, which converts `Date` objects to strings. The following listing shows how the same date can be displayed in multiple formats using `formatDate()`.

Listing 3.5 Formatting dates with `formatDate()`

```
var date = new Date( 2014, 0, 2 );    ◄— Creates a Date object for January 2, 2014

                 $.datepicker.formatDate( "d / m / y", date );      ◄— 2/1/14
02/01/2014 —▷   $.datepicker.formatDate( "dd / mm / yy", date );
                 $.datepicker.formatDate( "dd-mm-yy", date );       ◄— 02-01-2014
Thu Jan 2, 2014 —▷ $.datepicker.formatDate( "D M d, yy", date );
                 $.datepicker.formatDate( "DD M d, yy", date );        ◄┐ Thursday
Thursday —▷      $.datepicker.formatDate( "DD MM d, yy", date );        │ Jan 2, 2014
January 2, 2014 │
```

See how easy it is to output dates in a variety of formats? Also notice that characters in the format strings that aren't recognized are transferred to the output string directly—for example, the commas, slashes, and dashes. One warning: if you want to include characters in your formatted date that are also special formatting characters, you need to quote them. Suppose you wanted to output the day number of the year. You might try

```
$.datepicker.formatDate( "Day o of yy", new Date( 2014, 0, 2 ) );
```

but this unexpectedly outputs "Thua14 2 2f 2014", because the "D" in "Day" and "o" in "of" are interpreted as formatting characters. The following code outputs the expected "Day 2 of 2014":

```
$.datepicker.formatDate( "'Day' o 'o'f yy", new Date( 2014, 0, 2 ) );
```

`formatDate()` converts `Date` objects to strings, but `parseDate()` does the opposite: it converts strings back to `Date` objects. All these statements return a `Date` object representing January 2, 2014:

```
$.datepicker.parseDate( "d / m / y", "2 / 1 / 14" );
$.datepicker.parseDate( "dd / mm / yy", "02 / 01 / 2014 " );
$.datepicker.parseDate( "dd-mm-yy", "02-01-2014" );
$.datepicker.parseDate( "D M d, yy", "Thu Jan 2, 2014" );
$.datepicker.parseDate( "DD M d, yy", "Thursday Jan 2, 2014" );
$.datepicker.parseDate( "DD MM d, yy", "Thursday January 2, 2014" );
```

parseDate() throws an exception if the string can't be parsed into a valid Date object, making it perfect for determining whether user-inputted values are valid dates. The following function determines the validity of a date:

```
function isValidDate( date ) {
    try {
        $.datepicker.parseDate( "yy-mm-dd", date );
        return true;
    } catch( error ) {
        return false;
    }
}

isValidDate( "2014-01-01" );
isValidDate( "2012-02-29" );
isValidDate( "2014-02-29" );
isValidDate( "2014-10-31" );
isValidDate( "2014-09-31" );
```

Because parseDate() can throw an exception, it must be wrapped in a try/catch block. If parseDate() does throw an exception, the date isn't valid. If it executes successfully, the date is valid.

True

True, 2012 was a leap year.

False, 2014 isn't a leap year.

True, October has 31 days.

False, September doesn't have 31 days.

That's it. You don't need to manually check for leap years or the number of days in September. You can use this approach to validate the date in your appointment form. This is shown in the following code:

Listens for form submission ❶

Determines whether the user-provided date is valid ❷

```
$( "form" ).on( "submit", function( event ) {
    var date;

    try {
        date = $.datepicker.parseDate( "mm/dd/yy", $( "#date" ).val() );
    } catch ( error ) { }

    if ( !date ) {
        event.preventDefault();
        alert( "Please provide a valid date." );
    }
    if ( date && !checkDate( date )[ 0 ] ) {
        event.preventDefault();
        alert( "Cannot select a weekend or Tuesday for Dr. Smith." );
    }
});
```

❸ If date is defined...

❹ ...prevents the form from submitting...

❺ ...and notifies the user of the problem

Checks for weekends and Dr. Smith ❻

You attach a submit event listener to your appointment form ❶, then call parseDate with the user-provided date in a try/catch block ❷. If the date can be parsed, it's assigned to the date variable. If the date can't be parsed, date remains undefined and you go to the conditional ❸. If you have an error, you prevent the default event action (submission of the form) ❹, and then display an error to the user ❺. Finally, you use the checkDate() function you created earlier to ensure that the user didn't select Dr. Smith on Tuesday, or a day on the weekend ❻.

> **TIP** Although alert() works well for examples, in a production application you should display text error messages on the screen and highlight inputs that have errors. Not only do these best practices make your form look more professional, they also make it significantly more usable. Currently, when you close the alert, you have no way of knowing what the problem is. You'll dig deeper into form validation when you build a more complex example in chapter 11.

Although parsing and formatting dates are tricky problems, you have one final problem to tackle: globalization.

Datepicker and the widget factory

Datepicker is some of the oldest code in jQuery UI and therefore doesn't follow some of the modern conventions used by the library. It is the only widget in jQuery UI that isn't built with the widget factory. Not to worry; a lot of work has been done to mimic the widget factory's APIs so that datepicker works like the other widgets of jQuery UI.

One difference is that datepicker has no events. It does, however, have five callbacks that can be specified as options: beforeShow, beforeShowDay, onChangeMonthYear, onClose, and onSelect. Because these are options and not events, this works

```
$( "#datepicker" ).datepicker({ onClose: function() {} });
```

but this doesn't:

```
$( "#datepicker" ).datepicker().on( "datepickeronclose", function() {} );
```

3.5.2 Handling date globalization

Collecting dates from users of varied languages and cultures is a difficult task. You need to use different words for the days of the month and the months of the years, but you also need to deal with the structure of the date. Should the month or the day be displayed first? Does the culture read from left to right or right to left?

Although you need to handle only English and Spanish in your form, the jQuery UI datepicker handles 70+ locales. A few of these locales are shown in figure 3.9.

The datepicker widget stores locale information in $.datepicker.regional: an array of locale information indexed by language code. $.datepicker.regional["fr"] and $.datepicker.regional["ja"] contain the information needed to build the datepicker for the French and Japanese languages, respectively. The default locale is English and is stored at $.datepicker.regional[""].

Figure 3.9   The jQuery UI datepicker widget supports over 70 different locales. This figure shows three: French, Hebrew, and Japanese (left to right).

You can set the locale for a datepicker in multiple ways. At datepicker initialization you can pass the locale information to the plugin. The following code creates a datepicker using the French locale:

```
$( "#datepicker" ).datepicker( $.datepicker.regional[ "fr" ] );
```

Additionally, you can call the `option()` method to change the datepicker's locale after initialization. The following example changes the datepicker's locale to Japanese:

```
$( "#datepicker" ).datepicker( "option", $.datepicker.regional[ "ja" ] );
```

Datepicker provides a `setDefaults()` utility function to set the default values all future datepickers should use. You can use this function to default all datepickers to a given locale, such as defaulting all datepickers to the Hebrew locale:

```
$.datepicker.setDefaults( $.datepicker.regional[ "he" ] );
```

Due to file size considerations, the locale information that datepicker needs to build locale pickers isn't packaged in the main jQuery UI CDN file and has to be imported separately. If you download the jQuery UI zip archive from https://github.com/jquery/jquery-ui/releases, the locale information is in the ui/i18n folder (ui/i18n/datepicker-fr.js, for example, contains French locale data).

> **NOTE**   *i18n* stands for internationalization and *a11y* stands for accessibility. These terms have become common because "internationalization" and "accessibility" are painful to type.

Let's bring this back to your example. The following code takes your language radio buttons and updates them to change the locale of the datepicker in a change event:

```
<span id="buttonset">
    <label for="language-en">English</label>
    <input type="radio" id="language-en" name="language"
      value="" checked>
    <label for="language-es">Español</label>
    <input type="radio" id="language-es" name="language" value="es">
</span>
```

**Your language
buttonset from
earlier**

```
<label for="date">Date:</label>
<input type="text" name="date" id="date">

<script src="scripts/jquery-ui/i18n/datepicker-es.js"></script>
<script>
    $( "#buttonset" ).buttonset();
    $( "[name='language']" ).on( "change", function() {
        $( "#date" )
            .datepicker( "option", $.datepicker.regional[ this.value ] );
    });
    $( "#date" ).datepicker( $.datepicker.regional[ "" ] );
</script>
```

Imports the locale ❶
information

❷ **Attaches a change event**
to the radio buttons

Updates the
locale with
option() ❸

Sets the ❹
default
locale to
English

You first import the Spanish locale data ❶. This line assumes you have jQuery UI accessible in a scripts folder in the same directory as the HTML for the example. (Remember that the locale data is not available on the jQuery CDN.) Then you attach a change event to the language buttonset's radio buttons ❷; it's invoked whenever the selected radio button changes. You call the option() method to change the locale to the selected value ❸. Outside of the change event, you create the datepicker widget and set the default locale to English ❹.

This concludes our whirlwind tour of the datepicker widget. Because datepicker has a ton of options, it may be helpful to peruse its API documentation at http://api.jqueryui.com/datepicker/ to see some other things that are possible. Next, we'll look at the final widget for your form: spinner.

3.6 Spinner: enhancing native *<input>* elements to collect numeric data

Like dates, numbers are another common piece of information to collect from users. Normal text inputs offer little control over the data that users input. What's the maximum value allowed? The minimum? How do you handle more complex values like decimals and currency?

The spinner widget solves these problems by providing an easy way for users to input numbers in any format. You'll use the spinner to build the last field in your form: an input to collect the number of days the user has been sick.

To create spinner widgets, select <input> elements and invoke the widget's plugin. The following code shows this:

```
<input id="spinner" value="1">
<script>
    $( "#spinner" ).spinner();
</script>
```

The display of this spinner is shown in figure 3.10.

The spinner widget has two controls to increase and decrease the value of the spinner by one step. When the <input> has focus, the user can additionally use the up and down arrow keys to do the same.

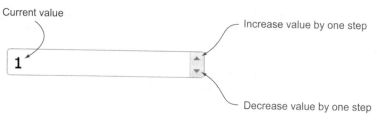

Current value

Increase value by one step

Decrease value by one step

Figure 3.10 The spinner widget adds two buttons that allow the user to increment and decrement the value of an `<input>`.

The default step value of spinner controls is 1. In figure 3.10 if the user clicks the up arrow the value changes from 1 to 2. But this step value can be changed with the `step` option. The following example creates a spinner that steps by values of 10:

```
<input id="spinner">
<script>
    $( "#spinner" ).spinner({ step: 10 });
</script>
```

Now the user can choose values of 0, 10, 20, 30, and so forth. But the user can also choose values of -10, -20, and so on. To cap the range of a spinner, the widget provides `min` and `max` options. The following spinner allows the user to select multiples of 10 from 0 to 100:

```
<input id="spinner">
<script>
    $( "#spinner" ).spinner({
        min: 0,
        max: 100,
        step: 10
    });
</script>
```

The HTML5 specification added `min`, `max`, and `step` as valid HTML attributes, and the spinner widget uses them if they're present. You can declaratively specify the `min`, `max`, and `step` options in HTML rather than passing them to the plugin:

```
<input id="spinner" min="0" max="100" step="10">
<script>
    $( "#spinner" ).spinner();
</script>
```

> **WARNING** If `min`, `max`, and `step` are specified as both attributes *and* options, the option values will be used. Make sure you only use one for clarity.

To create a spinner for your number-of-days-sick control, you only need to prevent the user from picking numbers less than one:

```
<label for="days">Number of Days Sick:</label>
<input type="text" id="days" name="days">
<script>
    $( "#days" ).spinner({ min: 1 });
</script>
```

But, like datepicker, the user can still submit any value for this field—including negative numbers, fractional numbers, and alphabetic characters. To prevent this, let's add another check to your submit event handler:

```
$( "form" ).on( "submit", function( event ) {
    if ( !$( "#days" ).spinner( "isValid" ) ) {
        event.preventDefault();
        alert( "Please provide a valid number of days." );
    }
});
```

① Checks whether the spinner's value is valid

You call spinner's isValid() method **①** to determine the validity of the spinner's value. The method checks that the value is a valid number that adheres to the widget's min, max, and step constraints.

You now have a complete number picker to use in your form. The spinner has more to offer, including support for decimal, currency, and time pickers in over 350 cultures. We'll cover those in appendix D.

3.7 *Completing the appointment form*

You've made it through all the pieces of the appointment form, so let's see how it all comes together. The source of the form is shown in listing 3.6.

NOTE The full example is available at http://jsfiddle.net/tj_vantoll/Dt8pW/.

Listing 3.6 The complete appointment form

```
<form method="POST" action="/path/to/server">
    <fieldset>
        <legend>Request Doctor Appointment</legend>
        <div>
            <label>Language:</label>
            <span id="buttonset">
                <label for="language-en">English</label>
                <input type="radio" id="language-en" name="language"
                  value="" checked>
                <label for="language-es">Español</label>
                <input type="radio" id="language-es" name="language"
                  value="es">
            </span>
        </div>
        <div>
            <label for="doctor">Doctor:</label>
            <select id="doctor" name="doctor">
                <option>No Preference</option>
                <optgroup label="Doctors">
                    <option>Adams</option>
                    <option>Crowley</option>
                    <option>Smith</option>
                    <option>VanToll</option>
                </optgroup>
                <optgroup label="Nurses">
                    <option>Davis</option>
```

```
                    <option>Johnson</option>
                    <option>Jones</option>
                    <option>White</option>
                </optgroup>
            </select>
        </div>
        <div>
            <label for="date">Date:</label>
            <input type="text" name="date" id="date">
        </div>
        <div>
            <label for="insurance">Insurance:</label>
            <input type="text" name="insurance" id="insurance">
        </div>
        <div>
            <label for="days">Number of Days Sick:</label>
            <input type="text" id="days" name="days">
        </div>
        <div>
            <button>Make Appointment</button>
        </div>
    </fieldset>
</form>
<script>
    $( "#buttonset" ).buttonset();
    $( "[name='language']" ).on( "change", function() {
        $( "#date" )
            .datepicker( "option", $.datepicker.regional[ this.value ] );
    });

    $( "#doctor" ).selectmenu();

    $( "#insurance" ).autocomplete({
        minLength: 2,
        source: "search.php"
    });

    $( "#date" ).datepicker({
        beforeShowDay: function( date ) {
            var isWeekday = date.getDay() > 0 && date.getDay() < 6;
            if ( $( "#doctor" ).val() === "Smith" ) {
                return [ isWeekday && date.getDay() != 2 ];
            } else {
                return [ isWeekday ];
            }
        }
    }).datepicker( "option", $.datepicker.regional[ "" ] );

    $( "button" ).button({
        icons: {
            primary: "ui-icon-calendar"
        }
    });

    $( "#days" ).spinner({ min: 1 });

    $( "form" ).on( "submit", function( event ) {
        var date,
```

1 Converts the radio buttons to a buttonset widget that changes the datepicker's locale

2 Converts the dropdown to a selectmenu widget

3 Converts the doctor fields to an autocomplete widget

4 Converts the date field to a datepicker that restricts the available days

5 Converts the Submit button to a button widget with a calendar icon

6 Converts the days field (number of days sick) to a spinner widget

```
        daysValid = $( "#days" ).spinner( "isValid" );

    try {
        date = $.datepicker.parseDate( "mm/dd/yy",
          $( "#date" ).val() );
    } catch ( error ) { }

    if ( !date ) {
        event.preventDefault();
        alert( "Please provide a valid date." );
    }
    if ( date && !checkDate( date )[ 0 ] ) {
        event.preventDefault();
        alert( "You cannot select a weekend or Tuesday " +
          "for Dr. Smith." );
    }
    if ( !daysValid ) {
        event.preventDefault();
        alert( "Please provide a valid number of days." );
    }
  });
</script>
```

Converting the language `<input type="radio">` controls to a buttonset ❶ overcomes the impossibility of styling native radio buttons with a themeable control.

Converting the doctor `<select>` to a selectmenu ❷ overcomes the difficulties of styling the native element. You have a themeable and customizable control that matches the other elements in the form and groups the options.

Converting the insurance company `<input>` to an autocomplete ❸ presents users with a list of potential insurance companies after they type. This is helpful for users who may not remember the name of their company or know what options are available. It also helps server load, because you only look up options as you need to.

Converting the date `<input>` to a datepicker ❹ gives the user a calendar control to select a date from. You also restrict the available appointment days and change the locale based on the user's language.

Converting the submit `<button>` to a button widget ❺ gives a button that looks the same as the rest of the form controls with an easily customizable icon.

Converting the sick days `<input>` to a spinner ❻ gives the user buttons and keyboard shortcuts to increment and decrement the value of the `<input>`. By setting the min to 1, you indicate to the user that you're looking for a positive value.

But wait, don't you have two requirements left?

- All controls in the form should match the current website's black and white color scheme.
- The form should work in all browsers.

Because you built the form with jQuery UI, these last two requirements have taken care of themselves. All widgets in the form conform to the jQuery UI theming framework; therefore, changing the form's theme is a matter of changing the style sheet imported. This is great for pesky clients who say they want a black-and-white form, but suddenly have a thing for green the next day. You'll look at the specifics of swapping out themes in chapter 7.

What about browser support? As you saw in chapter 1, jQuery UI supports all modern browsers as well as Internet Explorer 7 and above. But this client said they wanted "all" browsers. You're in luck. This form works everywhere because of the progressive enhancement approach jQuery UI takes for building widgets.

The initial HTML is a functional form that works fine without JavaScript. If JavaScript fails because of an authoring error, if the user has JavaScript disabled, or if the user is using a relic of the past like Internet Explorer 5.5, the form still works. If JavaScript is enabled and functioning, the form is enhanced with more functional controls that are easier on the eyes.

Now that you've seen how to build an appointment form using jQuery UI widgets, let's look at how these widgets compare to the controls in HTML5.

3.8 *HTML5 elements vs. jQuery UI widgets*

The HTML5 specification added several components to the HTML platform that were inspired by JavaScript libraries such as jQuery UI. This includes new elements like `<progress>` and `<datalist>`, as well as a slew of new input types: `color`, `date`, `datetime`, `datetime-local`, `email`, `month`, `number`, `range`, `search`, `tel`, `time`, `url`, and `week`. Because the specification was inspired by JavaScript libraries, the functionality of the new native controls and libraries overlap—both `<input type="date">` and the datepicker widget can be used to collect a date from the user.

What's a web developer to do? We'll focus on two of the elements from your appointment form—the datepicker and the number picker—and discuss the pros and cons of using the HTML5 control versus the jQuery UI widget. Although this doesn't provide a comprehensive overview of all HTML5 elements and jQuery UI widgets, the arguments for and against each is similar with each of these controls.

Here is the HTML that you turned into datepicker and spinner widgets:

```
<label for="date">Date:</label>
<input type="text" name="date" id="date">

<label for="days">Number of Days Sick:</label>
<input type="text" id="days" name="days">
```

The equivalent elements from the HTML5 specification are `<input type="date">` and `<input type="number">`. Let's swap in the HTML5 controls by changing the `type` of the `<input>` elements:

```
<label for="date">Date:</label>
<input type="date" name="date" id="date">

<label for="days">Number of Days Sick:</label>
<input type="number" id="days" name="days">
```

That's it. The main appeal of the HTML5 controls is that they're simple to use and dependency free. Another advantage is that the browser determines how input is presented to the user. Why is this a big deal? Check out figure 3.11, which shows the display of `<input type="date">` and `<input type="number">` on various platforms.

TIP On iOS Safari, you can use a keyboard that only shows numbers 0–9 by including a `pattern` attribute set to `"[0-9]*"`—that is, `<input type="number" pattern="[0-9]*">`.

Note the highly customized keyboard display used on the mobile browsers. These controls are optimized to make it easy for users to input data quickly. With all this power, why are you reading a chapter on jQuery UI form widgets?

As it turns out, along with the advantages of HTML5 form controls, there are also some serious (and usually show-stopping) disadvantages. For one, although giving the browser the ability to control how the input is displayed leads to the custom mobile inputs, it also means that you have little to no control over the display on desktop browsers. Need to change the spacing in the calendar? It's not possible. Need to change the colors to match your application's look and feel? That's not possible either.

The second major disadvantage of the native controls is that they only handle basic use cases. Need to collect a date from the user? The native control *can* do that. Need to disable days, show multiple months, or show the picker on the click of an icon? You're out of luck.

The third major disadvantage of the native controls is browser support. As of this writing, `<input type="date">` isn't supported in Internet Explorer (any version), Firefox,

Figure 3.11 The display of HTML5 date and number inputs on iOS Safari, Chrome, and Chrome for Android. Notice how the two mobile browsers—iOS Safari and Chrome for Android—optimize the UI to make it easy to input values.

Safari, or the default Android browser. `<input type="number` isn't supported in Internet Explorer, and isn't fully implemented in Android or iOS Safari (no `min`, `max`, or `step` attribute support). Therefore, unless you're writing the rare web application that only has to work on one platform, you're going to run into issues using these new elements.

To conclude, the major advantages of the HTML5 controls are

- They're easy to use.
- They're dependency free.
- The browser controls how data is inputted (helpful mobile UIs).

The main detriments are

- You have little control over the display.
- They handle only trivial use cases.
- Limited browser support.

Although we've addressed only a few of the many form controls of HTML5, the same arguments hold true for the others; the only real difference is that some HTML5 features are better supported by browsers than others.

For the vast majority of applications, the native controls aren't a viable option yet due to their limited support and functionality. But you have one additional option. If you have a basic use case, and your only problem is browser support, you can use jQuery UI to polyfill the native functionality. We'll discuss this, and a number of additional HTML5 elements, in chapter 11 and appendix F.

3.9   *Summary*

The jQuery UI form widgets assist with the complex task of building modern web forms. Specifically, they

- Provide accessible replacements for elements that are nearly impossible to style, such as dropdowns and radio buttons
- Add functionality that is not natively available on the web, such as robust calendar controls and server-backed autocompletes
- Apply a consistent and configurable theme
- Are accessible to all users—even users on assistive technologies such as screen readers
- Work in IE versions 7+ and all modern browsers
- Take a progressive enhancement approach, so that even users in unsupported browsers get a functional form

HTML5 includes a number of controls with functionality that overlaps that of the jQuery UI form widgets. The new controls are easy to use and great for input on mobile devices, but they're not customizable and suffer from limited browser support. You'll look more at how to practically use these HTML5 controls in chapter 11.

jQuery UI has widgets for more than form building. Next, you'll look at the layout and utility widgets included in the library.

Enhancing interfaces with layout and utility widgets

This chapter covers

- Organizing content with layout widgets
- Organizing actions into menus
- Opening content in interactive dialogs
- Replacing the browser's native tooltips
- Building a message composer

In chapter 3, you looked at using the jQuery UI form widgets to build powerful web forms. In this chapter, you'll focus on the jQuery UI widgets dedicated to displaying content and utility functionality.

The jQuery UI layout widgets—accordion and tabs—provide an easy means of organizing content in panels that can be shown and hidden. These widgets can organize content in digestible chunks, or present content in a limited amount of space. You'll look at the structure of these widgets, then see how to add advanced functionality, such as loading remote content and dynamically creating panels.

The jQuery UI utility widgets—menu, dialog, progressbar, slider, and tooltip—bring a number of desktop UI controls to the web. Although these controls have been on the desktop for years, they remain nontrivial to create on the web. You'll see that the jQuery UI utility widgets make it not only possible but easy to create powerful interactions such as displaying content in animated pop ups, selecting values in a range, and building tooltips with complex markup. On top of all this, you still get the themeability and accessibility that is built into all the jQuery UI widgets.

We'll get started by looking at the first of the jQuery UI layout widgets: accordion.

4.1   Accordion: creating toggleable content panels

Accordions are common UI elements that allow you to organize content and display information in a limited amount of space. Accordions associate headers with content panels. By default, when a header is clicked, its content expands and all other content panels collapse. This simultaneous expanding and collapsing is the effect that gives the accordion widget its name.

Because accordions work by associating headers with content, the accordion widget expects pairs of headers and content elements for HTML markup. Although not required, typically the headers are <h1>, <h2>, ... <h6> elements and the content panels are <div> elements, as shown in the following example:

```
<h3>Header One</h3>
<div>Content One</div>
<h3>Header Two</h3>
<div>Content Two</div>
```

For a more practical example, suppose you run a site that displays information on box office movies. The site lists popular movies with detailed descriptions and statistics such as their budgets and box office proceeds.

For your movie site you'll use movie names as headers and place the more detailed information in their associated content panels, shown next:

```
<div id="accordion">
    <h3>Ghostbusters</h3>
    <div>
        <p>Ghostbusters is a 1984....</p>
    </div>
    <h3>Titanic</h3>
    <div>
        <p>Titanic is a 1997 epic...</p>
    </div>
    <h3>Top Gun</h3>
    <div>
        <p>Top Gun is a 1986 action...</p>
    </div>
</div>
<script>
    $( "#accordion" ).accordion();
</script>
```

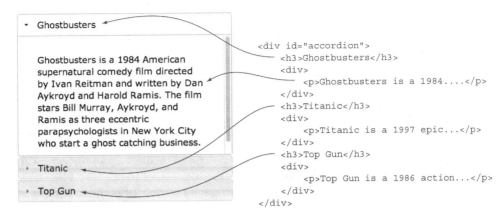

Figure 4.1   jQuery UI accordion widget used to display movie information. The accordion widget automatically activates the first panel.

Note that to create the accordion widget, you have to call the `accordion()` plugin on the parent of the headers and content panels. The display of this accordion is shown in figure 4.1. Note that the widget opens the first content panel automatically by default.

> **TIP**   The accordion widget accepts any arbitrary markup pattern; therefore, you're free to use whatever HTML elements you'd like for headers and content panels. The only requirement is that the content panels must be the siblings immediately after their associated headers in the DOM. For more information, see the `header` option documentation at http://api.jqueryui.com/accordion/#option-header.

In this example, you accomplish two things by displaying the content in an accordion. First, by organizing the widget as header and panel pairs, the content is easily skimable; users can scan to find the movie they're interested in and click for more details. Second, the example presents a lot of content in a limited amount of space.

By default, the accordion widget allows a single content panel to be displayed at a time. Clicking on the Titanic header shown in figure 4.1 causes the first content panel (Ghostbusters) to collapse and the second (Titanic) to expand simultaneously. By default, the user can't close all content panels; clicks on the open panel's header do nothing. Although this is the default behavior, you can customize it—and a lot more—using the accordion's options.

4.1.1   Configuring the accordion widget

The accordion widget has options to configure its appearance and behavior; we'll cover the most common ones here.

As you saw in the previous section, the accordion displays exactly one content area to the user. If this behavior isn't desired, you can set the `collapsible` option to `true` to let the user collapse all content panels, as shown next:

```
<div id="accordion">
    <h3>Header One</h3>
    <div>Content One</div>
    <h3>Header Two</h3>
    <div>Content Two</div>
</div>
<script>
    $( "#accordion" ).accordion({ collapsible: true });
</script>
```

The user can collapse all sections, but the first panel is still opened by default when the widget is created. This behavior is controlled by the `active` option—a zero-based index that determines the currently displayed content panel. The following example creates an accordion in which the second panel is opened on initialization:

```
<div id="accordion">
    <h3>Header One</h3>
    <div>Content One</div>                 ⟵── Content panel at index 0
    <h3>Header Two</h3>
    <div>Content Two</div>                 ⟵── Content panel at index I
</div>
<script>
    $( "#accordion" ).accordion({ active: 1 });   ⟵┐ Sets the active option to I (the
</script>                                           └  second content panel)
```

If you set the `collapsible` option, you can additionally set `active` to `false`, which initializes the accordion with all panels collapsed. This is shown in the following code:

```
<div id="accordion">
    <h3>Header One</h3>
    <div>Content One</div>
    <h3>Header Two</h3>
    <div>Content Two</div>
</div>
<script>
    $( "#accordion" ).accordion({
        active: false,
        collapsible: true
    });
</script>
```

Changing the `active` option after initialization changes the content panel displayed and animates it as if the user had clicked the corresponding header. The following listing creates two buttons that programmatically modify the displayed content panel by setting the `active` option using the `option()` method.

Listing 4.1 Modifying the active option to programmatically change panels

```
<div id="accordion">
    <h3>Header One</h3>
    <div>Content One</div>                 ⟵── The first content panel
    <h3>Header Two</h3>
    <div>Content Two</div>                 ⟵── The second content panel
</div>
```

```
<button>Show One</button>
<button>Show Two</button>
<script>
    $( "#accordion" ).accordion();

    $( "button:first" ).on( "click", function() {
        $( "#accordion" ).accordion( "option", "active", 0 );
    });
    $( "button:last" ).on( "click", function() {
        $( "#accordion" ).accordion( "option", "active", 1 );
    });
</script>
```

Shows the first content panel

Shows the second content panel

These are the most common accordion options, but you can also set icons to use on the headers with the `icons` option, show content on hover (rather than click) of the headers using the `event` option, and control the height of the content panels using the `heightStyle` option.

Before we finish our look at accordions, we'll look at how another problem is solved: adding and removing panels.

4.1.2   Adding and removing panels

If you look through the accordion's API, you'll notice that it has no options, methods, or utility functions to explicitly add or remove panels. Instead, accordion—as well as the tabs and menu widgets—implements this functionality through a generic `refresh()` method. The widget expects you to add new elements or remove existing ones on the DOM, and *then* call `refresh()`. The following listing shows a form that can be used to create new panels.

Listing 4.2   A form to create new accordion panels

```
<div id="accordion"></div>

<form>
    <label for="header">Header:</label>
    <input type="text" id="header" required>

    <label for="content">Content:</label>
    <textarea id="content" required></textarea>

    <button>Add Panel</button>
</form>

<script>
    var accordion = $( "#accordion" ).accordion();

    $( "form" ).on( "submit", function( event ) {
        event.preventDefault();
        accordion.append(
            "<h3>" + $( "#header" ).val() + "</h3>" +
            "<div>" + $( "#content" ).val() + "</div>"
        ).accordion( "refresh" );
        this.reset();
    });
</script>
```

➊ An empty accordion container

➋ Adds a new header and content panel

Calls the refresh() method ➌

Resets the form to its initial (empty) state

You start with an empty accordion container ❶ and a form to add new panels. When the form is submitted, you append new <h3> and <div> elements with the entered values for the header and content ❷. Finally, you call the refresh() method ❸ to tell the widget to render and style the panels you added.

Although the accordion widget gives you a variety of ways to display content, it requires the panels to be vertically stacked on top of each other. Your next layout widget—tabs—works similarly to accordion. It associates headers with content panels, but it offers more positioning flexibility and adds several powerful options.

4.2   Tabs: toggling between content areas

The same as accordions, tabs are common UI elements used to organize content into multiple sections in a limited space. Because these widgets serve similar functions, they were designed to have a similar API. In fact, the tabs' active, collapsible, disabled, event, heightStyle options and refresh() method work exactly the same as the accordion's.

The tabs widget, however, offers more flexibility in how the content is organized and presented. In this section, you'll see this flexibility by looking at how to load remote content and create user-closeable panels.

You start by creating tabs. Like accordions, tabs require a specific set of markup, as shown next:

```
<div id="tabs">
    <ul>
        <li><a href="#one">One</a></li>
        <li><a href="#two">Two</a></li>
    </ul>
    <div id="one">One Contents</div>
    <div id="two">Two Contents</div>
</div>
<script>
    $( "#tabs" ).tabs();
</script>
```

The display of the tabs widget is shown in figure 4.2.

The main requirement of the markup pattern is that the href attribute of the <a> tag must match the id attribute of the content panels. This is done for progressive enhancement; if JavaScript fails, the user still has a functioning list of links to content.

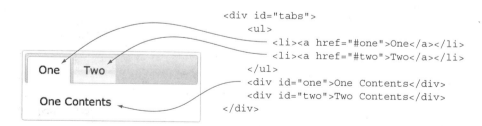

Figure 4.2   A jQuery UI tabs widget with two panels. The widget opens the first panel by default.

Like accordion, the first content panel is open by default, and you can configure that with the `active` option.

Now that you know the basics, let's do something more interesting.

> **TIP** Because the widget uses hash-based links, you can provide a hash in the URL to load a page with a given tab preselected. If the previous example were located at http://example.com, then http://example.com#two would load the page with the second tab activated.

4.2.1 Loading remote content

In the previous example, all your content was in HTML in the tabs control. Although this works for most use cases, the tabs widget also allows you to load remote content from a server.

Why would you use this? It could be that generating the content is resource intensive—perhaps because of expensive database queries or accessing third-party services. Or there may be a lot of content, and loading it all on page load is not only expensive on your servers, but also challenging for your users to sift though.

In these cases, you can use the tabs widget's ability to load remote content. Refer to the following example:

```
<div id="tabs">
    <ul>
        <li><a href="#intro">Introduction</a></li>        ❶ Local tab
        <li><a href="step-one.html">Step One</a>          ❷ Remote tab
    </ul>
    <div id="intro">Welcome, click "Step One" to get started.</div>
</div>
<script>
    $( "#tabs" ).tabs();
</script>
```

You have two links: one that references a local tab ❶ and another ❷ that doesn't appear to reference anything. In fact, the second link references a remote file that isn't included in the page. When the user clicks the link, the tabs widget fetches step-one.html via an AJAX call, creates a new content panel, and displays the HTML in the remote file within it. To see how this can be useful, let's return to the movie site example.

4.2.2 Loading movie information in a tabs widget

Recall that the site lists popular movies with statistics such as the movies' budgets and box office proceeds. Assuming your site lists a large number of movies, retrieving every statistic on every movie when the page loads puts a lot of load on your servers. It also creates a poor experience for the user; the page loads slowly, and the user is shown an overwhelming amount of information all at once. How can you fix this? You could use traditional HTML links, but you don't want users to load a full page to view a movie's information.

Figure 4.3 A tabs widget used to display information on movies. When the user clicks a movie in the list, its information is retrieved from the server and displayed in a new tab.

By using the tabs widget, you get the best of both worlds; users see movie information instantly, and you ease the load on your servers and bandwidth by displaying movie details only on user request.

Figure 4.3 shows the UI you'll build in this example. The following listing shows the implementation of this UI. There's a lot here, but don't be overwhelmed; we'll go over each piece individually.

Listing 4.3   A movie listing with jQuery UI

```
<div id="movie-list" class="ui-widget">                          Static list of ❶
    <h2>Movie List</h2>                                          movie links.
    <ul>
        <li><a href="movie.php?movie=ghostbusters">Ghostbusters</a></li>
        <li><a href="movie.php?movie=titanic">Titanic</a></li>
        <li><a href="movie.php?movie=top_gun">Top Gun</a></li>
    </ul>
</div>
                                                        Initial markup for ❷
                                                         the tabs control.
<div id="tabs">
    <ul>
        <li><a href="#intro">Introduction</a></li>
    </ul>
    <div id="intro">
        Welcome, select movies and their information will appear here.
    </div>
</div>

<script>
    var tabs = $( "#tabs" ).tabs();
                                                        ❸ Handler for
                                                           clicks on the
    $( "#movie-list" ).on( "click", "a", function( event ) {   static movie list.
        event.preventDefault();

    var index,
        movie = this.innerHTML,
        existing = tabs.find( "[data-movie='" + movie + "']" );
```

Looks for ❹
an existing
tab for this
movie.

Calls the refresh() method. ⑥

Activates the appropriate tab. ⑨

Attaches a click and keydown event handler to the Close buttons. ⑩

```
        if ( existing.length == 0 ) {
            tabs.find( ".ui-tabs-nav" )
                .append( "<li data-movie='" + movie + "'>" +
                    "<a href='" + this.href + "'>" + movie + "</a>" +
                    "<button class='ui-icon ui-icon-close'>" +
                    "Remove Tab</button>" +
                    "</li>" );
                tabs.tabs( "refresh" );
        }

        existing = tabs.find( "[data-movie='" + movie + "']" );
        index = tabs.find( ".ui-tabs-nav li" ).index( existing );
        tabs.tabs( "option", "active", index );
    });

    tabs.on( "click keydown", ".ui-icon-close", function() {
        if ( event.type === "keydown" && !(
            event.keyCode === $.ui.keyCode.ENTER ||
            event.keyCode === $.ui.keyCode.SPACE ) ) {
            return;
        }
        var panelId = $( this ).closest( "li" ).remove()
            .attr( "aria-controls" );
        $( "#" + panelId ).remove();
        tabs.tabs( "refresh" );
    });
</script>
```

If there isn't an existing tab, make one. ⑤

Finds the appropriate tab to activate. ⑦

⑧ **Determines the tab's index.**

⑪ **In a keydown event, only remove if the Enter or space bar keys are pressed.**

⑫ **Removes the appropriate elements from the DOM.**

⑬ **Calls the refresh() method to update the widget.**

You start with a static list of movies ❶ and a container for the tabs ❷ that are positioned on the left- and right-hand sides of the screen, respectively. The tabs container contains one local tab with introductory text for the user.

Next, you listen for clicks on the static list of movie links ❸. When clicks occur, you check whether a tab for the selected movie is already open (you don't want to open two Titanic tabs). To find a potentially existing tab, you use this check ❹:

```
tabs.find( "[data-movie='" + movie + "']" )
```

This query assumes that the movie for the tab is stored in an HTML5 `data-*` attribute; you'll see how this works when you add new tabs.

> **TIP** HTML5 `data-*` attributes are a quick and standards-compliant way of storing data on DOM elements. Here you're storing the movie name on an `<li>` element using `<li data-movie="Titanic">Titanic</li>`. You can retrieve that value using `$( "li" ).attr( "data-movie" )`, get all elements with that custom attribute using `$( "[data-movie]" )`, or get all elements with that custom attribute equal to "Titanic" using `$( "[data-movie='Titanic']" )`.

If you can't find an existing tab ❺, you add a new one by adding an `<li>` element to the tab's `<ul>` (which has a class name of `ui-tabs-nav`). Note that you add a `data-movie` attribute with the name of the movie the user clicked. This is the hook that the tab ❹ uses to determine whether the tab is currently open. You also add a button for users to close tabs using one of the jQuery UI built-in icons: `ui-icon-close`. You'll learn more about using the jQuery UI icons in chapter 7.

After adding the new tab, you have to call the `refresh()` method for the tabs widget to render the new tab ❻. Note that you didn't have to create a panel that corresponds to the new list item. Because these tabs are remote, the tabs widget automatically creates the panel when the remote link is activated.

Your final step in the click handler is to activate the tab for the movie the user clicked. You run the same query you ran earlier to find the tab for the movie that was clicked ❼:

```
existing = tabs.find( "[data-movie='" + movie + "']" )
```

This time, you know an `<li>` with a corresponding `data-movie` attribute exists because if it didn't, you just created one. Because the tabs widget uses a numeric index to determine which tab is active, you must determine the index of the clicked movie's tab to activate it ❽. Finally, you set the `active` option to this index to activate the tab ❾ (more on what that does momentarily).

In the last bit of code, you use a delegated event handler to handle user clicks on the Close buttons ❿. The handler finds the button's corresponding `<li>` element and panel, removes both from the DOM ⓬, and calls the tabs' `refresh()` method to update the display ⓭. There is one additional twist here: to make this UI keyboard accessible, you also listen for `keydown` events that occur on the close icons. Normally this is unnecessary on buttons—because the browser fires `click` events on Enter and space bar key presses—however, in this case, the tabs widget internally prevents the default action of Enter and space bar key presses (to implement its own keyboard functionality). Therefore you must explicitly listen for `keydown` events to make the Close buttons work with the keyboard—including a check to make sure you close tabs only when the Enter and space bar keys are pressed (and not "a", "b", and so forth) ⓫.

> **NOTE** Wondering about the key code constants (`$.ui.keyCode.ENTER` and `$.ui.keyCode.SPACE`)? jQuery UI provides several of these constants so you don't have to memorize the numeric codes that browsers use—for instance, 13 for Enter and 32 for the space bar. You can view a full list of the constants provided at http://api.jqueryui.com/jQuery.ui.keyCode/.

Let's go back to the tab activation, or what happens after you set the `active` option. Activating the tab causes the tabs widget to load the HTML for the tab via an AJAX call and display it to the user. Therefore, when the user clicks Titanic, `movie.php ?movie=titanic` is requested, and the HTML response is placed in a newly created content panel and displayed. A sample implementation of a server-side resource that builds this HTML—movie.php—is shown in the following code:

```php
<?
    $movies = array(
        "ghostbusters" => array(
            "title" => "Ghostbusters",
            "box_office" => "238",
            "budget" => "30",
```

```
                "release" => "June 8th, 1984"
            ),
            "titanic" => array(
                "title" => "Titanic",
                "box_office" => "658",
                "budget" => "200",
                "release" => "December 19th, 1997"
            ),
            "top_gun" => array(
                "title" => "Top Gun",
                "box_office" => "179",
                "budget" => "15",
                "release" => "May 16th, 1986"
            )
        );

    $movie = $movies[ $_GET[ "movie" ] ];
?>

<h3><? echo $movie[ "title" ] ?></h3>

<ul>
    <li>
        <strong>Box Office</strong>:
        <? echo $movie[ "box_office" ] ?> million USD
    </li>
    <li>
        <strong>Budget</strong>:
        <? echo $movie[ "budget" ] ?> million USD
    </li>
    <li>
        <strong>Released</strong>:
        <? echo $movie[ "release" ] ?>
    </li>
</ul>
```

> **WARNING** Although it works well for a demo, hardcoding a large list of information as in this example is generally a bad idea. A more robust implementation of this server-side component would get the movie information from a database instead of hardcoding the information in arrays. Such an approach would be more reusable (the movie data could be consumed elsewhere) and more maintainable.

You now have a UI that's both server and user friendly. The user gets two things: fast page loads and the ability to toggle between movies to compare information. Your servers benefit from reduced load; they only have to load detailed information when users request it.

Now that you know how to use the jQuery UI layout widgets to organize content, let's move on to the jQuery UI utility widgets, starting with one that groups actions together: menu.

> **TIP** Although tabs are shown on top of their content panels by default, you can use CSS to position them on the bottom or side of their content. We'll look at an example of this in chapter 7.

4.3   *Menu: creating web menus with semantic markup*

The menu is a UI element that needs no introduction; nearly any interface you interact with uses menus to group actions. jQuery UI makes it easy to create this common control on the web with the menu widget. With it, tasks such as creating nested menus, adding icons to options, and using dividers to separate actions are simple. And like all the jQuery UI widgets, you get a themeable and accessible widget with no extra effort.

As with the layout widgets, the menu widget enhances semantic markup—in this case an unordered list—to create a customizable and themeable control. The following listing builds a menu control to showcase the menu widget's features.

Listing 4.4   A menu widget

```
<style>
    .ui-menu { width: 200px; }
</style>
<ul id="menu">
    <li>
        <span class="ui-icon ui-icon-star"></span>
        Star
    </li>
    <li></li>
    <li>
        Options
        <ul>
            <li>One</li>
            <li>Two</li>
        </ul>
    </li>
</ul>
<script>
    $( "#menu" ).menu();
</script>
```

The width of menus is 100% by default, which is rarely what you need. This sets the width of all menus to 200 pixels.

Any of the jQuery UI icons can be used in menu options.

Empty list items create dividers.

Lists can be nested to create nested menus.

Figure 4.4 shows the display of this menu widget.

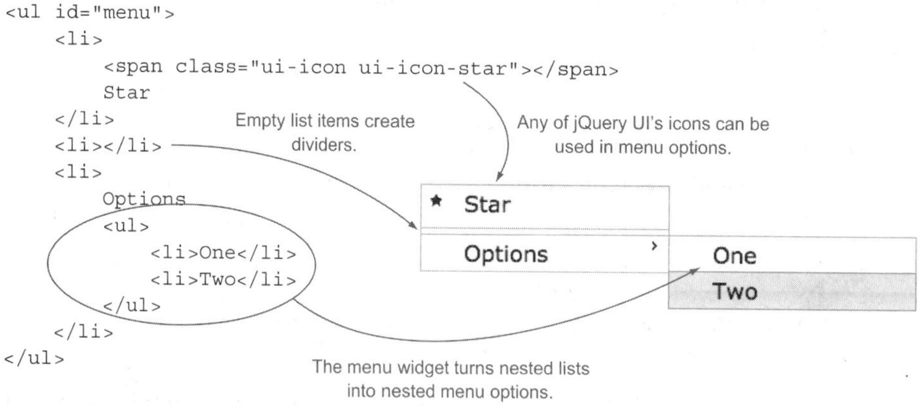

The menu widget turns nested lists into nested menu options.

Figure 4.4   A menu showcasing three features of the menu widget: the ability to turn nested lists into nested menus, the ability to create dividers from empty `<li>` elements, and the ability to add jQuery UI icons to individual menu items.

Now that you have a menu in place, you need it to do something when the user selects options. To show how this is done, let's build an example.

Suppose you want to build a UI to compose a message and store it in the browser. On its own, this UI isn't practical (there are easier ways to store messages). But you could incorporate this approach in a more complex scenario where it would be valuable. Email clients, CMS services, blog commenting services, and online text editors all preserve messages. Although simple, this message composer is an ideal way to introduce the jQuery UI utility widgets.

> **NOTE** The final version of the message composer is available at http://jsfiddle .net/tj_vantoll/jAwrA/. If may be helpful to refer to the complete example throughout the chapter for context.

You'll start with a menu that has options to save a message, load its previous state, and delete its saved state. Figure 4.5 shows the UI you'll build for this.

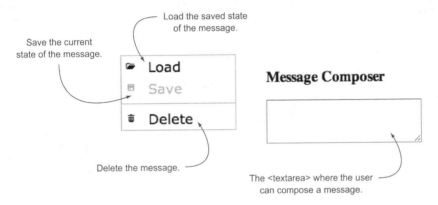

Figure 4.5   The message composer you'll build with the jQuery UI utility widgets. The user can compose a message, save it, load a previously saved message, and delete the message.

The following listing shows an implementation of this UI. As in the previous example, we'll go over each piece of this individually.

Listing 4.5   Implementation of a message composer

```
<style>
    .ui-menu { width: 200px; }
</style>

<div id="composer">
    <h3>Message Composer</h3>
    <textarea id="message"></textarea>
</div>

<ul id="menu">
    <li>
        <span class="ui-icon ui-icon-folder-open"></span>Load
```

```
    </li>
    <li class="ui-state-disabled" id="save-option">
        <span class="ui-icon ui-icon-disk"></span>Save
    </li>
    <li></li>
    <li>
        <span class="ui-icon ui-icon-trash"></span>Delete
    </li>
</ul>

<script>
    var menu = $( "#menu" ).menu({
        select: function( event, ui ) {
            var selection = $.trim( ui.item.text() ),
                message = $( "#message" ).val();

            switch( selection ) {
                case "Load":
                    message = localStorage.getItem( "message" );
                    $( "#message" ).val( message );
                    break;
                case "Save":
                    localStorage.setItem( "message", message );
                    break;
                case "Delete":
                    $( "#message" ).val( "" );
                    localStorage.removeItem( "message", "" );
                    break;
            }
        }
    });

    $( "#message" ).on( "keyup", function() {
        var message = $( this ).val();
        if ( message.length === 0 ) {
            $( "#save-option" ).addClass( "ui-state-disabled" );
        } else {
            $( "#save-option" ).removeClass( "ui-state-disabled" );
        }
        menu.menu( "refresh" );
    });
</script>
```

❶ The Save option is disabled by default.

❷ Attaches a select event callback.

❸ Determines which option was selected.

❹ Loads the message from localStorage.

❺ Saves the message to localStorage.

❻ Deletes the message from localStorage.

❽ Disables the Save option if the message is empty.

❼ Listens for keypresses on the message <textarea>.

❾ Calls the menu's refresh() method.

The menu has three items: Load, Save, and Delete. The Save option ❶ is given a ui-state-disabled class name. The menu widget automatically disables any option that has this class name when the widget is created—which is what you want here, as users can't save a message until they type one.

You then attach a callback for the menu's select event ❷. The event is invoked every time the user selects an option from the menu. The second argument of the callback, ui, has an item property set to the user-selected <li> element. You use the textual content of that element to determine which option the user selected ❸.

Next, you do a switch over the potential menu options. If the user selects Load, you retrieve the value from localStorage and set the value of the <textarea> to the retrieved value ❹; if the user selects Save, you store the value of the `<textarea>` in `localStorage` ❺; if the user selects Delete, you remove the value from `local-Storage` ❻.

> **NOTE** `localStorage` is an easy-to-use means of storing key-value pairs in the browser that are persisted across sessions. Its main three methods—`getItem()`, `setItem()`, and `removeItem()`—allow you to get, set, and remove strings, respectively, from an in-browser data store for your domain. For more information on `localStorage`, check out http://diveintohtml5.info/storage.html.

The last block of code prevents the user from saving an empty message. You attach a `keyup` handler to the `<textarea>` ❼. If the message is empty, you add the `ui-state-disabled` class name to the Save option; otherwise, you remove it ❽. The same as accordion and tabs, in order for markup changes to take effect on menus you need to call its `refresh()` method ❾.

Menus make it easy to create a powerful widget of grouped actions. You'll extend this menu with additional functionality later in this chapter, but for now we'll revisit a utility widget you first saw in chapter 2: dialog.

4.4 *Dialog: displaying content in a pop-up container*

The dialog is another UI element that needs no introduction. Most UIs use dialogs to display messages, confirm actions, or let the user select options. Despite their ubiquitous presence in desktop interfaces, dialogs are difficult to create on the web. Internet Explorer 4 introduced `window.showModelessDialog()` and `window.showModalDialog()` to show modeless and modal dialogs, respectively (we'll look at what those terms mean momentarily). Unfortunately, these APIs were verbose and fraught with issues; they haven't been implemented in all browsers. HTML 5.1 introduces the `<dialog>` element, but it'll be a long time before this gets implemented everywhere, and longer yet before it provides the functionality that web developers need.

Luckily, the jQuery UI dialog widget provides an easy and elegant means to display content in dialog windows. You saw some of what you can do with dialogs in chapter 2. Here we'll look at the advanced use of dialogs. We'll start with a common use case for dialogs: confirmation.

Confirmation dialogs are used to ensure the user wants to perform an irreversible action. Recall that your menu example from the previous section had a Delete action that removed the user's message without confirmation. Let's use the dialog widget to add a confirmation step to the delete process. Figure 4.6 shows the confirmation dialog you'll add.

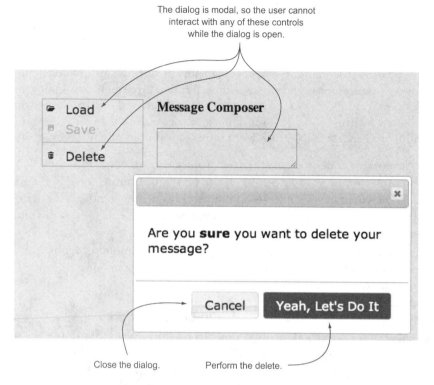

Figure 4.6   Prior to deleting the user's saved message, you'll present this confirmation dialog. This dialog allows the user to abort the action with the Cancel button, or proceed with the Yeah, Let's Do It button. This dialog is modal, which prevents the user from interacting with the rest of the screen until the user interacts with the dialog.

For reference, here's a condensed version of how you're currently handling a delete:

```
select: function( event, ui ) {
    var selection = $.trim( ui.item.text() );

    switch( selection ) {
        ...
        case "Delete":
            $( "#message" ).val( "" );
            localStorage.removeItem( "message", "" );
            break;
    }
}
```

To start this conversion, let's move the delete functionality to a function:

```
function deleteMessage() {
    $( "#message" ).val( "" );
    localStorage.removeItem( "message", "" );
};
```

Next, let's add the following <div> to your example's HTML to serve as the confirmation dialog:

```
<div id="confirmDelete">
    <p>Are you <strong>sure</strong> you want to delete your message?</p>
</div>
```

Now that you have this <div> on the DOM, you convert it to a dialog widget. This is shown in the following code:

```
$( "#confirmDelete" ).dialog({
    autoOpen: false,
    buttons: [
        {
            text: "Cancel",
            click: function() {
                $( this ).dialog( "close" );
            }
        },
        {
            text: "Yeah, Let's Do It",
            click: function() {
                deleteMessage();
                $( this ).dialog( "close" );
            },
            class: "primary"
        }
    ],
    minWidth: 400,
    modal: true
});
```

❶ Sets the dialog to NOT auto-open

❷ Calls the close() method

❸ Calls the deleteMessage() function, defined earlier

❹ Makes the dialog modal

Applies a primary CSS class name that you use to make the confirmation button visually stand out

NOTE If you're having trouble putting the pieces of this example together, don't worry. We'll return to the full source at the end of this chapter.

By default, dialogs automatically open when they're created. Here you don't want that behavior, as the dialog shouldn't display until the Delete option is clicked. Therefore, you set the autoOpen option to false ❶, preventing the automatic open.

Next, you define the buttons you want with the buttons option. Each object in the array can contain any attributes, properties, or event handlers the buttons should have. For the Cancel button, you assign a click event handler that closes the dialog ❷. Note that the context of the event handler (this) was automatically set to the dialog's DOM element. Therefore, you call the close() method with $(this).dialog("close").

The confirmation button also closes the dialog but first calls the deleteMessage() function you defined earlier to perform the delete ❸.

The final property you configure is the modal option. By default, dialog widgets are *modeless*—which means you can interact with other controls on the page while dialogs are open. In this case, you don't want users to be able to interact with the menu or alter the message while the confirmation message is displaying, and you want users to focus on the dialog rather than the rest of the UI; you set the modal option to true ❹. The dialog widget completely prevents users from interacting with content behind modal dialogs—including both mouse- and keyboard-based input.

After you create the dialog, your last step is to change the `Delete` handling to open your new dialog instead of performing the delete. To do this, you change the code that previously performed the delete to invoke your new dialog's `open()` method:

```
case "Delete":
    $( "#confirmDelete" ).dialog( "open" );
    break;
```

And that's it! You now have a functioning confirmation dialog that verifies the user wants to perform the irreversible delete action. We'll continue looking at the dialog widget throughout the book—we'll even build a few dialog extensions in chapter 9—but for now let's move on to a utility widget that displays the status of a process: progressbar.

4.5   Progressbar: displaying the progress of a task

Progressbar is another common UI element in desktop applications. When you install an application, your OS displays a bar indicating how far along in the process you are. When you download a file, your browser displays a bar that shows the progress.

The jQuery UI progressbar widget provides an easy way of implementing this functionality on the web. The progressbar widget has two modes: determinate and indeterminate. Determinate progressbars are used to display exact values—10%, 20%, and so forth. They should be used when you know the exact status of the process the progressbar is being shown for. An example of a determinate progressbar is shown in the following code:

```
<style>
    .ui-button { margin-top: 1em; }
    .ui-progressbar { position: relative; }
    #progressbar-label {
        position: absolute;
        left: 50%;                          Positions the label
        top: 4px;                           in the center of the
        font-weight: bold;                  progressbar
    }
</style>

<div id="progressbar">
    <div id="progressbar-label">0%</div>
</div>
<button>Make Progress</button>

<script>
    $( "#progressbar" ).progressbar();          ❶ Creates the      ❷ Creates a
                                                   progressbar        button
    var button = $( "button" ).button().on( "click", function() {    widget, and listens
        var value = $( "#progressbar" ).progressbar( "value" );      for clicks

                        Increments            value += 10;
                        the value                                   ❸ Gets the current
                                                                       value
```

❶ Creates the progressbar widget

❷ Creates a button widget, and listens for clicks

❸ Gets the current value

Increments the value

```
                $( "#progressbar" ).progressbar( "value", value );
Updates   ┌─►   $( "#progressbar-label" ).html( value + "%" );
the label │     if ( value === 100 ) {
          │         button.button( "disable" );
          │     }
        });
        </script>
```

Updates the label

Sets the incremented value ❹

If progress is complete, disables the button

You create a progressbar without setting any options ❶. The value option defaults to 0, which creates a determinate progressbar.

NOTE You create indeterminate progressbars by setting the value option to false. We'll look at those shortly.

You also create a button widget and attach a click event handler to it ❷. On every click you call the progressbar's value() method as a getter to retrieve the widget's current numeric value ❸. Then, you increment the value by 10 and call the value() method as a setter ❹ to update the displayed value. With this approach, the progressbar moves from 0 to 100 by increments of 10 with each click of the button. The display of this progressbar after three clicks is shown in figure 4.7.

Figure 4.7 A determine progressbar that advances 10% every time you click the Make Progress button.

Using determinate progressbars is appropriate when you know how far along in the process the user is, such as when a user fills out a form with multiple parts. But often this isn't the case. For these situations, you need indeterminate progressbars.

Indeterminate progressbars should be used to convey that some process is occurring and you don't know how long the process will take. To create indeterminate progressbars, you set the value option to false. Let's return to your message composer to see how you use an indeterminate progressbar.

In this example, you store and load data from localStorage. Interacting with localStorage is nearly instantaneous when dealing with small amounts of data like a single message. Suppose, however, you have a more common and complex case of loading and storing data in a server-side database. In this case, you don't know how long the user will have to wait while the data is retrieved and saved. Let's simulate this scenario and add an indeterminate progressbar to your example.

Recall that previously you've been retrieving the stored message directly in the select event:

```
select: function( event, ui ) {
    var selection = $.trim( ui.item.text() );

    switch( selection ) {
```

```
        ...
        case "Load":
            message = localStorage.getItem( "message" );
            $( "#message" ).val( message );
            break;
    }
}
```

As with the delete functionality, let's move this processing to its own function:

```
function loadMessage() {
    var message = localStorage.getItem( "message" );
    $( "#message" ).val( message );
}
```

To simulate more intensive processing, you wrap this functionality in a `setTimeout` to delay it by a few seconds:

```
setTimeout(function() {
    var message = localStorage.getItem( "message" );
    $( "#message" ).val( message );
}, Math.random() * 5000 );
```

⟵ **Delay processing by 0 to 5 seconds.**

Because the user has to wait, you show an indeterminate progressbar while the processing occurs. Furthermore, to prevent the user from interacting with the page during this time, you also place the progressbar in a modal dialog. This is shown in the following example:

```
function loadMessage() {
    var message,
        dialog = $( "<div>" ).dialog({
            modal: true,
            title: "Loading..."
        }),
        progressbar = $( "<div>" ).progressbar({ value: false });
    dialog.append( progressbar );
    setTimeout(function() {
        message = localStorage.getItem( "message" );
        $( "#message" ).val( message );
        dialog.remove();
    }, Math.random() * 5000 );
};
```

❸ **Adds the progressbar to the dialog**

❶ **Creates a modal dialog**

❷ **Creates an indeterminate progressbar**

❹ **Loads the message**

❺ **Removes the dialog**

You create a new `<div>` and convert it to a modal dialog ❶. Because dialogs auto-open, this dialog is instantly displayed to the user. Next, you create a new `<div>` and convert it to an indeterminate progressbar ❷. You append the progressbar to the dialog so the bar displays in the dialog ❸. Finally, when the timeout finishes you load the message as you did before ❹, and then remove the dialog from the DOM ❺.

This pattern of showing an indeterminate progressbar in a modal dialog is a convenient means of indicating to the user that some processing is occurring. The display of this progressbar is shown in figure 4.8.

With the progressbar in place, let's move on to the next of the utility widgets: slider.

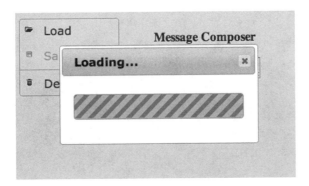

Figure 4.8 An indeterminate progressbar displayed in a modal dialog to indicate that processing is occurring—in this case you're loading a message.

4.6 *Slider: selecting a value using moveable handles*

Sliders are UI elements that let the user select a value between a min and a max. They let the user quickly visualize the range of potential values and easily experiment with values in that range. Because values are selected in a range, this automatically prevents the user from selecting invalid values.

As a realistic example, consider volume controls. They have a finite minimum value (mute) and a finite maximum value (the loudest that the hardware can produce); therefore, volume controls are typically represented as sliders. This not only gives the user an easy way to configure the volume level, but it also prevents the user from choosing ridiculous values—like a negative volume.

The jQuery UI slider widget brings this functionality to the web. The following code shows a slider control with the min, max, step, and value options set:

```
<div id="slider"></div>
<script>
    $( "#slider" ).slider({
        min: 0,
        max: 10,
        step: 2,
        value: 4
    });
</script>
```

This creates a slider to select a value between 0 and 10 that's a multiple of two. Because the value option is set to 4, the slider's handle starts there.

If this example seems familiar, it's because the min, max, and step options are also options on the spinner widget. The spinner widget enhances a textbox to accept numeric values, and the slider widget creates a range to select a value from. The difference is shown in figure 4.9.

So when do you use a slider and when do you use a spinner? In general, sliders are best at collecting approximate values and spinners are best at collecting precise values. For example volume controls make good sliders because you want an approximate level (quiet or loud) rather than an exact numeric value. Most thermostats function as spinners because you want an exact value—such as 72 degrees Fahrenheit.

```
<input id="spinner" value="4">
<script>
    $( "#spinner" ).spinner({
        min: 0,
        max: 10,
        step: 2
    });
</script>
```

```
<div id="slider"></div>
<script>
    $( "#slider" ).slider({
        min: 0,
        max: 10,
        step: 2,
        value: 4
    });
</script>
```

Figure 4.9   A comparison of the spinner (top) and slider (bottom) widgets. Although both widgets accept min, max, **and** step **options, the spinner enforces them within a textbox, and the slider enforces them using a visual range.**

When you do want to use a slider, the widget allows more powerful customization than putting a single handle on a range. Next, we'll look at how to configure the slider to collect a range of values.

4.6.1   *Building range sliders*

If you've ever shopped online, you've likely seen a range slider. Online retailers use range sliders to let you filter items between a minimum and a maximum price, such as all items between $25 and $75. To handle such a selection, you need the ability to place multiple handles on the range.

Building range sliders is tricky. You have to build multiple handles, prevent them from overlapping, style the range in between the handles, and ensure keyboard interactions continue to work. Fortunately, creating range sliders with the slider widget is as easy as setting the range option.

The range option accepts three values: true, "min", and "max". We'll look at an example to see what these values do. The following code shows three sliders with each type of range slider:

```
<div id="spinner-range"></div>
<div id="spinner-range-min"></div>
<div id="spinner-range-max"></div>

<script>
    $( "#spinner-range" ).slider({
        range: true,
        values: [ 25, 75 ]
    });
    $( "#spinner-range-min" ).slider({
```

```
        range: "min",
        value: 25
    });
    $( "#spinner-range-max" ).slider({
        range: "max",
        value: 75
    });
</script>
```

The display of this example is shown in figure 4.10.

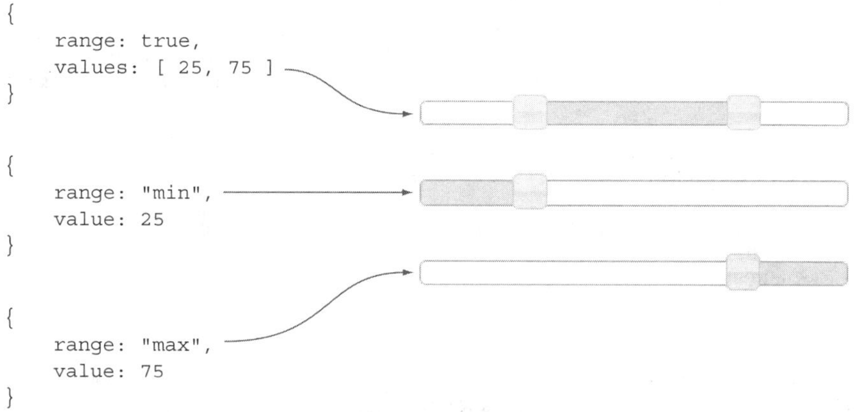

```
{
    range: true,
    values: [ 25, 75 ]
}
```

```
{
    range: "min",
    value: 25
}
```

```
{
    range: "max",
    value: 75
}
```

Figure 4.10   The three different types of range options provided by the jQuery UI slider widget. When the `range` option is `true` (top), the widget creates two handles and highlights the area between the two; when the range is `"min"` (middle), the widget highlights the area between the `value` and the `min`; when the range is `"max"` (bottom), the widget highlights the area between the `value` and the `max`.

As you can see from figure 4.10, a range option set to true creates a slider with two handles. The values option can be passed an array to configure the starting points of the two handles. The slider widget automatically styles the range between the handles.

On the other hand, the min and max ranges use only one handle. A "min" range highlights the area between the slider's min option (which defaults to 0) and the value; a "max" range highlights the area between the value and the slider's max option (which defaults to 100). Let's use this functionality to add a range slider to your message-composing example.

4.6.2   Adding a font size range

To show how to use a range slider, let's add a setting so that the user can change the font size of a message. This new control is shown in figure 4.11.

Recall that the message itself is in a `<textarea>` with an id of `"message"`:

```
<textarea id="message"></textarea>
```

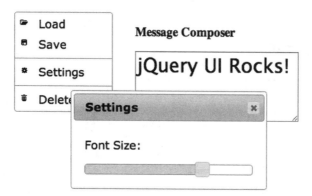

Figure 4.11   A slider to let the user change the message's font size

You start by defaulting the font size of this `<textarea>` to `1em` and giving it a set height and `width`:

```
#message {
    font-size: 1em;
    width: 250px;
    height: 100px;
}
```

Concrete dimensions prevent the `<textarea>` from resizing as you change the `font-size`. Next, you add a new Settings option to your example's menu:

```
<ul id="menu">
    ...
    <li>
        <span class="ui-icon ui-icon-gear"></span>Settings
    </li>
    ....
</ul>
```

When the user clicks this option, you have it open the following dialog:

```
<div id="settingsDialog">
    <p>Font Size:</p>
    <div id="slider"></div>
</div>
<script>
    $( "#settingsDialog" ).dialog({
        autoOpen: false,
        title: "Settings"
    });
</script>
```

NOTE   In this case, there's no need to make the dialog modal. There's no harm in letting the user interact with the rest of the interface while the settings dialog is open.

Your last step is to convert the `<div id="slider"></div>` in the dialog to a slider:

```
$( "#slider" ).slider({
    range: "min",
    value: 1,
    min: 0.5,
    max: 2.5,
    step: 0.1,
    slide: function( event, ui ) {
        $( "#message" ).css( "font-size", ui.value + "em" );
    }
});
```

Because this slider controls a font size in ems, and 1 em = 16 pixels by default, you set the step to 0.1 so the steps on the range are gradual. Along the same lines, you cap the minimum font-size at 0.5em and the maximum at 2.5em (8 pixels – 40 pixels by default).

You use the slider's slide event to change the font-size of the message. The event is triggered every time the user changes the slider's value. The new value is provided in the event's ui argument; you use it to call jQuery Core's css() method to perform the change.

The slider widget makes a nice fit for this example as it lets the user see the minimum and maximum font size at a glance and play with a variety of values. Next, we'll look at the last of the jQuery UI utility widgets: tooltip.

4.7 *Tooltip: enhancing native tooltips with a customizable control*

Like the other UI elements we've looked at in this chapter, tooltips are common on desktop applications. Hover over any icon in a word processor, image editor, or mail client and you'll likely be shown text describing what the icon does.

Unlike the other UI elements we've looked at, this behavior has been available on the web nearly since its inception. If you give an element a title attribute, all browsers display a tooltip after the user hovers over the element for approximately 1 second:

```
<input id="tooltip" title="Hover over me for a second and this message appears">
```

Although this behavior is easy to add, it's also limited. You have no control over the following things:

- The look of the tooltip.
- When the tooltip appears and disappears.
- Where the tooltip is positioned (above the element, below it, and so on).
- What displays in the tooltip. (You can't use HTML in a title attribute.)

The jQuery UI tooltip widget provides a customizable and themeable replacement for native tooltips that makes all items in this list possible. Because it's a direct replacement, the tooltip widget uses the title attribute directly by default:

```
<input id="tooltip" title="tooltip">
<script>
    $( "#tooltip" ).tooltip();
</script>
```

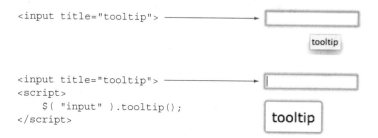

```
<input title="tooltip">
```

```
<input title="tooltip">
<script>
    $( "input" ).tooltip();
</script>
```

Figure 4.12   Comparison of a native tooltip (top) and the jQuery UI tooltip (bottom). The display of the native tooltip is controlled by the browser itself (this screenshot was taken in Chrome on OS X). The display of the jQuery UI tooltip is consistent across all browsers, and is highly configurable.

Figure 4.12 shows the effect of applying the tooltip widget to an `<input>`.

Although you can create tooltip widgets on individual elements, you can also instantiate the widget on any parent element. This approach adds tooltip functionality to any descendent element with a `title` attribute by default. The following code adds tooltip behavior to both `<input>` elements:

```
<div id="parent">
    <input title="tooltip">
    <input title="tooltip2">
</div>
<script>
    $( "#parent" ).tooltip();
</script>
```

This technique can be extended to the topmost container of an HTML document, the document object:

```
$( document ).tooltip();
```

That one line of code is all you need to create a direct replacement for native tooltips with the jQuery UI tooltip widget! Internally, the tooltip widget uses event delegation to determine which elements to display tooltips on and when. Event handlers are therefore attached only once, to the element the tooltip widget is created on. These handlers listen for mouse and focus events on descendent elements and display tooltips appropriately.

With delegated tooltips, the widget is smart enough to display tooltips on items you dynamically add to the DOM. Consider the following example that dynamically adds an `<input>`:

```
$( document ).tooltip();
document.body.innerHTML += "<input title='tooltip'>";
```

Because of the delegated approach, even though the `<input>` is added *after* the widget is created, tooltips display on the dynamically added element.

> **NOTE** The `items` option configures which elements display a tooltip. By default, this is set to any element with a `title` attribute, or `[title]`. If you wanted to display only tooltips on anchor elements with `id` attributes, you could change the `items` option to `[id]`. You'll see an example of this momentarily.

Although the tooltip widget provides an elegant replacement for the native control, sometimes you need more. The tooltip widget supports more powerful customization such as displaying HTML content, dynamically determining the content to display, and getting content from an external server. Let's see how.

4.7.1 Using custom tooltip content

The jQuery UI tooltip widget provides functionality far beyond what's capable with native `title` attributes. A `title` attribute, for example, can't contain HTML; therefore, something as simple as bolding a word isn't possible. With jQuery UI, you can use HTML by setting the `content` option.

The `content` option accepts a string with HTML to use as the message, or a function that returns the HTML to use. The following code shows how you can use the string version of the tooltip to display bold text:

```
<input id="tooltip">
<script>
    $( "#tooltip" ).tooltip({
        content: "<strong>Hi!</strong>"
    });
</script>
```

> **WARNING** jQuery UI doesn't parse HTML in a `title` attribute as it presents a cross-site scripting vulnerability. When `<input title="<strong>Hi!</strong>">` is converted to a tooltip widget, it literally displays `<strong>Hi!</strong>` in the tooltip presented to the user.

The function version of the `content` option adds the ability to customize the tooltip's behavior. The function is called before the tooltip is displayed to the user, and must return the content to display in the tooltip. The default version of the `content` option is a function that returns the element's `title` attribute. The following example shows how you can alter this behavior to display the `id` attribute of all elements in a tooltip:

```
<input id="I show!" title="I don't.">
<script>
    $( document ).tooltip({
        content: function() {
            return this.id;          ⟵——❶ Displays the id
        },
        items: "[id]"                ⟵──┐
    });                                  ❷ Uses tooltips for all
</script>                                   elements with an id
```

You instantiate a tooltip widget on the document object itself to ensure all elements on the DOM can potentially use tooltips. Then, you specify a function for the content option that returns the element's id ❶.

Next, you set the items option, which identifies the elements that display delegated tooltips. For consistency with the native tooltips, the items option defaults to [title], which tells the widget to show a tooltip on all items with a title attribute; for example, <input title="title">. Because this example is driven by id attributes, you change items to show a tooltip on all elements that have an id ❷; for example, <input id="id">.

Now that we've taken a tour of the tooltip widget's functionality, let's return to the message composer example to see how the tooltip widget can enhance your UI.

4.7.2 *Displaying a preview in a tooltip*

Recall that the first option in the message composer menu was an option to load a previously stored message:

```
<ul id="menu">
    <li>
        <span class="ui-icon ui-icon-folder-open"></span>Load
    </li>
    ...
</ul>
```

Unfortunately, the user currently has no way of previewing the saved message before loading. Let's use the tooltip widget to add this behavior. This is implemented in the following code:

```
                                    The first menu option is
                                    the Load option. Attach
                                    a tooltip widget to it.
$( "#menu li:first" ).tooltip({  ◁──
    content: function() {
        var message = localStorage.getItem( "message" );          ❶ Builds the message
        if ( message && message.length > 20 ) {                      to display in the
❸ Shows the     return message.substring( 0, 20 ) + "...";           tooltip.
tooltip after } else {
a I-second       return message;
delay.     }                      ❷ Ensures the element
    },                              displays despite having
    items: "*",              ◁──   no title attribute.
    show: { delay: 300 },
    position: {                     ❹ Positions the element on
        my: "left center",            the right of the menu.
        at: "right center"
    }
});
```

You create a tooltip on the Load menu option. The tooltip is for a preview, not for displaying the entire message. The content function grabs the actual message from localStorage, then conditionally substrings long messages and adds an ellipsis (...) to them ❶.

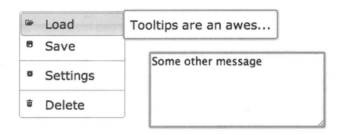

Figure 4.13   To give users a way to preview their stored message, you show a tooltip when they hover over the Load menu option.

Because the Load menu item doesn't have a `title` attribute, you override the default items option of `[title]` ❷. The star selector (`"*"`) selects all elements. Because only one element is eligible here—the selected `#menu li:first`—it's the only element matched.

Finally, you set options that we'll be taking a deeper look at in later chapters. The show option uses the jQuery UI effects configuration to show the tooltip after a 1-second delay ❸. We'll dig deeper into the full functionality of effects in chapter 6.

The `position` option sets the tooltip to display on the right-hand side of the Load menu option ❹. We'll look at the position utility and how this option can be configured in chapter 12.

The resulting tooltip that shows a message preview is shown in figure 4.13. This example assumes the user has previously saved a message of "Tooltips are an awesome UI control."

As a reminder, the full source of the message composer example is available at http://jsfiddle.net/tj_vantoll/jAwrA/. There you can play with all the options the tooltip widget provides. We'll look at additional uses of the tooltip widget throughout this book, including adding pointers to the tooltips in chapter 7, and using tooltips to display accessible form validation messages in chapter 11.

Using AJAX to retrieve tooltip content

The function form of the `content` option has one final variation that can be used to support content retrieved asynchronously. To use this variation, instead of returning a value directly, you invoke the function's first argument with the content to use. This is easier to see in an example. The following code displays a message tooltip for all elements with a `title` attribute:

```
$( document ).tooltip({
    content: function( response ) {
        response( "message" );
    }
});
```

(continued)

To use AJAX-loaded content, perform the server-side call and then invoke the same callback function with the results, as shown in the following code:

```
$( document ).tooltip({
    content: function( response ) {
        $.ajax({ url: "/path/to/server" })
            .then(function( data ) {
                response( data );
            });
    }
});
```

4.8   Summary

jQuery UI provides a collection of widgets that make building complex web UIs simple. The layout widgets—accordion and tabs—help you organize content in digestible chunks. You used the tabs widget to load remote data and create panels the user could toggle between and close. The jQuery UI utility widgets made it easy to replicate common desktop UI elements on the web. You used the utility widgets to build a demo for composing messages in the browser.

You'll continue to look at these widgets throughout the book. You'll see how to add effects to UI widgets in chapter 6, style UI widgets in chapter 7, and extend UI widgets in chapter 9. You'll also dig under the hood to see how these widgets are built in chapter 12. For now though, we'll shift from UI widgets to widgets that add mouse-based interactions.

Adding interaction to your interfaces

jQuery UI provides two types of widgets: the themeable widgets you've spent the last two chapters on, and a set of mouse-based widgets collectively known as interactions. Rather than changing the appearance of DOM elements, interactions let you perform various actions on DOM elements using the mouse. Applying the draggable widget to a DOM element, for example, lets the user drag the element around the screen using the mouse.

Despite being a different type of widget, interactions are still widgets implemented using the widget factory. The same conventions for options, methods, and events that you've learned still apply.

These mouse-based interactions are powerful tools when building interfaces. Suppose you need users to rank five movies from best to worst in a web form. You could provide text boxes to let users manually type in the rankings, but it's far easier—and more intuitive—to use the mouse to rearrange the movies. The sortable widget makes this interaction possible.

One major limitation of these interactions is that they don't currently support touch events; by default, the examples presented in this chapter don't work on iOS or Android devices. We'll explain why, and then look at a workaround to get touch events working in jQuery UI right now.

Let's begin our look at the jQuery UI interactions with the most commonly used one: draggable.

5.1 Draggable: allowing users to move elements

Draggable elements are ubiquitous in modern computer interfaces. Your OS of choice undoubtedly lets you drag files to move them around in the filesystem.

Although draggable interfaces are common, implementing them on the web still isn't easy. The HTML5 specification includes a `draggable` attribute that has now been implemented in all desktop browsers. Although the `draggable` attribute is great for dragging an element around the screen, it—like many native HTML5 features—suffers from limited customizability and extensibility.

The draggable widget shines because it makes it easy to perform complex interactions. To show how, let's build a few. Because interactions are widgets, they follow the same initialization conventions you've learned. The following code creates a red box you can drag around the screen:

```
<style>
    #draggable {
        width: 100px;
        height: 100px;
        background: red;
    }
</style>
<div id="draggable"></div>
<script>
    $( "#draggable" ).draggable();
</script>
```

First of all, it's pretty cool that one line of JavaScript is all you need to make an element draggable. But you can do more. The following code makes two draggables—one that can be moved only on the x-axis, and one that can be moved only on the y-axis:

```
<style>
    #x, #y {
        width: 100px;
        height: 100px;
    }
    #x { background: red; }
    #y { background: blue; }
</style>
<div id="x"></div>
<div id="y"></div>
```

```
<script>
    $( "#x" ).draggable({ axis: "x" });
    $( "#y" ).draggable({ axis: "y" });
</script>
```

It's powerful to see what you can do with a small amount of code. Let's look at one more example. Another common use case for draggable elements is constraining the area in which they're draggable. The draggable element makes this easy to implement with the `containment` option, as shown in the following code:

```
<style>
    #parent {
        border: 1px dotted black;
        width: 400px;
        height: 200px;
    }
    #draggable {
        background: red;
        height: 50px;
        width: 50px;                    Contains the parent
    }                                   element—a 400 x 200-
                                        pixel box with a l-pixel    Contains the draggable
</style>                                dotted black border         element—a red 50 x
<div id="parent">                                                  50-pixel-square box
    <div id="draggable"></div>
</div>
<script>
    $( "#draggable" ).draggable({ containment: "#parent" });
</script>
                                                   Contains the element in the
                                                   element with id "parent"
```

Here, because the `containment` option is set to `"parent"`, the draggable widget automatically prevents the draggable element from leaving its parent's boundaries. This behavior is shown in figure 5.1.

TIP The `containment` option also accepts a DOM element, the strings `"parent"`, `"document"`, and `"window"`—and even an array of coordinates in the document, such as in the form of (x1, y1, x2, y2). For more details, see http://api.jqueryui.com/draggable/#option-containment.

The draggable widget
contains the element
within its parent.

Figure 5.1   The draggable widget enforces the containment of the draggable box within its parent.

There's more to draggable than this, but before we delve too deep into draggable functionality, we need to introduce its sister widget: droppable.

5.2   *Droppable: creating containers that accept draggables*

Most UIs that use draggables also use droppables. Consider the OS's file interface. When you start dragging files, you can move them to alternate directories, move them to the trash bin, move them to other applications, and more.

The jQuery UI droppable widget makes it seamless to create drop targets for draggable widgets. As a short example, the following code has two `<div>` elements, the first of which is turned into a draggable widget and the second into a droppable widget. A `drop` event is fired whenever a draggable is dropped onto a droppable. You use a `drop` event callback to change the droppable's `background` to red, indicating that a drop occurred:

```
<style>
    #draggable {
        width: 100px;
        height: 100px;
        border: 1px solid black;
    }
    #droppable {
        width: 200px;
        height: 200px;
        border: 1px solid black;
    }
</style>
<div id="draggable"></div>
<div id="droppable"></div>
<script>
    $( "#draggable" ).draggable();
    $( "#droppable" ).droppable({
        drop: function() {
            $( this ).css( "background", "red" );
        }
    });
</script>
```

The draggable element, a 100-pixel-square box.

The droppable element, a 200-pixel-square box.

Set to the droppable element. Change its background to red after the draggable box is dropped on it.

That's all there is to detecting a drop. The widget handles all the complex mouse events and collision detection for you. Although this example shows what you can accomplish with a small amount of code, chances are you'll need to build something more complex than a box that turns red. To build something more useful, and to show off what draggable and droppable make possible, let's build something fun—a game.

5.2.1   *Building a drag-and-drop game*

Although drag and drop has many applications, one of the most prominent is in games. Dragging and dropping items on the screen builds a far more user-friendly experience than interacting with a series of form controls.

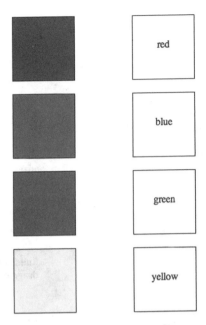

Figure 5.2   A game where children must match the colored boxes on the left to the word boxes on the right. To implement this, you convert the colored boxes to draggable widgets and the word boxes to droppable widgets.

For the purpose of this example, let's suppose you're a company that develops web games for children. You'll build a game in which kids have to match colors to words (matching a blue box to the word blue). Figure 5.2 shows the game you'll build.

The source for this example is shown in the following listing. Don't worry about the details; we'll go over each part individually.

NOTE   Some of the visual CSS is omitted from this example for clarity. You can check out the full source and play with this example live at http://jsfiddle.net/tj_vantoll/S7pdy/.

Listing 5.1   A children's word-matching drag-and-drop game

```
<style>
    #colors {
        position: absolute;
    }
    .ui-draggable {
        width: 100px;
        height: 100px;
        cursor: move;
        border: 1px solid black;
    }
    #drop-zones {
        position: absolute;
        left: 200px;
    }
    #drop-zones > div {
        width: 100px;
        height: 100px;
```

```
        border: 1px solid black;
    }
</style>

<div id="colors"></div>
<div id="drop-zones"></div>

<script>
    function randomize( array ) {
        return array.sort(function() {
            return 0.5 - Math.random();
        });
    };

    var i = 0,
        colors = randomize([ "red", "blue", "green", "yellow" ]);

    for ( ; i < colors.length; i++ ) {
        $( "<div>", { id: colors[ i ] } )
            .css( "background", colors[ i ] )
            .appendTo( "#colors" )
            .draggable({ revert: "invalid", zIndex: 2 });
    }

    randomize( colors );
    for ( i = 0; i < colors.length; i++ ) {
        $( "<div>", { text: colors[ i ] })
            .appendTo( "#drop-zones" );
    }

    $( "#drop-zones > div" ).droppable({
        accept: function( draggable ) {
            return $( this ).text() == draggable.attr( "id" );
        },
        drop: function( event, ui ) {
            var color = ui.draggable.css( "background-color" );
            $( this ).css( "background", color ).addClass( "filled" );
            ui.draggable.hide( "puff" );

            if ( $( ".filled" ).length === colors.length ) {
                $( "<div><p>Nice job! Refreshing game.</p></div>")
                    .dialog({ modal: true });
                setTimeout(function() {
                    window.location = window.location;
                }, 3000 );
            }
        }
    });
</script>
```

❶ Randomizes the list of colors used

❷ Builds the color draggables

❹ Builds the drop zones

❸ Rerandomizes the colors before building the droppables

❺ Determines the types of draggables each droppable accepts

❻ Sets the background of the droppable on success

❼ Hides the draggable with a puff effect

❽ Shows a confirmation dialog on game completion

This first thing to note in this example is the list of colors ❶. To ensure all games are different, you define a randomize() function that sorts this array in a random order.

Next, for each color in your array, you create a new <div> and set its id and background to that color, such as <div id="red" style="background: red;">. You then append the newly created <div> to the colors container (<div id="colors">) and convert it to a draggable widget ❷.

In doing so, you set two options: `revert` to `false` and `zIndex` to 2. The `zIndex` option controls the `zIndex` CSS property applied to the element being dragged. By setting it to 2, you ensure that the dragged element always displays on top of all other elements (because no elements have `zIndex` rules applied).

The `revert` option controls whether a draggable element returns to its starting position when dragging stops. When set to `false` (the default), the element never reverts; when set to `true`, it always reverts. You set it to `"invalid"`—which means the draggable reverts when not dropped on a droppable. This behavior is advantageous for your game, as the reversion provides visual feedback to the user that the selection was invalid.

> **TIP** You can control the duration of the revert animation using the `revert-Duration` option. If you were to set `revertDuration` to 2000, invalid draggable elements would take two full seconds to return to their starting positions.

Now that you've created the draggables, you have to create the droppable areas. You again randomize the list of colors ❸. If you didn't do this, the draggables would always be aligned with their appropriate droppable, which wouldn't be much of a challenge for your users!

After this, you again create a new `<div>` for each color. This time, though, you append the newly created elements to the drop zone container (`<div id="drop-zones">`) and set each color as their text ❹.

The last step is to convert these new drop zones to droppable widgets. You set an `accept` option and a `drop` event callback. The droppable widget's `accept` option controls which draggable widgets should be accepted. It supports two types of arguments. The first is a CSS selector—for example, `"*"` allows all draggables and `"#foo"` only allows draggables with an `id` of `"foo"`. The second, and the one you use ❺, is a function that must return a Boolean indicating whether the draggable should be accepted. Your version is shown here:

```
accept: function( draggable ) {
    return $( this ).text() == draggable.attr( "id" );
}
```

The context of the `accept` option (`this`) is set to the droppable element and is passed the draggable element as an argument. Recall that you set both the content of the droppables and the `id` of the draggables equal to the color's name. With that in mind, this function is saying, "when the text of the droppable matches the `id` of the draggable, the draggable should be accepted; otherwise, it should be rejected."

Because the `accept` option enforces the color section, your `drop` event is called only after the user makes valid selections. The `drop` event's `ui` parameter contains a reference to the draggable object in its `draggable` property. You grab the background-color from the draggable element and set it as the background of the droppable one as shown in the following code and at ❻. A `"filled"` class name is also added; you'll use that later to determine when the game is complete:

```
var color = ui.draggable.css( "background-color" );
$( this ).css( "background", color ).addClass( "filled" );
```

NOTE   As with the `accept` option, the context of the `drop` event is automatically set to the droppable's DOM element.

The background change gives the user a visual indication that the drop was successful, and because it was, you also no longer need the draggable. Therefore, you hide it ❼:

```
ui.draggable.hide( "puff" );
```

You use one of the jQuery UI effects—puff—to add a small effect that makes the draggable grow slightly as it fades away. We'll look more at how these effects can be configured in chapter 6.

The last thing you need to do is determine when the game is complete. Recall that you added a `"filled"` class name to each droppable in the `drop` event. Therefore, when the number of filled droppables matches the number of colors (`$( ".filled" ).length === colors.length`), the game is complete. At this point you show the user a congratulatory message ❽ then refresh the page to restart the game.

And with that, you have a fully functional matching game! Although there's a decent amount of code here, think about all the code the draggable and droppable widgets save you. You didn't have to write any code to implement dragging, detect collisions, or animate the draggables on invalid selections. Also, because you wrote this in a manner that looped over the colors, it's easy to alter the number of colors in this game to adjust the difficulty level. Try adding to the `colors` array, and note how the game still functions fine.

Although this is cool, you may be "I don't build children's games; how is this useful to me?" Dragging and dropping elements has all sorts of practical use cases, including a common feature on most e-commerce sites: the shopping cart.

5.2.2   *Building a shopping cart*

If you've ever shopped online, you've almost certainly used a shopping cart. In this section, let's imagine that you need to build an online shopping cart for a local grocery store. Due to the nature of grocery shopping, users tend to end up with a nontrivial number of items in their cart. Due to the number of transactions, you want to give the user an easy and intuitive way to add items. Therefore, you'll add a twist to the normal online shopping cart experience and let the users drag and drop available items to their cart.

We'll use this cart to explain a few more of the common configuration options in the draggable and droppable widgets. Figure 5.3 shows the cart that you'll build with the draggable `helper` and `cursor` options annotated.

The following listing shows the implementation of the shopping cart.

NOTE   A live demo of this example is available at http://jsfiddle.net/tj_vantoll/PUVXn/

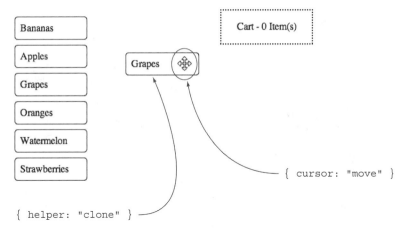

Figure 5.3   A shopping cart implemented with the jQuery UI draggable and droppable widgets

Listing 5.2   A grocery store shopping cart implementation

```
<style>
    #items { list-style: none; }
    #items li {
        border: 1px solid black;
        border-radius: 5px;
        width: 100px;
        cursor: move;
    }
    #cart {
        position: fixed;
        top: 0;
        right: 0;
        height: 55px;
        width: 150px;
        border: 2px solid black;
    }
    #cart.active {
        border: 2px dotted black;
    }
    #cart.hover {
        opacity: 0.5;
    }
</style>

<ul id="items">
    <li>Bananas</li>
    <li>Apples</li>
    <li>Grapes</li>
    <li>Oranges</li>
    <li>Watermelon</li>
    <li>Strawberries</li>
</ul>
<div id="cart">
    Cart - <span id="count">0</span> Item(s)
```

```
</div>

<script>
    $( "#items li" ).draggable({
        cursor: "move",
        revert: "invalid",
        helper: "clone"
    });
    $( "#cart" ).droppable({
        activeClass: "active",
        hoverClass: "hover",
        drop: function( event, ui ) {
            var count = parseInt( $( "#count" ).text(), 10 );
            $( "#count" ).text( count + 1 );
        },
        tolerance: "touch"
    });
</script>
```

1 Uses the CSS move cursor

2 Uses a clone of the item as the draggable helper

3 Applies this class name to the droppable on hover

4 Applies this class name to the droppable on activation

Accepts draggables on any overlap

5 Increments the cart's item count

You use CSS to position the cart in the top-right corner of the screen and the list of grocery items on the left. In JavaScript, you convert the items to draggable widgets and the cart to a droppable widget.

When converting the grocery list items to draggables, the first option you set is the cursor option to "move" **1**. This tells the widget to set the CSS cursor property to "move" while the draggable is dragged by the user. Although the cursor property has many potential values (see https://developer.mozilla.org/en-US/docs/Web/CSS/cursor for a list), "move" is the most appropriate choice for draggable elements. Because the cursor option only determines the cursor during a move, you also set { cursor: move; } on #items li in CSS. This provides the move cursor for users when they hover before they begin dragging. Setting these properties is important as the cursor change helps the user discover that the element in question can be dragged.

Next, you set the revert option to "invalid" as you did in the previous example. This is a common selection as it provides feedback to users that they missed the intended target.

Last, you set the helper option, which controls the element that the user drags. By default, helper is set to "original", which means the element converted to a draggable widget is used as the helper. You used this behavior in your matching game in the previous section. But in this case, you want to give the user the ability to drop multiple items of the same type in the cart; therefore, you leave the original draggable element in place. When the helper option is set to "clone" **2**, the draggable widget automatically clones the draggable when a drag starts, and removes the clone after a drag completes.

TIP   You can also pass a function for the helper option that returns a DOM element to use as a helper while dragging. This is useful when the original element is large or complex, and you only want to show a simplified representation while dragging.

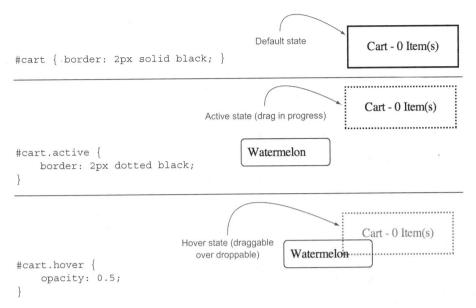

```
#cart { border: 2px solid black; }
```

```
#cart.active {
    border: 2px dotted black;
}
```

```
#cart.hover {
    opacity: 0.5;
}
```

Figure 5.4   The default, active, and hover states of a droppable as applied to the shopping cart

Now that the items are draggables, you need to turn the cart into a droppable widget. The first two options you set are activeClass to "active" ❸ and hoverClass to "hover" ❹. These options represent CSS class names to apply to the droppable element whenever an acceptable draggable is being dragged or hovered over the droppable, respectively. In this case, because you didn't specify an accept option, all draggable elements are considered acceptable. Like the cursor option, you use these class names to provide feedback to users. The display of the cart name under the various states is shown in figure 5.4.

If the feedback provided by these class names is so important, why didn't you use it in the matching game? Because activeClass and hoverClass apply class names only to acceptable droppables, they would affect only the correct color droppable in the matching game. Styling with these options would give away the correct answer!

The last option you set is tolerance ❺, which determines which algorithm the widgets should use for determining whether a draggable is indeed over a droppable. It has four possible values:

- "fit"—Drop is valid if the draggable overlaps the droppable *completely.*
- "intersect"—Drop is valid if the draggable overlaps the droppable by at least 50% vertically and horizontally. This is the default setting.
- "pointer"—Drop is valid if the mouse cursor is over the droppable.
- "touch"—Drop is valid if the draggable overlaps the droppable in any amount.

For your cart you want to make it as easy as possible for users to add items, so you set tolerance to the most permissive value: "touch".

And that's it for this example. In a few lines of code, you created a simple drag-and-drop shopping cart. Because it requires so little code, this functionality can easily be added to just about any existing shopping cart application.

With that, our look at the draggable and droppable widgets is complete, but we're just getting started with jQuery UI interactions. Next, we'll look at a close relative of the draggable and droppable widgets: sortable.

5.3 *Sortable: rearranging elements in a list*

One of the more common applications of draggable interfaces is the ability to sort items in a list. Although common, the sortable interaction is shockingly difficult to implement. You have to implement the logic to enable the mouse events for dragging, and then the collision detection from droppable, and then you need to reposition the items in the list to account for the rearranged list. Because of this, the sortable widget is the most complex widget in jQuery UI.

Fortunately, this complexity has all been abstracted to an easy-to-use widget. To create sortables, you call the plugin on an unordered list:

```
<ul id="sortable">
    <li>Item 1</li>
    <li>Item 2</li>
    <li>Item 3</li>
</ul>
<script>
    $( "#sortable" ).sortable();
</script>
```

That's all it takes to make the items in a list sortable by the user.

> **TIP** Although `<ul>` elements are the most common, you can turn any element into a sortable widget. The widget element's immediate children are converted to sortable items. This can be customized using the `items` option.

This interaction leads to all sorts of possibilities. Recall your movie site that you worked on in the last chapter. Let's suppose that the owners of this site contact you with a new feature in mind. They want to conduct a poll and have their users rank five popular movies from best to worst.

Think for a moment about how you'd implement this. Radio buttons are often used for polls, but they can gather only one selection, not capture the order of five items. You could use text boxes, but that's not user friendly. Let's see how you can build this poll using the sortable widget.

Figure 5.5 shows the poll that you'll build.

The implementation of this poll is shown in the following listing.

> **NOTE** Some visual CSS is not shown in the listing. The full source is available online at http://jsfiddle.net/tj_vantoll/5N6h9/.

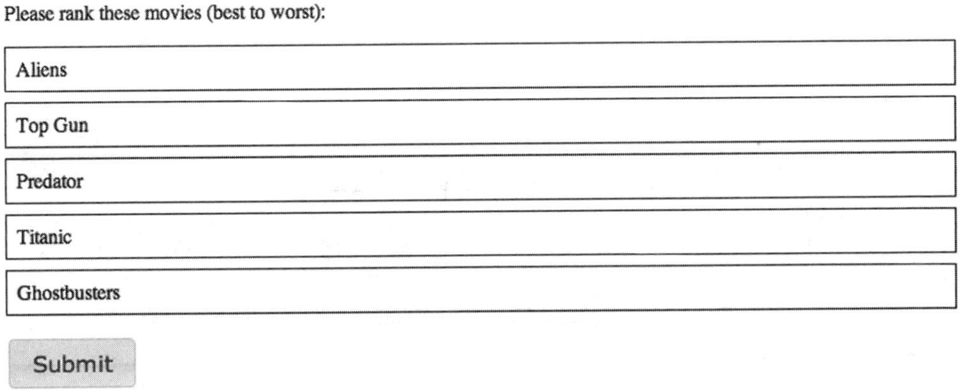

Please rank these movies (best to worst):

| Aliens |
| Top Gun |
| Predator |
| Titanic |
| Ghostbusters |

Submit

Figure 5.5   A poll that asks users to rank five movies from best to worst. The poll is implemented with the sortable widget; meaning, the user can rearrange movies with the mouse.

Listing 5.3   A movie-ranking poll

```
<style>
    #movies li:hover { cursor: move; }
    #movies .movie-placeholder {
        border: 1px dotted black;
    }
</style>

<p>Please rank these movies (best to worst):</p>
<ol id="movies"></ol>
<button>Submit</button>

<script>
    var movies = [ "Ghostbusters", "Titanic", "Top Gun",
        "Aliens", "Predator" ].sort(function() {
            return 0.5 - Math.random();
        }),
        i = 0,
        list = $( "#movies" ).sortable({
            placeholder: "movie-placeholder"
        });
    for ( ; i < movies.length; i++ ) {
        list.append( "<li>" + movies[ i ] + "</li>" );
    }
    $( "button" ).button().on( "click", function() {
        var movies = [];
        $( "#movies li" ).each(function() {
            movies.push( this.innerHTML );
        });
        alert( "Selection: " + movies.join( ", " ) );
    });
</script>
```

❶ Randomizes the movie order

❷ Creates the sortable widget

❸ Shows the user's selections in a pop up

You start with a list of movies that you rearrange in a random order ❶. You do this so the initial ordering of the list doesn't influence your users's selections.

Please rank these movies (best to worst):

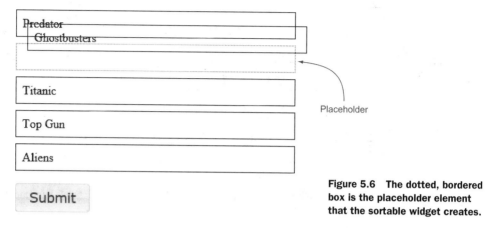

Figure 5.6   The dotted, bordered box is the placeholder element that the sortable widget creates.

Next you set one of the sortable's most common options: placeholder ❷. While a sortable item is being dragged, the sortable widget adds a filler element to the list. The sortable adds the filler where the item would be if it were dropped. This filler element is known as a placeholder and is far easier to show in a picture. Figure 5.6 shows the display of the placeholder during a sort.

The placeholder *option* specifies a class name to apply to this element so it can be styled with CSS. In your example you apply a movie-placeholder class name with an associated border: 1px dotted black CSS rule so your placeholder in figure 5.6 displays with a dotted border.

The last thing you do is attach a click event handler to your Submit button to gather the results. In the handler, you loop over each list item sequentially ($("#movies li").each(…)) and push each item's innerHTML—which is the name of the movie—to an array. At the end of the handler, you alert the user to show the results were collected successfully ❸. In a more realistic scenario, you'd send this data to a server that would aggregate these rankings and show the totals to the user.

This example shows how to use the sortable widget to build a practical UI control with a limited amount of code. Think of how painful and user unfriendly it would be to build a ranking control with regular HTML form elements. Next, we'll show a more powerful use of the sortable widget: connecting multiple lists.

Draggable vs. sortable

Even though much of the functionality is the same, the draggable and sortable widgets are not dependent on each other; but they do share a similar API. The sortable widget uses the following options that are also in draggable: axis, cancel, containment, cursor, cursorAt, delay, disabled, distance, grid, handle, helper, opacity, revert, scroll, scrollSensitivity, scrollSpeed, and zIndex.

(continued)
The sortable widget's `tolerance` option is similar to the droppable widget's; however, droppable offers four choices—`"fit"`, `"intersect"`, `"pointer"`, and `"touch"`; sortable offers only `"intersect"` and `"pointer"`.

5.3.1 Building connected lists

A common requirement of sortable lists is to connect multiple lists to each other. Consider a scheduling application where people or supplies need to be divided into multiple groups, or a to-do app that lets users move items from To Do to Done (and, unfortunately, vice versa). The jQuery UI sortable widget makes it easy to connect lists with the `connectWith` option.

To show how to do this, let's build another children's game with a different twist. This time you'll present the user with two lists with mismatched items—in this case, fruits and vegetables. The user's job is to move each item to the appropriate list.

To start, you create lists and connect them with the `connectWith` option. The following example builds two connected lists:

```
<h3>Fruits</h3>
<ul>
    <li>Banana</li>
    <li>Carrot</li>
    <li>Grape</li>
</ul>

<h3>Vegetables</h3>
<ul>
    <li>Apple</li>
    <li>Pea</li>
    <li>Spinach</li>
</ul>
<script>
    $( "ul" ).sortable({
        connectWith: "ul"
    });
</script>
```

The `connectWith` option takes a selector of sortable elements that the current list should be connected to. Therefore, `$( "ul" ).sortable({ connectWith: "ul" })` converts all `<ul>` elements to sortable widgets and connects them all. The user can then drag items from the fruits list to the vegetables list and vice versa. Let's see how you can take this basic functionality and turn it into a complete game.

5.3.2 Building a fruit and vegetable sorting game

To create a game, you need to do more than build lists. You need to validate the correctness of the lists, and ideally add a bit of randomness so the user isn't playing the same game every time. The sortable widget gives you the hooks to make this possible.

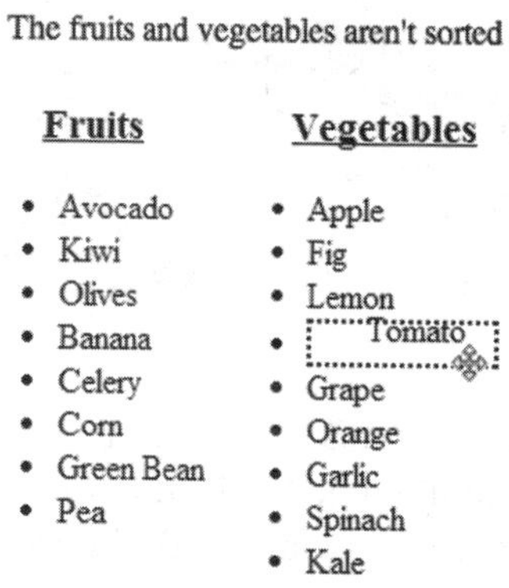

The fruits and vegetables aren't sorted correctly—rearrange them!

<u>**Fruits**</u>   <u>**Vegetables**</u>

- Avocado   - Apple
- Kiwi   - Fig
- Olives   - Lemon
- Banana   - Tomato
- Celery   - Grape
- Corn   - Orange
- Green Bean   - Garlic
- Pea   - Spinach
               - Kale

Figure 5.7 A fruit and vegetable sorting game implemented with the sortable widget. The user must move all fruits into the fruits list and all vegetables into the vegetables list to win.

As with previous examples, we'll show an implementation of the game, and then walk through it step by step. Figure 5.7 shows the display of the game, and the implementation is shown in listing 5.4.

NOTE   The CSS for this example is omitted here for brevity. You can view it in the book's downloadable code samples, or view this example live at http://jsfiddle.net/tj_vantoll/nCjwc/.

Listing 5.4 A children's game to sort fruits and vegetables

```
<p>The fruits and vegetables are not sorted correctly—rearrange them!</p>
<div id="game">
    <div id="fruits-container">
        <h3>Fruits</h3>
        <ul id="fruits"></ul>
    </div>
    <div id="vegetables-container">
        <h3>Vegetables</h3>
        <ul id="vegetables"></ul>
    </div>
</div>
<script>
    var fruits = [ "Avocado", "Banana", "Apple", "Cherry", "Fig", "Grape",
            "Kiwi", "Lemon", "Olives", "Orange", "Pumpkin", "Tomato" ],
        vegetables = [ "Broccoli", "Carrot", "Celery", "Corn", "Garlic",
            "Green Bean", "Kale", "Lettuce", "Onion", "Pea", "Spinach",
            "Turnip" ];

    $.each( fruits.concat( vegetables ), function( index, item ) {
        var type = fruits.indexOf( item ) >= 0 ? "fruit" : "vegetable";

        if ( Math.random() < 0.6 ) {
            $( "<li data-type=" + type + ">" + item + "</li>" )
                .appendTo( Math.random() >= 0.5 ? "#fruits" :
                    "#vegetables" );
        }
    });

    $( "#fruits, #vegetables" ).sortable({
```

Creates a new list item for each fruit and vegetable ❷

❶ Randomly determines whether each item is included

Connects the fruit and vegetable lists

Checks for completion in a stop event ④

③ Creates a `<div>` to use as a helper

```
connectWith: "#fruits, #vegetables",
cursor: "move",
helper: function( event, item ) {
    return $( "<div>", { text: item.text() } );
},
placeholder: "sortable-placeholder",
stop: function() {
    if ( isValid() ) {
        $( "<div>" ).append( "<p>Correct! Refreshing game.</p>" )
            .dialog();
        setTimeout(function() {
            window.location = window.location;
        }, 3000 );
    }
}
});

function isValid() {
    var valid = true;
    $( "#fruits li, #vegetables li" ).each(function() {
        var item = $( this ),
            actual = item.parent()[ 0 ].id == "fruits" ? "fruit" :
              "vegetable",
            correct = item.attr( "data-type" );

        if ( actual != correct ) {
            valid = false;
        }
    });
    return valid;
};
</script>
```

You start with an array of fruits and vegetables, and loop over them to create the sortable items. You wrap the addition of each fruit and vegetable with a `Math.random()< 0.6` call ❶. Because `Math.random()` returns a number between 0 and 1, each fruit and vegetable is present in the game 60% of the time. This adds randomness so that users aren't bored after their first play.

For each fruit and vegetable that passes your check, you then create a list item as shown in the following code ❷:

```
$( "<li data-type=" + type + ">" + item + "</li>" )
    .appendTo( Math.random() >= 0.5 ? "#fruits" : "#vegetables" );
```

Two interesting things are going on here. First, you store the type of the list item (fruit or vegetable) in a `data-type` attribute. You use that later when you verify that the user's selections are correct. Next, you call `Math.random()` again. Because this call uses 0.5, there's a 50% chance you'll append this new list item to the fruits list and a 50% chance you'll append it to the vegetables list.

Now that the lists are populated, you turn them into widgets. The `cursor` and `placeholder` options should look familiar from the previous example, but the `helper` option is new. Whenever a drag starts on a sortable item, the element being dragged is referred to as a helper element, and is given a class name of `ui-sortable-helper` for styling purposes. By default, the helper is the sortable element itself, which corresponds to a `helper` option of `"original"`. The `helper` option also accepts `"clone"`, which clones the element and uses it as a helper, or a function that returns a new element to use as a helper. In this example, you use this option and create a new helper `<div>` ❸:

```
helper: function( event, item ) {
    return $( "<div>", { text: item.text() } );
}
```

Why did you do this? Because these sortable elements are `<li>` elements, by default they're displayed with bullets next to them in the list—for example, • Banana. Dragging an element with the bullet looks a little odd, and creating a new `<div>` to use as a helper works around this.

> **NOTE** A cleaner solution would've been to apply `list-style-type: none` to the `ui-sortable-helper` class name in CSS. But the function-based helper works just as well and serves as a nice introduction to the option.

You've now completed all setup needed for the game, so the last thing to do is to check when the user has successfully sorted all items. The sortable widget's `stop` event is called when any sort completes; it's the perfect place to check whether the user has finished ❹. The implementation of this check is in the `isValid()` function, which you call immediately. Don't worry too much about the implementation of `isValid()`. All it does is use the `data-type` attribute you set on each list item to determine whether all items are in the correct list. If `isValid()` returns `true`, you display a confirmation dialog to the user and refresh the page to start a new game.

With that, you have a functioning sorting game in a few dozen lines of JavaScript. Think about how hard this would've been to set up without any help from jQuery UI. You'd have to recreate the draggable items, the collision detection, helper and placeholder management, and more. It's no wonder the sortable widget is the most complex widget in the library.

Building sortable tables

One little-known feature of the sortable widget is that you can use it to make table rows sortable. There's one small caveat, though: you need to convert the table's `<tbody>` to a sortable widget rather than the `<table>` itself, as shown in the following code:

```
<style>
    td { border: 1px solid black; }
</style>
<table>
    <tbody>
        <tr><td>One</td></tr>
        <tr><td>Two</td></tr>
    </tbody>
</table>
<script>
    $( "tbody" ).sortable();
</script>
```

Let's move on to another common, yet tricky, interaction that jQuery UI makes easy: resizing elements.

5.4   *Resizable: allowing users to change the size of elements*

Resizable elements are another common desktop interaction. Resizable elements have two use cases. The first is to give the user control over the size of the display. Consider the windows in a desktop OS; users can change the size of each individual window to meet their needs. The other use case for resizable elements is to add additional functionality. Most calendar applications, as an example, let you resize entries to increase the duration of an appointment in either direction.

The jQuery UI resizable widget makes it easy to create resizable elements on the web, with several options that make advanced and tricky use cases possible. Like all the jQuery UI widgets, to create a resizable element you invoke the widget's plugin. The following code creates a resizable `<div>`:

```
<style>
    #resizable {
        width: 100px;
        height: 100px;
        border: 1px dotted black;
    }
</style>
<div id="resizable"></div>
<script>
    $( "#resizable" ).resizable();
</script>
```

This displays as shown in figure 5.8.

The resizable widget automatically adds an icon to the bottom right-hand side of the element. By default, resizable elements can be resized to the south, east, and southeast. The `handles` option lets you configure this behavior.

Figure 5.8   A 100 x 100 `<div>` element converted to a resizable widget. By default the element can be resized to the south, east, and southeast.

> **TIP**   If the icon in the bottom corner is undesirable, you can remove it by adding `.ui-resizable-se { background: none; }`. After you do this, the functionality remains, but the icon is gone.

The `handles` option is set to `"e, s, se"` by default, which explains the behavior you see. You can set the option to a comma-delimited string containing any of the following in any order: n, e, s, w, ne, se, sw, nw. You can also pass the string `"all"` to make an element that can be resized in any direction. The handles are shown in figure 5.9.

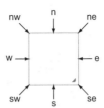

Figure 5.9   The resizable widget lets you configure the directions the element can be resized with the `handles` option. The eight potential handles are shown on an element. The `handles` option also accepts `"all"`, which uses all eight handles.

To allow for more customization, you can also build custom handles.

5.4.1   *Using custom resize handles*

The final version of the `handles` option lets you specify your own DOM elements to use as the handles. This allows you to build custom resizable interactions. Figure 5.10 shows a resizable element with a custom east handle.

Figure 5.10   A resizable element with a custom resizing handle on its east side. You build this by explicitly providing markup for the east handle, as shown in listing 5.5.

The following listing shows the code used to build this element.

Listing 5.5   Resizable element with a custom east handle

```
<style>
    #resizable {
        width: 100px;
        height: 100px;
        border: 1px solid black;
    }
    .ui-resizable-e {
        background-color: skyblue;
        width: 18px;
        right: 0;
    }
</style>

<div id="resizable">
    <div class="ui-resizable-handle ui-resizable-e">
        <span class="ui-icon ui-icon-triangle-1-e"></span>
        <span class="ui-icon ui-icon-triangle-1-e"></span>
        <span class="ui-icon ui-icon-triangle-1-e"></span>
        <span class="ui-icon ui-icon-triangle-1-e"></span>
        <span class="ui-icon ui-icon-triangle-1-e"></span>
        <span class="ui-icon ui-icon-triangle-1-e"></span>
    </div>
</div>

<script>
    $( "#resizable" ).resizable({
        handles: {
            e: ".ui-resizable-e"
        },
        minWidth: 50
    });
</script>
```

1 The element that you use as the east handle

2 Specifies the custom handle in the handles option

3 Ensures the element is at least 50 pixels wide

The first thing to notice here is the class names on your custom handle **1**. The resizable widget requires that a custom handle have class names `ui-resizable-handle` and `ui-resizable-{direction}`—in this case, `ui-resizable-e`.

To tell the resizable widget about your custom handle, you pass an object in as the `handles` option ❷. The keys of the object are the directions in which the user can resize. In this case, you specify `"e"` because the user should only be able to resize to the east. The value of each handle can be a selector that matches a child element of the resizable element, a DOM element, or a jQuery object. In this case, your handle is a child of the resizable element, so you pass a selector that matches it.

As a last step, you set the `minWidth` option to 50 ❸. This prevents the user from resizing the element to a size smaller than 50 pixels. The resizable widget also provides `maxWidth`, `minHeight`, and `maxHeight` options for similar constraining functionality.

With custom handles you can build a highly customized display for your resizable controls. To see at what the resizable widget makes possible, let's look at a common use of resizable UI elements: a calendar control.

5.4.2 Building an appointment scheduler

Most desktop calendar programs give you the ability to drag and resize appointments using the mouse. Although writing a full-featured web-based scheduler is a complex topic well out of the scope of this book, let's look at how the resizable and draggable widgets make building the grid portion of the calendar easy. Figure 5.11 shows the calendar grid you'll build.

In this grid the black box represents an appointment and each column represents a day of the workweek. The vertical gray lines are spaced 50 pixels apart and are used to represent half-hour time slots. To build this scheduler, suppose you have the following requirements:

- The appointment can resize only in the north and south directions.
- The appointment can resize only in certain intervals, corresponding to a half hour (50 pixels).
- Appointments can be dragged anywhere within a day or into other days.
- The appointment can't be dragged or resized outside of the calendar.

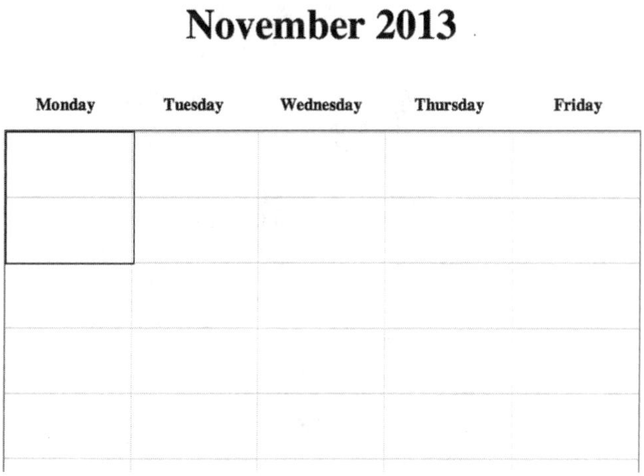

Figure 5.11 A scheduler for creating appointments. The black box represents an appointment, and the vertical lines represent half-hour time slots. The user can drag the appointment to different days and times— and resize the appointment to change its length.

Consider how tricky these requirements are to meet without the help of any widgets or plugins. With the jQuery UI interactions, you can meet these requirements with nine lines of JavaScript! The following listing shows an implementation of this grid.

> **NOTE** This example is available online at http://jsfiddle.net/tj_vantoll/ yUs44/.

Listing 5.6   Building a calendar grid with resizable and draggable

```
<style>
    #appointment {
        width: 100px;
        height: 100px;
        border: 1px solid black;
    }
    #appointment:hover { cursor: move; }
    #calendar {
        border: 1px solid red;
        height: 500px;
        width: 500px;
        position: relative;
        background-color: #fff;
        background-image:
            linear-gradient( 90deg, transparent 99%, #ddd 100% ),      Creates the
            linear-gradient( #eee .1em, transparent .1em );            grid lines
        background-size: 20% 100%, 100% 50px;
    }
</style>

<h1>November 2013</h1>
<div id="headers">
    <h3>Monday</h3>
    <h3>Tuesday</h3>
    <h3>Wednesday</h3>
    <h3>Thursday</h3>
    <h3>Friday</h3>
</div>
<div id="calendar">
    <div id="appointment"></div>
</div>
<script>
    $( "#appointment" ).resizable({          ❶ Resizes the
        handles: "n, s",                       appointment only to
        grid: [ 0, 50 ],                       the north and south
        containment: "parent"
    })
    .draggable({                             ❸ Contains the resizable
        grid: [ 100, 50 ],                      in its parent
        containment: "parent"
    });
</script>
```

Resizes only by increments of 50 pixels ❷

❹ Makes the element draggable

WARNING   The grid lines are drawn using CSS gradients. Although most browsers now support CSS gradients, they're not supported in Internet Explorer versions 9 and earlier. In these browsers, the grid doesn't appear. For a full list of browsers that support CSS gradients, see http://caniuse.com/#feat=css-gradients. For more information on how this grid works, as well as how to create other cool patterns with CSS gradients, see http://lea.verou.me/2010/12/checkered-stripes-other-background-patterns-with-css3-gradients/.

Let's look at how this example meets all your criteria. First, by setting the appointment's `handles` option to `"n, s"` ❶, you enforce the requirement that the resizable element can only be resized vertically, not horizontally or diagonally.

Your next criterion was to allow the user to resize the appointment only in a set interval. You want to let the user resize appointments by the hour or half hour, rather than by minutes or seconds.

To implement this, you use the resizable widget's `grid` option ❷. The `grid` option takes an array of pixels, with the x and y values as the resizing increments. The x value of the array is irrelevant, as the user can't resize the appointment horizontally. By setting the y value to `50`, the resizable widget allows the appointment's height to be changed only by increments of 50 pixels—50 pixels, 100 pixels, 150 pixels, and so on—which corresponds to half hours, per the example's convention.

Next, you prevent the user from resizing an appointment outside of the calendar itself. This is easy as the resizable widget has the same `containment` option as the draggable widget. By setting `containment` to `"parent"`, the resizable widget automatically contains all resizing actions in its parent widget—the calendar ❸. As with the draggable widget, the resizable widget's `containment` option can also be set to a selector or a DOM element to contain the element within.

This takes care of your resizable criteria. Next, you make the appointment draggable ❹.

TIP   A DOM element can be initialized with multiple widgets. Although some combinations make no sense—for instance, an element that's a dialog and a datepicker—some, such as draggable and resizable, can be quite useful.

To keep draggable in sync with resizable, you also set the draggable `grid` option. Unlike resizable, the x value of the grid is relevant here, as you want to let the user drag appointments horizontally to different columns. You specify an x value equal to the width of the columns: `100`. For the y value, you use the same value as resizable (`50`) so the user can drag appointments to reschedule by the half hour.

That's all there is to it. You built a powerful appointment scheduler that met your criteria with a few lines of configuration for the draggable and resizable widgets. This brings us to the last of the jQuery UI interactions: selectable.

Dialog, resizable, and draggable

Whether or not you realized it, you saw the draggable and resizable widgets in action before this chapter. The dialog widget uses these interactions to make dialog elements draggable and resizable by default. Whether dialog elements are draggable and resizable can be configured using the `draggable` and `resizable` options, respectively. The following code shows how to create a dialog that's neither draggable nor resizable:

```
$( "<div>" ).dialog({
    draggable: false,
    resizable: false
});
```

5.5   *Selectable: allowing users to select elements from a group*

Selectable elements should be familiar to anyone who has used a file browser GUI in any OS. Almost invariably the OS lets you select a file by clicking on it, select additional files by clicking with a modifier key held down (Control on Windows, Command on OS X), and select multiple files simultaneously by dragging your mouse to create a box or lasso.

The jQuery UI selectable widget brings this paradigm to the web. Selectable is one of the simplest widgets of jQuery UI. Although it has options, methods, and events like other widgets, for the vast majority of use cases the default behavior is all you need. Therefore, we'll only be looking at a single example that replicates the file GUI behavior in the browser.

Like sortable, when the selectable's plugin is called on an element, its immediate children are converted to selectable items. The following code converts a list to a selectable widget:

```
<ul id="selectable">
    <li>book.pdf</li>
    <li>image.png</li>
    <li>portrait.jpg</li>
    <li>paint.bmp</li>
    <li>words.doc</li>
    <li>text.txt</li>
</ul>
<script>
    $( "#selectable" ).selectable();
</script>
```

Although this does create a selectable widget, it gives no visual indication of what files are selected. This is because instead of styling the selectable elements directly, the widget adds CSS class names to the appropriate items and the author is responsible for styling them. The following four class names are applied by the selectable widget:

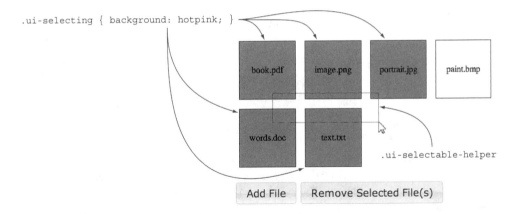

Figure 5.12 A browser representation of an OS's file GUI implemented with the selectable widget. The user can add new files and remove any selected files. The selectable widget's helper is styled with a dotted line, and files selected with the lasso are styled with a background in color.

- `ui-selectee`—Applied to all selectable elements, regardless of state
- `ui-selecting`—Applied to elements selected by the lasso before the user releases the mouse
- `ui-selected`—Applied to selected elements
- `ui-selectable-helper`—Applied to the lasso created by the mouse

To see how these class names work, you'll add a little CSS to your example. You'll also add a Remove button to make the example a bit more useful. Figure 5.12 shows the updated display of your example.

The following listing shows the final code of this example.

NOTE Some CSS is omitted from this example to focus on the selectable interaction. You can view the full source and play with this example at http://jsfiddle.net/tj_vantoll/Bd57U/.

Listing 5.7 Mimicking a filesystem GUI with jQuery UI

```
<style>
    .ui-selecting { background: hotpink; }
    .ui-selected { background: red; color: white; }
</style>

<ul id="selectable">
    <li>book.pdf</li>
    <li>image.png</li>
    <li>portrait.jpg</li>
    <li>paint.bmp</li>
    <li>words.doc</li>
    <li>text.txt</li>
</ul>
```

① Styles selectables hot pink during selection

② Styles selectables red with white text after selection

```
<button id="add">Add File</button>
<button id="remove">Remove Selected File(s)</button>

<script>
    var selectable = $( "#selectable" ).selectable();
    $( "#add" ).button().on( "click", function() {
        selectable.append( "<li>new</li>" );
    });
    $( "#remove" ).button().on( "click", function() {
        $( ".ui-selected" ).remove();
    });
</script>
```

❸ **Adds a new list item to the list**

❹ **Removes all selected items**

You style selectables as hot pink during mouse selection ❶ and red with white text after they have been selected ❷. You don't touch the `ui-sortable-helper` class name, leaving it as its default display defined by the widget (`border: 1px dotted black`).

After creating the selectable widget, you convert the Add button to a button widget and attach a `click` handler to it. The `click` event handler adds a new `<li>` element to the list ❸—and that's it. There's no `refresh()` method call or any call that tells the widget of the new element. How does the widget know that a new element was added?

The selectable widget is unique because it checks for new elements in the list whenever a select operation begins. Because this is a potentially expensive operation, the widget exposes an `autoRefresh` option that you can set to `false` to disable it. If you set `autoRefresh` to `false`, the widget has a `refresh()` method you can call after adding and removing elements. Because you have only a handful of items here, it makes sense to leave `autoRefresh` set to `true`.

The last thing you do is convert the Remove button to a button widget and attach a `click` event handler to it as well. In the `click` handler, you select all elements with the `ui-selectable-selected` class name and remove them from the DOM ❹.

If you run this example, you'll notice that you can perform all the actions that you're used to with a desktop OS with this small amount of code.

Before we end our discussion of jQuery UI interactions, there's one last thing we need to discuss. If you've happened to test any of the examples in this chapter to this point on an iOS or Android device, you may have noticed that they don't work. In the next section we'll discuss why that is, and what you can do to make them work.

5.6 Creating multidevice interactions: the importance of touch

Unless you have been living under a log, you're likely aware of the mobile explosion that has taken the web development industry by storm. Despite this, the latest release of jQuery UI still doesn't support touch events out of the box.

Why is this?

5.6.1 Why doesn't jQuery UI support touch events?

The answer is complicated and requires a short history lesson. In 2007 the iPhone was released and with it came touch events: a new event model for handling interactions on the web. Android soon followed with an implementation, and Firefox for Android, Chrome for Android, BlackBerry, and Opera Mobile would soon follow as well.

Despite the number of implementations, Apple's model has two major problems. First, it forces web developers to explicitly handle two types of events: mouse-based ones and touch-based ones. Unfortunately, the two event models have subtle differences that make this a nontrivial task.

The second issue is that Apple owns a number of patents related to its touch event implementation. These patents have (thus far) prevented touch events from becoming a W3C standard.

Because of these issues, the Internet Explorer team came up with a new approach known as pointer events, which shipped in Internet Explorer 10. Microsoft submitted this model to the W3C, and it's now a candidate recommendation spec—http:// www.w3.org/TR/pointerevents/.

> **NOTE** The candidate recommendation status means that the major features of the spec are locked down and the spec authors are waiting for feedback on the finer points before the spec enters its next state: proposed recommendation.

The pointer event model addresses the single largest problem with the touch event model: it handles multiple input types. If you're on a Windows touch screen tablet, you can handle mouse, touch, and stylus-based input, all with a single set of pointer events.

The jQuery UI team feels this model is the best way to move forward with events on the web; the team is currently working with others to create a polyfill of pointer events for browsers that don't natively support them, which will make the interactions work on any device. Expect it to be included in the library in a future release of jQuery UI.

> **NOTE** You can read a more thorough history of touch events at http:// blog.jquery.com/2012/04/10/getting-touchy-about-patents/.

Although this history lesson provides background, you're likely interested in getting the jQuery UI widgets to work for you now. Fortunately, there's a quick workaround to make that possible.

5.6.2 *Introducing jQuery UI Touch Punch*

jQuery UI Touch Punch is a tiny script that adds touch event support to all the jQuery UI widgets. It listens for touch events, then uses a DOM specification known as custom events to fire the corresponding mouse events that the jQuery UI widgets are looking for.

> **TIP** Custom events allow you to trigger native events (click, keypress, mousemove, touchstart, and so on) as if the user had taken that action. To read more about custom events, see https://developer.mozilla.org/en-US/docs/ Web/Guide/API/DOM/Events/Creating_and_triggering_events.

What's nice about Touch Punch is it requires no configuration to make it work. You download Touch Punch's script from http://touchpunch.furf.com/ and include it after `jquery-ui`:

```
<script src="jquery.js"></script>
<script src="jquery-ui.js"></script>
<script src="jquery.ui.touch-punch.js"></script>
```

That's it. This approach adds touch support for the jQuery UI widgets in any browser that supports the touch event model (iOS Safari, Android, Chrome for Android, Firefox for Android, Opera Mobile, and BlackBerry).

Although having to include an external plugin isn't ideal, Touch Punch provides an elegant stopgap solution until true pointer event support is released in jQuery UI.

Interactions on Windows 8 touch devices

Even though the jQuery UI interactions do not support pointer events, as of version 1.11, the interactions *do* support Windows 8 touch devices running Internet Explorer 10 and Internet Explorer 11. How? When you apply an interaction widget to an element, the widget sets the element's `touch-action` CSS property to `"none"`, which makes Internet Explorer 10+ fire the mouse events that make the interactions work— even on touch screens. You can read more about what the `touch-action` property does at http://msdn.microsoft.com/en-us/library/windows/apps/hh767313.aspx.

To summarize, the jQuery UI interactions work in all desktop browsers, as well as Windows 8 devices. The interactions do not work on mobile browsers that use the touch event model, but you can use Touch Punch to add support for those browsers. Between the two you get comprehensive device coverage.

5.7   *Summary*

In this chapter, you looked at the five interaction widgets provided by jQuery UI. You used them to create a number of practical UIs—from children's games to a shopping cart to an appointment scheduler.

Currently, these interactions don't work on mobile browsers that use the touch event model, such as iOS Safari and Chrome for Android. The jQuery UI team is working on creating a polyfill for pointer events that will bring support to all browsers, but in the meantime, you can use jQuery UI Touch Punch to make sure the interactions work on all devices today.

With this chapter, we've now completed our look at all the jQuery UI widgets. Although we'll continue to explore the inner workings of widgets throughout the book, for now we'll switch our focus to the jQuery UI animation components, collectively known as effects.

Creating rich animations with effects

6

This chapter covers

- Building animations with effects
- Using effects in the jQuery UI widgets
- Animating CSS class name changes

jQuery UI includes 15 built-in animations, that provide ways to show and hide elements, draw the user's attention to elements, or add visual appeal to your UIs. These effects stand on their own with the `effect()` method, tie into existing widgets such as dialog, and work with jQuery Core methods such as `show()` and `hide()`. But it doesn't stop there. jQuery UI also adds powerful abilities to animate CSS class name changes, transition between colors, and a whole lot more.

The jQuery UI effects are so powerful they've helped inspire changes made to the CSS specification, and you can now perform transitions and animations directly in CSS. At the end of this chapter, you'll explore what you can do with CSS directly, and compare that to the APIs in jQuery UI.

It's important to note that just because jQuery UI lets you make an element explode into 50 pieces over 10 seconds (yes, you can do that), it doesn't mean that you should. As we go through this chapter, we'll discuss where these effects make sense for *practical* use.

Let's get started with the core method of the jQuery UI effects: `effect()`.

6.1   Using effects and the effect() method

The most common—and easiest—way to run the jQuery UI effects is through the `effect()` plugin method. In its simplest form, you pass the `effect()` plugin the name of the effect to use. The following code shakes a blue box:

```
<style>
    div {
        background: blue;
        height: 100px;
        width: 100px;
    }
</style>
<div></div>
<script>
    $( "div" ).effect( "shake" );
</script>
```

What effects are there? As of jQuery 1.11, the following 15 effects are available:

- blind
- bounce
- clip
- drop
- explode
- fade
- fold
- highlight
- puff
- pulsate
- scale
- shake
- size
- slide
- transfer

As with widgets, each effect has detailed API documentation on how the effect is used and the available configurations. The URL to use is http://api.jqueryui.com/{NAME}-effect/. For example, http://api.jqueryui.com/shake-effect/ takes you to the API documentation for the shake effect and is shown in figure 6.1.

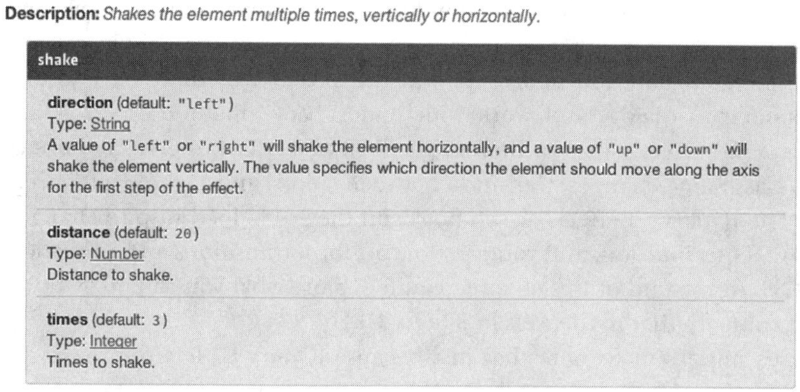

Description: *Shakes the element multiple times, vertically or horizontally.*

---

shake

direction (default: `"left"`)
Type: String
A value of `"left"` or `"right"` will shake the element horizontally, and a value of `"up"` or `"down"` will shake the element vertically. The value specifies which direction the element should move along the axis for the first step of the effect.

distance (default: `20`)
Type: Number
Distance to shake.

times (default: `3`)
Type: Integer
Times to shake.

Figure 6.1   The API documentation for each jQuery UI effect lists the options that can be used to configure the animation. For the shake effect (shown here), you can configure the direction of the shake, the distance to shake, and the number of times to shake.

The values listed in bold—direction, distance, and times—are options that config-ure the effect. To pass these options, provide them as objects as the second argument to effect(). The following code alters the previous example to shake the blue box 10 times over a distance of 100 pixels:

```
$( "div" ).effect( "shake", {
    times: 10,
    distance: 100
});
```

If you test this example, the effect runs so fast that it looks like a blur. This is because the next parameter of effect()—duration—defaults to 400 milliseconds, which isn't nearly enough time to shake a box 10 times. The following code increases the dura-tion to 3 full seconds:

```
$( "div" ).effect( "shake", {
    times: 10,
    distance: 100
}, 3000 );
```

**Defines the duration:
3000 milliseconds =
3 full seconds**

Now your animation has plenty of time to do its shaking. The final argument of the effect() plugin is a function that runs as a callback when the animation completes. The following code adds a callback to your example that makes the box red after the shaking finishes:

```
$( "div" ).effect( "shake", {
    times: 10,
    distance: 100
}, 3000, function() {
    $( this ).css( "background", "red" );
});
```

Although this is powerful, the API is starting to feel messy; the previous code certainly isn't clear to read. Because of this, the effect() plugin offers an alternative signature in which all arguments are passed as a single object. The following code alters your example to use the object signature:

```
$( "div" ).effect({
    effect: "shake",
    times: 10,
    distance: 100,
    duration: 3000,
    complete: function() {
        $( this ).css( "background", "red" );
    }
});
```

**Provides the name
❶ of the effect.**

Take note of two changes here. First, the name of the effect to use is passed as an effect property ❶. This is the only required property when using the effect() object signature. The other change is the properties that apply only to the shake effect (times and distance) are no longer in a separate "options" argument; they're included directly in the object passed to effect().

The object form of `effect()` takes one additional property we haven't discussed: an easing.

6.1.1   *Customizing effects with easings*

What are easings? An *easing* is a function that dictates the rate at which an animation progresses. jQuery Core includes two of them: `linear` and `swing`. The `linear` easing runs the entire animation at a constant pace, and the `swing` easing starts the animation slowly and speeds up toward the end. The `swing` easing is the default easing used in both jQuery Core and jQuery UI. A full list of easings in jQuery UI can be found at http://api.jqueryui.com/easings/ and is shown in figure 6.2.

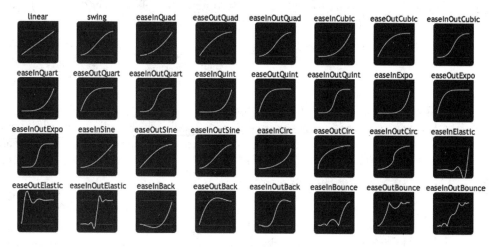

Figure 6.2   A list of the easings provided by jQuery UI from http://api.jqueryui.com/easings/. Each graph plots the progress of the animation (the y-axis) against time (the x-axis). Clicking on each graph runs an animation with the corresponding easing. If you're having trouble understanding easings, it's worth taking a minute to run these; easings are far easier to understand visually.

Each graph in figure 6.2 plots the progression of the animation (the y-axis) against time (the x-axis). The `linear` easing is the easiest to understand as the rate of the animation remains constant throughout. Some easings—such as `easeOutElastic`—run the animation beyond its final value before the animation completes. Although these easings offer plenty of options, why would you want to use any of them?

To answer, let's look at a few examples. The following code uses the jQuery UI explode effect to split a green box into four pieces over 5 seconds:

```
<style>
    div {
        background: green;
        height: 100px;
        width: 100px;
    }
</style>
```

```
<div></div>
<script>
    $( "div" ).effect({
        effect: "explode",
        pieces: 4,
        duration: 5000
    });
</script>
```

Uses the default swing easing because no easing is explicitly provided

Although this effect is cool, the default easing—swing—doesn't provide the ideal, realistic exploding experience. And if you're going to make an element explode, you may as well do it right.

What would be better is an easing that starts off slow, and then builds to a fast finish. If you look at figure 6.2, you see a few easings that meet this criterion, but the best choice looks to be easeInExpo. To use this easing, include it as a property on the object passed to effect(), as shown in the following code:

```
$( "div" ).effect({
    effect: "explode",
    easing: "easeInExpo",
    pieces: 4,
    duration: 5000
});
```

Easings are a nice way of configuring any animation to meet your needs, and they're not used only in the effect() method. You can use these easings with any of the jQuery Core animation methods: animate(), hide(), fadeIn(), fadeOut(), fadeToggle(), hide(), show(), slideDown(), slideToggle(), slideUp(), and toggle().

Suppose you need to move an element in your interface from one side of the screen to the other over 1 second:

```
<style>
    div {
        background: green;
        height: 100px;
        width: 100px;
        position: absolute;
    }
</style>
<div></div>
<script>
    $( "div" ).animate({
        left: $( window ).width() - 100
    }, 1000 );
</script>
```

The second argument of animate() is a duration—in this case, 1 second.

This works, but is rather boring. Let's liven it up with animation using the easeOut-Elastic easing (the third argument to animate() is an easing):

```
$( "div" ).animate({
    left: $( window ).width() - 100
}, 1000, "easeOutElastic" );
```

It's worth running this example to see how changing the easing can have a great effect. By using an `easeOutElastic` easing, the box swings out past its final value, then gradually settles back into it.

Why do this? By changing the easing, you create a more lively animation that's more fun and more engaging for users. And you can do this by playing with a few property names—no math required!

Next, let's look at another practical use of effects: making visual associations.

6.1.2   *Making visual associations with the transfer effect*

The interfaces you build on the web today are increasingly complex, and it can be difficult for users to learn how the various controls work. One of the jQuery UI effects, transfer, lets you assist users with an easy-to-use animation. Consider the grocery list builder application shown in figure 6.3.

Figure 6.3   A small application that builds grocery lists. You will use the transfer effect to help the user associate the Add Groceries form with the Grocery List.

From the screenshot, this UI seems easy to use. When you click the Add button, the grocery item is added to the list. But suppose this functionality were integrated in a more complicated example—such as a site that additionally manages coupons or personal expenses. In this type of situation—when more information is on the screen—users may not instantly recognize where the grocery list is after they add items. The user may be confused about what the application is doing.

Using the transfer effect, you help users make this association. The effect works by transferring the outline of one element to another. As it's easier to see this visually, figure 6.4 shows the effect you'll add.

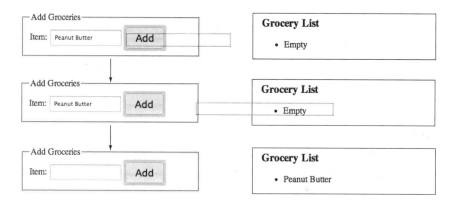

Figure 6.4   Progression of the transfer effect to associate the form with the grocery list

The code to build this is shown in the following listing. Some of the visual styling has been removed to keep this example succinct. The full source is available in the book's code samples or online at http://jsfiddle.net/tj_vantoll/7HQDK/.

Listing 6.1   A grocery list builder that uses the transfer effect

```
<style>
    .ui-effects-transfer { border: 1px dotted black; }         ◁──┐  Styles the transfer
</style>                                                          ❶ DOM element

<div id="grocery-list">
    <h3>Grocery List</h3>
    <ul><li class="empty">Empty</li></ul>
</div>
<form>
    <fieldset>
        <legend>Add Groceries</legend>
        <label for="item">Item:</label>
        <input id="item" required>
        <button>Add</button>
    </fieldset>
</form>

<script>
    function addToList( value ) {                          Adds the new
        var list = $( "#grocery-list ul" );                item to the list
        list.append( "<li>" + value + "</li>" );      ◁──
        list.find( ".empty" ).remove();               ◁──┐ Removes the "empty"
    };                                                   │ list item

    $( "form" ).on( "submit", function( event ) {    ❸ Ends the
        event.preventDefault();                          transfer on the
        $( "input" ).effect( "transfer", {               grocery list
            to: "#grocery-list ul",               ◁──┘
            complete: function() {                ◁────
                addToList( $( this ).val() );            On completion, updates
                $( this ).val( "" );              ❹     the grocery list
            }
        } );
    } );
</script>
```

Starts the ❷ — *Starts the transfer on the input* → `$( "form" )...` / `$( "input" ).effect(...)` annotations (left margin)

You start by applying a dotted border to the `ui-effects-transfer` CSS class name ❶. The transfer effect creates and animates this element, but it leaves the styling up to you. The CSS you apply creates the look of the dotted box shown in figure 6.5.

Next, in your HTML, you have a form for the user to add items and a list to display those items in. In JavaScript, you listen for the form to be submitted, select the `<input>` in the form, and perform a transfer effect on it ❷. The transfer effect takes a required `to` property that determines an element that the selected element's outline is transferred to. You set the `to` property to `"#grocery-list ul"` ❸, which tells the transfer effect to animate an outline from the `<input>` to the grocery list's `<ul>` element.

When the animation completes, you add the new item to the list and empty the contents of the `<input>` ❹.

The example showcases how you can use effects to teach users how an interface works. Instead of assuming users knows where the cart is, you use a transfer effect to draw their eyes in that direction.

Although these types of effects can be powerful, they can also annoy users if used excessively. As a future enhancement of this form you might consider performing the animation only on the first one or two additions to the list. After this, the effect is no longer useful, and may annoy power users who just want to build a grocery list.

In the next section, we'll continue to look at practical applications of the jQuery UI effects. This time, instead of looking at the `effect()` method, we'll look at how effects tie into familiar methods from jQuery Core.

6.2   *Animating visibility changes*

One of the most common tasks performed by JavaScript in the browser is showing and hiding elements. In jQuery Core this is done using three methods: `show()`, `hide()`, and `toggle()`. jQuery UI enhances these same APIs with the ability to use the effects and easings you saw in the previous section.

The enhanced APIs for `show()`, `hide()`, and `toggle()` work almost exactly like the `effect()` method. As with the transfer effect, this is easier to see in an example.

6.2.1   *Building form validation messages*

Let's return to the appointment form you built in chapter 3. Recall that you had a few errors that the user could run into—specifically, invalid dates and numbers. In chapter 3, you used alerts to show these errors, which isn't user friendly. Let's build a more robust means of displaying these errors in a list, and use effects to show the list at the appropriate times. The list you'll build is shown in figure 6.5.

As the form from chapter 3 is lengthy, we won't dig back into the full source here. You can view the final state of this example at http://jsfiddle.net/tj_vantoll/Rc4J2/ to follow along. To implement an error box for this form, you add the following HTML:

```
<div class="ui-state-error">
    <ul></ul>                          The list to contain
</div>                                  the error messages
```

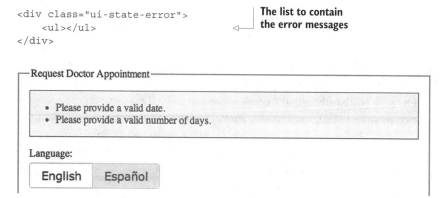

Figure 6.5   The contact form you built in chapter 3 with a formatted list of error messages. You'll use the jQuery UI shake effect to draw the user's eyes to these messages.

You place this <div> in the appointment <form>, and set its display to none so the user doesn't see the error box by default:

```
.ui-state-error { display: none; }
```

> **TIP** The ui-state-error class name applies all the styling for the "Please provide..." box in figure 6.5; no custom CSS is used. This is one of the many class names that the jQuery UI CSS framework provides. You can view a full list at http://api.jqueryui.com/theming/css-framework/, and we'll discuss these class names when we talk about themes in chapter 7.

Now that you have a box, you have to fill it with error messages. Let's define a handle-Errors function for managing error messages. handleErrors accepts an array of error messages—[], ["Invalid date."], and so on—and figures out how to display them appropriately. An implementation of this function is shown in the following code:

```
function handleErrors( errors ) {                      ❶ Gets a reference
    var container = $( ".ui-state-error" ).hide(),        to the container
        list = container.find( "ul" ).empty();           and hides it

    if ( errors.length === 0 ) {                        ❸ Exits if there
        return;                                             are no errors
    }

    $.each( errors, function( index, error ) {
        list.append( "<li>" + error + "</li>" );         ❺ Shows the
    });                                                     container with
    container.show( "shake", { times: 2 }, 100 );         a shake effect
};
```

❷ Gets a reference to the list and empties it

❹ Adds a list item for each error

You start by getting a reference to the error container ❶ and list ❷. You hide the container and empty the list to return each element to its initial state. Next, because you don't want to show the error box with no errors in it, you check whether you received an empty errors array ❸. If so, there's nothing more to do, and you return.

If you did get errors, you have to display them, so you create a new <li> for each message and add it to the list ❹.

The last thing you do is show the error box, and you use the jQuery UI version of the show() method to do it ❺. The arguments you pass to show() may look familiar as they're the same ones that the effect() method accepts. The first argument is the name of the effect, the second is the effect-specific options, and the third is the duration to use. The fourth argument to show() is a function to run when the animation finishes, but you don't need to use it here.

Like effect(), the show() method accepts a single object as an argument. The same call to show() could be written as follows:

```
container.show({
    effect: "shake",
    times: 2,
    duration: 100
});
```

Although the effects tie into many of jQuery UI and jQuery Core APIs, they use the same consistent API. You haven't specifically looked at how `hide()` and `toggle()` work because the API is identical. The following code hides the same container using the shake effect

```
container.hide( "shake", { times: 2 }, 100 );
```

and the following toggles it (shows it if it's hidden, hides it if it's visible):

```
container.toggle( "shake", { times: 2 }, 100 );
```

Why use an effect? Isn't it easier to show and hide the error box without any effects?

This example demonstrates the same use of effects you saw in the previous section: drawing the user's eyes. Have you been frustrated when you attempt to submit a web form? This is a common occurrence, and it's often because forms don't make error messages obvious to the user. It helps to use a bright color such as red, but often it's not enough. By using a shake effect, you attempt to make the error messages more obvious by drawing the user's eyes to them on each failed submission.

> **Accessible form validation**
>
> Although making form validation messages visually stand out improves the usability of your form, the messages aren't announced to screen readers; blind users have no idea there was an issue.
>
> After an invalid form submission, a more robust implementation would move focus to the first invalid field, and give it an `aria-invalid` attribute set to `true`. The implementation would also place the error message in an alternative DOM element, and link the message element to the invalid form element using the `aria-describedby` attribute. If the date were the only invalid field, you could do that with the following code:
>
> ```
> $( "#date" )
>     .attr( "aria-invalid", true )
>     .after( "<span id='message'>Please provide a valid date.</span>" )
>     .attr( "aria-describedby", "message" )
>     .focus();
> ```
>
> You'll look at how to implement accessible form validation when you build a more complex form in chapter 11.

To show another use of the jQuery UI effects with the jQuery Core visibility methods, let's look at one more example.

6.2.2 Building portlets with jQuery UI

Portlets are web UI elements that are made to look like desktop application windows. Like desktop windows, most portlets can be dragged, minimized, and maximized. Portlets frequently appear in large web portals and can be used to display anything from static content to highly dynamic content such as weather reports or sports scores.

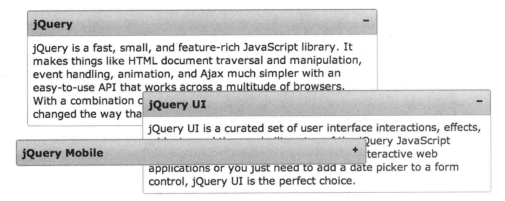

Figure 6.6 Three portlets, or web UI elements made to look like desktop windows, built using jQuery UI. The user can expand or collapse the content of each portlet using the icon in the top-right corner.

Let's look at how you create portlets using jQuery UI. Figure 6.6 shows an example of the portlets you'll build.

The following listing shows the implementation of these portlet controls. The listing only includes the HTML for one portlet window and omits the CSS. The full demo shown in figure 6.7 is available at http://jsfiddle.net/tj_vantoll/5caqN/.

Listing 6.2 Implementation of portlet controls

```html
<div class="portlet ui-widget ui-widget-content ui-corner-all">
    <div class="portlet-header ui-widget-header">
        <button>minimize</button>
        jQuery
    </div>
    <div class="portlet-content">
        <p>jQuery is a...</p>
    </div>
</div>

<script>
$( ".portlet" )
    .draggable({ handle: ".ui-widget-header", stack: ".portlet" })      ❶
    .each(function() {
        $( this ).find( "button" )
            .button({
                icons: { primary: "ui-icon-minusthick" },                ❷
                text: false
            })
            .on( "click", function() {
                var maximized = $( this ).button( "option",
                    "icons" ).primary === "ui-icon-minusthick";
                $( this )
                    .button( "option", {                                 ❸
                        label: maximized ? "maximize" : "minimize",
                        icons: { primary: maximized ? "ui-icon-plusthick":
                            "ui-icon-minusthick" }
                    })
```

❶ Makes each portlet draggable

❷ Attaches a click handler to each minimize/maximize button

❸ Updates the minimize/maximize button's options

```
                       .parents( ".portlet" )
                       .find( ".portlet-content" ).toggle( "blind", 200 );    ◁
           });
       });
</script>
```

Toggles the visibility of the content with the blind effect ❹

> **NOTE**   Confused about the ui-* class names being used here? Don't worry, we'll cover what each of these do when we talk about the jQuery UI CSS framework in chapter 7.

You start by making each portlet draggable and set two options: `handle` and `stack` ❶. The `handle` option controls which portion of a draggable the user can initiate a drag from. Because you want to allow users to drag a portlet only by its header, you set `handle` to a CSS class name that matches it. The `stack` option manages the CSS `z-index` property of draggables so that the currently dragged item is always brought to the front. If you didn't use this, and the user were to drag a second portlet on top of the first, the second would appear behind the first.

Now that the portlets are draggable, you have to make them collapsible. To do this, you convert their header buttons to button widgets and attach a `click` event handler to them ❷. Inside the handler, you first change the clicked button's options such that its icon is switched from plus to minus (or vice versa), and its label is changed from maximize to minimize (or vice versa) ❸. Why do you bother updating the `label` option—which is the button's text—for a button with no visible text? Even though the text is invisible, jQuery UI ensures that it remains accessible to assistive technologies such as screen readers. The library also places the text in the button's `title` attribute, so even sighted users see the text when they hover over the button. It's very important to keep this text up to date, even though it doesn't visually appear within the button.

After this, you get a reference to the clicked button's associated content and toggle it using the blind effect ❹. The blind effect shows and hides an element by altering its height vertically or horizontally, much like an accordion widget. Using this effect helps to mimic the desktop behavior of minimizing windows. Also, the animation helps tell the user that the content is being collapsed, and not being removed completely. To ensure this animation doesn't get in the user's way, you set the duration to a quick 200 milliseconds.

> **NOTE**   In addition to changing an element's height, the blind effect uses the CSS `overflow` property to prevent the browser from repositioning the element's text as its height changes—producing a smoother animation. As such, the blind effect works well on elements that contain text.

And that's all it takes to build portlet controls using jQuery UI. As the API to create these effects is so simple, it's easy to experiment with different effects and easings to customize the experience. Try using the explode or pulsate effects on this example for a little fun.

To continue our look at how effects tie into existing APIs, let's look at how you can use them directly in the jQuery UI widgets.

6.3 Using effects with the jQuery UI widgets

If you've perused the jQuery UI API documentation, you may have noticed that some widgets—specifically dialog, tabs, and tooltip—have `show` and `hide` options that use the jQuery UI effects. These options give you an easy way to configure how these widgets are shown and hidden. The values they accept are similar to the arguments you invoked `show()`, `hide()`, and `toggle()` with, but with a few differences.

6.3.1 The show and hide options

To explore these, let's use the dialog widget as an example. By default, the dialog widget uses no animations when it opens and closes. Internally, this is because its `show` and `hide` options are set to `null`. Like all effect-based methods, you can pass an effect name for these two options. The following code opens a dialog with the puff effect and closes it with the blind effect:

```
$( "<div>" ).dialog({
    show: "puff",
    hide: "blind"
});
```

Similar to other effect methods, you can pass an object with the full configuration of the effect. The following code uses objects for `show` and `hide`:

```
$( "<div>" ).dialog({
    show: {
        effect: "puff",
        percentage: 200,
        duration: 3000,
        easing: "linear"
    },
    hide: {
        effect: "blind",
        direction: "horizontal"
    }
});
```

> Configuration specific to the puff effect. It controls the size to "puff" out to. In this case, the dialog puffs out to twice its size when it opens.

> Configuration specific to the blind effect. It controls the direction the element is pulled when it's hidden. Using "horizontal" means this dialog is hidden from right to left.

You can see that the syntax here is the same as the object you can pass to `effect()`, `show()`, `hide()`, and `toggle()`. The dialog opens with a puff effect over 3 seconds with a linear easing. The dialog closes with a blind effect, the default duration (`400`), and the default easing (`"swing"`).

Thus far, the `show` and `hide` options have used the exact same syntax you've already seen. So what's different? Unlike the effect methods—`effect()`, `show()`, `hide()`, and `toggle()`—the `show` and `hide` options offer Boolean and number shorthand.

The Boolean shorthand determines whether a preconfigured animation should be used. If set to `true`, the widget uses the jQuery Core `fadeIn()` or `fadeOut()` methods (for `show` or `hide`, respectively) with the default duration and easing.

The number shorthand determines the duration to use for the animation. It also uses `fadeIn()` or `fadeOut()` and the default easing.

The following example creates a dialog that uses each of these shorthands. It opens with a fade-in animation over the default 400 milliseconds and closes with a fade-out animation over a full second:

```
$( "<div>" ).dialog({
    show: true,
    hide: 1000
});
```

The Boolean and number shorthand for these options are provided because they're the most common animations used. Setting `show` and `hide` to `true` is a way to use a small animation to improve the visual appeal of your widgets. But if this is the case, why might you want to use the more advanced options? Let's look at an example where they make sense.

> **NOTE**   Although we didn't specifically look at the tabs and tooltip widgets, the configuration for the `show` and `hide` options is identical. In fact, the implementation of these options is in the widget factory directly. You can use these options and effects in custom-built widgets. We'll start looking into custom widgets in chapter 8.

6.3.2   Showing a message in a dialog

To show more advanced options in actions, let's return to the fruit and vegetable sorting example you built in the previous chapter. To help you remember the game, an image of it is shown in figure 6.7.

In your implementation of the game, we didn't discuss the instructions, which are a sentence located above the game itself. The current instructions have one problem: they don't stand out in any way; therefore, users can easily miss them. Although you could make the instructions stand out visually—with bright colors or a bigger font size—that would distract the user during the game itself. Let's try a different approach: showing the instructions in a dialog.

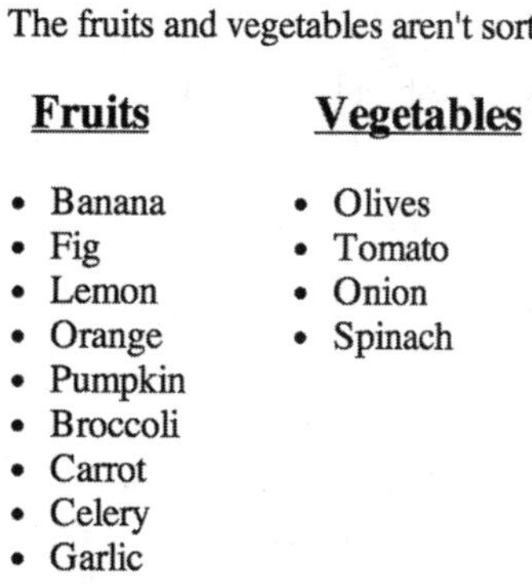

The fruits and vegetables aren't sorted correctly—rearrange them!

<u>Fruits</u>

- Banana
- Fig
- Lemon
- Orange
- Pumpkin
- Broccoli
- Carrot
- Celery
- Garlic

<u>Vegetables</u>

- Olives
- Tomato
- Onion
- Spinach

Figure 6.7   The fruit and vegetable game you built in chapter 5. Notice that the instructions are not especially noticeable—a user can easily miss them.

The HTML for the instructions is a paragraph tag:

```
<p>The fruit and vegetables aren't sorted correctly—rearrange them!</p>
```

You'll start by converting this paragraph to a dialog as the first thing in your game's JavaScript:

```
$( "p" ).dialog();
```

The display of this dialog is shown in figure 6.8.

Although this does make the instructions stand out, several things aren't ideal here:

- The user can interact with the game while the dialog is still open.
- The user can only close the dialog using a small 20-pixel-wide close button.
- The user sees this dialog every time a new game starts. You want users to see the dialog only once.

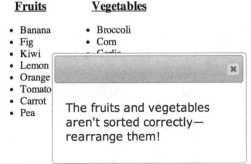

Figure 6.8 Showing the instructions for the game pulls them out of the main content and makes them stand out to the user.

Let's add effects and options to your dialog to improve the user experience. The next listing shows an updated dialog.

> **NOTE** You can view the updated game at http://jsfiddle.net/tj_vantoll/ MaKKX/. Note that the sessionStorage check is commented out because it makes the example difficult to test. You can uncomment the check to see its effect.

Listing 6.3 A message dialog with instructions

```
if ( !sessionStorage.getItem( "messageViewed" ) ) {          ❶ Shows the message only
    $( "p" ).dialog({                                            if it hasn't been viewed
        show: {
            effect: "scale",
            easing: "easeOutElastic",
            duration: 750                                     ❷ Shows the
        },                                                       dialog with a
        hide: {                                                  scale effect
            effect: "scale",
            duration: 100                                     ❹ Uses a modal
        },                                                       dialog
        modal: true,
        title: "Fruit & Vegetable Sorter",
        width: 400,                                           ❺ Creates an
        buttons: {                                               OK button
            "OK": function() {
                $( this ).dialog( "close" );
            }
```

Hides the dialog with a scale effect ❸

```
        },
        close: function() {
            sessionStorage.setItem( "messageViewed", true );
        }
    });
}
```

Records that
the message has
6 been viewed

You start with a check to make sure that the user hasn't already seen the message ❶. We'll discuss how this works momentarily.

Next, you create your dialog with several more options set. First, you define a scale effect to use when showing ❷ and hiding ❸ the dialog. Using a scale effect when displaying the dialog makes it jump out and grab the user's attention. To make the dialog stand out even more, you use an `easeOutElastic` easing, which runs the first part of the animation quickly.

When the dialog closes, you also use the scale effect. The goal here is slightly different than when you opened the dialog. Because the scale effect shrinks the dialog to hide it, it draws the user's eyes in the direction of the game, which is where the user should look after reading the instructions. You set the duration to a tiny 100 milliseconds to get the dialog out of the way of the game quickly.

After this, you set the `modal` option to `true` ❹ to prevent the user from interacting with the game until the dialog is closed. Modal dialogs place a semitransparent overlay over the content behind the dialog while it's displayed. Because the overlay grays out the game a bit, this is yet another technique for grabbing the user's attention.

Next, you set the `buttons` option to create an OK button that allows the user to close the dialog ❺. This gives the user a far bigger target to close the dialog with, which is important on small screens such as mobile devices.

As a last step, you specify a `close` event callback that sets a `"messageViewed"` variable in `sessionStorage` ❻. How does `sessionStorage` work?

You may recall from earlier chapters that `localStorage` is a means of storing key-value pairs in the browser. `sessionStorage` and `localStorage` share an identical API and behave the same way, with one important difference: `localStorage` is persisted indefinitely, but `sessionStorage` is only persisted for the user's session. After the user closes the browser, or the page's tab, `sessionStorage` is emptied. If you open the game, close the instructions, and refresh the page, you don't see the instructions again. But if you open the game in a new tab, you do.

`sessionStorage` makes sense for your example because, although you don't want the user to see the instructions on subsequent plays of your game, you do want the user to see them when returning to the game the next day, or next month.

The updated version of your dialog is shown in figure 6.9.

This example shows how the jQuery UI effects can be used in a practical manner to enhance an application. In this case, with a few lines of configuration you took static instructions and made them bounce out and grab the user's attention. To avoid annoying users, you showed the instructions once per session, made the instructions easy to close, and used a short duration on the hide effect.

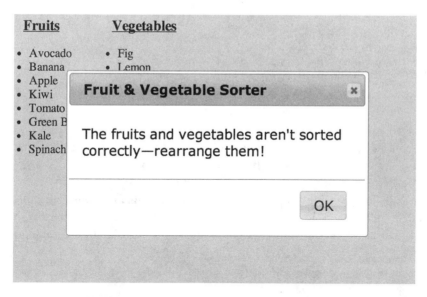

Figure 6.9   **The updated version of the instructions dialog does two things to draw the user's attention: it uses an effect to jump off the page, and it uses a modal dialog to gray out the rest of the content. This dialog includes an OK button, which makes it easy for the user to close the dialog to get to the game.**

Before we complete our look at effects, we need to look at one last way they integrate with existing APIs.

6.4 *Animating CSS class name changes*

Like showing and hiding elements, another extremely common operation in web development is managing CSS class names to control the display of DOM elements. Up until CSS3 transitions—which we'll look at in the next section—it was impossible to transition between the values specified by the class name. If you have a <div> with a top of 100px, and then add a class name that changes it to 200px, the <div> doesn't animate to its new position; it instantly hops 100 pixels.

jQuery UI makes these transitions easy by extending familiar methods from jQuery Core. Specifically, it extends the addClass(), removeClass(), and toggleClass() methods. Let's see how.

6.4.1 *Enhancing addClass(), removeClass(), and toggleClass()*

As an example of how jQuery UI enhances jQuery Core, the following code animates a <div> from a 50 x 50-pixel box to a 100 x 100-pixel box over a full second:

```
<style>
    div {
        height: 50px;
        width: 50px;
        background: red;
    }
```

```
    div.big {
        height: 100px;
        width: 100px;
    }
</style>
<div></div>
<script>
    $( "div" ).addClass( "big", 1000 );
</script>
```

The same as the other effect methods you've seen, each of the three class name manipulation methods that jQuery UI extends has two forms.

The first—and the one used in the previous example—specifies each property individually in the order of class name, duration, easing, and complete callback function. The following code also increases the size of the <div>, but does so over 2 seconds with a linear easing and logs a message when the animation completes:

```
$( "div" ).addClass( "big", 1000, "linear", function() {
    console.log( "complete" );
});
```

The other form of the class name manipulation method takes an object. The previous example could also be written as follows:

```
$( "div" ).addClass( "big", {
    duration: 1000,
    easing: "linear",
    complete: function() {
        console.log( "complete" );
    }
});
```

> **TIP**   To hit the jQuery UI extensions of the jQuery Core class name methods, you must pass at least two arguments. $("div").removeClass("big", 1000) performs a transition, but $("div").removeClass("big") doesn't. If you want a transition but don't need any customization, you can pass an empty object, for instance, $("div").removeClass("big", {}).

If you've used the jQuery Core animate() function before, you may know that you can perform these exact same effects with it. The following code has the same functionality—growing the <div> to 100 x 100 with a linear easing and logging when it finishes—using animate() instead of addClass():

```
$( "div" ).animate({
    height: 100,
    width: 100
}, 1000, "linear", function() {
    console.log( "complete" )
});
```

Because the end result is exactly the same, why use CSS class names? To explore this, let's look at an example that has become popular lately: off-canvas navigation.

Animating multiple class names simultaneously

One little-known fact about the jQuery Core class name manipulation methods is that they can operate on multiple class names simultaneously. The following adds three class names to all paragraphs. In accordance with the HTML `class` attribute, the class names need to be space delimited:

```
$( "p" ).addClass( "red big spaced" );
```

The jQuery UI class name–based animations also work with multiple class names, and provide a powerful means to combine several class names in a single animation. The following code performs a single animation that transitions the `color`, `font-size`, and `padding` on a paragraph over 3 seconds:

```
<style>
    .red { color: red; }
    .big { font-size: 5em; }
    .spaced { padding: 1em; }
</style>
<p>jQuery UI Rocks!</p>
<script>
    $( "p" ).addClass( "red big spaced", 3000 );
</script>
```

6.4.2 *Building an off-canvas navigation menu for mobile*

If you've browsed the web on a mobile device, you're almost certainly familiar with off-canvas navigation menus. These menus are initially hidden and "fly-out" over the main content after the user takes an action—usually clicking a link or button. Because the menus are initially hidden, they're popular on mobile and responsive sites as they help conserve limited space.

The off-canvas navigation menu you'll build is shown in figure 6.10.

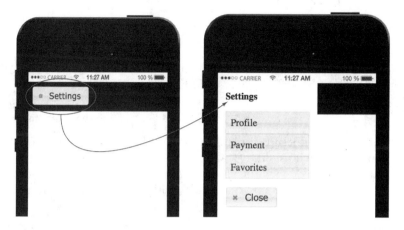

Figure 6.10 An off-canvas navigation menu for settings shown on a mobile device. Clicking the Settings button displays the menu. Clicking the Close button hides it.

How do these menus work? The most common way of implementing them is by animating the CSS `left` property. You give the menu an initial, negative `left` value that positions it off the screen, then update it to `0` after the button is clicked to show it.

Your implementation of this menu uses this approach and is shown in listing 6.4.

NOTE Some of the visual CSS and boilerplate HTML is omitted from this listing for simplicity. The full source of this demo can be viewed online at http://jsfiddle.net/tj_vantoll/4ytAn/ or in the book's code examples.

Listing 6.4 An off-canvas navigation menu

```
<style>
    #menu {
        position: absolute;              ❶ The initial left
        left: -200px;                       of the menu
        top: 0px;
        width: 200px;
    }
    #menu.visible {                      ❷ The updated left
        left: 0;                            of the menu
    }
</style>

<header>                                   The button to
    <button>Settings</button>             open the menu
</header>
<div id="menu">
    <h3>Settings</h3>
    <ul>...</ul>                            The button to
    <button>Close</button>                 close the menu
</div>
<script>
    $( "header button" ).button({
        icons: { primary: "ui-icon-gear" }
    });
    $( "#menu button" ).button({
        icons: { primary: "ui-icon-closethick" }
    });                                                      ❸ A click handler
    $( "button" ).on( "click", function() {                    for each button
        $( "#menu" ).toggleClass( "visible", 300, "easeOutQuint" );
    });
</script>
                                          Toggles the visible class to
                                          show and hide the menu  ❹
```

NOTE This example doesn't display correctly in Internet Explorer versions earlier than 9 because it uses the HTML5 `<header>` element. You can add support for the new HTML5 semantic elements in Internet Explorer versions earlier than 9 using the HTML5 shiv. See https://github.com/aFarkas/html5shiv for details.

You start with the menu positioned at a `left` of `-200px` ❶, which—because the menu is 200 pixels wide—places it off the screen. Next, you define a `visible` CSS class name that has a `left` value of 0 ❷, which, when applied, places the menu completely within the visible viewport on the left-hand side of the screen.

In this example's JavaScript, you attach a `click` event handler to each of the two buttons on the page ❸. In the handler, you toggle the `"visible"` class name using the `toggleClass()` method ❹. This uses the jQuery UI extension to the jQuery Core `toggleClass()` methods, and jQuery UI animates all properties associated with the change—in this case, `left`. You use a short duration (300 milliseconds) and an easing that accelerates the first part of the animation (`"easeOutQunit"`) so that the user sees the menu quickly.

This example demonstrates why the class name changes are cleaner than using a more low-level method such as `animate()`. For one, your JavaScript code is easier to read. Someone unfamiliar with this codebase will have an easier time understanding code that adds a `"visible"` class name than code that hardcodes individual CSS properties.

More importantly, using CSS class names to drive animations helps you group your code and separate your concerns. The JavaScript controls the state of the menu (whether or not it's visible), and your CSS defines what that state means visually. This gives you more flexibility with the maintenance of this application. If you want this menu to come in from the right-hand side of the screen, you don't have to change any JavaScript code.

This CSS-driven approach to animations is so powerful that jQuery UI effects have inspired changes to the web platform directly, via CSS3 animations and transitions. In the next section, we'll look at how the native transitions work and whether you should be using them today.

Animating colors with jQuery UI

jQuery Core doesn't have the ability to animate the color of elements. For example, if you run `$( "*" ).animate({ color: "red" })` on a page with only jQuery Core loaded, nothing happens. jQuery UI adds this support through the jQuery color plugin, which is packaged with the library.

You can animate colors using the jQuery Core `animate()` function or with the CSS class manipulation methods we looked at in this section. The color plugin supports colors as hex values, `rgb()`, `rgba()`, and valid CSS color names like `"red"` and `"blue"`. The following code animates a number of CSS color properties on a `<div>` over 2 seconds:

```
<style>
    div {
        border: 10px solid black;
        outline: 10px solid black;
    }
    div.rainbow {
        background: #FF0000;         ◁— Red
        border-color: yellow;
        color: rgb(0, 0, 255);       ◁— Blue
        outline-color: green;
    }
```

(continued)
```
</style>
<div>jQuery UI Rocks!</div>
<script>
    $( "div" ).addClass( "rainbow", 2000 );
</script>
```

A full list of the properties supported and additional documentation can be found on the color plugin's documentation at https://github.com/jquery/jquery-color.

6.5 Effects vs. CSS3 animations and transitions

Like many of the jQuery UI widgets, some of the functionality offered by the jQuery UI effects is now natively implemented in many browsers. Whereas the widget equivalents have been incorporated in the HTML specification, the effect equivalents have inspired changes in the CSS specification—specifically, CSS animations and transitions. Let's look at CSS3 transitions first.

6.5.1 CSS3 transitions vs. the jQuery UI class name methods

CSS3 transitions provide a way to control changes to CSS properties. Transitions are often associated with class names; they're best compared to the jQuery UI versions of the addClass(), removeClass(), and toggleClass() methods.

The following listing shows two identical transitions of text from black to red. One uses the jQuery UI class name animations, and the other uses CSS3 transitions.

Listing 6.5   Comparison of class name animation in jQuery UI and CSS3

```
<style>
    #css {
        -webkit-transition: color 5000ms linear;        ┐  CSS rule
        transition: color 5000ms linear;                │  declarations
    }                                                    ❶  for transition
    .red { color: red; }
</style>
<p id="ui">jQuery UI</p>
<p id="css">CSS3</p>
<script>
    $( "#ui" ).addClass( "red", {
        duration: 5000,
        easing: "linear",
        complete: function() {
            console.log( "ui animation complete" );      Event handler
        }                                                transitionend
    });
    $( "#css" ).addClass( "red" )
        .on( "webkitTransitionEnd transitionend", function() {  ┐  jQuery UI class
            console.log( "css transition complete" );           ❷  name-based
        });                                                     │  transition
</script>
```

The jQuery UI method should look familiar, as it's the same code you've looked at in this chapter. The CSS-based transition, however, may look a bit odd at first. To start, the configuration for the transition is in CSS rather than JavaScript. Let's look at each of the pieces of the `transition` CSS rule ❶:

- `color`—The property name to transition. This can list specific property names as is done here, or the keyword `all` to transition all property changes.
- `5000ms`—The equivalent of the duration property from jQuery UI. The one difference is that in CSS you must also provide the unit (`s` for seconds and `ms` for milliseconds).
- `linear`—The equivalent of the easing property from jQuery UI. CSS provides `ease`, `ease-in`, `ease-out`, `ease-in-out`, and `linear` easings. The default value is `ease`.

This one line is all you need to configure the transition. But the code has two lines of CSS: a `transition` and a `-webkit-transition`. What is this about?

Originally, most major browsers—specifically, Firefox, Chrome, Safari, Opera, the default Android browser, and iOS Safari—implemented CSS3 transitions behind a vendor-specific prefix. The prefixes have now been removed in the latest version of all browsers, although older versions of several WebKit-based browsers still receive significant use—most notably the default Android browser, which didn't remove the prefix until Android 4.4, and has a considerable market share. For this reason, the `transition` rule must be explicitly stated twice—once with the `-webkit-` prefix and once without it.

NOTE You can view more thorough documentation on which browser versions use vendor prefixes for CSS transitions at http://caniuse.com/#feat=css-transitions. Note that Internet Explorer implemented transitions without a prefix in Internet Explorer 10.

The last part of this example is the equivalent of the jQuery UI effect `complete` property: the `transitionend` event ❷. As the name implies, the `transitionend` event is fired when a CSS transition completes. As with the `transition` CSS property, you must additionally listen for a vendor-specific event name for more comprehensive browser support.

Which approach should you use?

In general, CSS3 transitions are preferred over jQuery-based transitions as the browser can execute the CSS-based ones faster. On desktop browsers, the performance difference is of little concern, as the browser can perform most JavaScript and CSS-based transitions effortlessly, but on mobile browsers, the device's limited processing power makes the performance difference pronounced. If you're developing applications for the desktop, it makes sense to use whichever approach works best for you; but if you're developing for mobile use, lean toward CSS-based transitions for optimal performance.

Computer scientist Donald Knuth famously said that "premature optimization is the root of all evil," and that sentiment applies here. Test your applications on the devices that you support. Start with the transition approach that you prefer, and if you don't notice any performance issues, then it's not worth worrying about.

Although browser support for CSS transitions is good, you need to provide vendor prefixes for some browsers, and Internet Explorer versions earlier than 10 have no support. If it's important to you to have functioning transitions in these browsers, stick with the jQuery UI class name–based transitions.

Next, we'll compare another CSS3 feature, animations, to the jQuery UI effects.

6.5.2   CSS animations vs. effects

CSS3 animations offer more power than simple transitions. Instead of changing a property from one value to another, you can control the value of multiple properties at different intervals. In this sense, CSS animations are more like the jQuery UI effects. Consider the shake effect. One of the positioning properties (`left`, `right`, `top`, or `bottom`) must be changed in several directions over the course of the animation. It's not as simple as changing a property from one value to another.

The best way to compare effects to animations is with an example. The following listing shows two paragraphs. One is shaken with the jQuery UI shake effect, and the other is shaken with a CSS animation.

Listing 6.6   Comparing CSS animations to the jQuery UI effects

```
<style>
    @-webkit-keyframes shake { ... }                    ◁──┐ The same content as the
    @keyframes shake {                                       unprefixed @keyframes
        0% { left: 0; }                                      declaration
        12.5% { left: -20px; }
        25% { left: 0; }
        37.5% { left: 20px; }
        50% { left: 0; }
        62.5% { left: -20px; }                              Defines the shake
        75% { left: 0; }                                    CSS animation
        87.5% { left: 20px; }                          ❶   keyframes
        100% { left: 0; }
    }
    #css {
        position: absolute;
        -webkit-animation: shake 1s linear;            ❷   Specifies the
        animation: shake 1s linear;                         animation
    }                                                       rule
</style>
<p id="css">CSS3</p>
<p id="ui">jQuery UI</p>
<script>
    $( "#ui" ).effect( "shake", {
        times: 2,                                          Uses a jQuery
        duration: 1000,                                    UI shake effect
        easing: "linear",
```

```
        complete: function() {
            console.log( "ui shake complete" );
        }
    });
    $( "#css" ).on( "webkitAnimationEnd animationend", function() {
        console.log( "css shake complete" );
    });
</script>
```

Uses a jQuery
UI shake effect

Attaches an animationend
event handler ❸

The jQuery UI–based shake effect should look familiar. You shake a paragraph two times over a second with a `linear` easing. As with CSS transitions, CSS animations can be tricky to understand if you haven't seen them before.

The `@keyframes` declaration defines the animation and gives it a name—in this case, shake ❶. Each keyframe, or entry in the `@keyframes` declaration, defines the CSS rules to be applied to selected elements during the animation. For the shake animation, you see that the `left` property is moved in 20-pixel increments back and forth to mimic the jQuery UI shake effect (whose default `distance` property is set to `20`).

After you have a CSS animation defined with `@keyframes`, you apply `animation` rules to elements. The syntax for `animation` is similar to that of the `transition` property you saw earlier. The shake `1s` `linear` value specified tells the browser to perform the shake CSS animation on this element over 1 second using a `linear` easing ❷.

Finally, you listen for the `animationend` event to show the equivalent of the jQuery UI `complete` function ❸.

As with CSS transitions, most browsers initially implemented CSS animations behind a vendor prefix. However, many browsers have yet to drop the prefix. As of this writing, the latest versions of Chrome, Safari, Opera, the default Android browser, and iOS Safari all use the `-webkit-` prefix for CSS animations. Firefox dropped its `-moz-` prefix in version 16, and Internet Explorer 10 shipped with CSS animations unprefixed. The `@keyframes` declaration, `animation` property, and `animationend` event used in this example all include a WebKit vendor-prefixed version.

Because the example creates identical animations, this again begs the question of whether you should be using jQuery UI or CSS. Unfortunately, there is no easy answer.

As with CSS transitions, the browser can perform CSS animations quicker, so if you're experiencing performance issues, you should look to CSS animations first. Desktop browsers can run the majority of JavaScript-based animations without issue, but mobile browsers may have issues—particularly with complex animations that require a great deal of processing power.

Although CSS transitions are succinct, CSS animations are verbose and more difficult to configure than the convenient APIs provided by jQuery UI. You need to do math to configure the `@keyframes` in the previous example, but not with the jQuery UI effect. The jQuery UI APIs are more convenient when they hook directly into widgets. Although you could configure a CSS animation to open a dialog with a blind effect, using `$( "<div>" ).dialog({ show: "blind" })` is much easier and more maintainable in a large application.

To complicate things further, some things can be done using the jQuery UI effects that can't be done with CSS animations, and vice versa. You can't write a CSS animation that makes a <div> explode into 100 pieces:

```
$( "<div>" )
    .appendTo( "body" )
    .css({ height: 500, width: 500, background: "red" })
    .effect( "explode", { pieces: 100, duration: 10000 });
```

On the flip side, no jQuery UI effect lets you infinitely spin a <div> in three dimensions, as this code does:

```
@-webkit-keyframes spin-3d {
    50% {
        -webkit-transform: rotateX( 360deg ) rotateY( 360deg )
            skewY( 180deg );
    }
    100% {
        -webkit-transform: rotateX( 0deg ) rotateY( 0deg ) skewY( 0deg );
    }
}
@keyframes spin-3d {
    50% {
        transform: rotateX( 360deg ) rotateY( 360deg ) skewY( 180deg );
    }
    100% {
        transform: rotateX( 0deg ) rotateY( 0deg ) skewY( 0deg );
    }
}
div {
    height: 500px;
    width: 500px;
    background: red;
    position: absolute;
    -webkit-animation: spin-3d 10s linear infinite;
    animation: spin-3d 10s linear infinite;
}
```

TIP   For more examples of using 3D in CSS, as well as an excellent tutorial on how to build your own, see http://desandro.github.io/3dtransforms/.

Unfortunately, it's not easy to handle this overlapping behavior. To summarize, the advantages of using CSS-based animations are

- They provide optimal performance.
- They're defined in CSS and can be used without JavaScript.

and the detriments are

- They can be verbose, especially for complex animations.
- You must specify vendor prefixes when using them.
- They don't work in older browsers.

If performance is critical, use CSS animations. If browser support is important, stick to jQuery UI. Otherwise, use whichever makes more sense for you and your projects.

> **TIP** If you need the performance of CSS transitions and animations, but prefer the jQuery syntax for performing animations, there are several plugins that provide a jQuery-like animation syntax, but use CSS under the hood for optimal performance. The two most popular of these plugins are Velocity.js (https://github.com/julianshapiro/velocity) and jQuery Transit (http://ricostacruz.com/jquery.transit/).

6.6 *Summary*

jQuery UI includes 15 effects that can be used with the `effect()` method, integrate with jQuery UI widgets, and even tie into jQuery Core methods such as `show()` and `hide()`. The jQuery UI effects also add functionality such as advanced easings and the ability to animate class name changes. But just because these effects let you do crazy things doesn't mean that you should.

You saw a number of reasons why effects are practical in real-life applications. You built a small grocery list builder that used the transfer effect to help the user learn the interface. You added the shake effect to an error box in a form to draw the user's attention. You also moved a game's instructions into a dialog for a similar effect.

As with many of the jQuery UI widgets, the jQuery UI effects have inspired similar functionality on the web natively as CSS transitions and animations. You looked at how these worked and compared them to the jQuery UI effects. CSS-based transitions and animations are faster, but they can be more verbose and don't work in all browsers yet.

Now that you've seen the powerful ways jQuery UI lets you animate elements, let's look at the tools the library provides to style elements with themes.

Theming and styling applications with jQuery UI

This chapter covers

- Using the jQuery UI themes
- Building custom themes with ThemeRoller
- Styling with the jQuery UI CSS framework

We've discussed the widgets in jQuery UI and how they work, but we've yet to discuss an important part of any set of UI widgets: how they look.

jQuery UI includes a theming system that makes it easy to apply a consistent look to all widgets. The library includes 24 prebuilt themes, as well as an online tool for customizing them.

The library's theming system is implemented as a series of CSS class names, collectively known as the jQuery UI CSS framework. The class names in the CSS framework let you create themeable components, as well as perform a number of common web development tasks such as styling error messages, using any of the jQuery UI icons, and styling widgets based on their state. We'll discuss what these class names are, how to use them, and the powerful things you can do with them.

Each individual widget uses a separate set of class names to allow for widget-specific customization. We'll end the chapter by looking at what widget-specific class names are available and how they work.

Before digging into the jQuery UI CSS class names, let's look at how to use the themes built in to jQuery UI.

7.1 Using built-in and custom themes

Thus far, all widgets you've used in this book have had a grayish appearance because you've been using the default jQuery UI theme: smoothness. The smoothness theme, and its grayish appearance, was designed to easily integrate into existing sites because it's a lot easier to drop a gray datepicker into an existing design than a bright red one. But wait, how did you specify which theme to use?

Recall the example boilerplate introduced in chapter 1:

```
<!doctype html>
<html lang="en">
<head>
    <meta charset="utf-8">
    <title>…</title>
    <link rel="stylesheet" href="http://code.jquery.com/ui/1.11.0/themes/
    smoothness/jquery-ui.css">                    ⟵┐
</head>                                              │ Imports the
<body>                                              │ smoothness theme
    …
</body>
</html>
```

The smoothness string in the path is what selects the theme to use for this page. To use a different theme, replace smoothness with the name of another theme. Importing http://code.jquery.com/ui/1.11.0/themes/le-frog/jquery-ui.css uses the le-frog theme.

The one limitation of changing the file names is you can't view multiple themes simultaneously to compare them, but don't worry—for that there's ThemeRoller, an online tool for previewing the provided themes as well as designing your own. ThemeRoller is available at http://jqueryui.com/themeroller/ and is shown in figure 7.1.

When you first visit ThemeRoller, the best place to begin is the Gallery tab ❶. The tab lets you preview all 24 jQuery UI themes and see the effect they have on each jQuery UI widget live. Despite the many options, it's unlikely that a theme will work perfectly for you without any alterations.

After you've found a theme you like, switch to the Roll Your Own tab. Here you can make customizations—including font, colors, and borders ❷—to the theme you selected.

> **WARNING** Despite years of trying, your author's artistic skills remain comparable to the average five-year-old with a box of crayons. As a result—as much as I would love to—this book won't give advice on how to choose colors for your apps. Several online resources can help you, though. Adobe Kuler provides a series of color selections that you can experiment with. See https://kuler.adobe.com/explore/.

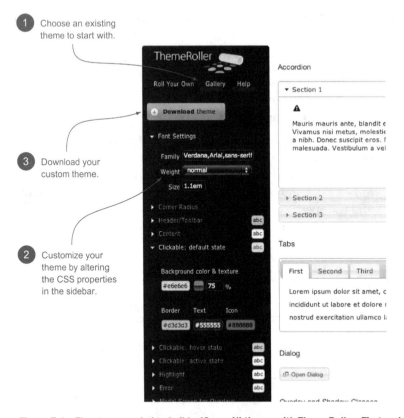

① Choose an existing theme to start with.

③ Download your custom theme.

② Customize your theme by altering the CSS properties in the sidebar.

Figure 7.1   The steps needed to build a jQuery UI theme with ThemeRoller. First, select a starting theme on the Gallery tab, then customize it by playing with CSS properties in the sidebar. As a final step, download the theme with the Download theme button.

The nice thing about ThemeRoller is you can visually see the effect a CSS property change has on all widgets instantly; they rerender themselves as changes are made. This is shown in figure 7.2.

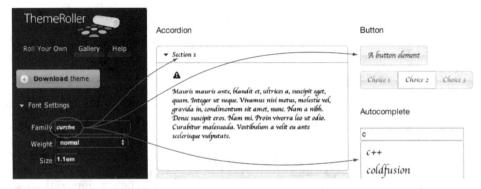

Figure 7.2   As you change CSS properties in ThemeRoller, all widgets are automatically updated to display the change. Here, the font family is changed to cursive, and all widget text changes to cursive instantly.

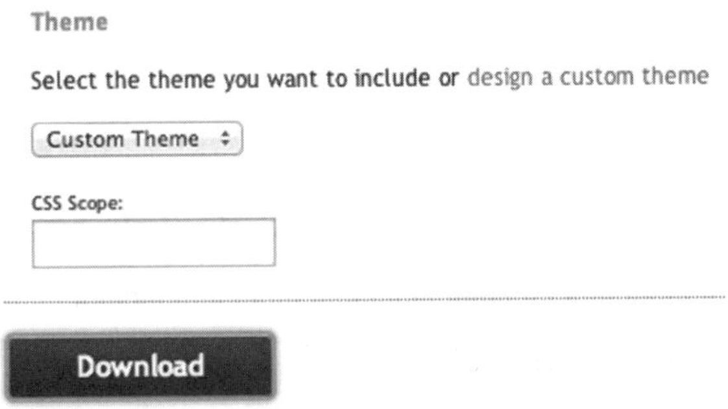

Theme

Select the theme you want to include or design a custom theme

[Custom Theme ⬍]

CSS Scope:

[   ]

Figure 7.3   The theme selector on the jQuery UI Download Builder with a custom theme from ThemeRoller selected. You can use a CSS Scope to scope the theme to a specific part of a page.

[**Download**]

If you like your changes and want to use them, click the Download theme button on the Roll Your Own tab ❸ (in figure 7.1). This sends you to the jQuery UI Download Builder with your custom theme preselected. If you scroll to the bottom of the Download Builder, you'll see the screen shown in figure 7.3.

The CSS Scope input sets a scope that the custom theme should be limited to. If you use a CSS scope of `div#sidebar`, the theme's CSS rules only apply in a `<div id="sidebar">` element. In the vast majority of situations, you won't need a CSS scope; it makes sense only if you want to use multiple themes on one page.

Clicking the Download button downloads a zip file containing the files shown in figure 7.4.

What are those jquery-ui.structure.css and jquery-ui.theme.css files? jQuery UI breaks its CSS rules into two categories: structural (margin, width, height, and so forth) and theming (the ones you configured in ThemeRoller). These rules are placed into jquery-ui.structure.css and jquery-ui.theme.css, respectively. This gives you

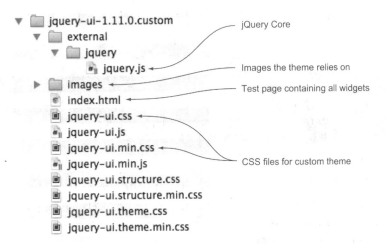

Figure 7.4   The contents of a jQuery UI download with a custom theme. The jquery-ui.css and jquery-ui.min.css files contain the CSS for the theme (jquery-ui.min.css is minified and jquery-ui.css is not), the `images` directory contains images that the theme depends on, and `index.html` is a demo page where you can see how all of the jQuery UI widgets look with your theme.

the ability to manage multiple themes without duplication, as jquery-ui.structure.css remains the same regardless of which theme you use. Unless you plan on managing multiple themes—and the majority of developers don't—use jquery-ui.css, as it's the structure and theme concatenated together.

If you open jquery-ui.css, you'll see that it starts with the following comment block:

```
/*! jQuery UI - v1.11.0 - 2014-01-01
* http://jqueryui.com
* Includes: core.css, draggable.css, ...
* To view and modify this theme, visit http://jqueryui.com/themeroller/
    ?ffDefault=Verdana...
* Copyright 2014 jQuery Foundation and other contributors; Licensed MIT */
```

The key part is the URL starting with http://jqueryui.com/themeroller/. If you navigate to this URL in your browser, you go to ThemeRoller with all your custom changes in place. This is great for keeping your theme up to date as new versions of jQuery UI are released. When jQuery UI x.y.z comes out, you can import your theme, see how it looks with the updated library, and then download an updated CSS file with your changes preserved.

TIP   In general, it's a bad practice to directly edit a ThemeRoller-built CSS theme file. Leaving the file intact makes it easier to upgrade when new versions of jQuery UI are released. Create a new CSS file for your application, and do any additional styling there.

Although ThemeRoller is a great starting point for styling applications, you can't do everything in it. You're limited to specific CSS properties, and you can't target individual widgets. ThemeRoller is just the beginning of the styling capabilities provided by jQuery UI.

To see other things that are possible, let's dig into the jQuery UI CSS framework.

> **Third-party themes**
>
> In addition to the themes provided in jQuery UI, a number of themes created by the jQuery community are available. The most popular of these is jQuery UI Bootstrap, which integrates the popular Bootstrap library with jQuery UI. You can learn more about Bootstrap at http://getbootstrap.com/ and check out jQuery UI Bootstrap at http://jquery-ui-bootstrap.github.io/jquery-ui-bootstrap/.

7.2   Using the jQuery UI CSS framework to customize applications

jQuery UI comes packaged with a full CSS framework with CSS class names that serve a variety of purposes. To get a sense of the names, a full list is documented at http://api.jqueryui.com/theming/css-framework/.

In this section, we'll go over the class names and what you can do with them. The main three categories of class names are widget containers, interaction states, and interaction cues. We'll go over each, starting with widget containers.

TIP To avoid naming conflicts, every class name used by jQuery starts with a `ui-` prefix. Names are lowercased, and words are separated with hyphens—for instance, `ui-widget-content`.

7.2.1 Styling widget containers

The first set of class names creates a visual consistency between the widgets used in an application. This set has only three class names, so they're not too hard to remember:

- `ui-widget`—Class name applied to the outer container of all widgets.
- `ui-widget-header`—Class name applied to header containers.
- `ui-widget-content`—Class name applied to content containers. The content container can be the parent or sibling of a `ui-widget-header`.

Internally, jQuery UI consistently applies these class names to all its widgets. Figure 7.5 shows how the class names are applied to a few widgets. The solid border is around the `ui-widget-header` element, and the dotted black border is around the `ui-widget-content` element.

In the case of the tabs, dialog, and datepicker widgets, the `ui-widget-content` class name is on the outer container of the widget. The accordion widget places `ui-widget-content` on each content pane.

NOTE In general, `ui-widget-content` is placed on the outer widget container as it's desirable to have a border around the whole widget. If you don't want a border—as with the accordion—it's placed on a separate child element.

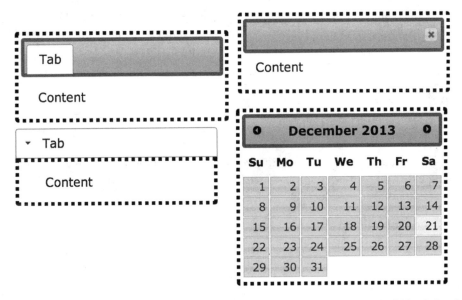

Figure 7.5 Locations of widget container class names `ui-widget-header` (solid border) and `ui-widget-content` (dotted border) on the tabs, dialog, accordion, and datepicker widgets. The accordion header uses neither because it is clickable; it uses the interaction states we'll cover in the next section.

Because the class names are consistently applied, you can write CSS rules that target all widgets at the same time. The following code shows an example of this:

```
.ui-widget {
    font-size: 1.2em;
    font-family: Tahoma;
}
.ui-widget-header {
    border: 5px solid blue;
    background: red;
    color: white;
}
.ui-widget-content {
    border: 2px solid green;
    background: purple;
    color: gray;
}
```

Although this example doesn't produce pretty widgets, it shows the types or rules that are safe to apply to these class names. Because the ui-widget class name is applied to all widgets, you can apply only a few CSS rules safely without breaking the display of some widgets. In fact, the jQuery UI themes internally specify only a font-size and font-family. For the header and content class names, border, background, and color are the most common rules used.

Unless you're a designer creating a custom look, it's uncommon to need to add CSS rules to these class names beyond the rules that are configurable in ThemeRoller. But as you'll see in the next chapter, if you know how to apply these class names to HTML elements, you can create custom widgets that work with the jQuery UI theming system automatically. If you want to add a container to your application that looks the same as your widgets, you can use the following markup:

```
<div class="ui-widget ui-widget-content">
    <div class="ui-widget-header">
        Hello
    </div>
    Content
</div>
```

The container class names handle the widget's default look, but they don't handle styling based on user interaction—such as the display of a tab after it's activated. The next category of framework classes addresses these states.

7.2.2 Styling interaction states

You may have noticed that when you hover over a button widget, its display changes. Or when you click an accordion header, it's automatically highlighted. What you may not have noticed is all these changes happen by manipulating a few core class names. The class names for the four widget states are

- ui-state-default—Applied to clickable elements such as a button, tab, or accordion header.
- ui-state-hover—Applied to clickable elements when the mouse hovers over them.
- ui-state-focus—Applied when clickable elements receive keyboard focus.
- ui-state-active—Applied when a clickable element is activated. The active tab and accordion header are given this class name.

To get a sense of how these class names work, consider the following example:

```
<style>
    .ui-state-default { color: blue; }        ◁—❶ Default styling
    .ui-state-hover { color: orange; }
    .ui-state-focus { color: green; }          ◁—❸ Focus styling
    .ui-state-active { font-size: 1.5em; }
</style>
<div id="buttonset">
    <label for="one">one</label>
    <input name="numbers" type="radio" id="one">

    <label for="two">two</label>
    <input name="numbers" type="radio" id="two">
</div>
<script>
    $( "#buttonset" ).buttonset();
</script>
```

Hover styling ❷—▷

Active styling ❹—▷

TIP This example is easier to see visually. You can try this example out at http://jsfiddle.net/tj_vantoll/78vQL/.

You have a buttonset widget containing two radio buttons. Because the buttons are clickable, the widget places the ui-state-default class name on each of them. As a result, your buttons start with blue text ❶.

If you hover over either button, its text changes to orange ❷. If you give either button focus with the keyboard, its text changes to green ❸. Finally, if you select either radio button, the selected button's font-size increases ❹.

As with the container class names, jQuery UI consistently applies the interaction state class names to all clickable elements in all widgets. By writing rules to target these states, you can again style widgets simultaneously.

Before we look at more comprehensive examples of how all these class names come together, we'll discuss one last category: interaction cues.

7.2.3 Styling interaction cues

Interaction *states* are directly related to clickable elements, but interaction *cues* can be applied to any element. The six interaction cue class names are

- ui-state-highlight—Represents a highlighted container element.
- ui-state-error—Represents an erred container element.

- ui-state-error-text—Utility class name to style error text without applying a background. It can be used on the labels of erred form fields.
- ui-state-disabled—Represents a disabled element.
- ui-priority-primary—Represents a higher priority element in a set, such as a button you want to stand out to the user.
- ui-priority-secondary—Represents a lesser priority element in a set, such as a button you *don't* want to stand out; for example, a cancel button.

Of these six, only ui-state-disabled is used by the jQuery UI widgets internally; the rest are intended for utility use in your applications. To show how, let's dig into more robust examples that use these class names.

Let's start by revisiting the accordion widget to add the ability to disable and display errors for individual headers. How could you use this functionality? Suppose you run an online service where users have accounts they can manage. An accordion provides an excellent way to divide the various settings into categories such as profile, billing information, preferences, and so forth.

With such a setup, erring individual headers lets you draw the user's attention to a collapsed panel to take some action—such as changing an expired password.

Disabling lets you prevent the user from interacting with individual headers. You have to be careful, though. In most situations, it's better to hide rather than disable elements; many users become confused when presented with controls they can't use. But in this example, you'll look at one way that disabling can be advantageous.

The accordion control you'll build is shown in figure 7.6.

The first tab displays with a red background, border, and text and contains a warning icon. The second tab appears disabled to the user. The following listing shows the code to build this accordion.

> **NOTE** The full source of this example is available at http://jsfiddle.net/tj_vantoll/z6w6P/.

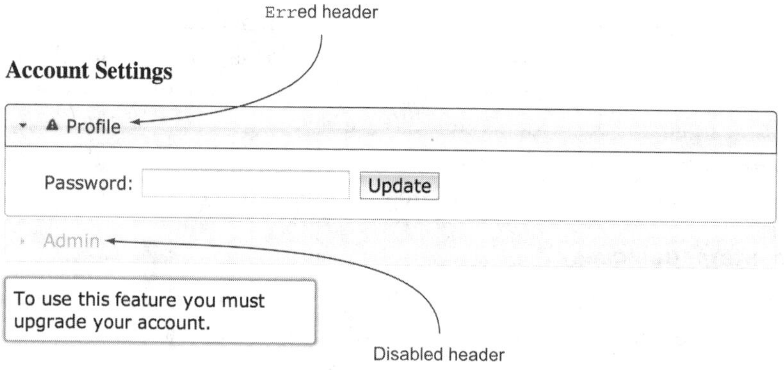

Figure 7.6   An accordion control with an erred header and a disabled header

Listing 7.1   Erring and disabling accordion panels

```
<style>
    .ui-state-error .ui-icon {
        display: inline-block;
    }
</style>
<div id="accordion">
    <h3 class="ui-state-error">
        <span class="ui-icon ui-icon-alert">
            This section has an error
        </span>
        Profile
    </h3>
    <div>
        <form>
            <label for="password"
              class="ui-state-error-text">Password:</label>
            <input id="password" required
              title="Your password has expired, please choose a new one">
            <button>Update</button>
        </form>
    </div>
    <h3 class="ui-state-disabled">Admin</h3>
    <div>Admin - Contents</div>
</div>
<script>
    $( "#accordion" )
        .accordion()
        .tooltip({
            items: ".ui-state-disabled",
            content: "To use this feature you must upgrade your account"
        });
    $( "#password" ).tooltip();
</script>
```

❶ Applies an erred state

❷ Shows an alert icon

❸ Disables the Admin header

❹ Shows a tooltip for disabled headers

For the first tab, you apply the erred styling by adding the `ui-state-error` class name ❶, which applies the red border, background, and text color to the header. The class name doesn't, however, apply the warning icon as shown in figure 7.6. This comes from the `<span>` in the header ❷.

You've used the jQuery UI icons several times throughout this book, but you've only looked at using icons as options of the jQuery UI widgets, such as the button widget's `icons` option. All the jQuery UI icons can be used in HTML directly by applying two class names: `ui-icon` and the name of the specific icon, in this case, `ui-icon-alert`. You can find a full list of the icons available at http://api.jqueryui.com/theming/icons/.

> **NOTE** If `<span class="ui-icon ui-icon-alert"></span>` creates the icon, why do you give the "This section has an error" text in it? The text is provided for screen reader users who can't see the red styling or the warning icon. The `ui-icon` class name hides this text from sighted users and leaves it accessible to assistive technologies such as screen readers.

That takes care of the first panel, so let's move on to the disabled panel. You disable an accordion panel by applying the `ui-state-disabled` class name to the appropriate header element ❸. The widget now automatically prevents this panel from being opened. This technique of disabling with `ui-state-disabled` works for several of the jQuery UI widgets—specifically, tabs, menu, and button.

But you need to take care of one last thing. Disabled UI elements can confuse users unless they're given an indication of why the elements are disabled. For this example you add a tooltip ❹ to the disabled accordion header to let the user know why the header is disabled—the user needs to upgrade the account to use this panel.

Although this is not a complete example, it shows how the jQuery UI CSS framework makes it easy to customize a widget's built-in behavior to meet your needs. The accordion widget has no built-in options to `error` or disable individual tabs, but you can build this display using a few of the framework's class names. Let's look at another example of how you can customize widgets with the jQuery UI CSS framework.

Layout helper class names

We haven't specifically looked at one category of class names: the layout helpers. The layout helpers are a series of utility class names you may have a use for in your applications:

- `ui-helper-hidden`—Hides the element visually and from screen readers.
- `ui-helper-hidden-accessible`—Hides the element visually but leaves it accessible to screen readers.
- `ui-helper-reset`—A CSS style reset. It resets `margin`, `padding`, `border`, `outline`, `line-height`, `text-decoration`, `font-size`, and `list-style` to a baseline value that's consistent across browsers. Read more about what CSS resets do at http://meyerweb.com/eric/tools/css/reset/.
- `ui-helper-clearfix`—Clears floating child elements. Learn more about CSS floats and clearing them at https://developer.mozilla.org/en-US/docs/Web/CSS/float.
- `ui-front`—jQuery UI uses this class name internally to manage the `z-index`-based stacking of elements on the screen. Read more about `ui-front` at http://api.jqueryui.com/theming/stacking-elements/.

7.2.4   *Building a styled confirmation dialog*

In chapter 4, you built a dialog to get the user's confirmation before you deleted the user's data. Now that you know about the CSS framework, let's see how you can use the CSS class names in jQuery UI to improve the look of a confirmation dialog. This time, you'll build a dialog for a different use case: confirming a money transfer. If you've ever banked online, a dialog such as that shown in figure 7.7 should look familiar.

The code to build this dialog is shown in the next listing.

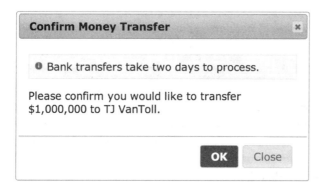

Figure 7.7 A confirmation dialog to show before a money transfer

NOTE The full source of this example can be found at http://jsfiddle.net/tj_vantoll/a3zkQ/.

Listing 7.2 Building a styled confirmation dialog

```
<style>
    .ui-dialog .ui-state-highlight { padding: 0.5em; }
    .ui-dialog .ui-icon-info { display: inline-block; }
    .ui-widget-content .ui-priority-primary {
        color: white;
        background: green;
    }
</style>
<div id="dialog">
    <p class="ui-state-highlight">
        <span class="ui-icon ui-icon-info">
            Informational message
        </span>
        Bank transfers take two days to process.
    </p>
    <p>Please confirm you would like to transfer $1,000,000 to TJ
        VanToll.</p>
</div>
<script>
    $( "#dialog" ).dialog({
        buttons: [
            {
                text: "OK",
                "class": "ui-priority-primary",
                click: function() {
                    // Process transaction
                    $( this ).dialog( "close" );
                }
            },
            {
                text: "Close",
                "class": "ui-priority-secondary",
                click: function() {
                    $( this ).dialog( "close" );
                }
            }
```

① Styles the primary button

② Highlights the informational paragraph

③ Uses an info icon

④ Uses the primary button class name

⑤ Uses the secondary button class name

```
        ],
        title: "Confirm Money Transfer",
        width: 500
    });
</script>
```

Let's start with the HTML. For the informational message about bank transfers, you use the jQuery UI `ui-state-highlight` class name to make the message stand out to the user ❷. Inside the message, you use another of the CSS framework icons, `ui-icon-info`, to visually indicate that this is an information message ❸. You also provide a text fallback for screen readers that can't read the icon.

In JavaScript, you create a dialog widget—using the widget's `buttons` option to create the two buttons. On each button's object, you include a `class` property to add the class names—`ui-priority-primary` ❹ and `ui-priority-secondary` ❺, respectively—to each button. The class names add emphasis to a primary action and reduce emphasis from a secondary action. You want to draw the user's eye and attention to the OK button to encourage the user to complete the transaction.

Internally, jQuery UI bolds the primary button and decreases the opacity of the secondary button to achieve this effect. To further draw the user's attention, you also change the background and text color of the primary button ❶.

> **TIP** The word *class* is a reserved word in JavaScript; to use it in code you must quote it as in this example. Although the language doesn't currently use *class*, it will be used in the next version of JavaScript (ECMAScript 6).

One last note before we move on: did you notice the difference between the three CSS rules you used?

```
.ui-dialog .ui-state-highlight { … }
.ui-dialog .ui-icon-info { … }
.ui-widget-content .ui-priority-primary { … }
```

See how the first two rules are prefixed with a `ui-dialog` class name and the third with `ui-widget-content`? The first two use widget-specific class names, and the last uses a framework-wide rule. As you saw in this section, framework-wide rules let you add CSS rules that apply to all widgets. Because you made your button green using `ui-widget-content`, any future widgets with primary buttons will be styled the same.

Although the ability to style all widgets at the same time is powerful, sometimes you don't want changes to apply everywhere. In this example, the highlighting changes are prefixed with `ui-dialog` because you want the CSS rules to apply only when `ui-state-highlight` is used in a dialog. `ui-dialog` is one of many class names that jQuery UI provides for each individual widget. Next, let's look at what class names are available and what you can do with them.

7.3   *Styling with widget class names*

Each widget uses a comprehensive set of CSS class names so you can easily target any section of any widget. The class names are documented in each widget's API

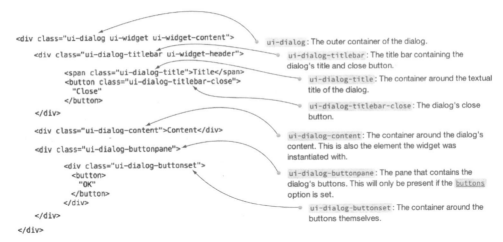

Figure 7.8 On the left is a simplified version of the markup the dialog widget uses. On the right is the dialog widget's class name documentation. Notice that the nesting in the documentation matches the nesting used in the rendered HTML markup.

documentation. The dialog class names are documented at http://api.jqueryui.com/dialog/#theming. The documentation uses nesting to show the structure of each widget's markup. The dialog widget's ui-dialog-titlebar, ui-dialog-content, and ui-dialog-buttonpane elements are direct children of the ui-dialog element. This relationship is shown in figure 7.8.

The widget-specific class names give you the ability to target specific parts of widgets without having to worry about affecting other widgets. Figure 7.9 shows how you could use the dialog class names to customize its appearance.

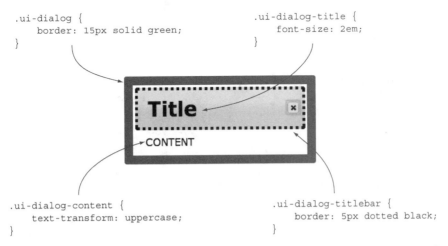

Figure 7.9 A sampling of the dialog-specific CSS class names available. The ui-dialog class name applies a solid border to the whole dialog; ui-dialog-title applies a larger font size to the title bar; ui-dialog-content uppercases the content's text; and ui-dialog-titlebar applies a dotted border to the title bar.

Admittedly, putting a 15-pixel green border around dialogs isn't practical for most applications, but you can do it! Let's look at how you can use the widget-specific class names to make powerful customizations to the jQuery UI widgets.

7.3.1 Building vertical tabs

Recall from chapter 4 that the jQuery UI tabs widget displays tabs horizontally on top of the active tab's content. Although this is the most common use case, suppose you want the tabs to display vertically on the side of the content, as shown in figure 7.10.

Figure 7.10   A jQuery UI tabs widget with CSS rules applied to the tabs-specific class names to stack the tabs vertically.

Although you may think you need JavaScript to rearrange elements to create this display, the class names provided by jQuery UI make it possible to do this in CSS alone. The key portions of the CSS are shown in the following listing. The full source and a live demo are available at http://jsfiddle.net/tj_vantoll/SL44T/.

Listing 7.3   Displaying tabs vertically

```
.ui-tabs { overflow: hidden; }
.ui-tabs .ui-tabs-nav {
    float: left;
    width: 10em;
    border-radius: 4px 0 0 4px;
    border-right: 1px solid gray;
}
.ui-tabs .ui-tabs-nav li {
    width: 100%;
    border: 1px solid gray;
    border-width: 1px 0 1px 1px;
    position: relative;
    right: -2px;
}
.ui-tabs .ui-tabs-nav li.ui-state-active {
    border-right: 1px solid white;
}
.ui-tabs .ui-tabs-panel {
    float: left;
    width: -webkit-calc(100% - 11em);
    width: calc(100% - 11em);
    box-sizing: border-box;
}
```

❶ Floats the navigation

❷ Relatively positions the list items

❸ Gives the active nav item a white border

❹ Calculates the width of the tab panels

The main tabs container has a class name of ui-tabs, and it has four immediate children: the navigation (ui-tabs-nav) and three panels (ui-tabs-panel), one for each of the tabs. The key to this example is that both the navigation and the panels are floated ❶, which makes them appear side by side. To make this work, you also need to give both the navigation and the panels an explicit width, which we'll get to momentarily.

After this is done, you need to replicate one visual detail from the default horizontal tabs by removing the border between the active tab and the content panel. If you look at figure 7.10, you can see that there's no border between One and One Contents.

To make this happen, you don't remove the border from the navigation; rather, you position the individual list items directly on top of it ❷. Notice how both the .ui-tabs-nav and .ui-tabs-nav li selectors are given the same border. Now all you have to do is remove the border from the currently active list item.

The tabs widget makes this easy as ui-state-active is automatically applied to the active tab; you use this selector to apply a white border ❸, which gives the appearance that the border has been removed.

Your last task is to determine the widths to use for both the tabs navigation and panels. In this example, you use a width of 10 em for the navigation and the default 100% width for the parent ui-tabs container. To make your content responsive to different screen sizes, and leave the width of the navigation a static 10 em, you use a new feature of CSS to calculate the width of the content panels: the calc() function.

By specifying a width of calc(100% - 11em) for the tab panels ❹, you tell the browser to take the default width of the panels, subtract 11 em (to account for the navigation), and use the result as the width of the panels. The calc() function makes it easy to calculate percentages based on widths and static values. Now you can resize the window to your heart's desire, and the content panels adapt to the screen size automatically.

> **WARNING** The calc() function isn't supported in Internet Explorer versions earlier than 9 as well as Android versions earlier than 4.4. If you need to support these browsers, you unfortunately need to hardcode widths for both ui-tabs and ui-tabs-panel to make this vertical tabs approach work.

As you can see from this example, the class names provided by the tabs widget give you the ability to perform complex customizations without any JavaScript. Although building vertical tabs is cool, you may have noticed one limitation of this approach: because ui-tabs is styled, you can't use vertical and horizontal tabs side by side. We'll return to this example to build a more robust implementation in chapter 9 when we look at widget extensions.

Next, let's look at another handy use of the jQuery UI widget class names.

7.3.2   *Building a mobile-friendly datepicker*

The jQuery UI datepicker is great for letting users select dates from a calendar, but on touch devices, the calendar days are small; it's too easy for fingers to accidentally select the wrong day. Let's see how you can use the CSS class names on the datepicker to make the widget mobile friendly.

You'll build the inline datepicker shown in figure 7.11. The code to build this datepicker is shown in the following listing.

Listing 7.4   A mobile-friendly inline datepicker

Applies changes only to devices that are < 600 pixels wide ❶ ➝

❷ Makes the datepicker take up the full screen width

Makes the dates ❸ easier to tap

```
<style>
    @media (max-width: 600px) {
        .ui-datepicker { width: 100%; }
        .ui-datepicker-calendar td a {
            text-align: center;
            padding: 0.5em;
        }
    }
</style>
<div id="datepicker"></div>
<script>
    $( "#datepicker" ).datepicker();
</script>
```

Because the datepicker displays appropriately on larger screens, you start your CSS with a media query to limit your changes to screens with a viewport of under 600 pixels wide ❶. Media queries are a quick way to scope CSS rules based on the characteristics of the browser it's running on—most commonly its width. Media queries aren't supported in Internet Explorer versions earlier than 9, although because you're building for mobile devices, this isn't a concern; older versions of the browser ignore the media query.

> **TIP** Media queries are the primary tool for building responsive web applications as they let you conditionally apply CSS rules based on the browser's height and width. A full exploration of media queries is outside the scope of this book, but a good place to get started is https://developer.mozilla.org/en-US/docs/Web/Guide/CSS/Media_queries.

Next, you use the datepicker-specific CSS class names to make the datepicker larger for mobile devices. Specifically, you first use the outer `ui-datepicker` class name to make the datepicker take up the full width of the screen ❷. Then, you increase the `padding` of all links in the `ui-datepicker-calendar` to make them bigger and easier to click with fingers ❸.

Figure 7.11   An inline datepicker displayed on an iPhone

Although this is great, most developers want to use a mobile datepicker tied to an `<input>`, not an inline one. Because this is a common requirement, you'll implement this use case as well. But because this is a nontrivial task that requires a decent amount of JavaScript, you'll build it in chapter 9 as a widget extension.

For now, let's look at one last use of the jQuery UI widget-specific class names.

7.3.3 Adding arrows to tooltips with CSS

The jQuery UI tooltip widget makes it easy to show additional information for controls on a web page. But the tooltip widget doesn't provide one common UI pattern out of the box: adding arrows. If you're not sure what I'm talking about, take a look at the image shown in figure 7.12.

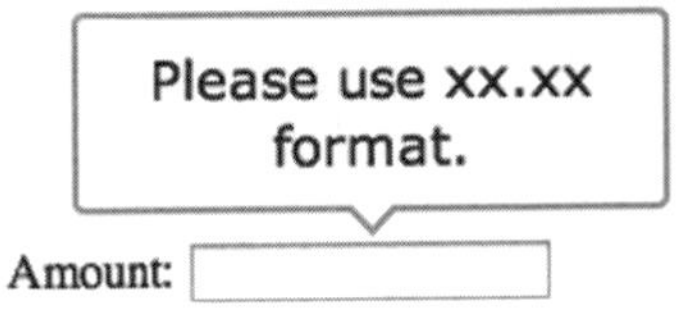

Figure 7.12 A jQuery UI tooltip with a CSS-drawn arrow

Notice how the arrow points from the tooltip to the form control itself. This small visual touch helps the user associate the tooltip with the input. And believe it or not, you can draw the arrow in CSS alone. This is shown in the following listing. You can view the example live at http://jsfiddle.net/tj_vantoll/cAz6T/.

Listing 7.5 Adding arrows to a tooltip widget

```css
<style>
    .ui-tooltip {
        text-align: center;
        padding: 0;
        box-shadow: none;
        width: 200px;
    }
    .ui-tooltip-content {
        position: relative;
        padding: 0.5em;
    }
    .ui-tooltip-content::after, .ui-tooltip-content::before {
        content: "";
        position: absolute;
        border-style: solid;
        display: block;
        left: 50px;
    }
    .ui-tooltip-content::before {
        top: -10px;
        border-color: #AAA transparent;
        border-width: 10px 10px 0;
    }
    .ui-tooltip-content::after {
        top: -7px;
        border-color: white transparent;
        border-width: 10px 10px 0;
    }
</style>
```

❶ Creates triangles using the border of pseudo-elements

```
<label for="amount">Amount:</label>
<input id="amount" title="Please use xx.xx format.">

<script>
    $( "#amount" ).tooltip({
        position: {
            my: "center bottom",
            at: "center top-10",
            collision: "none"
        }
    });
</script>
```

❷ Positions the tooltip

The tooltip widget provides only two CSS class names: ui-tooltip and ui-tooltip-content. But as it turns out, that's all you need to build this cool effect. Most of the magic here comes from using the ::before and ::after pseudo-elements on the ui-tooltip-content element. If you haven't used ::before and ::after, they're two bonus elements every DOM node has that you can use to add supplementary content or styling.

> **WARNING**   Although the two-colon syntax for ::before and ::after is now standard, Internet Explorer 8 supports only the now-outdated single-colon versions—:before and :after. The double-colon syntax is technically correct per the CSS specification, but all modern browsers support both the single- and double-colon syntax. Personally, because it's not a big deal if the pointers aren't present, I prefer sticking with the technically correct ::before and ::after.

Even if you understand how pseudo-elements work, this example is still likely a mystery. How in the world is this CSS turning into a pointer? This code uses an odd trick to draw triangles with a single element in CSS: if you give an element with no height and no width a border on three sides, it creates a triangle ❶. If this makes no sense to you, you're not alone; this is a nearly impossible thing to conceptualize. There's a great demo at http://codepen.io/chriscoyier/pen/lotjh that walks through exactly what's going on here. If you're near a computer or phone, watch this now.

If you're not able to watch the demo, just accept that by some CSS magic the ::before and ::after pseudo-elements on the ui-tooltip-content element are triangles. The ::before triangle is the same color as the border, and the ::after triangle is white. The white triangle obscures most of the dark triangle. This gives the appearance of a single, cohesive border for the tooltip.

> **TIP**   http://cssarrowplease.com is an online tool for building these CSS-based pointers without having to understand the magic going on.

Because you're using a pointer, you have to make sure the pointer points at the correct element. To do this, you use the tooltip's position option. As you saw in chapter 4, the position reads like an English sentence: position my (the tooltip's) horizontal center vertical bottom at the horizontal center vertical top (of the input) ❷. Don't worry about the positioning specifics here; we'll return to this example when we discuss the position utility in detail in chapter 12.

7.4 *Summary*

jQuery UI provides a number of tools to style and theme your applications. You started with ThemeRoller, an online tool to build themes. You can use it to build a theme from scratch, or one based on the 24 built-in themes. You can also import your theme back into ThemeRoller to make further changes.

From there, you can use the two sets of CSS class names that the library provides: framework-wide and widget-specific. The framework-wide class names let you change the look of all widgets at once, and the widget-specific class names let you write CSS that targets specific widgets. Between these two sets of class names, you have the ability to build highly customized UIs. You used the class names to build a vertical tabs UI, a mobile-friendly datepicker, and tooltips with CSS-based arrows.

We'll continue to discuss the jQuery UI CSS framework throughout the book. In the next chapter, you'll build a custom widget from scratch, and you'll see how applying the jQuery UI class names makes a widget automatically themeable.

Part 3

Customization and advanced usage

These final 5 chapters cover the more complex aspects of jQuery UI, starting with widgets. In chapter 8 you'll learn how to build your own widgets from scratch, using the same mechanism jQuery UI uses. In chapter 9 you'll see how to customize any widget's behavior using widget extensions.

You'll learn in chapter 10 how to optimize your applications for production use, including the most important optimizations for building mobile sites. In chapter 11 you'll build on this and create a complete application from scratch—one that runs fast on all devices. Chapter 12 looks under the hood of jQuery UI to uncover the tools that make jQuery UI work.

Using the widget factory to build stateful plugins

This chapter covers

- Creating widgets with the widget factory
- The benefits of using the widget factory
- Accessing a widget's data and inner workings

Throughout this book, you've looked at the widgets jQuery UI provides and all the things you can do with them. Although the jQuery UI widgets let you do a lot, the widgets don't cover all the UI controls you need to build modern web applications. Don't worry—the most powerful part of jQuery isn't its widgets, it's the mechanism that all its widgets are built with: the widget factory.

The widget factory evolved from the early days of jQuery UI. Recall that the jQuery UI project started as a collection of popular plugins from a variety of authors, coding styles, and APIs. Over time, common patterns and best practices emerged. Implementations of these patterns gradually moved out of individual plugins and into a common base, which eventually became the widget factory. The widget factory itself is a jQuery plugin that builds jQuery plugins that adhere to these common conventions.

The widget factory is also a standalone component; you can use it independently of the jQuery UI library. In fact, the widget factory serves as the basis of all the jQuery Mobile widgets and numerous third-party jQuery plugins. By learning to use the widget factory, you'll have the ability to build widgets that work anywhere that jQuery Core is available.

In this chapter, you'll walk through the development of a custom widget built from scratch. You'll see that, like all of jQuery UI, the widget factory packs a whole lot of functionality in a few, easy-to-use APIs.

Let's get started.

Why build a widget rather than a jQuery plugin?

A widget's differentiating feature is its concept of state. Many jQuery plugins don't have—or need—the concept of state. Consider the following jQuery plugin that replaces the selected element's contents with a random number:

```
$.fn.randomNumber = function() {
    return this.each( function( index, element ) {
        $( element ).html( Math.random() * 1000 );
    };
};
```

This plugin is designed to run once and be done. The plugin doesn't remember which elements it changed or anything about them. Contrast that with any of the jQuery UI widgets, such as the dialog widget created in the following code:

```
<div id="dialog"></div>
<script>
    $( "#dialog" ).dialog({ title: "Hello World" });
</script>
```

The `randomNumber()` plugin knew nothing about the element it operated on; the dialog widget knows a whole lot about the `<div id="dialog">` element. It knows that it's a dialog, that its title is `"Hello World"`, and more. (We'll look at how it remembers this information later in the chapter.)

Dialog is an excellent candidate for a widget because it has a state to manage; you can open it, close it, change its title, change its height, and so forth. Conversely, the `randomNumber()` plugin isn't a good widget candidate because it has no state. The general rule is this: use the widget factory when you want to build a plugin that maintains state.

8.1   Building a widget

Building a fully featured widget is a complex, multistep process; we'll break widget creation into a set of steps that you'll follow in this chapter. The nine steps are shown in the following checklist. Don't worry about what each step means; we'll walk through each individually.

1 `$.widget()`		**2** Markup structure		**3** `_create()`	
4 Make themeable		**5** Add options		**6** Expose methods	
7 Trigger events		**8** Enable/Disable		**9** `_destroy()`	

To walk through these steps, you need a widget to build, and in this chapter, you'll build a to-do list. In this case it will be a list of tasks that the user can check and uncheck. Such a list could be used for any set of tasks—for exam-

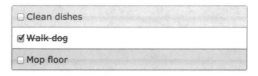

Figure 8.1 The to-do list you'll build in this chapter

ple, a grocery list or your widget-creation checklist. An image of the to-do list you'll build is shown in figure 8.1.

Let's dig right in with the API to create widgets: `$.widget()`.

> **NOTE** The finished version of this widget is available at http://jsfiddle.net/tj_vantoll/zStp7/ if you'd like to follow along or play with the examples as we go.

8.1.1 Constructing widgets with $.widget()

As discussed at the beginning of this chapter, the widget factory itself is a jQuery plugin located on the $ global object. To invoke it, call `$.widget()` as shown in the following code:

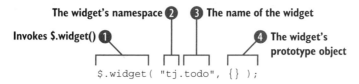

You invoke `$.widget()` with two parameters ❶. The first is the name of the widget: `"tj.todo"`. Why is the name in two parts, separated by a period?

The first half of the name determines the widget's namespace ❷. The namespace determines the location where the widget's constructor function and prototype are stored on the global $ object. All jQuery UI widgets use a `"ui"` namespace; therefore, they're accessible at `$.ui` (`$.ui.dialog`, `$.ui.tabs`, and so on).

The `"ui"` namespace is reserved for the jQuery UI widgets; you need to create your own namespace for your own widgets. In this example, the namespace is my first name: `"tj"`. We'll look at how the widget's constructor function works momentarily.

The second half of the name is the string to use as the plugin name ❸. Because you used `"todo"`, a `todo()` plugin was created for you.

The last parameter to `$.widget()` is an object to use as the widget's prototype object ❹. You can use the prototype object to override default widget behavior and expose methods to users of the widget. We'll go over how this object works in the next section when we look at `_create()`. For now, because it's a required argument, you pass an empty object.

NOTE `$.widget()` takes one additional, optional parameter: the constructor function of another widget to extend. This powerful feature lets you alter and build on top of existing widgets. We're skipping the parameter for now to focus on developing a widget from scratch. Chapter 9 covers widget extension in detail.

When you execute `$.widget( "tj.todo", {} )`, a lot happens. This is shown in figure 8.2; let's look at that figure in detail.

NAMESPACE CREATION

The widget factory created an object at `$.tj` to use as a namespace for the todo widget. `$.widget()` is smart enough to create the namespace only if it doesn't already exist. If you create another widget on the same namespace—for instance, `$.widget( "tj.awesome", {} )`—the original namespace isn't overridden.

CONSTRUCTOR FUNCTION

Although you haven't used constructor functions, they exist for each of the jQuery UI widgets. For example, you can create a new dialog using the following code:

```
new $.ui.dialog({ title: "The Widget Factory Rocks!" }, "<div>" );
```

The first argument is an object for configuring the widget's options.. The second argument determines the element to convert to a widget—in this case, a newly created `<div>`. When using constructor functions, you can optionally omit the new keyword:

```
$.ui.dialog({ title: "The Widget Factory Rocks!" }, "<div>" );
```

By running `$.widget()`, you get this behavior for free. The following creates a new `<ul>` and converts it to a todo widget:

```
$.tj.todo( {}, "<ul>" );
```

CHAINABLE PLUGIN

The chainable plugin should look familiar, as it's the mechanism you've used to initialize widgets up to this point. `$.widget()` created this plugin for you automatically; you can now initialize todo widgets by selecting elements and calling `todo()`. The following converts all `<ul>` elements to todo widgets:

```
$( "ul" ).todo();
```

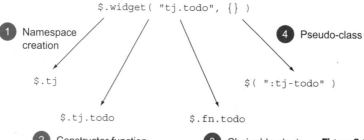

Figure 8.2 An overview of what happens when creating a widget

Because the plugin is also automatically chainable, you can append additional jQuery method calls. The following code initializes todo widgets and then hides them:

```
$( "ul" ).todo().css( "display", "none" );
```

PSEUDO-CLASS

The widget factory creates a pseudo-class with the widget's full name—in this case, ":tj-todo". CSS pseudo-classes are selectors that match elements based on the state they're in. For example, :focus matches the element that currently has focus. Pseudo-classes are always prefixed with a single colon. The pseudo-class can be used to find all elements that have a widget associated with them, or to determine whether a given element is a widget. This behavior is shown in the following listing.

Listing 8.1 Using the pseudo-class created by the widget factory

Creates a new `<ul>` element.

Selects and logs all elements that are todo widgets; in this case, the `<ul>` is logged.

```
$.widget( "tj.todo", {} );
var ul = $( "<ul>" ).appendTo( "body" );
ul.todo();
console.log( $( ":tj-todo" ) );
console.log( ul.is( ":tj-todo" ) );
```

Converts the element to a todo widget.

Determines whether the `<ul>` is a todo widget. It is, so true is logged.

> **WARNING** The pseudo-class created by the widget factory only works in jQuery's selector engine. $(":tj-todo") matches all todo widgets, but document.querySelectorAll(":tj-todo"), or a CSS selector such as :tj-todo { color: red; }, won't.

You've now seen all the functionality you get by running $.widget(), but your widget still doesn't do anything. The next step in your process is choosing the HTML markup structure for your widget to use.

8.1.2 Choosing a markup structure

All widgets built using the widget factory work by associating themselves with a DOM element. For most widgets, a single DOM node is all you need to build the widget. For instance, autocomplete, datepicker, and spinner require only an `<input>` element to be initialized.

Some widgets, however, require a more complex structure. Recall the expected markup to build a tabs widget shown in the following code:

```
<div>
    <ul>
        <li><a href="#one">One</a></li>
    </ul>
    <div id="one">One Contents</div>
</div>
```

What markup structure should you use for a to-do list? You need to consider two things when choosing the markup structure of your widget:

1 It should be as easy as possible to create a widget.
2 The markup should be semantic.

The first consideration means that you should aim to require as little markup as possible. For instance, the spinner widget *could* require developers to create DOM elements for the up and down arrows. But this would make the spinner far harder for developers to use; the widget generates these elements for you.

The second consideration means that the markup should make sense, even when the element isn't a widget. Consider the required markup of the tabs widget. If JavaScript were to fail, the user would still have a set of functioning links to content. This rule is applied across all the jQuery UI widgets. If the button widget fails, the user still has a functioning unenhanced button; if the spinner widget fails, the user still has a functioning <input>.

With these criteria in mind, you'll need the following markup to build your todo widget:

```
<ul>
    <li>First todo</li>
    <li>Second todo</li>
    <li>Third todo</li>
</ul>
```

As this is a to-do *list*, you use an HTML unordered list (<ul>) to represent it. You'll require that the initial items on the list be specified as list items (<li>s). That way, if something goes wrong in JavaScript, users can still view the items on the list, even if they can't edit them.

To build a complete todo widget, you need more markup than this—most notably, you need to add check boxes. How do the jQuery UI widgets add the extra markup they need when widgets are initialized? They use one of many hooks the widget factory provides: _create().

> **WARNING** Take note of the underscore prefix. The method name is _create(), not create(). We'll go over why an underscore prefix is used for most of the widget factory's methods in section 8.3.2 when we discuss methods; for now, make sure you include the underscore.

8.1.3   *Overriding _create() to initialize widgets*

In addition to the features you've seen, the widget factory also provides a number of methods and properties to aid with widget development. To add custom behavior to your new widget, you have to override a few of these methods—starting with _create(). To see how to do this, recall your call to $.widget():

```
$.widget( "tj.todo", {} );
```

The last argument to $.widget() is an object to use as the widget's prototype. If you don't understand the details of how prototype objects in JavaScript work, don't worry.

For now, know that the default set of methods and properties a widget uses is stored in `$.Widget.prototype` (note the capital W). When you pass methods and properties to `$.widget()`, they're used instead of those on `$.Widget.prototype`.

> **TIP** A full list of the methods and properties on `$.Widget.prototype` is documented at http://api.jqueryui.com/jquery.widget/.

This is easier to see with an example. The first method you override in any custom widget is the `_create()` method. The widget factory invokes `_create()` anytime an element is converted to a widget. The default `_create()` on `$.Widget.prototype` does nothing. To make your widget do something useful, you must provide your own `_create()`:

```
$.widget( "tj.todo", {
    _create: function() {
        this.element.addClass( "tj-todo" );
    }
});
```

You provide a `_create()` method for the todo widget's prototype, and the widget factory uses it instead of `$.Widget.prototype._create()`. Although the `_create()` method doesn't have any parameters, it does have `this.element` set to the element the widget was initialized on, and `this.options` set to any options that were passed. You use the `this.element` reference to add a CSS class name to the element that was converted to a widget.

The following example creates a new `<ul>`, appends it to the `<body>`, and initializes a todo widget on it:

```
$( "<ul><li>Walk dog</li></ul>" )          ❶ Initializes the todo widget
    .appendTo( "body" )                         on the new <ul>
    .todo();
```

When the todo plugin runs ❶, your `_create()` method is invoked, and a `"tj-todo"` class name is added to the `<ul>` element.

One other important thing takes place when an element is initialized with a widget. Under the hood, the widget factory invokes the widget's constructor function—in this case, `$.tj.todo`—which performs a number of initialization tasks, including calling `_create()`, and then returns an object with all properties and methods available on the widget. This object is known as the widget's *instance*.

The instance object gives direct access to the methods and properties on a widget without going through the widget's plugin. To see how it works, let's return to your todo widget.

Remember that for your to-do list, the markup you need to add is a check box for each item on the list. The following code alters your `_create()` method to do that:

```
_create: function() {
    this.element.addClass( "tj-todo" );
    this._renderList();
},
```

```
_renderList: function() {
    this.element.find( "li" ).each(function() {
        var li = $( this ),
            label = $( "<label></label>" ),
            checkbox = $( "<input>", {
                type: "checkbox",
                value: li.text()
            });

        label.append( checkbox ).append( li.text() );
        li.html( label );
    });
}
```

This code adds a `<label>` element and a check box to each `<li>` in the element. The `_renderList()` method—which does all the work here—is abstracted out of `_create()` because you're going to need it in other methods later.

Take note of one more thing: you were able to invoke `_renderList()` using a reference to `this`. In this case, `this` is set to the widget's instance object; you can use the `this` reference to invoke any widget methods directly. As you'll see throughout this chapter, the widget factory automatically sets `this` to the widget's instance object in most of its methods.

You now have the markup that you need, and a CSS class name to use for styling. But your to-do list still doesn't look like a jQuery UI widget. Next, let's see how to make this widget themeable.

Working with instances

If you're coding a widget, the widget's instance is easy to access as it's set as the context (a.k.a `this`) of most methods. But what if you need to access a widget's instance when using its plugin? The widget factory provides two external mechanisms for doing so.

The first is the `instance()` method. The following code creates a new dialog widget, and then accesses its instance using the `instance()` method:

```
$( "<div>" ).dialog().dialog( "instance" );
```

The second option relies on the fact that—internally—the widget factory stores the instance object using the `$.data()` method in jQuery Core, with the widget's full name as a key; you can use `$.fn.data()` to retrieve it:

```
$( "<div>" ).dialog().data( "ui-dialog" );
```

The widget factory utilizes this API to remember which elements have been initialized with a widget, which makes a number of things possible, including protection against multiple instantiation. If the widget's plugin is called multiple times on the same element, `_create()` will be invoked only once, as shown in the figure.

```
                    > $.widget( "tj.todo", {
                          _create: function() {
                              console.log( "create!" );
                          }
  _create() was       });
called only once
                        $( "<ul>" ).todo().todo();

                        create!
```

_create() was called only once

Plugin invoked twice on the same element

View of the JavaScript console where a widget is created and its plugin is invoked twice

8.1.4 *Making widgets themeable*

One of the major advantages of using jQuery UI widgets is that you get a consistent, easily configurable display. In chapter 7, you saw how to configure the theming hooks provided by the widgets. Let's look at how to add these hooks to your custom widget.

To make a widget themeable, you must correctly apply the appropriate class names from the jQuery UI CSS framework, specifically the following:

- *Widget containers*—ui-widget, ui-widget-header, ui-widget-content
- *Interaction states*—ui-state-default, ui-state-hover, ui-state-focus, ui-state-active

Let's start with the widget containers. For your to-do list, you have no header; ui-widget-header isn't relevant. But you do need to add ui-widget and ui-widget-content to the outer container of the list. You'll add these class names in _create():

```
_create: function() {
    this.element.addClass( "tj-todo ui-widget ui-widget-content " +
        "ui-corner-all" );
    this._renderList();
}
```

> **TIP** The jQuery UI CSS framework has helper class names for adding CSS border-radius values that are configurable in ThemeRoller. The previous example uses ui-corner-all to round all corners. The full list of corner class names is available at http://api.jqueryui.com/theming/css-framework/.

Next, you need to add the interaction states. But first you need to determine which elements in the widget are clickable. For your to-do list, the only clickable elements are the check boxes. But you may recall from chapter 3 that check boxes are nearly impossible to style with CSS. How can you theme a check box? How does the jQuery UI button widget make this possible?

To answer, let's start by looking at the markup you use for each item in the to-do list:

```
<li>
    <label>
        <input type="checkbox">
    </label>
</li>
```

Recall from chapter 3 that browsers have a built-in feature for interacting with form elements: clicks on an element's `<label>` are automatically transferred to the element itself. You can take advantage of this behavior to work around the styling limitations of check boxes.

Instead of styling the check box, you'll make its `<label>` the full height and width of the `<li>`, and style the whole `<li>` as clickable. With this setup, all clicks on the `<li>` also click the `<label>`, which toggles the underlying check box appropriately. The jQuery UI button widget uses this technique for styling check boxes and radio buttons. The native buttons themselves are hidden (in an accessible manner), and the button's `<label>` elements are styled instead.

This approach has one other advantage. Because check boxes are tiny, they're tough to click with a mouse, and painfully difficult to tap on touch devices. By styling the `<li>`, you give the user a much larger target.

To make the to-do list themeable, you alter your `_renderList()` to use the following code:

Adds class names ❶
to each `<li>`

```
var that = this;
this.element.find( "li" ).each(function() {
    var li = $( this ).addClass( "tj-todo-item ui-state-default" ),
        label = $( "<label>" ),
        checkbox = $( "<input>", {
            type: "checkbox",
            value: li.text()
        });

    label.append( checkbox ).append( li.text() );
    li.html( label );
    that._hoverable( li );
    that._focusable( li );
});
```

❷ **Handles the hover class names**

❸ **Handles the focus class names**

You add two class names to each `<li>` in the list: `ui-state-default` and `tj-todo-item` ❶. As you recall from the previous chapter, `ui-state-default` is the class name that indicates the default state of clickable elements in a widget. This applies the same clickable look as the jQuery UI buttons, tabs, and so forth.

You want to provide widget-specific class names. You already added a `tj-todo` class name to the `<ul>`, and here you add `tj-todo-item` to each `<li>`. Widget-specific class names give developers who use your widget flexibility in how they style it.

The `ui-state-default` class name takes care of the default display of the `<li>`, but remember that clickable elements can have three other states: active, hover, and focus.

For the hover and focus states, the widget factory provides two helper methods: `_hoverable()` ❷ and `_focusable()` ❸. These methods add event handles to the passed element—in this case, the `<li>`—such that the `ui-state-hover` and ui-state-focus class names are automatically managed. When the user mouses over the <li>, the <li> receives the ui-state-hover class name; when the user mouses out of the <li>, the class name is removed. The ui-state-focus is managed similarly on focus-in and focus-out of the element.

You have an almost fully themeable widget. You're missing only the ui-state-active class name. For the todo widget, you'll want to add the active class name to any checked items. And to do that, you need to listen for clicks on the check box. But where do you put that code? The widget factory has a helper method for this as well.

8.1.5 Listening for events with _on()

Throughout this book, you've been using the on() method to bind to DOM events. Although you can use on() to listen to events in widgets, the widget factory provides an additional method with a few widget-specific niceties: _on() (note the underscore prefix).

Remember that for your todo widget, you need to listen for clicks on check boxes, and then toggle the ui-state-active class name on the <li> appropriately. When the check box is checked, its <li> should have ui-state-active. When the check box is unchecked, it shouldn't. To keep your logic consolidated in one place, you'll want to manage the class name in _renderList(), but how do you call it?

Let's start with looking at how you would do it with on() (the jQuery Core one with no prefix). As a general rule, the _create() method is used to attach all event listeners; you'll add your code there:

```
_create: function() {
    ...
    this.element.on( "click", "input",
        $.proxy( this._renderList, this ) );
}
```

This code listens for clicks on the todo widget <ul>, and—when the target is an <input>—invokes _renderList(). The $.proxy() call is necessary so that this in _renderList() is set to the widget instance, instead of the DOM element the event occurred on.

Next, let's look at the same functionality implemented with _on():

```
_create: function() {
    ...
    this._on( this.element, {
        "click input": this._renderList
    });
}
```

Although the code for the two approaches is similar, _on() offers a few conveniences for widget development. First, it sets this to the widget instance automatically. There's no need for a $.proxy() call.

_on() also automatically suppresses events on disabled widgets and cleans up event handlers when a widget is destroyed. We'll get to the specifics of both later in this chapter.

Now that you call _renderList() when the user clicks check boxes, you have to make it toggle the ui-state-active class name. The updates to _renderList() are shown in the following code:

```
_renderList: function() {                              Determines whether  ❶
    this.element.find( "li" ).each(function() {            the item is active
        var li = $( this ).addClass( "tj-todo-item ui-state-default" ),
            active = li.find( ":checked" ).length === 1,
            checkbox = $( "<input>", { ... });

        li.toggleClass( "ui-state-active", active );
        ...                                 Toggles the ui-state-active
    });                                              class name  ❷
};
```

With this update, you determine whether the <li>'s check box is checked ❶, and then use that to decide whether the ui-state-active class name should be added or removed from the <li> itself ❷.

> **TIP**   The jQuery Core toggleClass() method takes an optional second parameter. When passed, as in _renderList(), true indicates the class name should be added and false indicates the class name should be removed.

You now have a widget that works seamlessly with all the jQuery UI built-in themes, as well as third-party ones. With all class names in place, let's add a bit of CSS to give the widget its final display:

```
.tj-todo {
    padding-left: 0;
}
.tj-todo .tj-todo-item label {          ❶  Takes up the full
    padding: 0.5em 0.3em;                   width and height
    display: block;                         of the <li>
}
.tj-todo .ui-state-active {                 Crosses out all completed
    text-decoration: line-through;          to-do items
}
```

The most important rule here is setting the display of the <label> to block. Your <label> elements need to take up the full dimensions of the parent <li> ❶ to ensure that all clicks toggle the appropriate check box (remember that clicks on <label> elements are transferred to their corresponding check box).

Now, not only is your widget themeable, but it also has its final look in place. But developers still can't do a lot with your widget. It's time to make it customizable.

8.2   *Customizing widgets with options, methods, and events*

We've covered a lot of territory, so let's review where we are. You created your widget using $.widget(), chose a markup structure to use, built your markup with _create(), and made your widget themeable. Your checklist shows your progress:

1	~~$.widget()~~	**2**	~~Markup structure~~	**3**	~~_create()~~
4	~~Make themeable~~	**5**	Add options	**6**	Expose methods
7	Trigger events	**8**	Enable/Disable	**9**	_destroy()

What you haven't yet tackled is how to make your widget customizable. You need to add the same options, methods, and events that the jQuery UI widgets have. Let's start with options.

8.2.1 Making widgets configurable with options

Options are properties you can provide to customize the behavior of a widget. You've been using them in the widgets presented so far. Let's look at how to add them to your custom widget.

For the to-do list, you'll implement an option that gives developers the ability to place the todo widget in a submittable form: a name attribute. Providing name as a configurable option lets developers choose the name of the key submitted to the server.

To start, you need to add an options object to your widget's prototype:

```
$.widget( "tj.todo", {
    options: {
        name: "todo"
    },
    ...
});
```

The options object should have a key-value pair for each option the widget has. Each key—in this case, name—is the name of the option, and each value—in this case, "todo"—is the default value of the option. Your widget has a single name option that defaults to "todo".

After you define the option, you have to use it. The following code adds it to your _renderList() method:

Saves a reference to the widget's instance ❶

```
var that = this;
this.element.find( "li" ).each(function() {
    ...
    checkbox = $( "<input>", {
        type: "checkbox",
        name: that.options.name,
        value: li.text()
    });
    ...
});
```

Adds a name attribute based on the option ❷

TIP The use of a variable named that is a JavaScript convention to store a reference to an outer function's this so it can be used in an inner function. In this example, you save a reference to the widget's instance as that ❶, and then use the reference to access the instance's options in an inner function ❷.

With this approach, all check boxes have a `name` of `"todo"` by default. To use a different value, you pass it when the widget is initialized. The following code uses a name of `"tasks"`:

```
$( "ul" ).todo({ name: "tasks" });
```

To see how this could be used, refer to the following code:

```
<form method="POST" action="/path/to/server">
    <ul>
        <li>Clean dishes</li>
        <li>Walk dog</li>
        <li>Mop floor</li>
    </ul>
    <button>Submit</button>
</form>
<script>
    $( "ul" ).todo({ name: "tasks" });
</script>
```

If the user were to check the first two tasks on the list and then submit, `tasks=Clean+dishes&tasks=Walk+dog` would be submitted to the URL at /path/to/ server. The formatting of the post-data string isn't specific to jQuery or jQuery UI. Per the HTML specification, only check boxes that are checked are serialized and sent on HTTP requests. You need to deduce unchecked check boxes by their omission—for example, "Mop floor" wasn't checked because it wasn't included in the post-data.

 You now have a functioning option, but you need to handle one more thing. Recall that the `option()` method lets you change any option at any time. Currently, if you call the `option()` method on your widget, it doesn't work. The name of this to-do list remains `"todo"`, when it should be changed to `"tasks"`:

```
$( "ul" ).todo()
    .todo( "option", "name", "tasks" );
```

To see how to respond to changes, you need to use another of the widget factory's methods: `_setOption()`. To add a `_setOption()` method, you pass it on the widget's prototype:

```
$.widget( "tj.todo", {
    options: { name: "todo" },
    _setOption: function( key, value ) {
        . . .
    },
    . . .
});
```

`_setOption()` is called every time an option is changed on the widget. It is passed the name of the option as `key` and the value of the option as `value`. If you run `todo( "option", "name", "tasks" )`, `_setOption()` is called with `"name"` and `"tasks"`. In `_setOption()`, you have to implement the code to alter the widget based on the option change.

In your case, you have a method that does that: `_renderList()`. (Remember how I said abstracting that method would come in handy later?) All you need to do is call `_renderList()` in `_setOption()`:

```
_setOption: function( key, value ) {
    this._super( key, value );
    this._renderList();
}
```

What about the `_super()` method call? This calls your parent widget's method, in this case `$.Widget.prototype._setOption()`, which updates the appropriate property on the instance's `options` object; for example, setting `this.options.name`. Because `_renderList()` uses `this.options.name`, the `_super()` call has to happen before the call to `_renderList()`. Don't worry about the specifics of `_super()`; extending widgets is the topic of the next chapter, and we'll go over the details then.

You now have a completely functional option, but that's only one way of letting developers configure a widget. We'll look at adding methods next.

What about _setOptions()?

If you have perused the widget factory's documentation, you may have noticed that both `_setOption()` and `_setOptions()` are methods. `_setOptions()` is always called first when options are changed, and it's responsible for invoking `_setOption()`. In fact, the base implementation in `$.Widget.prototype._setOptions()` loops over the options and calls `_setOption()` on each:

```
_setOptions: function( options ) {
    var key;
    for ( key in options ) {
        this._setOption( key, options[ key ] );
    }
    return this;
}
```

The only reason to provide your own `_setOptions()` method is if you want to perform optimizations when multiple properties are changed at the same time. Consider a hypothetical "box" widget with `height` and `width` options. Suppose both options are updated at the same time:

```
$( "div" ).box( "option", { height: 200, width: 200 });
```

Instead of resizing the box twice—once for `height`, once for `width`—you could perform the resizing in `_setOptions()` to ensure it happens only once:

```
_setOptions: function( options ) {
    this._super( options );
    if ( options.height || options.width ) {
        this.resize();
    }
}
```

The dialog widget performs a similar optimization for its numerous dimension-related options.

8.2.2 *Changing the widget's state with methods*

Options let you customize a widget, but they don't let you perform actions on it. If you were to use the to-do list you've built to this point, wouldn't you need some way of adding items to it? In this section, you'll add four methods to your widget: add(), check(), uncheck(), and remove().

To add a method, you add a function to the widget's prototype. The following code defines a hello widget with a single world() method. The hello("world") call invokes the method and the alert():

```
$.widget( "tj.hello", {
    world: function() {
        alert( "hello world" );
    }
});
$( "<div>" ).hello().hello( "world" );
```

Have you noticed that all the methods you've used in the todo widget thus far—_create(), _renderList(), and _setOption()—have been prefixed with an underscore? In widget methods, the underscore prefix determines whether the method can be invoked through its widget's plugin:

```
$.widget( "tj.hello", {
    available: function() {},
    _notAvailable: function() {}
});
$( "<div>" ).hello().hello( "available" );
$( "<div>" ).hello().hello( "_notAvailable" );
```

❶ This works fine.

❷ This throws an error.

You define two methods: available() and _notAvailable(). Invoking available() through the widget's plugin ❶ works fine, but attempting to invoke _notAvailable() throws a JavaScript error ❷.

Although they have similarities, don't think of underscore-prefixed methods like private members from other languages. The methods aren't available through the plugin, but they're still accessible on the widget's instance. The following code invokes the previous example's _notAvailable() method:

```
$( "<div>" ).hello().hello( "instance" )._notAvailable();
```

Use an underscore when it doesn't make sense to invoke the method through the plugin. _create() is a perfect example: explicitly invoking it is unnecessary (as the widget factory does it for you); it doesn't make sense to expose it.

Conversely, if developers could use the method's functionality—make it available. The methods you'll add in this section will all be publicly exposed. Let's start with the add() method; an implementation is shown in the following code:

```
$.widget( "tj.todo", {
    ...
    add: function( value ) {
        this.element.append( "<li>" + value + "</li>" );
```

```
        this._renderList();
    }
});
```

Because all your logic is consolidated in _renderList(), there's not much to this method. The widget factory sets this equal to the widget instance; you use the this.element reference to append a new list item.

Having an add() method makes it possible for developers to build UI elements that interact with the to-do list. The following listing shows a form that utilizes the new add() method.

Listing 8.2   Adding items to the to-do list

```
<ul>
    <li>Clean dishes</li>
    <li>Walk dog</li>
    <li>Mop floor</li>
</ul>
<form>
    <label>Add Item:<input required></label>          Converts the list
    <button>Add</button>                              to a todo widget
</form>
<script>
    var todo = $( "ul" ).todo();
    $( "form" ).on( "submit", function( event ) {
        event.preventDefault();                       ❶ Adds the typed item to
        var input = $( this ).find( "input" );           the list using add()
        todo.todo( "add", input.val() );
        input.val( "" );
    });
</script>
```

This example uses a form with a single text box. When the user submits the form, you take the value the user typed and invoke the to-do list's add() method with it ❶. This workflow is shown in figure 8.3.

One more question worth considering is, why didn't you build a <form> into the widget itself? You certainly could have _create() build a <form> that adds items to the list. The downside of this approach is that it makes the widget far less extensible. If you were to bake the <form> into the widget and a user wanted to fill the list with an alternative UI, the user would have to hide or remove the <form> to use the todo widget.

Figure 8.3   An external form that adds items to the to-do list

If you keep the widget minimal, and expose its API through methods, developers can build solutions on top of it. We'll look at some of those things in the next chapter, but before we end our methods discussion, you have three more methods to implement: check(), uncheck(), and remove(). The implementation of these three methods is shown in the following code:

```
remove: function( value ) {
    this.element.find( "[value='" + value + "']" )
        .parents( "li:first" )
        .remove();
},
check: function( value ) {
    this._toggleCheckbox( value, true );
},
uncheck: function( value ) {
    this._toggleCheckbox( value, false );
},
_toggleCheckbox: function( value, checked ) {
    this.element.find( "[value='" + value + "']" )
        .prop( "checked", checked );
    this._renderList();
}
```

❶ Removes the appropriate list item from the DOM

❷ Checks or unchecks the check box based on the argument

All three methods take the value of the item to operate on—for example, "Walk dog". The remove() method finds the check box with this value, and then removes its parent <li> from the DOM ❶.

> **WARNING** You're dealing with two different remove() methods here: the method you're adding to the to-do list ($.tj.todo.prototype.remove) and the jQuery Core $.fn.remove method, which removes elements from the DOM. Normally, I don't like introducing potentially confusing APIs, but in this case, I went with remove() because it's a direct antonym of add(). Also, I can't use delete because it's a JavaScript reserved word, and the other words the thesaurus gave me sound silly—for example, abolish(), eliminate(), or expel(). Because of the ambiguity, I'll try to clarify when this comes up to avoid confusion.

Because the implementation of the check() and uncheck() methods is so similar, you place the logic in a shared _toggleCheckbox() method. _toggleCheckbox() finds the appropriate check box and checks or unchecks it appropriately ❷. It then calls _renderList() so ui-state-active is added or removed from the appropriate <li>.

All these methods give developers flexibility when using your widget. In the next chapter you'll use the todo widget's remove() method to build an extension with which items can be removed from the list.

At this point your widget is configurable. Developers can add items with add(), check off items with check(), uncheck them with uncheck(), and remove them with remove(). Your next step is to allow developers to respond to changes that take place in the widget. You do that by triggering events.

8.2.3   Triggering widget events with _trigger()

Like options and methods, events need little introduction because you've been using them throughout this book. The jQuery UI widgets trigger events whenever their state changes—a dialog is closed, a tab is activated, and so on.

When writing a widget, you have to decide what events to trigger. This is a judgment call, but in general, you should trigger events for anything that could be useful for developers to subscribe to. For the to-do list, the most important use case is checking and unchecking items in the list, so let's start there.

Recall that you're using _on() to update your widget's markup whenever a check box is clicked:

```
this._on( this.element, {
    "click input": this._renderList
});
```

The following code alters this code to trigger "check" and "uncheck" events:

```
this._on( this.element, {
    "click input": function( event ) {
        this._renderList();
        this._trigger( event.target.checked ? "check" : "uncheck",
            event, { value: event.target.value } );
    }
});
```

Triggers a "check" or "uncheck" event using _trigger() ❶

The only addition here is another one of the widget factory's convenience methods: _trigger(). _trigger() takes three arguments: the name of the event, an event object, and an object with data associated with the event. You trigger either a "check" or an "uncheck" event (depending on whether the check box is checked), and you pass the value of the check box ❶.

As with all the jQuery UI widget events, you can now subscribe to events with callback functions or event handlers. For instance, when a user checks an item, each of these functions logs the value of the check box checked:

```
$( "ul" ).todo({
    check: function( event, ui ) {        ◁— Callback function
        console.log( ui.value );
    }
}).on( "todocheck", function( event, ui ) {        ◁— Event handler
    console.log( ui.value );
});
```

Before we move on, remember that in the last section you added check() and uncheck() methods; you need to trigger check and uncheck events there as well. The following code adds this behavior to the methods:

```
check: function( value ) {
    this._toggleCheckbox( value, true );
    this._trigger( "check", null, { value: value } );
},
uncheck: function( value ) {
    this._toggleCheckbox( value, false );
    this._trigger( "uncheck", null, { value: value } );
}
```

These examples use `null` in place of an event object. Whenever you provide data to an event (in this case, the `value` of the check box), you must provide all three parameters to `_trigger()`. In the `click` event handler, you had an event to pass along, but here you don't. In these situations, pass `null` to indicate that there's no native event.

You now have comprehensive coverage for the check and uncheck events; they'll be triggered regardless of whether the user clicks check boxes in the UI or a developer uses the `check()` or `uncheck()` methods.

This consistency gives developers flexibility in what they can implement with the todo widget. If you want to sync changes to a back-end database as they're made, you can use the `check` and `uncheck` events to do that.

Now that you're triggering events, you're near the end of your widget development checklist. The last things we need to cover are enabling, disabling, and destroying widgets.

Triggering cancellable events

You may recall from chapter 2 that some jQuery UI widget events are cancellable— that is, you can cancel an event to prevent some action from occurring. If you prevent the default action of the dialog widget's `beforeClose` event, the dialog does not close.

How do you implement your own cancellable events? The same `_trigger()` method you just used to trigger events returns a Boolean that indicates whether the default action was prevented. You can use that Boolean to determine whether to continue with the action.

As an example, you can make the todo widget's `check` event cancellable with the following change to the `check()` method:

```
check: function( value ) {
    if ( this._trigger( "check", null, { value: value } ) ) {
        this._toggleCheckbox( value, true );
    }
}
```

Now, if a user subscribes to the `check` event and prevents the default action, `_trigger()` will return `false` and the check box will not be checked. For instance, the following code creates a todo widget, appends it to the `<body>`, and invokes the `check()` method on its only item:

```
var list = $( "<ul><li>One</li></ul>" ).todo({
    check: function( event ) {
        event.preventDefault();
    }
});
list.appendTo( "body" );
list.todo( "check", "One" );
```

Because the `todo()` call includes a `check` event callback that calls `prevent-Default()`, the `_trigger()` call within the widget's `check()` method returns `false`, and the widget's checkbox is not checked.

8.3   Enabling, disabling, and destroying widgets

Let's take one last look at your widget checklist.

1	~~$.widget()~~	**2**	~~Markup structure~~	**3**	~~_create()~~
4	~~Make themeable~~	**5**	~~Add options~~	**6**	~~Expose methods~~
7	~~Trigger events~~	**8**	Enable/Disable	**9**	_destroy()

Your new widget is almost complete. The last two steps are allowing developers to disable and destroy widgets. As in most of the widget steps, much of the functionality to do this is baked into the widget factory, but you have to override a few methods for your todo widget. Let's get started by looking at how to enable and disable widgets.

8.3.1   Enabling and disabling a widget

Disabling UI elements is a common UI pattern to prevent users from interacting with a control. Native form elements <input>, <select>, <textarea>, and <button> can be disabled by adding a disabled attribute—for example, <input disabled>.

   Most of the jQuery UI widgets can be enabled or disabled. Some of the functionality is built in to the widget factory itself.

> **NOTE**   The two widgets that can't be disabled are datepicker and dialog. Datepicker doesn't support the same disabling mechanism because it's the only widget not built with the widget factory. The dialog widget doesn't support disabling because it doesn't make any sense to disable a dialog (more on this momentarily).

Specifically, the widget factory provides a disabled property, disable() method, and enable() method for all widgets. Let's look at how these work in a button widget example. The following code creates a disabled button by setting its disabled option:

```
var magicButton = $( "<button>Magic Button</button>" )
    .appendTo( "body" )
    .button({ disabled: true });
```

You can then enable the same button by calling its enable() method

```
magicButton.button( "enable" );
```

and call its disable() method to disable it again:

```
magicButton.button( "disable" );
```

How can you let developers disable your widget? First, let's look at what the widget factory provides. To start, your to-do list already has enable() and disable() methods. The following code creates a new to-do list and calls its disable() method:

```
$( "<ul><li>One</li></ul>" )
    .todo()
    .appendTo( "body" )
    .todo( "disable" );
```

If you were to try this out, you'd see that it has no visual effect on the widget. You can still check and uncheck the item on the list. To see why, let's look at the full implementations of the base enable() and disable() methods your widget uses: $.Widget .prototype.enable() and $.Widget.prototype.disable():

```
enable: function() {
    return this._setOptions({ disabled: false });
},
disable: function() {
    return this._setOptions({ disabled: true });
}
```

The default methods set only the widget's disabled option. To implement disabling logic, you must respond to the change in the disabled option. And—you'll recall from section 8.3.1—you do this with _setOption(). The following code alters your widget so it can be disabled and enabled:

```
_setOption: function( key, value ) {
    this._super( key, value );
    this._renderList();
    if ( key == "disabled" ) {                    ❶ If the disabled option
        this.element                                 is changing
            .find( "input" ).prop( "disabled", value );
        this.element
            .find( "li" ).toggleClass( "ui-state-disabled", value );
    }
}
```

...disable or enable the widget's check boxes ❷

...and toggle the ui-state-disabled class name on each <li>. ❸

The first addition to _setOption() is a check for the disabled option ❶. Remember that _setOption() is called for any option change, so you need this check to make sure your code runs only when dealing with the disabled option.

If you're dealing with disabled, you do two things: toggle the disabled property on all check boxes ❷, and toggle the ui-state-disabled class name on all <li>s ❸. Because this is the disabled option, when the value is true, you disable all check boxes and add ui-state-disabled. When the value is false, you enable all check boxes and remove ui-state-disabled.

Now that you have the functionality in place, what about styling your disabled widget? Because you're using the themeable ui-state-disabled class name, your disabled state is styled according to your theme. No extra work is needed!

If you do want to tweak the disabled look, you can target the disabled list items using .tj-todo .ui-state-disabled. The widget factory also adds a *namespace-widget-name-disabled* class name to the outer container of the widget. In the case of your todo widget, the outer <ul> has a tj-todo-disabled class name when disabled.

Now that you have a widget that can be enabled and disabled, you're nearing the end of your widget checklist. You have only one thing left to handle: destruction.

What if your widget can't be disabled?

Although most widgets can be disabled, there are exceptions. Disabling a dialog widget would be bizarre, for example; at the least, the jQuery UI team couldn't come up with a practical reason to allow it.

The dialog widget does two things. First, it sets the `enable()` and `disable()` methods it inherits from the widget factory to an empty function—specifically, `$.noop`, a convenience property provided by jQuery Core that's literally set to `function() {}`:

```
disable: $.noop,
enable: $.noop
```

The dialog widget still has `disable()` and `enable()` methods, but they do nothing. The second thing the dialog widget does is ignore the `disabled` option. The following code appears near the beginning of the dialog widget's `_setOption()` method:

```
if ( key === "disabled" ) {
    return;
}
```

If you're developing a widget that it doesn't make sense to disable, this approach is recommended.

8.3.2 Undoing a widget's effects with _destroy()

In the terms of the widget factory, destroying a widget is like hitting the undo button in a text editor. When a widget is destroyed on an element, any markup that was added is removed; any class names that were added are removed; any events that were bound are unbound. The element is returned to its prewidget state.

All the jQuery UI widgets provide a `destroy()` method that undoes their effects. As an example, the following code initializes a `<button>` with a button widget, and then destroys the widget using `destroy()`:

```
                $( "<button>Button</button>" )
                   .appendTo( "body" )
                   .button()
                   .button( "destroy" );
```

Destroys the button widget ⟶

Initializes the button widget ⟵

Now that you're on the implementing end, you have to provide this functionality as well. How do you do it? Like most of the topics in this chapter, the widget factory gives you a method to provide this functionality: `_destroy()`.

> **WARNING** Take note of the underscore prefix again—`destroy()` and `_destroy()` are different methods with different purposes. We'll get to that in a minute.

Here's the implementation of your todo widget's `_destroy()` method:

```
_destroy: function() :
    this.element
        .removeClass(
```

Removes all class names that were added. ❶

```
            "tj-todo ui-widget ui-widget-content ui-corner-all" )
        .find( "li" ).each(function() {
            var li = $( this ).removeClass(
                    "tj-todo-item ui-state-default" ),
                input = li.find( "input" ),
                text = li.text();
            if ( input.is( ":checked" ) ) {
                li.remove();
            } else {
                li.html( text );
            }
        });
    }
```

❷ **Removes checked items from the DOM.**

❸ **Leaves unchecked items. Sets their innerHTML to text only.**

Your first step is to remove all class names that the widget added. You first do that from your main `<ul>` element ❶, then for each `<li>`.

Next, you determine whether the check box of each `<li>` is checked. If it is, you remove the `<li>` from the DOM ❷. Because of this implementation, checked to-do items are removed from the list when it's destroyed. We'll look at why you take this approach in a moment.

Finally, you revert the contents of all list items that aren't checked. To see how this works, let's recall the HTML you used when you created the widget in `_create()`. You took a list item—for example, `<li>Walk dog</li>`—and turned it into the following markup:

```
<li>
    <label>
        <input type="checkbox" value="Walk dog">
        Walk dog
    </label>
</li>
```

To undo this, you set the `innerHTML` of each `<li>` (using jQuery Core's `html()` method) back to the text of the `<li>`, in this case, "Walk dog" ❸.

That's the end of your method. You may be wondering why you didn't need to do more. You didn't unbind any events, and there were some class names you didn't remove. As it turns out, the widget factory handles this for you.

Whenever a widget's `destroy()` method (no underscore prefix) is called, the widget factory performs common cleanup tasks in `$.Widget.prototype.destroy()` and then delegates to the widget's `_destroy()` method (with an underscore prefix) for widget-specific cleanup. The following code shows an abridged version of `$.Widget.prototype.destroy()`. Don't worry if you don't understand everything here; we're looking at the code to give an overview of the things `destroy()` does for you.

```
destroy: function() {
    this._destroy();

    this.element
        .removeData( this.widgetFullName );
```

❶ **Calls the widget-specific _destroy() method**

❷ **Removes all stored widget data**

Removes disabled state class names ❸

```
this.widget()
    .removeClass(
        this.widgetFullName + "-disabled " +
        "ui-state-disabled" );
```

❹ **Unbinds all events attached with _on()**

```
this.bindings.unbind( this.eventNamespace );
```

Removes all hover state class names ❺

```
this.hoverable.removeClass( "ui-state-hover" );
this.focusable.removeClass( "ui-state-focus" );
}
```

❻ **Removes all focus state class names**

destroy() invokes the _destroy() method for widget-specific cleanup ❶. This is the method you implemented for your to-do list earlier in this section.

To understand the next line ❷, remember that the widget factory stores instance data using $.data() with a key of the widget's full name—in this case, tj-todo. Calling removeData() removes the instance from jQuery's internal data store to avoid memory leaks.

Both disabled class names—ui-state-disabled and the widget-specific tj-todo-disabled—are removed from the widget ❸.

The next line may also seem a bit cryptic. this.bindings is a collection of elements in the widget with events bound to them with _on() ❹ The unbind() call removes those events. Remember earlier in the chapter when I said that if you use _on(), all events are cleaned up for you? This is the code that makes that happen.

The code at ❺ and ❻ removes the ui-state-hover and ui-state-focus class names from all elements that were made hoverable or focusable using _hoverable() and _focusable().

You only need to worry about cleaning up things specific to your widget in _destroy(). The widget factory takes care of all generic cleanup tasks for you. Before leaving the topic of widget destruction, we need to discuss one thing: why bother destroying a widget?

For one, it can be useful to have the ability to completely undo a widget's effect when building a UI. The following listing uses the todo widget to build an editable list of items.

Listing 8.3 An editable list built with the todo widget

```
<style>
    #update { display: none; }
</style>

<ul id="todo">
    <li>Clean dishes</li>
    <li>Walk dog</li>
    <li>Mop floor</li>
</ul>
<button id="edit">Edit</button>
<button id="update">Update</button>

<script>
```

```
var list = $( "#todo" ),
    editButton = $( "#edit" ).button(),
    updateButton = $( "#update" ).button();

editButton.on( "click", function() {
    list.todo();
    editButton.hide();
    updateButton.show();
});
updateButton.on( "click", function() {
    list.todo( "destroy" );
    editButton.show();
    updateButton.hide();
});
</script>
```

❶ Initializes a todo widget on the `<ul>`

❷ Destroys the todo widget on the `<ul>`

In this example, you have two buttons: Edit and Update. The Edit button converts the example's `<ul>` to a todo widget **❶**. The user can then check off items on the list.

When the user clicks Update, the todo widget's `destroy()` method removes the todo widget from the `<ul>` **❷**, leaving a list of items. Because of your implementation of `_destroy()`, items that the user checks are removed from the `<ul>` when it's destroyed. This workflow is shown in figure 8.4.

Beyond the UI niceties, there's one other good reason to implement `_destroy()` on your widgets: `destroy()` (which, as you recall, invokes `_destroy()`) is called when the widget's element is removed from the DOM using any of the jQuery Core methods. In the following code a button widget is initialized on a `<button>`, and then it's removed from the DOM because the `innerHTML` of its parent is changed using the jQuery Core `html()` method.

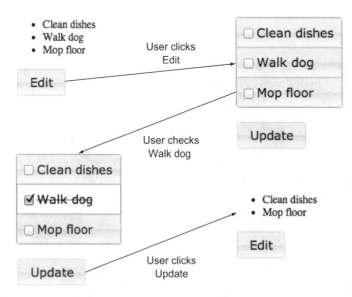

Figure 8.4   Workflow of the `destroy()` example. The user can check off items to remove them from the list.

```
<div>
    <button>Button</button>
</div>
<script>
    $( "button" ).button();
    $( "div" ).html( "Some other content" );
</script>
```

Even though the code doesn't explicitly call `destroy()`, it does invoke the button widget's `destroy()` (and `_destroy()`) methods. This is another piece of magic that the widget factory provides. Internally, the widget factory duck punches jQuery Core's internal `$.cleanData()` method. When it detects that a widget has been removed, it invokes its `destroy()` method to give the widget a chance to clean up and avoid memory leaks. Even if you have no intention of providing undo functionality, it's important to include a `_destroy()` method to avoid leaks.

TIP *Duck punching* refers to a technique of extending some piece of a library without altering its original source. (The technique is also sometimes known as monkey patching the proxy pattern.) Paul Irish has a great explanation of the technique and concrete implementations of it at http://www.paulirish.com/2010/duck-punching-with-jquery/. You'll use the duck punching technique to build datepicker extensions in the next chapter.

Evaluating third-party widgets

Although building a custom widget is powerful, it can also be a lot of work, and someone else may have built what you need. You can look for third-party widgets on jQuery's plugin repository at http://plugins.jquery.com/ or with a Google search.

Remember, though, that unlike the jQuery UI widgets, you have no idea what you're going to get from widgets you find on the internet. You can find robust widgets that save you time and development effort, and you can find widgets that don't work.

When evaluating unofficial jQuery widgets, here are a few questions to ask. The more of these questions you can answer affirmatively, the more likely the widget will work well in your application:

- *Does the widget use the widget factory?* If so, all the conventions we've discussed throughout the book for options, methods, events, and such still apply. Usually, widget maintainers mention whether the widget factory is used in the widget's documentation; if not, you can look for a call to `$.widget()` in the widget's code.
- *Is the widget themeable?* If it is, the existing jQuery UI themes will work fine with the new widget. To see if the widget is themeable, check for the CSS framework's class names (`ui-widget`, `ui-widget-content`, and so on) on the widget's markup.
- *Does the widget have tests?* Unit tests are a sign that the widget's code is stable and all its APIs work. Furthermore, because unit tests aid with code maintenance, their presence is a good sign that the widget will be updated as future versions of jQuery are released.

(continued)

- *Is it well documented?* This one is a bit self-explanatory; thorough documentation makes it easier to get started with a widget and to use it.
- *Is it maintained?* A widget that was last updated a month ago is more likely to be actively maintained than a widget that was last updated two years ago. Look for the release date of the latest version of the widget, and when the last few commits were.
- *Is it battle tested?* If you're the 10,000th person to use a widget, chances are you'll have a smoother experience than the 10th person to use it. Widgets that have been used in numerous production applications are more likely to have the kinks worked out. If the widget is on GitHub, look for projects that have a lot of watchers and stars. If the project isn't on GitHub, look for how much information is available with a Google search or on Stack Overflow.

8.4   Summary

That's it! In this chapter, you saw that the widget factory is used to build stateful plugins, and then you went through a nine-step process of building a widget with it. The nine steps you took were

1 Create the widget with `$.widget()`.
2 Decide on a markup structure to use.
3 Build the markup structure with `_create()`.
4 Make the widget themeable by applying the appropriate class names from the jQuery UI CSS framework.
5 Add options to make the widget configurable.
6 Expose methods.
7 Trigger events as the widget's state changes using `_trigger()`.
8 Allow developers to disable and enable the widget.
9 Undo the widget's effects using `_destroy()`.

You can refer back to this chapter and follow these nine steps anytime you want to build a stateful plugin with the widget factory.

But what if you don't want to build a complete widget from scratch? Sometimes you need to make a quick alteration to an existing widget, and the widget factory has an extension mechanism built in that does that. We'll spend the next chapter looking at how it works.

Extending widgets with the widget factory

9

This chapter covers

- Building on top of the jQuery UI widgets
- Using and creating extension points
- Extending datepicker

We've spent the greater part of this book looking at myriad things you can do with the jQuery UI widgets. But although the jQuery UI widgets handle the most common development use cases, real-life applications often have specific—often crazy—requirements. To give a few concrete examples: the jQuery UI team has had feature requests asking for accordions that store their open panel in a cookie, draggables that have a Cancel button, and autocompletes within autocompletes. (I'm not sure what those last two even mean, but someone asked for them.)

Widgets can't solve every niche problem that developers have, so to allow for highly customized solutions to these unique issues, the widget factory allows you to extend existing widgets. The ability to extend widgets lets you add, remove, or tweak the behavior of an existing widget without reinventing the wheel. Because of the customizability it provides, the widget factory's extensions mechanism is—in my opinion—the single most powerful feature in jQuery UI.

In this chapter, we'll look at how to create widget extensions, then we'll build a few examples to see what they make possible. We'll look at datepicker specifically, as it's the only jQuery UI widget that doesn't use the widget factory yet and requires tricky workarounds.

Let's dig in.

9.1   Building widget extensions

Widget extensibility is built directly into the widget factory; you can use all the widget mechanisms you've learned, along with a few mechanisms specific to widget extensions that you'll learn throughout this chapter. In fact, extending widgets is as easy as passing the constructor function of the widget to extend into $.widget(). The following builds an extension of the jQuery UI dialog widget named superDialog:

```
$.widget( "tj.superDialog", $.ui.dialog, {} );
```

superDialog is an exact clone of the dialog widget. You can use its constructor function to create a new dialog

```
$.tj.superDialog( "<div>" );
```

or you can use its plugin

```
$( "<div>" ).superDialog();
```

With the widget factory, you aren't limited to one level of inheritance; you can build extensions of extensions. The following creates a third superDuperDialog widget that extends the superDialog widget:

```
$.widget( "tj.superDuperDialog", $.tj.superDialog, {} );
```

All three widgets are complete widgets, each with its own plugin; each of the following creates a new dialog:

```
$( "<div>" ).dialog();
$( "<div>" ).superDialog();
$( "<div>" ).superDuperDialog();
```

Although it's cool that you can create a copy of a widget in one line of code, these extensions aren't useful; they're the same widget with different names. To make your widget extensions useful, you have to make them do something their parent widget doesn't. Let's start by altering options.

9.1.1   Changing existing and adding new options to a widget

With widget extensions you have the full power of the widget factory at your disposal. Anything you can do with a widget, you can do with a widget extension—including altering options, or adding new ones.

To show this, let's return to the confirmation dialog that you built in chapter 2. That example created a new <div> and converted it to a dialog widget with an OK button.

```
$( "<div>Your transaction processed successfully.</div>" ).dialog({
    options: {
        buttons: {
            OK: function() {
                $( this ).dialog( "close" );
            }
        }
    }
});
```

This works, but you repeat the five lines to create the OK button every time you want to create a confirmation dialog. You could change `$.ui.dialog.prototype` `.options.buttons`, but that would change the defaults of all dialogs, not just confirmation ones.

To consolidate this configuration, let's create a confirmationDialog widget extension:

```
$.widget( "tj.confirmationDialog", $.ui.dialog, {      ❶ Specifies the
    options: {                                            confirmationDialog's options
        buttons: {
            OK: function() {
                $( this ).confirmationDialog( "close" );
            }
        },
        close: function() {                                ❷ Destroys the dialog
            $( this ).confirmationDialog( "destroy" );        when it's closed
        }
    }
});
```

You define options for your confirmationDialog ❶ and when you extend another widget, the widget factory intelligently merges the widget's default options with its parent's defaults. So your widget still has all the dialog widget's options—height, width, modal, and so on—without needing to explicitly list them. Any options you do provide override those of the parent widget. The following creates a confirmation dialog using your new widget's plugin:

```
$( "<div>Your transaction processed successfully.</div>" )
    .confirmationDialog();
```

This dialog is shown in figure 9.1. Although you passed no options to confirmationDialog(), it automatically has an OK button that closes the dialog.

The other option you pass is a close event callback that calls the confirmationDialog's destroy() method ❷. Because you're creating a new <div> every time you build a confirmation dialog, this prevents the dialog from staying in the DOM when you no longer need it.

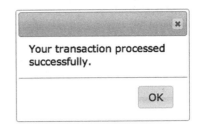

Figure 9.1 A confirmation dialog built with the confirmationDialog widget

The confirmation dialog sets the default value of its parent widget's options. Next, let's show a widget that adds a new option altogether. Remember the vertical tabs example that you built in chapter 7? You added CSS to the tabs widget to stack the tabs vertically instead of horizontally:

```
.ui-tabs {
    padding: 0;
    overflow: hidden;
}
.ui-tabs .ui-widget-header {
    border: none;
}
/* etc */
```

This works if all your tabs are vertical, but what if you want horizontal and vertical tabs in the same application, or even on the same page? We'll look at a couple of ways to make this possible, starting with adding a new option to the tabs widget.

For consistency with the jQuery UI slider widget (which can also display horizontally or vertically), you'll use an `orientation` option that can be set to `"horizontal"` or `"vertical"`. The final display of this widget is shown in figure 9.2.

To implement this widget, you need to change your custom CSS so that it no longer adds rules to the `ui-tabs` class name. Instead, you prefix all rules with a `ui-tabs-vertical` class name, as shown here:

```
.ui-tabs-vertical {
    padding: 0;
    overflow: hidden;
}
.ui-tabs-vertical .ui-widget-header {
    border: none;
}
/* etc */
```

Your widget extension now has to manage this class name to determine whether the tabs display horizontally or vertically. The first step is to add logic to conditionally add the `ui-tabs-vertical` class name when the tabs are initialized in `_create()`. But

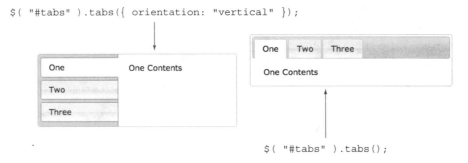

Figure 9.2 Display of a tabs extension that adds an `orientation` option

there's a problem with this. The tabs widget's existing _create() method already does a lot, and if you override it, you lose all that behavior.

No need to worry; the widget factory has a trick up its sleeve to make the parent widget's method available in all extended methods. To see this in action, look at the tabs extension shown in the following listing.

Listing 9.1 Tabs widget extension with an orientation option

```
$.widget( "tj.tabs", $.ui.tabs, {          ← Creates the extension
    options: {                              ❶  with name "tj.tabs"
        orientation: "horizontal"
    },
    _create: function() {
        this._super();
        this._handleOrientation();          ← Invokes the parent
    },                                      ❸  widget's _create() method
    _handleOrientation: function() {
        this.element.toggleClass( "ui-tabs-vertical",
            this.options.orientation === "vertical" );
    },
    _setOption: function( key, value ) {    ❹  Invokes the parent widget's
        this._superApply( arguments );      ←   _setOption() method
        if ( key === "orientation" ) {
            this._handleOrientation();
        }
    },
    _destroy: function() {
        this._super();
        this.element.removeClass( "ui-tabs-vertical" );
    }
});
```

Adds an orientation option that defaults to "horizontal" ❷

NOTE This example is available at http://jsfiddle.net/tj_vantoll/S6bCN/.

We'll start at the top before getting into _create(). The call to $.widget() defines the widget's full name as "tj.tabs" ❶. How can you have two widgets that have the same name? Because the widgets have different full names, "tj.tabs" and "ui.tabs", these two widgets can coexist; their constructor functions are available at $.tj.tabs() and $.ui.tabs(), respectively.

But because you can't have multiple jQuery plugins with the same name, the tabs() plugin is now associated with $.tj.tabs() and not $.ui.tabs(). This can be confusing; we'll look at a better way to handle this in the next section.

Next, you define a new option for your tabs widget extension: orientation, which defaults to "horizontal" ❷. Because your extension inherits all options from its parent widget—in this case $.ui.tabs—this is the only option you need to explicitly list.

After the options, you provide a few methods on your new widget's prototype—the first being _create(). In _create() you can see the utility function the widget factory provides for accessing the parent widget's method of the same name: _super() ❸.

_super() is incredibly useful in extensions because, instead of having to duplicate the logic in the jQuery UI tab widget's _create(), you can directly invoke it and then add your custom logic to manage the ui-tabs-vertical class name.

The rest of this example manages this class name. In _destroy() you ensure the class name is removed, and in _setOption() you ensure the class name is added or removed appropriately when the orientation option changes.

_setOption() uses one other method you haven't seen before: _superApply(). _superApply() and _super() both invoke the parent widget's method of the same name. The difference is in the arguments the methods accept; _super() accepts zero to many arguments passed individually, and _superApply() accepts an array of arguments. For example, you call _superApply(arguments) ❹, but you could have invoked _super() with the two arguments of _setOption() explicitly listed—that is, _super(key, value). Because the two methods do the same thing, which one you use is a matter of personal preference.

> **TIP**   The arguments object is an array-like local variable available in all functions. It contains the arguments passed to the function. For more information on arguments, see https://developer.mozilla.org/en-US/docs/Web/JavaScript/Reference/Functions_and_function_scope/arguments.

This extension approach added a new orientation option, but you could have taken other approaches. You could've used a different plugin name as shown in the following code:

```
$.widget( "tj.verticalTabs", $.ui.tabs, {
    _create: function() {
        this._super();
        this.element.addClass( "ui-tabs-vertical" );
    },
    _destroy: function() {
        this._super();
        this.element.removeClass( "ui-tabs-vertical" );
    }
});
```

This implementation creates two separate plugins: tabs() and verticalTabs(). Developers call tabs() to create horizontal tabs and verticalTabs() to create vertical ones. The only difference is this implementation doesn't let you change the orientation of the tabs using the option() method.

The widget factory makes different approaches possible so that you can create the widget that best meets your needs. In the next section you'll return to your initial vertical tabs implementation to see how you can clean it up.

9.1.2   Redefining widgets with the widget factory

Often you perform a small alteration to an existing widget, but you have no need to create a brand-new widget from scratch. Your first vertical tabs extension is the perfect example of this—you added a new option, but you had no need to create a new widget.

> ## Widgets extensions and method calls
>
> When you create widget extensions that define new plugins, such as the vertical-Tabs example, the parent widget's plugin cannot be used to invoke methods on elements that are instances of the child widget. This is a bit of a mouthful, so let's look at an example:
>
> ```
> $.widget( "tj.superDialog", $.ui.dialog, {} );
> var div = $( "<div>" ).superDialog();
> div.superDialog( "close" );       ←❶ This works.
> div.dialog( "close" );            ←
>                            ❷ This doesn't.
> ```
>
> Here, you create a superDialog widget that extends the dialog widget, and then create a superDialog instance on a newly created <div>. Because the <div> is a superDialog instance, you can invoke methods on it through the superDialog() plugin ❶, but you cannot use the parent widget's dialog() plugin ❷.

Before jQuery UI 1.9, there was no *good* way to do this. Your only option was to change the widget's methods on its prototype. The following example does this for the tabs widget's `_create()` method:

```
$.ui.tabs.prototype._create = function() {
    this.element.addClass( "some-class-name" );
};
```

The problem with this approach is that you have no access to the `_super()` and `_superApply()` methods; therefore, to invoke the tabs widget's original `_create()` method, you must store off a reference to it before overriding it:

```
var oldCreate = $.ui.tabs.prototype._create;
$.ui.tabs.prototype._create = function() {      ❶ Set this for the
    oldCreate.apply( this );                  ←    parent method.
    this.element.addClass( "some-class-name" );
};
```

This code is a lot of work to perform a single action in `_create()`. You have to manually set the context (`this`) of the parent method's `_create()` ❶—something that the widget factory handled for you.

The biggest problem with this approach is that it requires you to duplicate boilerplate code to store a reference to the parent method. You override only one method, but if you had more, you'd have to duplicate the same code for each.

To make this process easier, a new feature was added to the widget factory in the jQuery UI 1.9 release: the ability to redefine widgets. To see how this works, let's look at the same example implemented with the widget factory:

```
$.widget( "ui.tabs", $.ui.tabs, {
    _create: function() {
        this._super();
        this.element.addClass( "some-class-name" );
    }
});
```

This example is also four lines of code, but it's far cleaner. You don't have to worry about saving references to the parent widget's method—you just call _super(). This approach ends up being cleaner for more complex examples. Let's return to your widget that added an orientation option to the tabs widget:

```
$.widget( "tj.tabs", $.ui.tabs, {
    options: {
        orientation: "horizontal"
    },
    ...
});
```

As discussed, the issue here is that you're creating two widgets: $.tj.tabs and $.ui.tabs. To change this widget to redefine $.ui.tabs, you change the namespace from "tj" to "ui":

```
$.widget( "ui.tabs", $.ui.tabs, {
    options: {
        orientation: "horizontal"
    },
    ...
});
```

Instead of creating a new widget on a different namespace, you alter the jQuery UI tabs widget's behavior. Because of this, all instances of the tabs widget are affected—any new and existing tabs widget instances now have an orientation option.

In general, whether to build a new widget or redefine an existing one is a matter of personal preference and depends on the specific scenario, but I'll give a few recommendations. For quick changes, redefining a widget is preferred—as users of the widget don't have to remember two different widget names and plugins.

For more complex changes, a new widget is preferred. A different name helps to clearly differentiate the widget from its parent; otherwise, users of the widget might attribute the additional functionality to the parent. As an example, a developer using your updated tabs widget might assume that the orientation option is part of jQuery UI, and wonder why it's not documented on the API documentation.

Regardless of which approach you use, widget extensions make all sorts of powerful customizations possible. Let's look at a few more practical examples of this, starting with your todo widget from the last chapter.

9.1.3 *Extending a custom widget*

Widget extensions aren't limited to the jQuery UI widgets. Any widget built with the widget factory can be extended, even completely custom widgets like the to-do list you built in the previous chapter. To show this, you'll build two extensions of this widget, one that makes items in the list removable and another that makes them sortable.

Let's start with the removable example. Remember from chapter 8 that each item in the list could be checked and unchecked, but there was no way to remove items from the list; therefore, you'll build an extension that adds this functionality. The display of this widget is shown in figure 9.3.

Figure 9.3 A todo widget extension that adds remove icons

The implementation of this widget is shown in the following listing.

Listing 9.2 A todo widget extension with removable items

```
$.widget( "tj.todo", $.tj.todo, {
    _create: function() {
        this._super();
        this._on({
            "click button": function( event ) {
                var value = $( event.target ).parents( "li:first" )
                    .find( "input" ).val();
                this.remove( value );
            }
        });
    },
    _renderList: function() {
        var listItems = this.element.find( "li" );
        listItems.find( "button" ).remove();
        this._super();
        listItems.each(function() {
            var button = $( "<button>Close</button>" ).button({
                icons: { primary: "ui-icon-closethick" },
                text: false #4
            }); #4
            $( this ).append( button );
        })
    },
    _destroy: function() {
        this.element.find( "button" ).remove();
        this._super();
    }
});
```

① **Listens for clicks on the list's buttons**

② **Calls the remove() method**

③ **Removes all buttons from the list**

④ **Creates a new <button>**

⑤ **Removes all buttons from the list**

> **NOTE** This example is available at http://jsfiddle.net/tj_vantoll/umrmm/. If you need to reference the code for the original todo widget, you can view that at http://jsfiddle.net/tj_vantoll/zStp7/.

This example works by adding a `<button>` element to each `<li>` in the list. In `_create()`, after calling `_super()`, you use `_on()` to attach an event listener for buttons in the list ①. The listener determines which item was clicked, then calls the todo widget's `remove()` method you added in chapter 8 to remove the `<li>` from the DOM ②.

Next, you have to inject the `<button>` elements into each `<li>`. Because the todo widget's `_renderList()` method is called every time the list is manipulated (when items are added, removed, checked, or unchecked), it makes for a perfect extension point for the todo widget. We'll discuss extensions points in more detail in the next section, but for now know that extensions points are methods that are convenient to extend.

You remove all buttons from the list ❸, before you call _super(). You do this because the parent widget relies on getting the text of each <li>, and having button elements in the <li> messes with that logic. I'm specifically using this approach to show that there's no rule for where to call _super() in an extension. You can call it in the beginning, the middle, or the end of a method—you can avoid calling it completely if you don't need the parent widget's behavior.

After the _super() call, your list's markup structure is in place, so you can now add your buttons. You do so by looping over each <li>, creating a new button for each ❹, and appending the new button to the <li>.

Your last task is to eliminate the buttons when the widget is destroyed. You accomplish this by extending the todo widget's _destroy() method, removing all <button> elements ❺, and invoking the parent widget's _destroy() with _super().

To get the display you need, you have to add a little CSS to make your buttons look right. The following CSS handles the positioning and sizing of the buttons:

```
.tj-todo .tj-todo-item {
    position: relative;
}
.tj-todo .tj-todo-item button {
    position: absolute;
    right: 5px;
    height: 1.5em;
    width: 1.5em;
    top: 0.4em;
}
```

And with that, you have a todo widget in which users can remove items from the list—all in about 25 lines of code. This example shows off the true power of the widget factory. Because you're building on top of an existing solution, you don't have to write much code to create a custom UI component.

Let's look at one more extension example: a sortable list. Figure 9.4 shows the sortable to-do list in action.

The implementation of the sortable todo widget is shown in the following listing.

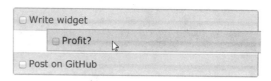

Figure 9.4 An extension of your to-do list widget that lets users reorder items in the list

Listing 9.3 A sortable todo widget

```
$.widget( "tj.todo", $.tj.todo, {
    options: {
        sortable: false
    },
    _create: function() {
        this._super();
```
                          Defines a
                        ❶ sortable option

```
        if ( this.options.sortable ) {
            this.element.sortable();
        } #2
    },
    _setOption: function( key, value ) {
        this._super( key, value );
        if ( key === "sortable" ) {
            if ( value ) {
                this.element.sortable();
            }
            if ( !value && this._isSortable() ) {
                this.element.sortable( "destroy" );
            }
        }
    },
    _isSortable: function() {
        return this.element.is( ":data(ui-sortable)" );
    },
    _destroy: function() {
        if ( this._isSortable() ) {
            this.element.sortable( "destroy" );
        }
        this._super();
    }
});
```

② Makes the element sortable if the option is set

③ Makes the element sortable

Destroys the widget if necessary **④**

⑤ Determines whether the element is sortable

⑥ Destroys the widget if necessary

NOTE This example is available at http://jsfiddle.net/tj_vantoll/vfJ65/.

The code here is similar to the vertical tabs extension. You define a sortable option and default it to false **❶**. In _create(), when the option is set, you convert the todo widget's element to a sortable widget **❷**. (Remember that there's no reason a single element can't be associated with multiple widgets.)

To handle the sortable option being changed, you override _setOption(). When sortable is set to true, you make the todo widget's element sortable **❸**. Because the widget factory prevents dual instantiation, there's no harm in calling sortable() on an element that's already sortable; it has no effect.

When the sortable option is set to false, the situation is a bit more complex. Before calling destroy() to remove the sortable functionality, you first must make sure that the todo widget's element has been initialized with a sortable widget **❹**. You need this check because calling a widget method before the widget is initialized—in this case sortable("destroy")—throws an error.

To determine whether the element is sortable, you use this.element.is (":data(ui-sortable)") **❺**. We'll look at how the :data() selector works in chapter 12, but for now know that it selects elements that have data stored under the specified key. If the element has data stored with the widget's name, then that element has that widget initialized on it. (Remember that destroy() cleans up that data.)

In the todo widget's _destroy() method, you need to clean up the sortable widget **❻**. You use the same _isSortable() method you defined earlier to determine whether the element is a sortable and, if so, call its destroy() method.

Now you can create sortable to-do lists by setting the `sortable` option to `true`:

```
<ul>
    <li>Write widget</li>
    <li>Post on GitHub</li>
    <li>Profit?</li>
</ul>
<script>
    $( "ul" ).todo({ sortable: true });
</script>
```

You can change whether the list is sortable by changing the option:

```
$( "ul" ).todo( "option", "sortable", false );
```

Just as in the vertical tabs example, this is only one possible implementation. You also could've created a new widget that's always sortable. An implementation of this is shown here:

```
$.widget( "tj.sortableTodoList", $.tj.todo, {
    _create: function() {
        this._super();
        this.element.sortable();
    },
    _destroy: function() {
        this.element.sortable( "destroy" );
        this._super();
    }
});
```

With this approach, you can create a sortable to-do list by calling this new widget's plugin:

```
<ul>
    <li>Write widget</li>
    <li>Post on GitHub</li>
    <li>Profit?</li>
</ul>
<script>
    $( "ul" ).sortableTodoList();
</script>
```

As before, neither approach is *better*; they're different ways of extending the todo widget with additional behavior. If you prefer having a separate plugin with a different name, then create a new widget; if you have no need for a completely different widget, then redefine the original widget.

Before we end this section, there's one final question worth discussing: why didn't you implement removable and sortable items directly in the todo widget? Why build this functionality as extensions?

The answer is one the jQuery UI team itself has learned the hard way: widgets with lots of options are difficult to use and maintain. For every option you add to a widget, you have to think about how it interacts with every other option. Worse, every option you add makes extending your widget harder (extensions also have to worry about supporting every single option).

The interaction between options is a consistent source of bugs and code complexity in jQuery UI. Think of all the combinations of datepicker's 50 options! Plus, the vast majority of use cases don't require more than a couple of options. I've yet to see a datepicker that required a quarter of datepicker's 50 options.

Because of this, from now on the jQuery UI team will attempt to implement only commonly needed options. To make the jQuery UI widgets customizable for highly specific situations, the library has recently implemented a brand-new means of customization: extension points.

Options that depend on other options

Limiting the number of options a widget has is a widget API design best practice. Another is to avoid creating options that depend on other options.

jQuery UI itself violates this best practice in a few places for backward compatibility. As an example, the resizable widget has `animate`, `animateDuration`, and `animateEasing` options. These APIs are confusing because `animateDuration` and `animateEasing` are irrelevant when `animate` isn't set to `true`.

If you need multiple values for a single option, the preferred approach is to accept an object. For instance, the dialog widget's `show` and `hide` options accept an object with multiple properties set, as shown here:

```
$( "<div>" ).dialog({
    hide: {
        duration: 500,
        easing: "linear",
        effect: "puff"
    }
});
```

9.2 Customizing widgets with extension points

Although any method in a widget can be overridden with the widget factory, the jQuery UI team has realized that it's useful to create methods specifically for extension. These methods are designated as extension points and have the same API stability as options, methods, and events—meaning jQuery UI will never rename or remove an extension point in a bug fix release.

The extension point mechanism doesn't apply only to jQuery UI. By adding extension points to custom widgets, you make them easier to use, and easier for other developers to build widgets on top of. We'll look at examples of this later in the section.

The jQuery UI extension points are now listed on each widget's API documentation—right alongside the widget's options, methods, and events. Figure 9.5 shows the dialog widget's single extension point.

Options	Methods	Events
appendTo	close	beforeClose
autoOpen	destroy	close
buttons	isOpen	create
closeOnEscape	moveToTop	drag
closeText	open	dragStart
dialogClass	option	dragStop
draggable	widget	focus
height		open
hide	**Extension Points**	resize
maxHeight	_allowInteraction_	resizeStart
maxWidth		resizeStop

Figure 9.5   The dialog widget's extension points list on http://api.jqueryui.com/dialog/. Not all widgets have extension points, but the ones that do will always show up in this location on the API docs.

As discussed, extension points are nothing more than widget methods; you know the mechanism to override the dialog's `_allowInteraction()` method:

```
$.widget( "ui.dialog", $.ui.dialog, {
    _allowInteraction: function() {}
});
```

The dialog widget's `_allowInteraction()` method is specifically used for modal dialogs. Normally, modal dialogs don't allow users to interact with elements outside of the dialog. This behavior is almost always what you want, but suppose you have an element outside the dialog that's positioned to look as if it's inside the dialog.

Many third-party plugins take this approach. Consider the following code that uses the third-party Select2 jQuery plugin in a modal dialog:

```
<div id="dialog">
    <label for="country">Country:</label>
    <select id="country">
        <option>Afghanistan</option>
        <option>Albania</option>
        <option>Algeria</option>
        ...
    </select>
</div>
<script>
    $( "#dialog" ).dialog({ modal: true });
    $( "#country" ).select2();
</script>
```

The display of this example is shown in figure 9.6.

As you can see from figure 9.6, the Select2 plugin automatically provides an `<input>` for the user to filter options in the list. Unfortunately, the dialog widget blocks this `<input>` from getting focus. Why? Take a look at the generated markup structure of this example, shown here:

Figure 9.6   Display of the Select2 plugin with a modal dialog

```
<body>
    <div id="dialog" class="ui-dialog" ...></div>
    <div class="select2-drop" ...>
        <input class="select2-input">
        ...
    </div>
</body>
```

Although the `<input>` looks as if it's inside the dialog, it's actually in a sibling `<div>`, and is absolutely positioned on top of the dialog: the dialog widget blocks any interactions with this `<input>`.

This is where the `_allowInteraction()` method comes in. The method lets you whitelist elements the user can use that aren't children of modal dialogs. The following code uses the `_allowInteraction()` extension point to allow the use of the Select2 plugin:

```
$.widget( "ui.dialog", $.ui.dialog, {
    _allowInteraction: function( event ) {
        return $( event.target ).is( ".select2-input" ) ||
            this._super( event );
    }
});
```

You perform two checks here. First, you see if the element that received the event has a `select2-input` class name. This is what allows the Select2 `<input>` to receive focus. Second, you call `_super()` so that you still do the checks in the parent widget's method. `$.ui.dialog.prototype._allowInteraction()`, for instance, has a workaround to ensure datepickers work within dialogs.

> **TIP** The autocomplete and selectmenu widgets automatically work within modal dialogs because of their use of the `ui-front` class name and `appendTo` option. Read more about the technique these widgets use at http://api.jqueryui.com/theming/stacking-elements/. The datepicker widget will take the same approach when its rewrite is complete, which will remove the need for the workaround in the dialog widget's `_allowInteraction()` method.

Now you have a Select2 plugin that works in a jQuery UI modal dialog, and, because `_allowInteraction()` is a documented extension point, you can feel comfortable that this fix will work in future releases.

Because extension points are a relatively new mechanism in jQuery UI, there are still few documented extension points. What do you do if you want to extend an undocumented method?

9.2.1 *Using undocumented extension points*

If you use jQuery UI long enough, you'll almost certainly want to extend a method that isn't an official extension point. Although only some methods are documented as extension points, any widget method can be overridden using the widget factory. And sometimes it can be advantageous to override the undocumented methods (we'll look at an example in a bit).

Despite this, overriding undocumented methods should always be considered a last resort during development. Because jQuery UI is free to rename or replace any undocumented method during any release (even a bug fix release), you risk having your application break as new versions of jQuery UI come out.

But sometimes it can be worth the risk to truly customize the behavior of the widget. To give a concrete example of this, let's return to the dialog widget. The dialog widget does some logic to manage focus for you. When you open a dialog, focus is automatically set to the first of the following:

1 An element with the `autofocus` attribute
2 A tabbable element in the dialog's content
3 A tabbable element in the dialog's button pane
4 The dialog's close button
5 The dialog itself

This is done for accessibility purposes. Shifting focus lets screen reader users know that there is new content to interact with.

> **NOTE**   The dialog widget also moves focus when a dialog is closed. When you open a dialog, the widget remembers which element had focus, and when you close the dialog, focus is returned to that element.

Usually, this behavior gives focus to an appropriate element in the dialog, but not always, for instance, in the following example:

```
<div id="dialog">
    <p>The transaction processed successfully. For details,
       see <a href="/account">your account</a>.</p>
</div>
<script>
    $( "#dialog" ).dialog({
        buttons: {
            OK: function() {
                $( this ).dialog( "close" );
            }
        }
    });
</script>
```

The display of this dialog is shown in figure 9.7. Notice that the your account `<a>` received focus.

If you refer to the dialog's focus algorithm, you'll see why. Because there's no element with an `autofocus` attribute, the dialog looks for a tabbable element in the dialog's content.

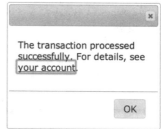

Figure 9.7   Display of a dialog widget with focus placed on a link in the content

Because `<a>` tags with `href` attributes are tabbable, the dialog widget selects the link and gives it focus.

Here this isn't desirable behavior. Because this is a simple confirmation dialog, you want to focus the OK button so the user can easily close the dialog with the Enter key. Having focus on the link also draws the user's attention to the link, and you have no reason to do that in this example.

How do you change this behavior? Although there are no documented extension points to control this, if you look at the source of the dialog widget (https://github.com/jquery/jquery-ui/blob/master/ui/dialog.js), you'll see that there is a method that controls this behavior: `_focusTabbable()`.

You can use this method to alter the focus logic in your example. The following code shows an extension that does that:

```
$.widget( "ui.dialog", $.ui.dialog, {
    _focusTabbable: function() {
        var okButton = this.uiDialog.find( "button:contains('OK')" );
        if ( okButton.length > 0 ) {
            okButton.focus();
        } else {
            this._super();
        }
    }
});
```

Finds any buttons with text "OK" ❶

Focuses the OK button if found ❷

Calls the parent method if not ❸

This extension overrides one method: `_focusTabbable()`. You use a reference to the dialog's outer DOM element (`this.uiDialog`) to look for any `<button>` elements that contain the text `"OK"` ❶.

If you find one, you give it focus ❷; otherwise, you call the parent widget's `_focusTabble()` with `_super()` to let it determine which element should receive focus ❸.

With this extension in place, your example dialog now gives focus to the OK button when opened rather than to the link. You could've written this extension other ways. You could've looked for the first button in the button pane, regardless of its text. You also could've assumed there would always be an OK button and given it focus without checking whether it exists.

The point here isn't the specific implementation, as what you'll need to do is specific to what you're building. The point is that you could change the widget's behavior only by extending an undocumented method of the dialog widget.

Is this all right? Although developers coming from a server-side background may cringe at using undocumented APIs, it's sometimes the only option you have to implement your requirements. As we discussed, using undocumented extension points should always be a last resort.

Creating extensible widgets is an important goal of the jQuery UI project. If you think a specific method should be listed as an extension point, let us know! Or if you think some logic in a widget could be refactored to make it more extensible, create a ticket requesting it. Better yet, after you create the ticket, submit a pull request implementing the new extension point! For more information on contributing to jQuery UI, see appendix E.

9.2.2 Adding your own extension points

Extension points make a widget more extensible, and therefore it's easier to build complex solutions on top of the widget. Because jQuery UI tries to adhere to this methodology in its widgets, you should try to do the same in your own custom widgets as well. As a general rule, if you think someone may want to change the behavior of something you're writing, put it in a method.

Let's return to the extension you built earlier in this chapter that added remove buttons to your to-do list. For a refresher, the code for that extension is shown again here:

```
$.widget( "tj.todo", $.tj.todo, {
    ...
    _renderList: function() {
        var listItems = this.element.find( "li" );
        ...
        listItems.each(function() {
            var button = $( "<button>Remove</button>" ).button({
                icons: { primary: "ui-icon-closethick" },
                text: false
            });
            $( this ).append( button );
        })
    }
});
```

The code that builds the remove `<button>` elements is embedded in the `_renderList()` method. If you want to customize how the buttons work, you need to reimplement the entire, nontrivial `_renderList()` method. Let's move the button creation to its own method to make it an extension point.

The following code implements a new `_buildRemoveButton()` extension point:

```
$.widget( "tj.todo", $.tj.todo, {
    ...
    _renderList: function() {
        var listItems = this.element.find( "li" ),
            that = this;
        ...
        listItems.each(function() {
            var button = that._buildRemoveButton();
            $( this ).append( button );
        })
    },
    _buildRemoveButton: function() {
        return $( "<button>Remove</button>" ).button({
            icons: { primary: "ui-icon-closethick" },
            text: false
        });
    }
});
```

Functionality-wise, this implementation does the exact same thing, but you now have the ability to alter the code that builds the remove `<button>` elements without needing to reimplement `_renderList()`. This extension shows text on the button instead of an icon. (Notice that the `text` option is no longer set; it takes its default value of `true`.)

```
$.widget( "tj.todo", $.tj.todo, {
    _buildRemoveButton: function() {
        return $( "<button>Remove</button>" ).button({
            icons: { primary: "ui-icon-closethick" }
        });
    }
});
```

Is this an extension of an extension? Yes, it is. With the widget factory you can extend or redefine the same widget as many times as you'd like.

Because of the power of extending widgets, it's important to think about extension points during the development of a widget. By putting your button-creating code in its own method, you allow developers to customize the button's creation without having to repeat code from your widget.

Before we end our discussion of widget extensions, there's one last widget we need to discuss: datepicker.

9.3 Extending the datepicker widget

Remember that datepicker is the only widget in jQuery UI that isn't built with the widget factory. Because of this, it also can't be extended using the widget factory—which unfortunately means that none of the techniques we've discussed throughout this chapter will work on datepicker.

You can do some things, although the implementations aren't nearly as clean as widgets built with the widget factory. To show this, let's tackle one common datepicker request: changing what the Today button does.

Recall that setting the datepicker's `showButtonPanel` option to `true` displays the datepicker along with the two buttons shown in figure 9.8.

If you had to guess, what do you suppose the Today button does? Most people, including me, believe that it should select today's date, place today's date value in the `<input>`, and close the calendar. Alas, this isn't the behavior of the Today button—instead, the button *links to today's date.*

Figure 9.8 A datepicker with a button pane. The button pane contains two buttons: Today and Done.

To understand what this means, you have to know that there's always an active date when the datepicker is open. The active date is today's date by default, but it can be altered with datepicker's keyboard shortcuts, the next and previous month buttons, or by typing dates directly in the datepicker's <input>. You can select the active date at any time using the Enter key.

When you click the Today button, it makes today's date the active date. If you navigate the datepicker in figure 9.8 to February and click Today, you're taken back to January, but today's date isn't selected.

This behavior confuses almost everybody who uses the datepicker; it's counterintuitive. So how do you change it?

There are no options to control the behavior, and no events triggered when the Today button is clicked; you must resort to a technique mentioned in the last chapter: duck punching.

Internally, datepicker runs $.datepicker._gotoToday() whenever the Today button is clicked. You still need $.datepicker._gotoToday() to run—as you need to make Today's date active—but you need to add to what it does.

With the widget factory this was simple; you used _super() to call the parent's method, then did your custom logic. But because datepicker isn't built with the widget factory, that's not an option here. So what do you do?

This is where the duck-punching technique comes into play. Duck punching lets you extend a function while maintaining a reference to the original function. Let's look at the implementation:

```
$.datepicker._gotoToday = (function( orig ) {
    return function( id ) {
        orig.call( this, id );
        this._selectDate( id );
    };
})( $.datepicker._gotoToday );
```

Let's break this down, starting with the first and last lines:

```
$.datepicker._gotoToday = (function( orig ) {
    ...
})( $.datepicker._gotoToday );
```

This is an assignment; you're assigning a new value to $.datepicker._gotoToday. *What* is being assigned is where this gets tricky.

function(orig) {} defines an anonymous function and ($.datepicker ._gotoToday) immediately invokes that function—passing it a reference to $.datepicker._gotoToday; after this executes, orig is set to the original version of $.datepicker._gotoToday. Because this whole block of code is an assignment, whatever you *return* from this anonymous function will become the new value of $.datepicker._gotoToday.

Here's the function that you return:

```
return function( id ) {
    orig.call( this, id );
    this._selectDate( id );
};
```

Because you have a reference to the original `$.datepicker._gotoToday` as `orig`, you invoke that first, then you add your custom behavior: calling another internal method `$.datepicker._selectDate()`, which selects the active date and places it in the `<input>`. Now your datepicker's Today button selects today's date instead of linking to it.

Duck punching is a clever technique to implement a new version of a function, while maintaining the ability to call the original version. The widget factory's `_super()` and `_superApply()` methods are implemented using a similar approach internally.

Although this technique is clever, is this approach to extending datepicker safe to add to your production applications? Like undocumented extension points, there's a definite risk when altering undocumented methods in datepicker. jQuery UI can change the name, behavior, or the existence of these methods at any time.

But unlike other jQuery UI widgets, a long-term rewrite of the datepicker is in progress, which means two things:

1 You shouldn't have to keep these hacks in long-term. Eventually, there will be far easier ways to alter the datepicker.
2 The API of the current datepicker isn't changing in any way.

In many ways, datepicker is a victim of its own success. Datepicker is such a popular widget—easily the most popular in jQuery UI—that *any* change is a breaking change for many users; therefore, the team is focusing almost exclusively on the rewrite. Because of this, however crazy it may seem, duck punching datepicker's methods is a reasonable solution to customize datepicker's behavior until it's rewritten.

The technique of duck punching functions is a bit tricky to wrap your head around, but it's incredibly powerful. It lets you add to the behavior of any JavaScript function without needing to change the original function. Internally, jQuery UI duck punches a few of jQuery Core methods to add to their behavior.

Never change the jQuery UI source code!

If you find a bug in jQuery UI, or there's some behavior you want to modify that isn't part of a public API, you may be tempted to alter the jQuery UI source code to change the behavior to meet your needs. Resist that urge. Modifying the library's source code makes upgrading difficult, because as each new version of jQuery UI is released, you have to remember every change you have made, and reapply each of those changes to the new version—which is a manual and error-prone task.

Using undocumented extensions points and duck punching, albeit not ideal, provide appealing alternatives to modifying the source code. These techniques let you alter the library's internal behavior without having to reapply your changes at every upgrade.

To help drive the duck punching concept home, let's look at one more example.

9.3.1   *Building a mobile-friendly datepicker extension*

In chapter 7 you used CSS to make an inline datepicker that displayed nicely on mobile devices. We avoided discussing a datepicker that's tied to an `<input>` because it requires nontrivial customization using the duck-punching technique we just discussed. To show the problem, consider the following example:

```
<label for="date">Date:</label>
<input id="date">
<script>
    $( "#date" ).datepicker();
</script>
```

Figure 9.9 shows how this example looks on an iPhone running iOS7.

Obviously, this behavior isn't ideal; the user sees only a portion of the datepicker, and the positioning of everything is off. And unfortunately, changing a few options isn't going to fix this situation.

The code to improve the mobile experience requires a variety of changes, including duck punching a few more of datepicker's methods. I'll present the implementation first, then we'll go over each piece individually. The updated datepicker implementation is shown in listing 9.4.

Figure 9.9   Display of a vanilla datepicker widget when its `<input>` receives focus on iOS

> **NOTE**   Some of the visual CSS is omitted to focus on the JavaScript aspect of this example. To view the full source of this example, see http://jsfiddle.net/ tj_vantoll/RZVKS/.

Listing 9.4   A mobile-friendly datepicker

```
<style>
    input { font-size: 1em; }
</style>

<label for="date">Date:</label>
<input id="date" placeholder="mm/dd/yyyy">

<script>
    $.datepicker._findPos = (function( orig ) {
        return function( obj ) {
            var position = orig.call( this, obj );
            position[ 0 ] = 0;
            return position;
        };
    })( $.datepicker._findPos );
    $.datepicker._attachments = (function( orig ) {
```

1 Prevents the browser from zooming in

2 Adds a placeholder with the date format

3 Overrides _findPos() for custom positioning

4 Overrides _attachments() to change the datepicker's button

```
                    return function( input, inst ) {
                        orig.call( this, input, inst );
                        input.next( "button" ) #6
                            .text( "toggle calendar" )
                            .button({
                                icons: { primary: "ui-icon-calendar" },
                                text: false #6
                            }); #6

                    };
                })( $.datepicker._attachments );

                $( "#date" ).datepicker({
                    showOn: "button"
                });
            });
</script>
```

Calls the parent _attachments() method ⑤

⑥ Converts the button to a button widget

⑦ Only shows the datepicker when its button is clicked

The first problem to fix is the zoom issue. The reason the `<input>` and datepicker are so large in figure 9.9 is that mobile browsers automatically zoom in to `<input>` elements that have a computed `font-size` under 16 pixels when they receive focus. The fix for this is making sure the `<input>` has a font size of at least 16 pixels ❶.

> **TIP** By default, 1 em is equivalent to 16 px; because em values cascade, parent elements have the ability to alter this value. For more on how ems work, see http://css-tricks.com/css-font-size/.

Even with this change, seeing a full datepicker on focus can be disorienting to users on a small screen; because of this, you set the datepicker's `showOn` option to `"button"` ❼. This tells the datepicker to generate a `<button>` and to show the datepicker only when that button is clicked—not on focus of the `<input>`. Because the datepicker no longer shows on focus, you add a `placeholder` attribute to the `<input>` to tell the user the format you're expecting ❷. (You can see the display of the placeholder in figure 9.10.)

Although the button the datepicker builds from `showOn: "button"` can be configured with the `buttonImage`, `buttonImageOnly`, and `buttonText` options—and is given a `ui-datepicker-trigger` class name—you have no means of controlling the creation of the `<button>` itself. You can't, for instance, use a themed jQuery UI button widget.

To work around this, you duck punch the method that datepicker uses to generate the button: `$.datepicker._attachments()` ❹. You call the original `$.datepicker._attachments()` ❺ and convert the `<button>` it created to a button widget with a calendar icon ❻.

There's one last workaround to discuss, this time for positioning. The datepicker always attempts to align the calendar's left edge with the left edge of its `<input>` and gives you no means of configuring this position. This is almost always fine on desktop browsers, but on mobile browsers this has a tendency to push the calendar outside of the browser's viewport, and having any portion of a calendar off the screen renders it unusable.

To work around this, duck punch another of the datepicker's methods: $.datepicker._findPos()  _findPos() returns an array in which the first value is the calendar's left coordinate and the second value is its top coordinate. In your override, you first call the original method and then set the left coordinate to 0. This ensures the calendar is positioned on the left edge of the screen and takes up the full viewport.

The updated version of your mobile datepicker is shown in figure 9.10.

Although this example works, the implementation is less than ideal because you can't use the widget factory. Because you altered the datepicker's methods directly, this isn't an extension of datepicker; all datepicker instances are affected by your changes. You can't use a mobile datepicker alongside a desktop one, for example.

In many ways, looking at how hard it is to customize datepicker is the best way to show how much the widget factory does for you.

Figure 9.10   The improved datepicker widget display on iOS—with a new placeholder, a button widget, and CSS to make the datepicker more mobile friendly

---

Evaluating third-party widgets

As you'll recall from the HTML5 discussion in chapter 3, most mobile browsers now have a native means of collecting dates from the user—without any JavaScript or configuration you used in the preceding example.

Remember that if all you need is a date from a mobile user, you should attempt to use the HTML5 input first, as it's going to use the same picker the user is accustomed to.

But also remember that the HTML5 datepicker is extremely limited; if you need to make customizations—disabling individual days, highlighting individual days, controlling the formatting, custom styling, and so on—you can use the approach we just discussed.

9.4   Summary

In this chapter, you looked at extension, the most powerful feature of the widget factory. You saw that extending an existing widget is as easy as passing the widget's constructor function to $.widget(). A widget can even redefine itself to change its behavior without generating a new widget with a different name.

Although you can extend any method in a widget extension, jQuery UI is moving toward documenting its extensible methods as extension points. These extension points appear on each widget's API documentation alongside the widget's options, methods, and events. You also saw how to add extension points to the todo widget you built in the previous chapter.

Although sticking to the publicly documented extension points is recommended, in unique situations you can override any method in any of the jQuery UI widgets. If you believe an existing method in a widget should be an extension point, let the jQuery UI team know! Creating extensible widgets is an important goal of the project, and it's feedback that we'd love to have. For more, see appendix E.

Finally, you looked at how to extend the only widget in jQuery UI not using the widget factory: datepicker. You saw that it's messy, but you can use a technique known as duck punching to alter the behavior of the widget.

Now that you've built and extended widgets, let's look at how to get your application using jQuery UI ready for production.

Preparing your application for production

This chapter covers

- Managing dependencies with AMD
- Building your files for production
- Adding AMD support to jQuery UI extensions

So far, we've discussed all the components (widgets, effects, utilities, and more) that make up the jQuery UI library. Although these components offer a lot of functionality, there are a few problems associated with having this many components. The biggest problem is, because jQuery UI is a client-side library, the browser must download all the JavaScript code to implement this functionality over the network—which increases the amount of time it takes your application to load.

To make things worse, because JavaScript is an interpreted language, the browser also has to convert the text contents of these JavaScript files to executable byte code—which leads to a longer wait for your users. Load times are important. Studies have shown that over 25% of people abandon a website if it takes over 4 seconds to load. An amazon.com spokesman famously stated that a one-second delay on its load times represents a loss of over $1.5 billion a year!

The mobile explosion has exacerbated these issues. Users on mobile devices, especially ones on rural networks, have much higher latency and much lower download speeds than more traditional desktop computers.

The sheer size of jQuery UI coupled with mobile's surge in importance has led to a perception that jQuery UI is too big to be used on mobile. Although jQuery UI is big, it's also written modularly, meaning that it's easy to include only the parts of the library you need. And because jQuery UI has so much in it (enough to write a whole book on!), few applications use even half of the library.

In this chapter, we'll look at the tools jQuery UI provides to include only the parts of the library you need, and how to package them so your applications are optimized for production usage.

We'll start by digging deeper into why the setup you've used to this point isn't ideal for production.

10.1 The problem with third-party CDNs

In chapter 1, we introduced boilerplate to use in all your examples. It contained the following three lines to download jQuery Core and jQuery UI from jQuery's CDN:

```
<link href="http://code.jquery.com/ui/1.11.0/themes/smoothness/
           jquery-ui.css" rel="stylesheet">
<script src="http://code.jquery.com/jquery-1.11.1.js"></script>
<script src="http://code.jquery.com/ui/1.11.0/jquery-ui.js"></script>
```

Third-party CDN downloads like this are great for testing; you can access the files you need without having to grab the files and store them on your own servers. But unless you're developing the rare application that only ever runs on a blazing fast internal network, third-party CDNs aren't appropriate for use in production. To explain why, we have to dig deeper into how the browser handles these three lines of code.

The browser has to figure out where the web server that hosts these files resides on the internet. Specifically, it has to perform a DNS lookup to find the IP address associated with the domain code.jquery.com. The browser and OS cache these lookups for a limited time to limit redundant trips, but if the user doesn't have the domain cached, your application must perform the lookup before your application loads.

Once the browser knows where the web server is located, it must establish a TCP connection to the external server and transfer data across it. This again has a time cost to the end user.

The browser issues an HTTP GET request for jquery-1.11.1.js and ui/1.11.0/jquery-ui.js from the web server located at code.jquery.com (or, as the browser sees it, 108.161.188.209). This workflow is shown in figure 10.1.

No need to worry if this is too much information; the point is to show how network-intensive <link> and <script> tags can be.

The time it takes for each trip to the network is known as *round-trip time* (RTT). One round trip on a desktop browser with a fast internet connection takes a matter of a few milliseconds, but on mobile, a single round trip can easily take hundreds of

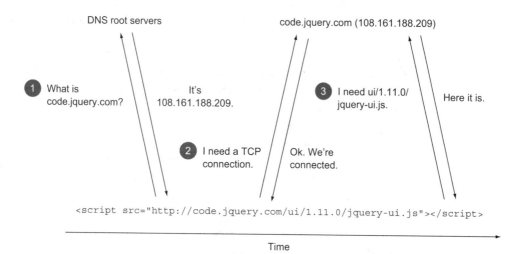

Figure 10.1   Round trips the browser must take when it parses a `<script>` tag from an external domain

milliseconds—and sometimes up to a full second in an extreme edge case (trying to access a server in Asia on a 3G network in rural Michigan, for example). Because of this, reducing RTTs is the top web-performance best practice listed on both Google and Yahoo's performance best-practice lists. (See https://developers.google.com/speed/articles/ and http://developer.yahoo.com/performance/rules.html, respectively.) Reducing RTTs is the single most important thing you can do to improve the performance of your web applications—especially on mobile devices.

What does this have to do with third-party CDNs? Because the third-party CDN is on a different domain, the browser must perform at least one round trip to establish a TCP connection, and possibly a second to perform a DNS lookup. These are extra round trips that aren't necessary if you host jQuery and jQuery UI on your own domain.

There's one additional issue with third-party CDNs that we need to discuss: the sheer size of the download. Because you can't tell the external CDN which parts of jQuery UI you need, you must download the entirety of the library. And because jQuery UI does a lot of stuff, that can be a whole lot of code. If you only need to use an autocomplete, you shouldn't subject your users on slow connections to download sortable's collision-detection algorithms, or datepicker's globalization logic.

Although third-party CDNs are great for testing, they aren't appropriate for use in production in the majority of applications. Throughout the rest of this chapter, you'll rework your boilerplate project structure to perform better in a production setting. To overcome the issues with third-party CDNs, we have two goals: reduce the number of round trips and ensure users download only the parts of jQuery UI that they need.

Luckily, jQuery UI has tools to make both of these optimizations possible. We'll start with Download Builder.

What about caching?

An oft-cited benefit of using third-party CDNs is the potential for the user to enter your site with the external resource already cached, eliminating the need for any network trips at all. Unfortunately cache hits in the wild are extremely rare.

Why?

Browsers cache files by their complete URL; for a user to have jQuery or jQuery UI cached, they would need to have visited another site that downloaded jQuery or jQuery UI using that *exact* same URL. Any change, however small, and the browser sees the file as a completely different resource. And there are three big differentiators in the URLs:

- *The CDN provider*—Google, the jQuery Foundation, Microsoft, and others provide CDNs with jQuery and jQuery UI. To the browser, http://code.jquery.com/ jquery-1.11.1.js and http://ajax.googleapis.com/ajax/libs/jquery/1.11.1/ jquery.min.js are different resources.
- *The version number*—There are dozens of versions of both jQuery and jQuery UI in the wild. In 2013, the most popular version was jQuery 1.4.2 (keeping in mind that the latest version released in 2013 was 1.10.2). To the browser, http:// code.jquery.com/jquery-1.10.1.js and http://code.jquery.com/jquery-1.10.2.js are different resources.
- *http versus https*—To the browser, http://code.jquery.com/jquery-1.11.1.js and https://code.jquery.com/jquery-1.11.1.js are different resources.

Because of these variations, the odds of a user arriving at your site with jQuery or jQuery UI already cached are too low to justify using third-party CDNs. For a more detailed write-up on the subject, see http://www.stevesouders.com/blog/2013/03/18/ http-archive-jquery/.

10.2 *Downloading jQuery UI from Download Builder*

The first tool we'll look at is the jQuery UI Download Builder, available at http://jqueryui.com/download/. Download Builder lets you configure a download of jQuery UI with only the pieces you need.

The page is set up as a series of check boxes for each of the widgets and utilities in jQuery UI. The check box for each feature is smart enough to know what the feature's dependencies are. Because of this, the recommended approach to using Download Builder is to deselect all check boxes, and then select widgets and utilities that you need. In figure 10.2. when the accordion widget is selected, its two dependencies— jQuery UI Core and the widget factory—are selected as well.

After you have the features you need selected, click the Download button to download a custom build of jQuery UI. The built JavaScript file is located at jquery-ui.min.js, and the built CSS file is located at jquery-ui.min.css in the downloaded build.

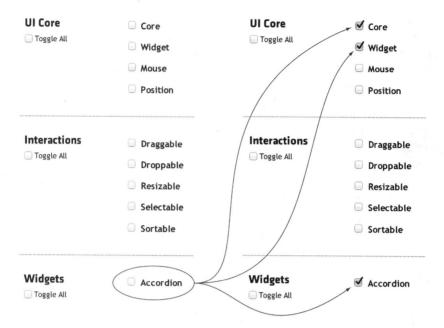

Figure 10.2   When Accordion is checked, its dependencies are as well.

You can see the difference the custom build made by looking at the sizes of your new files. jQuery UI 1.11 in its entirety is 232 K, and your custom build with the accordion widget is 19 K. A savings of 213 K! Although not quite as much of an impact, your CSS file was reduced from 27 K to 16 K. The savings are shown in table 10.1.

Table 10.1   The savings of configuring a custom build of the accordion widget

File	File size	File size after gzip
jQuery UI JS (full)	232 K	61 K
jQuery UI JS (accordion only)	19 K	6 K
jQuery UI CSS (full)	27 K	5.5 K
jQuery UI CSS (accordion only)	16 K	3.3 K

Although Download Builder can have huge benefits in reducing the size of jQuery UI, it can be a bit of a pain to use. If you decide to use a new widget, you have to go back to Download Builder, remember which dependencies you're using, generate a new build, and put the updated files in your project—a lot of work for us lazy web developers.

More importantly, Download Builder doesn't solve your biggest performance issue: reducing RTTs. The next technique solves both the download size and the RTT issues, but it's going to require a bit more work to set up.

The importance of gzip

All modern browsers support sending compressed resources over the network, with the most common means of compression being gzip. gzip compression has a drastic impact on the file size of HTML, CSS, and JavaScript files. Running gzip on jQuery UI 1.11 reduces its JavaScript from 232 K to 61 K, and its CSS from 27 K to 5.5 K!

The compression algorithm running under the hoods of gzip works by replacing repeated strings with symbols; files with lots of repeated strings—such as CSS files—tend to get the highest level of compression.

Because of gzip's dramatic impact, it's important to make sure that your web server is using gzip on JavaScript and CSS files. You can verify this by looking for a Content-Encoding: gzip response header on these files. The following figure shows this header on the Network tab of Chrome's developer tool.

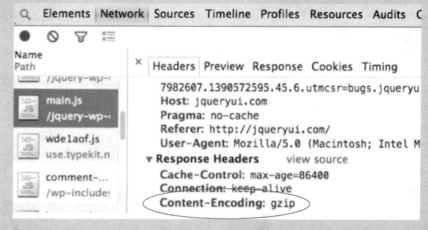

Chrome's developer tool showing that the Content-Encoding header is indeed sent on a JavaScript resource

For a more detailed explanation of gzip, see Chrome's gzip best practice documentation at https://developers.google.com/speed/docs/best-practices/payload#Gzip-Compression.

10.3 Managing JavaScript dependencies with AMD

Managing dependencies in JavaScript has always been a tricky subject. Because JavaScript has no native means of declaring dependencies, web developers have historically been limited to `<script>` tags and global variables, which are easy to mess up. For instance, to use the accordion widget, you must know what its dependencies are (jQuery Core, jQuery UI Core, and the widget factory) and include each of them before the accordion widget itself. If you get the order wrong, you get an error. Although explicitly managing dependencies for a single script isn't too bad, the practice can easily get out of control in big apps where you have hundreds of components with various codependencies.

The Asynchronous Module Definition (AMD) format attempts to solve dependency management on the web. Instead of relying on `<script>` tags that communicate through global variables, AMD modules declaratively specify their dependencies and return a function or object that other modules can use.

> **NOTE** ECMAScript 6, the upcoming version of JavaScript, includes an implementation of JavaScript modules, which will finally bring dependency management to JavaScript natively. But as of the time of this writing, the syntax hasn't been finalized; it will be a few years before enough browsers implement modules and they can be realistically used in production applications.

Although AMD defines APIs for how modules should be specified, it doesn't provide an implementation of the APIs. Think of AMD like the HTML specification which defines HTML elements and how they work, but it's up to the browsers to implement them.

In the same sense, to use AMD you need a script loader that implements the AMD APIs. Although a few AMD loaders are out there, by far the most popular one is RequireJS. RequireJS is a free, open source, and well-documented library, making it perfect for managing dependencies in any application.

In the rest of this section, we'll look at how to use RequireJS to load jQuery UI in your applications, how to switch your own application files to use AMD, and how to use RequireJS to optimize your files for production.

Do I have to use AMD?

Although AMD provides many benefits to managing dependencies and building your resources, it can be difficult to convince your boss or organization to switch to using it—especially in existing code bases.

But don't worry; you by no means have to use AMD. jQuery and jQuery UI both add all their modules to the global $ variable; therefore, you can reference these global variables as you always have.

Remember that your main performance goals were to reduce RTTs and the download size. If you can't use AMD, you can use some other process to concatenate and minify your scripts, and a variety of alternative solutions for this are out there. Ruby on Rails has the Asset Pipeline and Rakefiles; Java has Ant tasks; Node.js has Grunt and Gulp tasks.

In general, it's best to search for the best tool that matches your server-side environment.

Let's start by looking at how to change your boilerplate to use RequireJS.

10.3.1 *Setting up RequireJS for development*

Before introducing RequireJS, let's give an example showing how you've been doing things to this point. You'll start with two files: an index.html and an app.js:

```
├── index.html
└── js
    └── app.js
```

Your app's index.html includes jQuery, jQuery UI, and your application's functionality from jQuery's CDN in `<script>` tags:

```
<script src="http://code.jquery.com/jquery-1.11.1.js"></script>
<script src="http://code.jquery.com/ui/1.11.0/jquery-ui.js"></script>
<script src="js/app.js"></script>
```

Your app.js performs whatever logic you need your application to perform. In this case, you'll use it to create a new `<input>`, convert it to a spinner widget, and append it to the `<body>`:

```
$( "<input>" )
    .appendTo( "body" )
    .spinner({
        min: 0,
        max: 10
    });
```

Although this example is simple, it shows the disadvantages of using `<script>` tags and global variables. First, the three `<script>` tags must be in this exact order for this application to work. Second, this application downloads all of jQuery UI, and must perform numerous round trips to retrieve the three files it needs. So how are you going to improve this?

To get the improved example started, you're going to need to download the latest versions of the following three things:

- require.js from http://requirejs.org/docs/download.html
- jQuery Core from http://jquery.com/download/
- jQuery UI from https://github.com/jquery/jquery-ui/releases

You'll want to download the unminified, development versions of these libraries (jquery.js and require.js, not jquery.min.js and require.min.js). The development versions make your app easier to debug if things go wrong, and you'll take care of minifying the files for production later. For jQuery UI, you can get the development files at https://github.com/jquery/jquery-ui/releases. Download the latest zip file and grab the JavaScript files, which as of version 1.11 are in the `ui` directory.

After downloading these files, you'll want to create the following directory structure on your local development machine:

```
├── index.html
└── js
    ├── app.js
```

```
├── jquery-ui
│   ├── accordion.js
│   ├── autocomplete.js
│   ├── button.js
│   ├── ....
│   ├── spinner.js
│   ├── ...
├── jquery.js
└── require.js
```

With this setup, you place all your JavaScript assets in a js directory, and all the jQuery UI files in a jquery-ui subdirectory. For convenience, you include all the jQuery UI files even though you're not using every one. As you'll see, RequireJS takes care of bundling up only what you need. RequireJS is also flexible enough to handle any directory structure you'd like to use. You'll stick to this structure in your example for simplicity.

Now that you have your files set up, you have to use them.

10.3.2 *Loading jQuery UI components with RequireJS*

To start using RequireJS, change the three <script> tags in your index.html file to this:

```
<script src="js/require.js" data-main="js/app"></script>
```

This is a normal <script> tag that synchronously loads js/require.js. When require.js loads, it automatically performs an AJAX call to asynchronously load the file specified in its data-main attribute—js/app.js in this case—and executes it. Even though app.js loads and executes, you're still not loading jQuery or jQuery UI; you get an error that $ isn't defined.

To load your dependencies add an AMD-defined require() call in app.js:

```
require([ "jquery", "jquery-ui/spinner" ], function( $, spinner ) {
    $( "<input>" )
        .appendTo( "body" )
        .spinner({
            min: 0,
            max: 10
        });
});
```

The only thing different from before is the first line, and it can be tricky to understand at first. The require() function takes two parameters: an array of dependencies and a callback function. Our example's two dependencies are jQuery Core and the jQuery UI spinner widget. RequireJS resolves these dependency strings—"jquery" and "jquery-ui/spinner"—as the names of files in the project's directory structure. When require() runs, it asynchronously loads jquery.js and jquery-ui/spinner.js via AJAX requests. When these files both load, the callback function is invoked with the dependent modules as arguments.

RequireJS also does two important things on top of this. First, although it loads a module's dependencies in parallel (that is, multiple HTTP requests are sent out simultaneously), it ensures that all dependencies are loaded before the callback function is invoked. In the callback function, you can be absolutely sure that all declared dependencies are available.

Second, RequireJS resolves deep dependencies of modules. The jQuery UI spinner widget depends on a few other jQuery UI files, such as the widget factory and the button widget. Having the deep file dependencies be transparent—that is, you don't have to know the dependencies of dependencies—is incredibly useful. You can use modules without needing their dependencies. It's the same functionality you got from the jQuery UI Download Builder, without going through the manual process of checking check boxes.

Under the hood RequireJS still loads these deep dependencies asynchronously. Figure 10.3 shows the network activity from running this example.

Figure 10.3 showcases another important feature of RequireJS: it's smart enough to load dependencies only once. Every file in jQuery UI depends on jQuery Core, yet you can see that jquery.js was loaded only once. In fact, because the spinner widget depends on jQuery Core, you don't have to list the jQuery dependency in your example. The following removes the `"jquery"` dependency from your `require()` call:

```
require([ "jquery-ui/spinner" ], function( spinner ) {
    $( "<input>" )
        .appendTo( "body" )
        .spinner({
            min: 0,
            max: 10
        });
});
```

When loaded with AMD, jQuery Core still makes the global $ variable available for backward compatibility. In the same manner, all the jQuery UI modules append their APIs to the global $ variable. The spinner widget's constructor function is, for example, at `$.ui.spinner`.

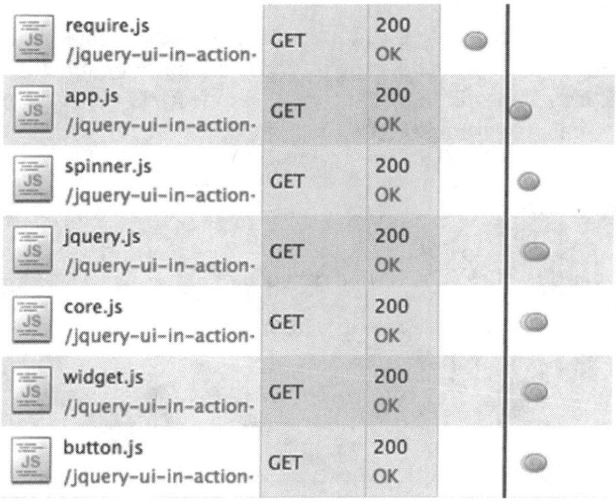

Figure 10.3 The Network tab of the Chrome developer tool showing the JavaScript files loaded by your AMD example

All AMD modules have the ability to return a value, and the jQuery UI widgets all return their constructor functions. You can optionally use the widget's constructor function instead of its plugin in the callback function:

```
require([ "jquery-ui/spinner" ], function( spinner ) {
    spinner({ min: 0, max: 10 }, "<input>" )
        .widget()
        .appendTo( "body" );
});
```

> **NOTE** All widgets have a `widget()` method that returns a jQuery object. For most widgets—such as accordion, menu, and tabs—the returned object contains the element the widget was initialized on. Other widgets return an element that they create internally; for instance, the autocomplete widget's `widget()` method returns the `<ul>` element it displays suggestions in. The spinner widget's `widget()` method returns a `<div>` it wraps around the `<input>` element it is initialized on. You can see what the `widget()` method returns for each widget on its API page.. The spinner widget's `widget()` method is documented at http://api.jqueryui.com/spinner/#method-widget.

Regardless of how you choose to create widgets, the big advantage of AMD is that you're loading only the parts of jQuery UI that you need. If your application needs only a spinner, you load only what you need to make a spinner. If your application suddenly needs an autocomplete, you can add `"jquery-ui/autocomplete"` to your `require()` call and not worry about what autocomplete depends on.

Although your example has solved your download size issues, there's still a big problem: you perform more round trips than before—and we discussed how that's the number-one thing you don't want to do!

RequireJS has a trick up its sleeve to help with that. And it has a cool name too: the optimizer.

Datepicker exception

Yet again the pesky datepicker widget is the exception to the rule. Because datepicker isn't written with the widget factory, it doesn't return a constructor function when required with RequireJS. You can still load datepicker as an AMD dependency, but you can't use the returned value as a constructor function; therefore, this doesn't work:

```
require([ "jquery-ui/datepicker" ], function( datepicker ) {
    datepicker({}, "<input>" );
});
```

For better or worse, you need to stick to initiating datepicker instances with its plugin:

```
require([ "jquery", "jquery-ui/datepicker" ], function( $ ) {
    $( "<input>" )
        .datepicker()
        .appendTo( "body" );
});
```

10.4   *Building your application's assets with the optimizer*

Although the AMD spec defines how to define and require resources, it doesn't define how to optimize those files for use in web browsers. In addition to its implementation of AMD, RequireJS has a separate optimization tool that does this, known as the *optimizer*.

The optimizer is written in JavaScript and runs on top of Node.js. To run the examples in this section you need to have Node.js installed on your machine, although you do not need to learn anything about it. Also, installing Node.js on Windows and OS X is now as easy as downloading and running an installer. If you don't have Node.js installed on your machine, grab the installer from http://nodejs.org/ and run it.

> **TIP**   If you're a Java developer, you might want to check out an alternative version of the optimizer written in Java. For more details, see https://github.com/jrburke/r.js.

You can verify the install worked by opening a new command-line session (Command Prompt on Windows, Terminal on OS X) and typing `node`. If you see something other than "command not found," it worked.

In addition to Node.js itself, the installer installs npm, or Node Package Manager: a package management system for Node.js modules. Because the RequireJS optimizer is implemented as a Node.js module, you'll use npm to install it.

To install the optimizer, run the following on your command-line session of choice:

```
> npm install -g requirejs
```

> **NOTE**   In this book, command-line code is displayed in bold text to differentiate it from browser code.

The –g flag tells npm to install the module globally—in other words, not specific to an individual project. You can verify that the installation worked by running r.js (r.js.cmd on Windows). You should see the following output:

```
> r.js
See https://github.com/jrburke/r.js for usage.
```

That's it for your installation; now you're ready to optimize your files.

10.4.1   *Optimizing JavaScript assets*

Before doing so, we need to set a few configuration variables to tell the optimizer *how* to optimize your code. You can specify the configuration as command-line arguments or a JavaScript file to use as a build profile. I find the separate file to be more readable and maintainable, so you'll use that for your example. If you're interested in learning about the command-line option, the optimizer's documentation (http://requirejs.org/docs/optimization.html) has a few examples.

You'll name your configuration file build.js and place it in the same `js` directory you've placed the rest of your JavaScript assets in:

```
├── index.html
└── js
    ├── app.js
    ├── build.js
    ├── jquery-ui
    │   ├── accordion.js
    │   ├── autocomplete.js
    │   ├── button.js
    │   ├── core.js
    │   ├── datepicker.js
    │   ├── ...
    ├── jquery.js
    └── require.js
```

There is an overwhelming number of options that you can provide the optimizer (a full list is available at http://requirejs.org/docs/optimization.html#options), but the vast majority of applications need only a few, which we'll walk through. For your example, you need only the following build.js:

```
({
    name: "app",
    out: "app.built.js"
})
```

You set two options: name and out. name is the filename of the JavaScript module to optimize, and out controls the filename of the output file generated by the optimizer.

Now that you have your installations done and your configuration in place, you can run the build. To do so, run this command in the root directory of your project (that is, the same directory containing your project's index.html). Remember that on Windows, you'll need to use r.js.cmd instead of r.js:

```
> $ r.js -o js/build.js
```

You should see the following output:

```
Tracing dependencies for: app
Uglifying file: js/app.built.js

js/app.built.js
----------------
js/jquery.js
js/jquery-ui/core.js
js/jquery-ui/widget.js
js/jquery-ui/button.js
js/jquery-ui/spinner.js
js/app.js
```

The optimizer starts at the file indicated by the name option (app.js), collects all its dependencies, concatenates them in a single file (named app.built.js because of the out option), and minifies that file. You now have a single js/app.built.js file that contains everything your application needs. Back in your app's index.html, remember that you currently use this `<script>` tag:

```
<script src="js/require.js" data-main="js/app"></script>
```

To switch to the built file for production, all you need to do is add "`.built`" to the `data-main` attribute:

```
<script src="js/require.js" data-main="js/app.built"></script>
```

With this, you've solved both your RTT and download size issues. This code performs only two round trips—one for require.js and one for app.built.js. Because app.built.js contains only the modules you're using, the user downloads only what is needed.

> **TIP** If performance is ultracritical and you want to get the RTT count down to one, the author of RequireJS provides an alternative AMD loader called almond. We'll look at how to use almond in the next chapter.

This example shows the benefits of managing dependencies with AMD and RequireJS. Need to add a new dependency? Add it to your `require()` statement, rerun your build, and it's there. Need to remove a dependency? Remove it from `require()`, rerun your build, and it's gone. There's no need to mess with configuration files or configure a new build on Download Builder.

We've now covered how to optimize your JavaScript assets for production, but we haven't said a thing about CSS files. The reason is that although there are some third-party plugins, neither RequireJS nor the AMD specification handles CSS dependencies. Although RequireJS doesn't manage CSS dependencies, its optimizer does let you concatenate and minify CSS files using the same build you used for JS files. We'll look at how to use that next.

10.4.2 *Optimizing CSS dependencies*

The build you created in the previous section works great for smaller apps, but more complex apps have to build multiple JS files, CSS files, and more. No worries, though; RequireJS has configuration options to meet these nontrivial requirements.

Let's return to your application's directory structure to show the location of CSS files:

```
├── css
│   ├── app.css
│   └── jquery-ui
│       ├── accordion.css
│       ├── images
│       │   └── ...
│       └── ...
├── index.html
└── js
    ├── app.js
    ├── build.js
    ├── jquery-ui
    │   ├── accordion.js
    │   └── ...
    ├── jquery.js
    └── require.js
```

The same as your JavaScript files, you're free to place your files in whatever directory structure you like (and RequireJS will support that structure), but for the sake of this example, you're going to use a CSS directory with the jQuery UI .css files in a `jquery-ui` directory.

For your application's code, you use a single app.css file in the same CSS directory. In it, you import your app's CSS dependencies and add any styling you need for your application. For this example, you'll load only your jQuery UI dependencies. To continue the same spinner example, place the following in your app.css:

```
@import "jquery-ui/core.css";
@import "jquery-ui/theme.css";
@import "jquery-ui/button.css";
@import "jquery-ui/spinner.css";
```

The only two required jQuery UI .css files are core.css and theme.css—which contain the jQuery UI CSS framework class names and the base theming rules, respectively. From there, all widgets in jQuery UI have a dedicated CSS file that's needed only if you use that widget. Because—unlike AMD—you have no dependency management in CSS, you need to explicitly list your dependencies.

Normally, including `@import` statements in CSS files is a bad practice. The browser performs a separate HTTP request to load each of these files—the very round trips we've been attempting to avoid. But don't worry; the same RequireJS optimizer you've been using to optimize your JS files can inline these `@import` statements as well.

Now that you have your CSS in place, let's return to your build. Here's the configuration you've been using:

```
({
    name: "app",
    out: "app.built.js"
})
```

This tells the optimizer to build the module in file app.js and place the output in app.built.js. To expand this to handle multiple files, including CSS files, you have to use additional build options. The following code is the updated build.js:

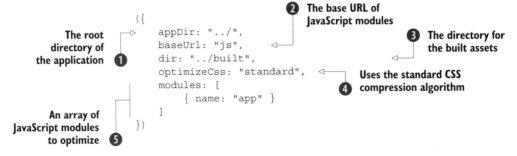

If you run this build from the command line again (`r.js -o js/build.js`), you'll see that it takes a slightly different approach than your previous build. When you specify a `dir` option, the optimizer clones the app's entire directory structure in a new directory. The name of the new directory is determined by the `dir` option—in this case, built ❸.

From there, the optimizer looks for any JavaScript or CSS files in the application—where the root of the application is determined by the `appDir` option **❶**—minifies them, and inlines any `@import` statements in CSS files. The type of compression the optimizer does on CSS files is determined by the `optimizeCss` option. You use `"standard"` compression **❹**, which removes all lines and unnecessary whitespace. If you want to preserve new lines or whitespace, you can set `optimizeCSS` to `"keepLines"` or `"keepWhitespace"`, respectively.

The optimizer does the same task you saw in the previous section: optimizes AMD modules. By passing a `modules` option **❺**, you can specify multiple files to optimize if your application requires it. The directory for the JavaScript modules is determined by the `baseUrl` **❷** option.

The cool thing about this approach is that it doesn't mix your source files with your built files. In the previous example, you had an app.built.js file that sat alongside app.js. Here, your source directories aren't touched; instead, you have an app.js in your main application's directory and another in the built directory, which gives the following structure:

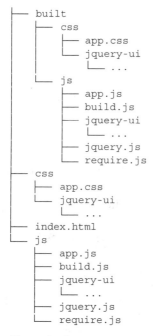

```
├── built
│   ├── css
│   │   ├── app.css
│   │   └── jquery-ui
│   │       └── ...
│   └── js
│       ├── app.js
│       ├── build.js
│       ├── jquery-ui
│       │   └── ...
│       ├── jquery.js
│       └── require.js
├── css
│   ├── app.css
│   └── jquery-ui
│       └── ...
├── index.html
└── js
    ├── app.js
    ├── build.js
    ├── jquery-ui
    │   └── ...
    ├── jquery.js
    └── require.js
```

If you look at your app.css in the built directory, you see that instead of being four `@import` statements, it's now a single line of minified code with the four jQuery UI CSS files embedded.

Use the following two lines to import resources in development

```
<link href="css/app.css" rel="stylesheet">
<script src="js/require.js" data-main="js/app"></script>
```

and the following two for production:

```
<link href="built/css/app.css" rel="stylesheet">
<script src="built/js/require.js" data-main="built/js/app"></script>
```

The only difference is the updated references to the `built` directory, because that's where your built assets are. In development, these two lines generate 10 HTTP requests for four CSS files and six JavaScript files. In production, these two lines generate 3 HTTP requests: one for app.css, one for require.js, and one for app.js. This is a major performance improvement, and this is for the simplest of examples. In large applications, a RequireJS build can easily reduce hundreds of requests down to a small handful.

The examples in this chapter were purposely simple to show how to use jQuery UI in an AMD setting. Because the topic of managing large applications and complex build configuration is so vast, a more comprehensive discussion is outside the scope of this book. If you're looking for more detailed material on the subject, *JavaScript Application Design: A Build First Approach* by Nicolas Bevacqua, to be published by Manning in 2015, is an excellent resource.

Although we won't dig deeper into AMD-based builds, we need to discuss one last thing, and that's how you can add AMD support to your own jQuery UI extensions. How does jQuery UI offer AMD support, *and* still work for users not using AMD? Let's explore that next.

10.5 *Supporting AMD in custom widgets*

If you're designing a module to be externally used—whether it's distributed online or distributed throughout your company—it's important to support common development environments. In this case, that means supporting developers who want to use AMD, and developers who don't.

Let's return to your todo widget you built in chapter 8. Let's suppose you want to use your todo widget in your AMD example from the previous section. You add its todo.js file to your `js` directory—right alongside `jquery.js` and the `jquery-ui` directory:

```
├── index.html
└── js
    ├── app.js
    ├── build.js
    ├── jquery-ui
    │   ├── accordion.js
    │   └── ...
    ├── jquery.js
    ├── require.js
    └── todo.js
```

You change your app.js to use todo.js with the following:

```
require([ "todo" ], function( todo ) {
    todo( {}, "<ul><li>One</li><li>Two</li><li>Three</li>" )
        .element
        .appendTo( "body" );
});
```

You expect this code to create a new <ul> with three items, convert it to a todo widget, and append it to the <body>. Instead, this example fails with a JavaScript error that $ isn't defined.

The problem is you never declared dependencies for your todo widget. RequireJS doesn't know that the widget depends on jQuery Core and the widget factory, so it never loads them. You can change that easily enough. The following code shows the todo widget updated to support AMD:

```
define([ "jquery", "jquery-ui/widget" ], function( $, widget ) {
    return widget( "tj.todo", {
        options: { ... },
        _create: function( ... ) { },
        ...
    };
});
```

Defines a module with its dependencies ❶

Returns the module's APIs ❷

Notice you're using `define()` instead of `require()` on the first line of your module. `require()` lets you load dependencies; `define()` lets you load dependencies, and then return an API that can be used by other modules. You should use `define()` whenever you want to define a new module.

The parameters of `define()` are the same as `require()`—an array of dependencies as strings and a callback function ❶. The todo widget depends on jQuery Core and the widget factory, so you pass them as the first argument. In the callback function—to be consistent with the jQuery UI widgets—you return the result of `$.widget()`, which is the widget's constructor function ❷. That same constructor function was what your previous example was using:

```
require([ "todo" ], function( todo ) {
    todo( {}, "<ul><li>One</li><li>Two</li><li>Three</li>" )
        .element
        .appendTo( "body" );
});
```

This code now works as expected. RequireJS loads jQuery, the widget factory, and the todo widget. Then, the code to create a new todo widget with the widget's constructor function executes successfully.

There's only one problem. Suppose the developers of another project don't use AMD and want to use the todo widget. They use code like this:

```
<script src="js/jquery.js"></script>
<script src="js/jquery-ui/widget.js"></script>
<script src="js/todo.js"></script>
<script>
    $( "<ul><li>One</li><li>Two</li><li>Three</li></ul>" )
        .todo()
        .appendTo( "body" );
</script>
```

This code worked fine before you introduced AMD support, but now it doesn't. Because this new example doesn't use AMD or RequireJS—which implements the necessary AMD functions—this code throws an error because `define` isn't defined. So when you added support for AMD, you also removed support for developers not using AMD. How do the jQuery UI modules support both?

What jQuery UI does, and what is the established solution to this problem, is a technique known as a UMD wrapper. UMD (Universal Module Definition) refers to a pattern for writing modules that work in multiple environments. jQuery UI uses a UMD wrapper in all its modules. If you look at the source code for the spinner widget you'll see the following:

```
(function( factory ) {                                          ①  First to execute.
    if ( typeof define === "function" && define.amd ) {
        define([                                                ←
            "jquery",          Third to execute.                    Registers as
            "./core",          Checks whether              ④       AMD module.
            "./widget",        AMD is being used.
            "./button"      ③
        ], factory );
    } else {
        factory( jQuery );
    }                                                           ②  Second to execute:
}(function( $ ) {          Only adds to     ⑤                        the factory.
    return $.widget( "ui.spinner", {  ←
        ...                                                         Creates the
    });                                                      ⑥     spinner widget.
}));
```

This code is a bit intimidating at first glance, so let's break it down piece by piece. I find it easiest to explain this in terms of the order in which these lines of code execute. Of course, the first line that executes is line one ①, which defines a function that immediately invokes itself. The function at ① passes itself a reference to the function at ② and sets it as a `factory` parameter. You may need to reread that sentence a few times or play with the code here before that sinks in. Don't worry if you continue to be confused. Just know that in the function at ①, the following is now true:

```
factory = function( $ ) {
    return $.widget( "ui.spinner", {
        ...
    });
}
```

`factory` is a variable that references a function that creates the spinner widget; it hasn't been invoked yet. Before invoking `factory`, you need to know whether the user is using AMD.

You check for AMD support by looking for a `define()` function available with an `amd` property ③. If this is the case, you call `define()` ④ with the spinner widget's dependencies—jQuery Core, jQuery UI Core, the widget factory, the button widget—and a reference to the factory. `define()` resolves the dependencies and invokes `factory` with its dependencies. The factory invocation causes `$.widget()` to run ⑥, which defines the spinner widget as an AMD module.

Backing up to ❸, if the user isn't using AMD, you invoke the factory with the jQuery global variable ❺. Note that this route doesn't resolve any dependencies. It requires all of the spinner widget's dependencies to be available before this code runs.

Although admittedly a bit convoluted, the UMD wrapper lets you support AMD users and non-AMD users without having to create separate files.

TIP Alternative versions of UMD also let you support use in Node.js environments. Because jQuery UI is exclusively browser-based code, it doesn't add the extra code to do this. If you're writing a module that would be useful in the browser as well as the server, check out the alternative UMD versions at https://github.com/umdjs/umd.

Let's take what we've learned back to the todo widget. To support both AMD and non-AMD users, all you need to do is add the same UMD wrapper, passing the appropriate dependencies—jQuery Core and the widget factory:

```
(function( factory ) {
    if ( typeof define === "function" && define.amd ) {
        define([
            "jquery",
            "jquery-ui/widget"
        ], factory );
    } else {
        factory( jQuery );
    }
}(function( $ ) {
    return $.widget( "tj.todo", { ... });
}));
```

Users can now use the todo widget regardless of whether or not they use AMD. Although the UMD wrapper is a bit verbose and tricky to understand, the ability to support multiple usage scenarios is valuable in any code you intend to distribute—whether it's on the web or in your company.

10.6 Summary

Performance is important to any web application. In the context of jQuery and jQuery UI, the two most important optimizations you can make to your application are reducing RTTs by concatenating scripts and reducing download size by configuring a build that includes only what you need.

Download Builder is a web-based tool that lets you configure a build of jQuery UI with only the pieces you need. Unfortunately, however, using Download Builder is a manual process. If you need another part of jQuery UI, you have to go back and create a new build.

AMD is a more complex, but more elegant solution to the performance problems. Using an AMD loader like RequireJS, you can specify your dependencies in your JavaScript files, and you can load only the code you need. When you're ready for production, you can run the RequireJS optimizer to minify and concatenate your files.

Even if you can't do every optimization laid out in this chapter, every little bit helps. If you can't convince your boss, team, or organization to make the switch to AMD, look into ways you can minify and concatenate scripts in your own server-side environment. Focus on reducing RTTs and HTTP requests, as that has the biggest performance benefit, especially in the context of mobile devices.

If you're building distributable code, support for both AMD and non-AMD usage makes it available to a wider audience of developers. Using a UMD wrapper is the preferred way of adding this support.

You've now made it through the core jQuery UI topics. You know how to wield widgets, customize themes, use effects, and now—how to get your code ready for production. It's time to put all this knowledge to use on a larger scale.

11

Building a flight-search application

This chapter covers

- Building mobile-friendly forms
- Connecting to a RESTful API
- Creating responsive forms
- Bundling a full application for production

Up to this point you've learned about jQuery UI and built a number of real-world applicable examples, but you have yet to build something at real-world scale—an application that you may actually need to build and deploy. And building a full-scale web application is no simple task. Depending on the application, it may require jQuery, jQuery UI, other utility libraries, as well as server-side components.

To learn how these pieces come together, you'll build a small flight-search application, similar to one on Orbitz, Travelocity, or any airline's site. In building this form, you'll get an idea of how these live sites work. Along the way, we'll look at concepts we haven't yet explored, such as client-side form validation, interacting with a RESTful API, and creating a responsive application. Figure 11.1 shows the finished version of the application that you'll build.

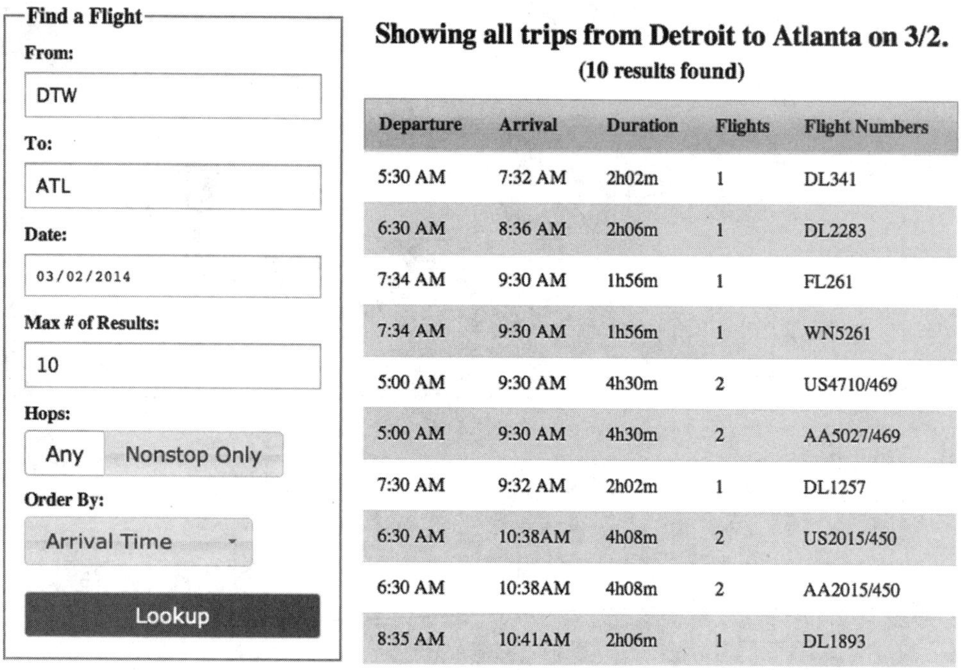

Find a Flight

From:

```
DTW
```

To:

```
ATL
```

Date:

```
03/02/2014
```

Max # of Results:

```
10
```

Hops:

| Any | Nonstop Only |

Order By:

```
Arrival Time        ▾
```

| Lookup |

Showing all trips from Detroit to Atlanta on 3/2.

(10 results found)

Departure	Arrival	Duration	Flights	Flight Numbers
5:30 AM	7:32 AM	2h02m	1	DL341
6:30 AM	8:36 AM	2h06m	1	DL2283
7:34 AM	9:30 AM	1h56m	1	FL261
7:34 AM	9:30 AM	1h56m	1	WN5261
5:00 AM	9:30 AM	4h30m	2	US4710/469
5:00 AM	9:30 AM	4h30m	2	AA5027/469
7:30 AM	9:32 AM	2h02m	1	DL1257
6:30 AM	10:38AM	4h08m	2	US2015/450
6:30 AM	10:38AM	4h08m	2	AA2015/450
8:35 AM	10:41AM	2h06m	1	DL1893

Figure 11.1   A flight-tracking application built using tools you've learned about throughout this book

NOTE   A functional version of the application is available at http://jsfiddle.net/ tj_vantoll/ujwWL/. Please note that, because jsFiddle examples can't use multiple files, there are small differences between the code shown on jsFiddle and the code shown in the book. For example, the jsFiddle code doesn't use AMD.

Let's get started.

11.1   Structuring your application

Before you can start coding, you need to get your directory structure in place. For consistency, you'll use a base structure that's identical to the examples you used in chapter 10:

```
├── css
│   ├── app.css
│   └── jquery-ui
│       ├── accordion.css
│       └── ...
├── index.html
└── js
    ├── app.js
    ├── build.js
    ├── jquery-ui
    │   ├── accordion.js
    │   └── ...
    ├── jquery.js
    └── require.js
```

As a reminder, app.css contains your application's CSS, app.js contains your application's JS, and build.js contains your application's RequireJS build configuration. You'll add more files to the project throughout the chapter, but for each we'll discuss what the file is and where it goes in this structure.

Your app's index.html file will start with the following boilerplate:

```html
<!doctype html>
<html lang="en">
<head>
    <meta charset="utf-8">
    <meta name="viewport" content="width=device-width, initial-scale=1">
    <title>Find a Flight!</title>
    <link href="css/app.css" rel="stylesheet">
</head>
<body>

<form>
    <fieldset>
        <legend>Find a Flight</legend>
        <!-- The form fields -->
    </fieldset>
</form>

<div id="flights-container"></div>

<script src="js/require.js" data-main="js/app"></script>

</body>
</html>
```

Shows the list of matched flights in this container

> **NOTE** The main two components of this page are `<form>` to collect search input from the user and `<div>` to show the results. We'll look at what to put in these two containers throughout this chapter.

At a high level, this application does three things: collects data from the user, contacts a third-party API to find flights that match the provided data, and displays the matches on the screen. You'll tackle these three sequentially in the next three sections, starting with how to gather data from the user.

11.2 Collecting user input

Before talking about what data you need, we have to discuss the API you'll use to find flights. The means of contacting a third-party API is always API-specific, and you have to start with the API provider's documentation. For your example, the folks at Mashape (https://www.mashape.com/) and FlightLookup (http://www.flightlookup.com/) have provided us access to their flight-lookup API. If you look at the documentation for their API at https://www.mashape.com/flightlookup/flight-schedules-one-day-rest-method#!documentation you'll see the following code at the top:

```
curl --include --request GET 'https://flightlookup-timetable-
rest.p.mashape.com/TimeTable/BOS/LAX/12/31/2012/?
    &Hops=NONSTOP&Count=10&SortOrder=0' \
  --header "X-Mashape-Authorization: ********************"
```

This may look like a mess, but it's fairly straightforward. It uses the curl command-line utility to perform an HTTP GET request to the given URL. It includes a custom X-Mashape-Authorization HTTP header that contains the API key Mashape needs to know that you have permission to use the API (which is obfuscated with asterisks here). Because you won't be using curl, don't worry about the specific syntax; instead, look at how the data you collect fits into the request you need to send. You need to format a URL as follows: https://…mashape.com/TimeTable/from/to/date/

Then, add a query string that contains the number of hops, a count, and a sort order. Your task is to collect the data you need to build this URL—which means you have to ask users for the following six pieces of information:

- *From*—Your departure airport
- *To*—Your arrival or destination airport
- *Date*—When do you plan to leave?
- *Number of results*—How many flights do you want to see at a time?
- *Hops*—Do you want a nonstop flight, or are you OK with making connections?
- *Order By*—How do you want the returned flights sorted?

The last two are going to be the easiest, so you'll code them first, using the following HTML for the *Hops* and *Order By* questions:

```
<div>
    <label>Hops:</label>
    <div id="hops">
        <label for="hops-any">Any</label>
        <input type="radio" name="hops" id="hops-any" value="" checked>
        <label for="hops-nonstop">Nonstop Only</label>
        <input type="radio" name="hops" id="hops-nonstop" value="NONSTOP">
    </div>
</div>
<div>
    <label for="order-by">Order By:</label>
    <select id="order-by">
        <option value="0">Arrival Time</option>
        <option value="1">Departure Time</option>
        <option value="2">Duration</option>
    </select>
</div>
```

Next, you turn these elements into jQuery UI widgets to make them themeable. The following code shows the initial version of your app.js. It converts the *Hops* and *Order By* form elements into buttonset and selectmenu widgets:

```
require([ "jquery", jquery-ui/button", "jquery-ui/selectmenu" ],
    function( $, button, selectmenu ) {
        var hops = $( "#hops" ).buttonset(),
            orderBy = $( "#order-by" ).selectmenu();
    }
);
```

You store off references to the two elements because you'll use them later when you connect to the API. For these widgets the code is straightforward because the default behavior does everything you need. The next three fields—*To, From,* and *Date*—require a bit more work; we'll devote a section to implementing each.

11.2.1 *Building an airport code autocomplete*

Per your FlightLookup API, the *To* and *From* fields need to be three-letter International Air Transport Association (IATA) airport codes. The IATA code is a unique identifier assigned to each airport around the world. Usually these codes are related to their city's name (ATL is the IATA code for Atlanta's airport), but not always (IAD is the IATA code for Dulles airport near Washington, DC). As a result, even seasoned travelers may not know the appropriate code to use, especially for new destinations.

Because you don't want to rely on users knowing the appropriate codes, you'll use an autocomplete that lets the user type the airport's code (ATL) *or* the destination's name (Atlanta). Recall from chapter 3 that the autocomplete widget has a built-in mechanism to associate the labels the user needs to type with an underlying code. This mechanism is perfectly suited for this airport-code use case.

In chapter 3 we talked about options to connect an autocomplete to a server-side back end. In this chapter we'll mix it up a bit and show a way of driving an autocomplete exclusively from the client.

> **NOTE** I retrieved the airport data from http://www.airportcodes.org/ and formatted it in a JSON file for use in this example.

You'll place a JSON file containing your data in your project's directory structure as follows

```
├── css
│   └── ...
├── index.html
├── js
│   └── ...
└── json
    └── airports.json
```

and the airports.json file is formatted like this:

```
{
    "airports": [
        { "label": "Aalborg, Denmark (AAL)", "value": "AAL" },
        { "label": "Aalesund, Norway (AES)", "value": "AES" },
        ...
    ]
}
```
⟵ ~3500 other airport entries

The JSON file contains a single `airports` property that contains an array of all airports in the world. Each object in the array contains two properties: a `label` (the text the user sees in the autocomplete menu) and a `value` (the text that ends up in the `<input>` after the user selects an option). Notice that in this case, you include the `value` in each

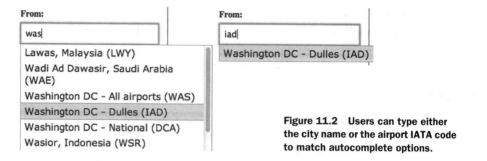

Figure 11.2   Users can type either the city name or the airport IATA code to match autocomplete options.

option's `label`. Users who know the airport codes can type them, and users who don't know the codes can type city names. This behavior is shown in figure 11.2.

Now that you have that data in place, you have to add the two airport fields to your form. You do that by adding the following HTML to your index.html

```
<div>
    <label for="from-airport">From:</label>
    <input id="from-airport" autocorrect="off">
</div>
<div>
    <label for="to-airport">To:</label>
    <input id="to-airport" autocorrect="off">
</div>
```

and the following to your app.js:

```
require([ ..., "jquery-ui/autocomplete" ], function( ..., autocomplete ) {
    var fromAirport = $( "#from-airport" ),
        toAirport = $( "#to-airport" );

    $.getJSON( "json/airports.json" ).then(function( data ) {
        fromAirport.add( toAirport ).autocomplete({
            source: data.airports,
            minLength: 2
        });
    });
});
```

Loads the JSON ❶

Converts both `<input>` elements to autocomplete widgets ❷

Ties the autocompletes to the airport data ❸

Shows results after two characters are typed ❹

> **TIP** You first saw this in chapter 3, but as a reminder, setting the autocorrect attribute to "off" prevents the browser/OS—most notably iOS and Android—from automatically correcting the user's input. This attribute is a good idea to add to any autocomplete field—as well as username fields, password fields, and email address fields.

You load the JSON file using the jQuery Core getJSON() method ❶. When it finishes, you convert the *To* and *From* `<input>` elements to autocomplete widgets ❷ using the airport data from your JSON file ❸ (recall that the JSON file was an object with a single airports property). Finally, because there are over 3000 airports, and you filter on the client, you set the minLength to 2 ❹. This forces the user to type two characters before seeing the results, which limits the number of potential matches to hundreds rather than thousands.

> **NOTE** Older browsers such as Internet Explorer <= 8 and Android < 3 have considerably slower JavaScript speeds than modern browsers. If you support these browsers, consider setting the `minLength` to 3 to avoid a sluggish experience.

With that you have functioning autocompletes for both your *To* and *From* fields. But there's one final question we have to ask before moving on: is building an autocomplete only on the client side a good idea?

Like most software development questions, the answer depends on the situation. In this case, the big advantage with being client-side only is that you don't have to set up a server to host and filter this data. This gives you more flexibility in how this application is used; it makes it possible for me to host this example on jsFiddle without setting up an external server. Because of the ease of use and flexibility of storing all data on the client, it's a realistic option for small- to medium-sized datasets, but is a bit too heavy for large datasets.

Your airport JSON file is 52 K after gzip compression. The file is loaded asynchronously, but that can still be a bit heavy for mobile devices; although this example could be more efficiently written to perform the filtering on a server-side back end, the flexibility of running only on the client makes it ideal for this example—as the current performance isn't bad. For a discussion of how you can connect an autocomplete widget to a server-side back end, refer to chapter 3.

Autocompletes and scrolling long lists of options

By default, the autocomplete widget doesn't display a scroll bar when displaying a long list of options, but it's easy to add one. Your example uses the following CSS to accomplish this:

```
.ui-autocomplete {
    max-height: 200px;
    overflow-x: hidden;
    overflow-y: auto;
}
```

Here, an `overflow-y` of `auto` tells the browser to add a vertical scroll whenever the height of the menu exceeds its `max-height`—which you set at 200 pixels. Setting `overflow-y` to `hidden` prevents the browser from creating a horizontal scroll bar.

11.2.2 Polyfilling HTML5 inputs with jQuery UI

The last fields to add to your form are a datepicker to pick a destination date and a number picker to choose the number of results to use. You may recall from chapter 3 that you have a choice here. Although the jQuery UI widgets offer functionality and extensibility, the HTML5 native controls—in this case, `<input type="date">` and

`<input type="number">`—are preferable for simple usage scenarios—mostly because mobile devices can provide an optimized keyboard for data entry. For your example, a simple usage scenario is exactly what you have. You don't need your date or number pickers to do anything special; you just need a date and a number.

But keep in mind that only some browsers support the new HTML5 controls, and you want a solution that works everywhere. To accomplish this, you use a technique known as polyfilling, or using native support where it's available, and falling back to a JavaScript-based solution where it's not. To start implementing this, let's add the following HTML to your form

```
<div>
    <label for="date">Date:</label>
    <input id="date">
</div>
<div>
    <label for="results">Max # of Results:</label>
    <input id="results" value="10" min="10" max="100" step="10">
</div>
```

and this JS to convert the two form elements to widgets in your app.js file:

```
require([ ..., "jquery-ui/datepicker", "jquery-ui/spinner" ],
    function( ..., datepicker, spinner ) {
        ...
        var date = $( "#date" ),
            results = $( "#results" );
        date.datepicker();
        results.spinner();
    }
);
```

At this point you have a familiar solution: both `<input>` elements are jQuery UI widgets that look and work the same in all browsers. The next step is to use the widgets only when needed, that is, only when the native controls aren't supported. To do that, first you have to change your HTML to use the new types. You can do that by switching your datepicker `<input>` to a type of "date" and your spinner `<input>` to a type of "number":

```
<input type="date" id="date">
<input type="number" id="results" value="10" min="10" max="100" step="10">
```

Now you have to switch your logic to create widgets only when necessary. You do that by making the following alteration to your app.js file:

```
function isTypeSupported( type ) {
    var input = document.createElement( "input" );
    input.setAttribute( "type", type );
    return input.type === type;
};

var date = $( "#date" ),
    results = $( "#results" );
```

❶ Detects whether the browser natively supports the type

```
if ( !isTypeSupported( "date" ) ) {
    date.datepicker({ dateFormat: "yy-mm-dd" });
}
if ( !isTypeSupported( "number" ) ) {
    results.spinner();
}
```

① Initializes a datepicker widget if necessary

② Initializes a spinner widget if necessary

You define a new function that determines whether native support of a given type is available **①**. In it, you create a new `<input>`, change its `type` attribute to the type passed in, and see if the change took. If it did, you have support; if not, you don't.

NOTE A more thorough discussion of polyfills, including how to use Modernizr to detect native features without having to write them yourself, is in appendix F.

You then use that function to determine whether you should initialize a datepicker widget on your `<input>`. If you do need a datepicker, you set its `dateFormat` to `"yy-mm-dd"`—which is the same format the HTML5 picker uses **②**. This ensures that, when it's time to call your API, your date is in the same format, regardless of whether the user is using the HTML5 control or the datepicker widget. You use the same approach to create a spinner widget only if necessary **③**. The end result of your polyfill approach for the date input is shown in figure 11.3.

With these last two fields added, your form is now complete. But before you call off to your API, you have one last task: validating the user's data.

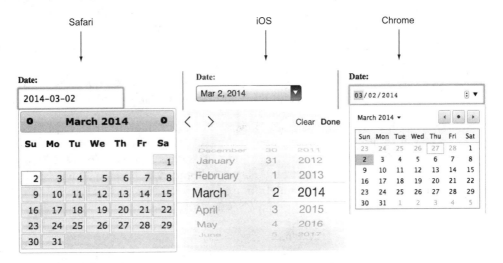

Figure 11.3 Safari doesn't have a native datepicker, so it uses the jQuery UI datepicker. iOS and Chrome have a native datepicker, so they use the native implementation.

11.2.3   *Validating user input with HTML5*

Client-side form validation is a notoriously painful development experience. Building a user-friendly, developer-friendly, and accessible validation mechanism is hard. HTML5 introduced a mechanism, known as constraint validation, designed to make form validation easier. *Constraint validation* refers to a series of HTML attributes, a DOM API, and a series of CSS hooks that the browser natively provides to validate form data.

Although constraint validation does make form validation easier, it's not without its drawbacks. Almost all browsers now support constraint validation, but some don't have it turned on—which sounds weird, but we'll talk about what this means and how to work around it.

We'll start with the HTML attributes of constraint validation, as they're easy to use. To make your first three form elements required, all you need to do is add a `required` attribute to them:

```
<input id="from-airport" required>
<input id="to-airport" required>
<input type="date" id="date" required>
```

When you try to submit this form without these fields filled in, supporting browsers will prevent the submission and provide an error message—you don't need to write any JavaScript! Furthermore, the browser will automatically validate the `type="date"`, `type="number"`, `min`, `max`, and `step` attributes that you already configured. Figure 11.4 shows this behavior in a few browsers.

If all browsers supported HTML form validation, you'd be done; unfortunately, this isn't the case. Here's where things get weird though. As mentioned, all popular browsers (except Internet Explorer <= 9) support the APIs of constraint validation; some WebKit-based browsers—specifically Safari, iOS Safari, and the default Android browser—don't have the APIs turned on. Even though these browsers recognize the new HTML5 attributes, they neither prevent form submission nor show validation bubbles to the user. To work around this odd behavior, you use the following code.

> **WARNING**   This approach works everywhere other than Internet Explorer <= 9; the form itself is still functional in Internet Explorer <= 9, but the validation doesn't work. If you need full support for older versions of Internet Explorer, check out more fully featured validation libraries such as the jQuery validation plugin (http://jqueryvalidation.org/) or Kendo UI's validator (http://demos.telerik.com/kendo-ui/web/validator/index.html).

Figure 11.4   From left to right: required field validation in Firefox, date validation in Chrome, and number validation in Internet Explorer

```
function validateForm() {
    var invalidFields,
        form = $( "form" );

    form.find( ".ui-state-error-text" )
        .removeClass( "ui-state-error-text" )
    form.find( "[aria-invalid]" ).attr( "aria-invalid", false )
    form.find( ":ui-tooltip" ).tooltip( "destroy" );

    invalidFields = form.find( ":invalid" ).each(function() {
        form.find( "label[for=" + this.id + "]" )
            .addClass( "ui-state-error-text" )
        $( this ).attr( "aria-invalid", true )
            .attr( "title", this.validationMessage )
            .tooltip({ tooltipClass: "ui-state-error" });
    }).first().focus();

    return invalidFields.length === 0;
};

$( "form" ).on( "submit", function( event ) {
    event.preventDefault();
    if ( validateForm() ) {
        // Call the API
    }
});
```

① Undoes the effects of previous invocations

② Loops over each invalid field

③ Adds a class name to the field's label

④ Sets the aria-invalid attribute

⑤ Initializes a tooltip widget on the element

⑥ Focuses the first invalid field

⑦ Listens for submit events

⑧ Only calls the API when the data is valid

This approach revolves around listening for submit events on the <form> **⑦**. On browsers with constraint validation implemented and enabled, you won't get a submit event until the user provides valid data. For these browsers, all this code is unnecessary and does nothing. But in browsers with constraint validation disabled, you use the validateForm() **⑧** function to highlight the appropriate fields and determine whether the data is valid. (You don't want to call the flight-lookup API with invalid data if you can avoid it.)

The validateForm() function is where things get fun. First, you reset the form to its initial state **①**—removing changes that the subsequent code in the function makes.

Next, you find all invalid fields in the form using the :invalid pseudo-class **②**. This is a pseudo-class the browser provides that matches all fields that are invalid per their constraints, such as the required and type attributes. This is one of those APIs that the WebKit family of browsers supports, even though they have constraint validation turned off.

For each invalid field, you do a few things. First, you add a ui-state-error-text class name to the invalid field's <label> element **③**. Then, you set the field's aria-invalid attribute to true **④**. This informs assistive devices such as screen readers that the field contains invalid data.

You have to tell the user what the problem with the field is. The browser has built that message for you and stored it the invalid element's validationMessage property. You take this message, set it as the element's title attribute, and convert it to a tooltip widget. The user sees a tooltip when hovering over the field and when it has focus **⑤**. The tooltip widget also ensures that screen readers read the validation message as well. To match the native validation behavior, you move focus to the first invalid element in the form ❻.

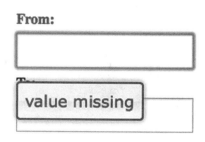

Figure 11.5 shows how your new validation mechanism looks in Safari.

TIP If you want to learn more about HTML5 form validation, including how to customize the validation messages, I have a more thorough discussion at http://www.html5rocks.com/en/tutorials/forms/constraintvalidation/.

Figure 11.5   The UI shown after the user attempts to submit the form without providing a required field in Safari on OS X

With this you have a form that collects the data that you need and validates that it's correct. The validation isn't 100% comprehensive—you don't ensure the user picks a valid airport—but you've protected against the most common mistakes users make, and built a feedback mechanism to inform them of the errors that they made.

Writing accessible form validation

Writing validation in an accessible manner can be tricky, but by making sure you follow a few best practices, you can ensure your forms are usable for everyone. Here's a list of the most important things to do:

- *Manage the* `aria-invalid` *attribute*—When a form element with invalid data has focus, screen-reader users need to know when there's a problem. You can do this by setting the element's `aria-invalid` attribute to `"true"` or `"false"` based whether its data is valid—`<input aria-invalid="true">` or `<input aria-invalid="false">`.
- *Ensure screen readers can read error messages*—Screen reader users not only need to know that fields are invalid, they also need to know why. Your previous example used a tooltip widget to accomplish this. Under the hood, the tooltip widget added an `aria-described-by` attribute to associate itself with the `<input>`, and to ensure its content is read by screen readers when the `<input>` receives focus. This is a little more in depth than most forms need, and a simpler solution is to set an `aria-label` attribute containing the error message, such as `<input aria-invalid="true" aria-label="Please enter a positive number">`. Make sure you remove the `aria-label` when the field becomes valid.
- *Don't rely on color to designate invalid fields*—Accessibility isn't only about screen readers, and in the case of form validation, you also have to be considerate of color-blind users. No matter how bright a red you add to your form, some users won't see it. Your previous example made the validation messages visually stand out with a tooltip widget. Other common techniques are error icons and drawing boxes around invalid fields.

Now that you have a form that collects the data you need, let's put it to use.

11.3 Connecting to a RESTful API

REST refers to Representational State Transfer, which Wikipedia defines as a "software architectural style consisting of a coordinated set of architectural constraints applied to components, connectors, and data elements." In the context of web services, RESTful APIs structure their URLs in a predefined manner and handle the core HTTP methods—GET, PUT, POST, DELETE, and so forth—appropriately. Let's see how this works in practice by connecting to your flight-lookup service.

> **NOTE** A more detailed discussion of what makes an API RESTful is available at http://en.wikipedia.org/wiki/Representational_state_transfer#Applied_to _web_services.

11.3.1 Looking up flights with $.ajax()

Although building RESTful APIs can be a complex task, connecting to them from the client side is relatively easy—especially in the case of your flight-lookup API, because it uses a single HTTP GET to retrieve data. You can look back to the API's documentation at https://www.mashape.com/flightlookup/flight-schedules-one-day-rest-method#!documentation, but the main thing you're interested in is the URL, such as the one we discussed earlier: https://flightlookup-timetable-rest.p.mashape.com/TimeTable/BOS/ LAX/12/31/2012/? &Hops=NONSTOP&Count=10&SortOrder=0.

Your job is to build this URL with user-provided data rather than hardcoded data, and to display the results on the screen. You'll start with the following code, which uses the jQuery Core $.ajax() method to connect to the flight-lookup API.

> **NOTE** Recall from earlier examples that the date, fromAirport, toAirport, hops, results, and orderBy variables correspond to jQuery objects containing the input elements of the form.

Sets the API key in a custom header ❶

```
var selectedDate = $.datepicker.parseDate( "yy-mm-dd", date.val() );
$.ajax({
    headers: { "X-Mashape-Authorization": "********************" },   ⟵
    url: "https://flightlookup-timetable-rest.p.mashape.com/TimeTable/" +
        fromAirport.val() + "/" +
        toAirport.val() + "/" +
        $.datepicker.formatDate( "mm/dd/yy", selectedDate ) + "/",   ⟵
    data: {
        Hops: hops.find( ":checked" ).val(),
        Count: results.val(),
        SortOrder: orderBy.val()
    }
});
```

Adds the two airport codes to the URL ❷

Adds the destination date to the URL ❸

Adds the query string ❹

jQuery's ajax() method lets you specify custom headers by providing a headers option. You use that to add your custom X-Mashape-Authorization header so Mashape knows it's you ❶. Next, you need to add the two airport codes to the URL; you can do this by appending them from the values of their respective <input> elements ❷.

After this comes the date, and here you have a little work to do. Remember that you specified a dateFormat of "yy-mm-dd" for consistency with the HTML5 date <input>, but your API needs the date in "mm/dd/yy" format. To convert the date from one format to another, you use a combination of datepicker's parseDate() and formatDate() utility functions. You use parseDate() to get a Date object representing the date that the user selected, then you output that date in "mm/dd/yy" by passing the Date object to the formatDate() method ❸.

The last part of the URL to add is the query string, and you can add that using the ajax() method's data property ❹. Internally, jQuery will URL-encode these values and turn it into a valid query string automatically.

And that's it. You don't have to tell $.ajax() that you need to make a GET request because that's the default. If you invoke this code, you'll see that it indeed performs a GET request and returns XML containing the results of the query, such as the following:

```
<?xml version="1.0" encoding="UTF-8"?>
<results>
    <query status="0" message="success" RouteCount="120" ... />
    <route ActualFrom='DTW' ActualTo='ATL'>
        <segment From.1='Detroit' From.2='DTW' To='ATL'
          To.1='Atlanta' To.2='ATL' />
    </route>
    <route>...</route>
</results>
```

The XML returns a lot of information, but I'm only showing a small segment here so you can get an idea of the structure. The core of what you're interested in are the attributes of the <route> tags nested in . Each <route> additionally has a for each flight that makes up the route, but to keep this example lean, we'll focus on the <route> elements for now. But how do you get the data you need from that XML?

11.3.2 *Parsing XML with jQuery*

XML parsing can seem like a scary task, but jQuery Core contains a number of methods that make traversing complex XML structures easy. Let's look at how you can use them to get the data you need.

We'll start by moving your AJAX call into its own method and adding a success callback:

```
function lookupFlights() {
    return $.ajax({ ... });
};

lookupFlights.then(function( data ) {
    ...
});
```

At this point, `data` is an XML string with the full results from the API call. To traverse the XML, you select the string using jQuery and use the `find()` method to select child tags. Here's the code you use to pull the information you need out of the XML:

```
var flights = []
$( data ).find( "route" ).each(function() {
    var route = $( this ),
        flight = {
            from: route.attr( "ActualFrom.1" ),
            to: route.attr( "ActualTo.1" ),
            departureDate: route.attr( "DepartureDate.3" ),
            departureTime: route.attr( "DepartureTime.1" ),
            arrivalDate: route.attr( "ArrivalDate.3" ),
            arrivalTime: route.attr( "ArrivalTime.1" ),
            duration: route.attr( "Duration" ),
            flights: route.attr( "FlightCount" ),
            flightNumbers: route.attr( "FlightNumbers" )
        };
    flights.push( flight );
});
```

Finds each `<route>` and loops through them ❶

❷ Selects the `<route>` with jQuery

❸ Picks individual attributes out of the XML tag

Adds the object to ❹ the array of routes

You select the XML string with jQuery, call its `find()` method to select all `<route>` tags, and use `each()` to loop over them ❶. Inside the loop, the context (`this`) is set to the `<route>` as a string. You pull information from the `<route>`, convert it to a jQuery object, and store it in the `route` variable ❷. Then, you use jQuery's `attr()` method to pluck individual attributes from the `<route>` tag and store all of them in the `flight` object ❸. Finally, you add that object to an array of flights ❹. You do this so that, after this code runs, instead of dealing with XML strings, you have an array of JavaScript objects with the data you need. The following is a sample version of the `flights` array with two routes:

```
[
  {"from":"Detroit","to":"Atlanta","departureDate":"2/26",
   "departureTime":"6:30 AM","arrivalDate":"2/26",
   "arrivalTime":"8:45 AM","duration":"2h15m","flights":"1",
   "flightNumbers":"DL2283"},
  {"from":"Detroit","to":"Atlanta","departureDate":"2/26",
   "departureTime":"7:34 AM","arrivalDate":"2/26",
   "arrivalTime":"9:30 AM","duration":"1h56m","flights":"1",
   "flightNumbers":"FL261"}
]
```

Now that you have the data you need, let's review where you stand. You built a form, connected it to your flight-lookup API, and parsed the data you needed into a JavaScript array. Now that you have the data ready to go, you need to build something with it.

11.4   *Displaying the results on the screen*

You can display flight data in countless ways, but as the data is tabular, it lends itself to an HTML <table>, so we'll use one for this example. You can also build <table> elements in JavaScript in countless ways, but the most maintenance-friendly option is to use a JavaScript templating engine to format your data into HTML. The JavaScript templating spectrum has several libraries available, but you'll use Underscore in this example because it's one of the more popular templating solutions; it's also simple to use.

> **TIP**   If you want to learn more about the basics of JavaScript templating, check out http://coding.smashingmagazine.com/2012/12/05/client-side-templating/. If you want to see what templating engines are out there and compare them, there's a good tool available at http://garann.github.io/template-chooser/.

The simplest way of using a JavaScript templating engine like Underscore is to place a <script> tag in your HTML with the template you want to use. The following code shows the <script> tag that you'll include in your index.html file:

```
                                    Tells the browser this is  ➊
                                    HTML, not JavaScript
                                                          ➋  Shows a nice message
<script type="text/html" id="flights-template">              if no flights are found
<% if ( flights.length === 0 ) { %>
    <p>There were no flights found that matched your selections.</p>
<% } else { %>
    <table id="flights">                                Outputs a heading  ➌
        <caption>                                       about the trips found
            Showing all trips from <%- flights[ 0 ].from %> to
            <%- flights[ 0 ].to %> on <%- flights[ 0 ].departureDate %>.
            <span>(<%- flights.length %> result
                <%- flights.length === 1 ? "" : "s" %> found)</span>
        </caption>
        <thead class="ui-widget-header">
            <th>Departure</th>
            <th>Arrival</th>
            <th>Duration</th>
            <th>Flights</th>
            <th>Flight Numbers</th>
        </thead>
        <tbody>
            <% _.each( flights, function( flight ) { %>
                <tr>
                    <td><%- flight.departureTime %></td>
                    <td><%- flight.arrivalTime %></td>
                    <td><%- flight.duration %></td>
                    <td><%- flight.flights %></td>
                    <td><%- flight.flightNumbers %></td>
                </tr>
            <% }) %>
        </tbody>
    </table>
<% } %>
</script>
```

If you haven't used JavaScript templating before, the initial `<script>` tag ❶ may seem a little odd. To tell the browser that this is an HTML template, and not JavaScript code, you have to set the `<script>` element's `type` attribute to something other than `text/javascript` (the default). By convention, you use `text/html` here.

The template itself is mostly straight HTML with a few special Underscore delimiters mixed in to add logic and to output your flight data. The first delimiter you use is `<% ... %>`, which is Underscore's way of letting you execute JavaScript code in the template. You use it to perform an `if` check that outputs a message if the `flights` array is empty ❷.

The other delimiter you use is `<%- ... %>`, which is Underscore's means of letting you output JavaScript values. You use it to output a heading for your table of flights ❸, and then to output the flight data itself (one flight per row).

Now that you have this template in place, you have to use it, and you add the following code to your `app.js` to do that.

NOTE Remember that the `flights` variable in your app.js is an array of flight data that you aggregated in the previous section. Also, remember your index.html has a `<div id="flights-container"></div>` element that's referenced in the following code.

Passes the flight ❷
data to the
template

```
var html = _.template(
    $( "#flights-template" ).html(),
    { flights: flights });
$( "#flights-container" ).html( html );
```

❶ **Retrieves the contents**
of your template

Fills your results
`<div>` with the
❸ **templated markup**

Underscore's `_.template()` function takes two arguments: a template string and data. Your template string is the contents of the `<script>` tag you defined earlier; you get a reference to the `<script id="flights-template">` element and use the jQuery Core `html()` method to grab its contents ❶. For the second data argument, you create an object with a `flights` property that contains the array of flight information you built earlier ❷.

Underscore then applies the data to the template, and you end up with an HTML string with a `<table>` full of flights (or a `<p>` if the flights array is empty). You set the HTML of your flights container `<div>` to this template markup ❸.

TIP If you don't like the delimiters Underscore uses—for example, `<% %>` and `<%- %>`—you can customize them by setting `_.templateSettings`. For more information, see http://underscorejs.org/#template.

This displays flight results in a `<table>` on the screen, but this implementation isn't ideal. Storing HTML templates in a `<script>` tag is odd, and because this implementation relies on that `<script>` tag being in the HTML, you can't share this template across multiple pages or multiple applications. Let's look at one technique to clean up your templating logic.

11.4.1 *Storing and resolving templates with RequireJS*

Up to this point you've used RequireJS only to resolve JavaScript dependencies, and that's how it's used the vast majority of the time. But RequireJS can load additional file types—such as CSS files, JSON files, and more—through plugins. Perhaps the most common plugin is the RequireJS text plugin, which lets you load an arbitrary text resource using the same `require()` and `define()` methods you know. The text plugin is also commonly used to manage HTML template dependencies—which is exactly what you need here.

You start by adding a few new files to your application:

```
├── index.html
├── js
│   ├── text.js
│   └── ...
└── template
    └── flight-list.html
```

The text.js file is the text plugin, which you can download from https://github.com/requirejs/text. The flight-list.html file is your flight HTML template minus the outer `<script>` tag, as shown here:

```
<% if ( flights.length === 0 ) { %>
    <p>There were no flights found that matched your selections.</p>
<% } else { %>
    <table id="flights">
        . . .
    </table>
<% } %>
```

To use the text plugin, you only need to know one rule: when loading text dependencies, you must prefix them with `"text!"`. You'll add the following to app.js to load the text plugin and your template:

```
require([ ..., "text", "text!../template/flight-list.html" ],
    function( ..., text, flightListTemplate ) {
        . . . .
    }
);
```

The `"text!"` prefix is needed so RequireJS knows that it doesn't need to interpret the file it loads as JavaScript code. Here, RequireJS loads the file at `../template/flight-light.html` and assigns its text to the `flightListTemplate` variable.

With this variable in place, you can switch your templating logic to use it rather than relying on a `<script>` tag. Remember that you're currently using the following code:

```
var html = _.template(
    $( "#flights-template" ).html(),
    { flights: flights });
$( "#flights-container" ).html( html );
```

Let's switch this up to use the `flightListTemplate` variable:

```
var html = _.template( flightListTemplate, { flights: flights } );
$( "#flights-container" ).html( html );
```

This approach has a few advantages. For one, you can now remove the `<script>` tag from your index.html as you no longer need it. (It still appears in the jsFiddle example because of the inability to split your example into multiple files in that environment.) Secondly, you can now share this template across multiple pages and even multiple applications. Other pages or applications just have to depend on the template file. Finally, you can build your templates into your optimized build file without any extra work. All this works when you run the RequireJS optimizer. No extra configuration is needed.

With that, you have a fully functional flight lookup with a solid implementation. With the behavior in place, let's look at some things you can do to clean up the user experience.

11.4.2 Showing a processing indicator while data loads

Between contacting your RESTful API, parsing the XML response, and templating the HTML results, the user could potentially have to wait a few seconds between clicking the Lookup button and seeing the results on the screen. Currently, the user receives no feedback that processing is occurring—which can make your application seem unresponsive.

The current implementation is doing nothing to prevent the user from hitting the Lookup button multiple times—which adds load to your API server and slows the experience for all users. It also frustrates users who wonder why their button clicks aren't doing anything. Let's see what you can do to fix this.

First, remember that your function to look up flights from your RESTful API was named `lookupFlights()`. For readability, you break the two pieces of functionality you added in the last two sections—parsing the flight data and templating it—into their own functions as well. This is shown in the following code:

```
function parseFlights( data ) {
    var flights = []
    $( data ).find( "route" ).each(function() {
        var flight = ...
        flights.push( flight );
    });
    return flights;
};

function templateFlights( flights ) {
    var html = _.template( flightListTemplate, { flights: flights } );
    $( "#flights-container" ).html( html );
};
```

With this in place, your code to perform the lookups looks like this:

```
lookupFlights().then(function( data ) {
    var flights = parseFlights( data );
    templateFlights( flights );
});
```

This code reads a bit like an English sentence. Look up the flights, parse the flight data, and template the flights onto the screen. But remember that you want to add code that provides feedback while this processing is happening.

You do so by combining a jQuery UI dialog with a progressbar. You start by adding the following to app.js:

```
require([ ..., "jquery-ui/dialog", "jquery-ui/progressbar" ],        Adds requires
    function( dialog, progressbar ) {                                for dialog and
        var processingDialog = $( "<div>" ).dialog({            ①   progressbar
            autoOpen: false,
            modal: true,
            title: "Looking up flights..."
        }),
        progressbar = $( "<div>" ).progressbar({ value: false });
        processingDialog.append( progressbar );
    }                                              Creates a new <div> and
);                                                 makes it a progressbar  ③
```

Creates a new <div> and makes it a dialog ②

First, you add the dialog and progressbar widgets to the list of module dependencies in app.js ①. In the callback you create two new widgets. The first is a dialog widget you create from a newly created `<div>` ②. You set its `autoOpen` option to `false` as you don't want the dialog to show right away, and you set `modal` to `true` because you don't want the user to interact with the UI while this dialog is open.

Next, you create a progressbar widget from another newly created `<div>` and set its `value` to `false`, so it renders as an indeterminate progressbar (that is, a progressbar that has no definite value) ③. Then, you append the progressbar to the dialog widget you just created. You'll see how this all comes together momentarily. Now if you return to the code that looks up and templates the flights, you can switch it to do the following:

```
processingDialog.dialog( "open" );
lookupFlights().then(function( data ) {
    var flights = parseFlights( data );                    ② Closes the
    templateFlights( flights );                                processing dialog
    processingDialog.dialog( "close" );
});
```

Opens the processing dialog ①

With your widgets in place, all you need to do is open the dialog before your processing begins ① and close it when processing completes ②. Now, instead of wondering what's happening, the user instantly sees the display in figure 11.6 after clicking the Lookup button.

Because the dialog is modal, and the user can't interact with elements while a modal dialog is open, this technique has the added advantage of preventing duplicate form submissions. Not bad for a few extra lines of code.

This solves one of your application's UX problems, but we can make more improvements. If you load this on a mobile device, you'll notice that the results

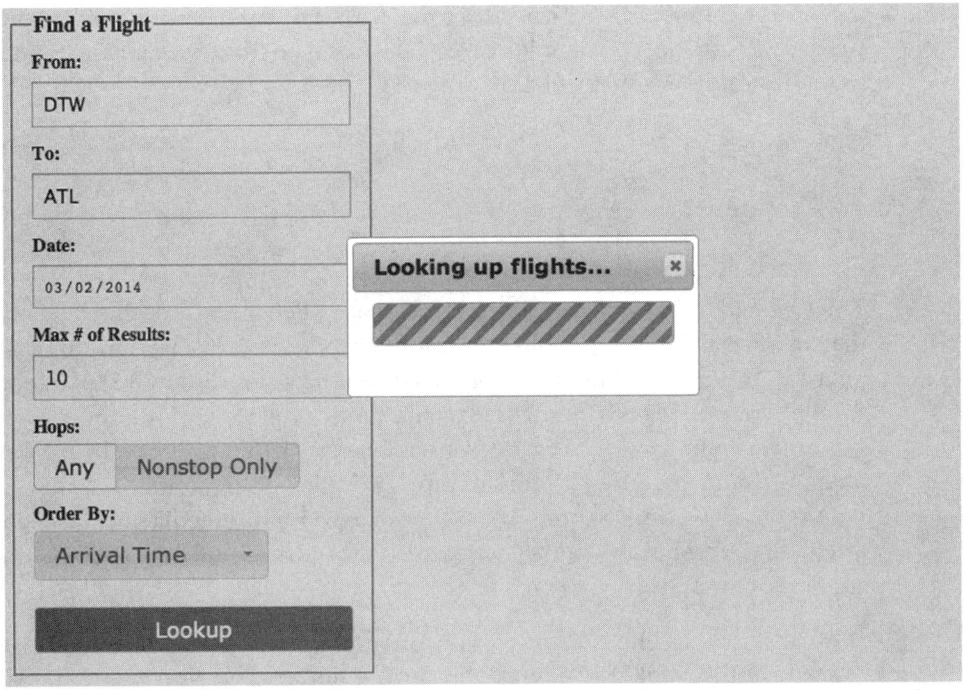

Find a Flight

From:

DTW

To:

ATL

Date:

03/02/2014

Looking up flights... ✕

////////////////

Max # of Results:

10

Hops:

Any   Nonstop Only

Order By:

Arrival Time ▾

Lookup

Figure 11.6   A processing indicator to show while you look up and process flight results

`<table>` doesn't fit very well. Figure 11.7 shows how the `<table>` looks on an iPhone running iOS7 by default.

Although the user can zoom out to see the data, this display isn't ideal for users on smaller screens. Let's see what you can do to make your application look good, regardless of what device it's viewed on.

11.5   Adding a responsive design

The release of the iPhone in 2007, and the explosion of mobile device usage that followed, fundamentally changed the way we develop for the web. No longer do we have the convenience of developing desktop-only applications; instead we must consider a full spectrum of devices—from a 320-pixel-wide iPhone screen to 2000+ pixel-wide high-resolution retina displays. Building applications for these screens can be overwhelming, but the web community has responded with a series of techniques to help, collectively known as responsive web design.

For your flight lookup, you'll use one of the core tenets of responsive web design, media queries, to optimize your

Figure 11.7   Your data goes off the screen of an iPhone.

application for different screen sizes. Personally, I find it easiest to think of media queries as a way of conditionally adding CSS rules based on the device's features—most commonly its width. Consider the following CSS:

```css
body {
    color: black;
}
@media ( max-width: 800px ) {
    body { color: blue; }
}
```

This CSS makes all text black in browsers that are > 800 pixels wide and blue in browsers that are <= 800 pixels wide. I like to read the `max-width: 800px` portion of the media query as, "Is the maximum width of the current browser window 800 pixels or less?" If so, apply the nested CSS rules. These media queries are live, so if you resize your browser window across the 800-pixel barrier, you can see the `color: blue` rule being applied and unapplied. You can play with this at http://jsfiddle.net/tj_vantoll/LHts7/.

Although you can use properties other than width in a media query (height, device orientation, resolution, and so on), this width check is all you need to make your application responsive.

> **NOTE** A comprehensive discussion of responsive web design is out of the scope of this book. For a more thorough guide see *The Responsive Web* (Manning, 2004) by Matthew Carver (http://www.manning.com/carver/).

Before we dig into how to make your app responsive, we have to discuss how your CSS is currently structured. All the CSS for your example is stored in a single app.css file, which starts by bringing in the CSS for jQuery UI:

```css
@import "jquery-ui/all.css";
```

> **NOTE** Notice that you bring in all of the jQuery UI CSS instead of managing the individual files that you need. Because the jQuery UI CSS is substantially smaller than its JS (~14 times smaller), and because you're using more than half of the jQuery UI CSS already, managing individual jQuery UI CSS files has a minimal performance benefit. It also would make the file more difficult to maintain, as every time you need to add or remove a widget to the project, you'd have to add or remove its entry from your app's CSS file.

After that, you configure your layout, which is controlled by the following code:

```css
form {
    float: left;
    min-width: 300px;
    width: 30%;
}
#flights-container {
    float: left;
    width: 70%;
}
```

Because of these rules, the sibling `<form>` and `<div id="flights-container">` elements appear next to each other, with the `<form>` taking up 30% of the width and the `<div>` taking up the other 70%. To keep the `<form>` from getting too small on small screens, you give it a `min-width` of `300px`. Because both of these containers are floating, when the `<form>` reaches its `min-width`, the `<div>` drops below `<form>`. But you're doing nothing to optimize the user experience after the flight container drops.

To improve this, you define two breakpoints, or maximum widths, where you want custom CSS to apply. For your purposes you use breakpoints of 800 and 500 pixels—which correspond to the widths of an average tablet and phone in portrait mode, respectively. Admittedly these numbers are a bit arbitrary, but it doesn't matter. Pick whatever values work best for your application—800 and 500 work well here as they're the points at which the current display isn't ideal. Let's add the following CSS to your example:

```
@media (max-width: 800px) {
    #flights-container, form {            ❶ Makes the form and table
        width: 100%;                        take up the full width
    }
    input, .ui-spinner {
        width: 200px;
    }
    fieldset > div {                      ❷ Shows the form elements
        float: left;                        next to each other
        margin-left: 0.5em;
        height: 70px;
        width: 210px;
    }
}
@media (max-width: 500px) {
    td, th {
        padding: 0.8em 0.1em;
    }
    #flights-container {                  ❸ Reduces the spacing
        padding: 0;                         for small screens
    }
}
```

If you're on a desktop browser, or have one available, you can see the effect of these breakpoints by starting with a large browser window and resizing to a small one. When your browser reaches 800 pixels wide, the first set of rules takes effect. The first thing you do is switch the application's `<form>` and flight list to take up the full width of the screen ❶. (Recall that they previously took up 30% and 70%, respectively.) This switches these two containers from appearing side-by-side to displaying stacked on top of each other.

Because the containers are stacked, you have a little extra room in the `<form>` that you can use; you additionally float each `<div>` containing a form element so that they display next to each other ❷. Figure 11.8 shows the updated tablet display of your application.

This approach works well for tablet-sized screens, but if you keep resizing your screen down, you see that the display breaks down on tiny phone screens. This is where your second breakpoint comes in. For displays 500 pixels and under, you reduce the padding in the flight container and in the flights table ❸.

The final display of your application on three screen sizes is shown in figure 11.8.

NOTE   As I'm not a designer, the display of the flights table on a mobile device could be improved. Tables are a difficult UI element to make look good on small screens. For a good roundup on ways to make tables work in a responsive context, see http://css-tricks.com/responsive-data-table-roundup/.

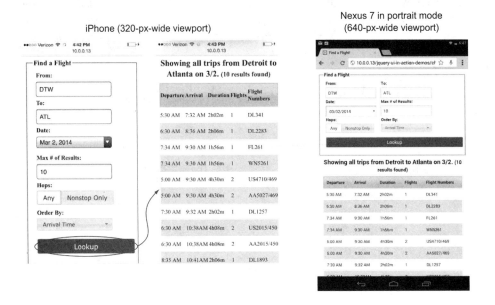

Figure 11.8   The display of your responsive design on three screen sizes: an iPhone 5 running iOS 7 (top left), a Nexus 7 tablet (top right), and a MacBook Pro (bottom)

The key takeaway of the responsive approach is the ability to have CSS rules conditionally apply based on the browser and device capabilities. Here you use the browser's width to rework your application to optimize the experience for users on different devices.

With the UI finalized, your application is now complete. The last thing you need to do is apply the lessons you learned in the last chapter and optimize your application's assets for production.

11.6   *Preparing the application for production*

In chapter 10, we discussed in detail the importance of optimizing front-end assets, but it's worth repeating. We mentioned that Amazon.com famously found that a one-second delay of load times resulted in a loss of $1.5 billion a year. And recall that the single most important thing you can do to improve the load time of your application is to reduce the number of HTTP requests that it performs.

Because you wrote your JavaScript using AMD, there's not much that you have to do here. You start by configuring a js/build.js file that's nearly identical to the one you built in the previous chapter:

```
({
    appDir: "../",
    baseUrl: "js",
    dir: "../built",
    optimizeCss: "standard",
    modules: [
        { name: "app" }
    ]
})
```

Like the one in chapter 10, this copies all your assets to a `built` directory, and then minifies and concatenates each of them. Refer to chapter 10 or http://requirejs.org/docs/optimization.html#options for details on what each individual option does.

To run the build, run the following from the command line in the root of the application:

```
> r.js -o js/build.js
```

The build creates a single concatenated CSS and JavaScript file for you to use in your application. You can go back to your index.html and switch the paths you use to import these files. Currently you're using the following two imports:

```
<link href="css/app.css" rel="stylesheet">
<script src="js/require.js" data-main="js/app"></script>
```

For production you can switch them to point at the `built` directories instead:

```
<link href="built/css/app.css" rel="stylesheet">
<script src="built/js/require.js" data-main="built/js/app"></script>
```

After the build, your app.js and app.css files are 78 K and 5.6 K gzipped, respectively—not bad considering you're using jQuery, several jQuery UI widgets, and Underscore for templating. These numbers don't include require.js, as it's not built into app.js.

require.js adds one additional (6.3 K gzipped) HTTP request, which is perfectly acceptable for the vast majority of applications; however, suppose your flight tracker is intended for mobile users, and a fast load time is paramount to the success of the application. With this prerequisite, you can take one extra step in your build and switch `require.js` out for a more lightweight AMD loader: almond.

11.7 *Getting the optimal performance with almond*

almond describes itself as a replacement AMD loader for RequireJS. It's lightweight, but because of that it doesn't do everything that require.js does. In fact, it's intended for use only *after* an optimized build is performed. But for production code, almond gives you the basic features of AMD loader with an extremely small footprint. Personally, I think it's easier to see how almond works by adding it to your application.

> **WARNING** If you're using certain advanced behaviors of RequireJS that aren't discussed in this book, you may not be able to use almond. For a full list of restrictions, see https://github.com/jrburke/almond#restrictions.

You'll start by adding almond.js from https://github.com/jrburke/almond to your `js` directory:

```
├── index.html
├── js
│   ├── almond.js
│   ├── app.js
│   ├── build.js
│   └── ...
└── ...
```

Then, you make one small alteration to your build.js configuration:

```
({
    appDir: "../",
    baseUrl: "js",
    dir: "../built",
    optimizeCss: "standard",
    modules: [
        {
            name: "app",
            include: [ "almond" ]    ←──①
        }
    ]
})
```

Each module in RequireJS can specify an `include` array, containing any modules that should be prepended to the output file. Because you include almond as an `include` ❶, it will be the first module present in the concatenated and minified built/js/app.js file.

To update your built files, you need to run r.js again from the root of this application:

```
> r.js -o js/build.js
```

Let's go back to your production `<script>` tag included from the last section:

```
<script src="built/js/require.js" data-main="built/js/app"></script>
```

Because an AMD loader (almond) is now is built in to your output file, you can switch this `<script>` tag to point directly at your app.js file:

```
<script src="built/js/app.js"></script>
```

That's all there is to using almond. With this approach you've eliminated a few bytes that the user has to download (remember almond.js is smaller than require.js), but more importantly, you've eliminated an HTTP request from your application. Instead of the browser downloading require.js, and then downloading app.js asynchronously, it can download app.js directly—and you still have all the advantages of using AMD to manage your dependencies.

To summarize, with this approach you can use this `<script>` tag during development

```
<script src="js/require.js" data-main="js/app"></script>
```

and this one in production:

```
<script src="built/js/app.js"></script>
```

Before leaving this topic, we have one more question to consider: how can you automate the switching between the two `<script>` tags? No programmer wants to manually alter them every time you need to develop or deploy to production.

You have a few different options for handling this situation, but my personal favorite is to use your server-side environment to detect whether you're in development or production. Consider the following PHP code:

```
<? if ( strpos( $_SERVER[ "HTTP_HOST" ], "localhost" ) ) { ?>
    <script src="js/require.js" data-main="js/app"></script>
<? } ?>
    <script src="built/js/app.js"></script>
<? } ?>
```

This code checks whether the server is running on the localhost domain. If it is, it outputs the development `<script>` tag; otherwise, it uses the production version. If you're developing in a Java/JSP environment, you could write the same check this way:

```
<% if ( request.getServerName().equals( "localhost" ) ) { %>
    <script src="js/require.js" data-main="js/app"></script>
<% } else { %>
    <script src="built/js/app.js"></script>
<% } %>
```

If you're in an environment where you're running on the client side only, you can use the following code:

```
<script>
    if ( window.location.hostname === "localhost" ) {
        document.write( '<script src="js/require.js" ' +
            'data-main="js/app"><\/script>' );
    } else {
        document.write( '<script src="built/js/app.js"><\/script>' );
    }
</script>
```

This code has the same flow as the previous examples, but there's one quirk in the way you include the <script> tags. Because you're already in a <script> tag, you can't use the character sequence "</script>", as it would prematurely close the outer <script> block; you escape the / character and write <\/script> instead of </script>.

As there are numerous server-side environments, I'm not going to include an exhaustive list of how to check for a domain in each of them, but the idea is the same: perform a check that you know will be true only in development and use it to output the appropriate <script> in each environment. The same technique can be used to include the appropriate CSS file as well:

```
<script>
    if ( window.location.hostname === "localhost" ) {
        document.write( '<link href="css/app.css" rel="stylesheet">' );
    } else {
        document.write( '<link href="built/css/app.css" rel="stylesheet">' );
    }
</script>
```

With all these in place let's summarize the performance of your application. The final version of the app loads with three HTTP requests: index.html (1 K gzipped), app.js (81 K gzipped), and app.css (5.6 K gzipped). These three resources amount to a mere 87.6 K being sent across the network to load the page—which should load quickly even on the worst of mobile networks. This page uses a few additional resources—specifically, the jQuery UI theme images and your airport JSON data—but those files are loaded asynchronously and don't delay the application's initial load.

Admittedly, getting all these optimizations into an existing project can be difficult if not impossible, but every little bit helps. Remember that the single most important thing you can do for mobile performance is reduce the number of HTTP requests your application performs; therefore, that's the best place to start.

11.8 Summary

Using jQuery, jQuery UI, and a few utility libraries, you built an application that contacted a RESTful API to present flight choices to an end user. Along the way, you put some of the widgets you've learned about throughout the book to use—and learned new techniques like polyfilling, templating, and building a responsive UI. You used RequireJS to optimize your front-end assets for production, making your application ideal for use on mobile devices.

Throughout the book, you may have noticed how every complex example you built, including this flight search, ended up involving very little of jQuery UI itself, and lots of other code. This is the goal of jQuery UI: to provide well-encapsulated widgets and utilities that just work, so you can focus on your applications. In the context of this chapter, jQuery UI let you focus on making a compelling flight search, without worrying about how to build UI components like autocompletes and dialogs.

Although you've now seen the core of what jQuery UI has to offer, and even built a small production application with it, we have a few topics left to cover. In the next chapter, we'll look at advanced stuff that you can do with jQuery UI.

Under the hood of jQuery UI

12

This chapter covers

- Advanced positioning of elements
- Tips and tricks for dealing with widget instances
- Working with widget properties
- Building declarative widgets

Although we've covered the core of jQuery UI, we have yet to dig into a series of utilities, methods, and properties intended for more advanced usage of the library. As you explore these utilities, you'll also get a look at how jQuery UI works under the hood. You'll learn things like how jQuery UI manages instances, how it structures prototype chains, and how some of jQuery Mobile works.

Let's start by looking at how the jQuery UI widgets handle positioning.

12.1 Positioning elements with the position utility

Positioning an element relative to another element on the web is surprisingly hard. Besides the brute-force mathematical computations—comparing heights, widths, and offsets—you also have to worry about CSS positioning mechanisms (static, relative, absolute, and fixed), not to mention accounting for the window's scroll offset, or collision detection if the element doesn't fit.

This is where the jQuery UI position utility comes in. The position utility provides an elegant API that makes positioning elements a trivial task. It's what the jQuery UI widgets use to perform all their positioning magic, including centering dialogs, showing tooltips, and placing nested menus in the right spots.

> **TIP**   The autocomplete dialog, menu, and tooltip widgets have a `position` option to configure how the widgets are positioned. We'll look at how those work momentarily.

We'll look at how to do cool things with the position utility, but let's start with an example to get the syntax down—because it can be tricky at first. The following code makes two boxes—one red and one blue:

```
<style>
    div { height: 100px; width: 100px; }
    #red { background: red; }
    #blue { background: blue; }
</style>
<div id="red"></div>
<div id="blue"></div>
```

Suppose you want to position the red box on the right-hand side of the blue box. The following code does that

```
$( "#red" ).position({
    my: "left",
    at: "right",
    of: "#blue"
});
```

What's cool about this API is that it reads like an English sentence. Position *my* (the red box) left side *at* the right side of the element with an `id` *of* `"blue"`. See how easy that was? There was no need to calculate the blue box's offset or either box's dimensions; it just worked. And we're just getting started with what the position utility can do. Using the same red-and-blue-box example, figure 12.1 shows different positioning options.

> **NOTE**   I highly recommend playing with this example to get a feel for how the options for the position utility works. Although I explain each option here, there's no substitute for experimentation with live code. You can play at http://jsfiddle.net/tj_vantoll/LgGQH/.

We'll start with the red box at the bottom of the blue box. This box shows that the `my` and `at` options of the position utility accept two positions, which—to be consistent with CSS conventions—are listed in the order of horizontal, vertical. If you were to read this code, it would read, "Position *my* (the red box) horizontal left, vertical top, *at* the horizontal right, vertical bottom *of* the blue box."

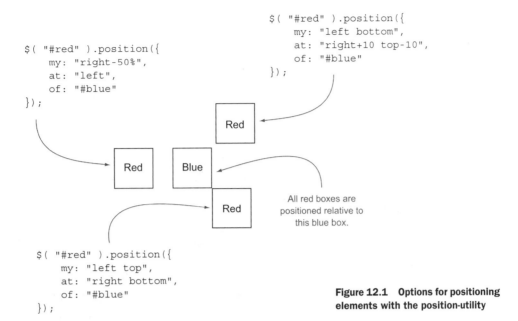

Figure 12.1   Options for positioning elements with the position-utility

If you specify only one position, that position is normalized using the same parsing rules CSS uses (for properties such as `background-position`). For instance, `"left"` equates to `"left center"`, or the horizontal left, vertical center of an element, and `"top"` equates to `"center top"`, or the horizontal center, vertical top of an element.

To show this in action, let's move on to the red box on the left-hand side of the blue box—the one that uses the following positioning:

```
$( "#red" ).position({
    my: "right-50%",
    at: "left",
    of: "#blue"
});
```

Here, because only one horizontal direction is specified, the my and at options are each assumed to be vertically centered. So this code reads, "Position *my* (the red box) horizontal right *at* the horizontal left *of* the blue box." But you'll notice there's one additional twist here: the use of -50%. This is an offset, which each direction of the my and at options optionally accepts as percentages or pixels. (We'll get to pixels momentarily.) The offset is relative to the element being positioned; 50% here refers to half the width of the red box, or 50 pixels. Offsets can be positive or negative. Your use of `"right-50%"` means that the right position of the red box should be adjusted by -50%; that is, the red box should be moved 50 pixels to the left.

Offsets can also be in pixels, which is what you use in your final box (the one on the top).

```
$( "#red" ).position({
    my: "left bottom",
    at: "right+10 top-10",
    of: "#blue"
});
```

This example reads, "Position *my* (the red box) horizontal left, vertical bottom 10 pixels beyond the horizontal right, and 10 pixels above the vertical top *of* the blue box." The position utility assumes that numbers without percentages are pixel values and uses them as an offset.

This gives you a sense of the things you can do with the position utility. If you're still having trouble understanding the syntax, it's worth taking a few minutes to play in jsFiddle and understand how the keywords work.

Although moving red boxes around the screen makes for a nice learning exercise, chances are you aren't building a production application full of blue and red boxes to move around the screen. (But if you are, that's awesome!) Let's look at useful applications of the position utility.

12.1.1 *Building a UI walkthrough with the position utility and dialog widget*

If you create an account on a web service, there's a decent chance you'll be given a tutorial or walkthrough of the UI. These walkthroughs are designed to introduce parts of the interface and what they do. Figure 12.2 shows part of the walkthrough you go through after creating a Gmail account.

With the position utility and dialog widget, building such a walkthrough is relatively easy. For simplicity, let's say your application includes the following three UI elements that you want to introduce to the user:

```
<header>My awesome header</header>
<aside>My awesome sidebar</aside>
<footer>My awesome footer</footer>
```

You'll use the following code to accomplish this.

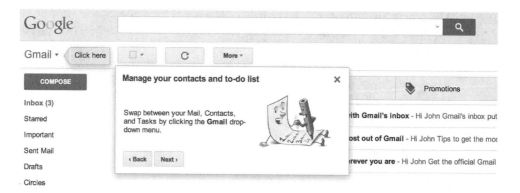

Figure 12.2   A UI walkthrough that Gmail gives new users

NOTE The following example is available at http://jsfiddle.net/tj_vantoll/ 59eZq/. Unless you're on a very large screen, it's easier to see this example in action at http://jsfiddle.net/tj_vantoll/59eZq/show (which runs the example outside of the jsFiddle development interface).

Hides all messages by default

Only shows the message for the current step ❶

```
<style>
    #dialog p { display: none; }
    #dialog[data-step="1"] #step-1 { display: block; }
    #dialog[data-step="2"] #step-2 { display: block; }
    #dialog[data-step="3"] #step-3 { display: block; }
</style>
<div id="dialog" data-step="1" title="Walkthrough">
    <p id="step-1">1) This is the header!</p>
    <p id="step-2">2) This is the sidebar!</p>
    <p id="step-3">3) This is the footer!</p>
</div>
<script>
    var positions = [
        {
            my: "center top",
            at: "center bottom",
            of: "header"
        },
        {
            my: "left center",
            at: "right center",
            of: "aside"
        },
        {
            my: "center bottom",
            at: "center top",
            of: "footer"
        }
    ];

    $( "#dialog" ).dialog({
        modal: true,
        buttons: {
            "Next": function() {
                var step = parseInt( $( this ).attr( "data-step" ), 10 );
                if ( step === 3 ) {
                    $( this ).dialog( "close" );
                } else {
                    $( this )
                        .dialog( "option", "position",
                            positions[ step ] )
                        .attr( "data-step", ++step )
                }
            }
        },
        position: positions[ 0 ]
    });
</script>
```

An array of coordinates for the dialog ❷

Gets the current step ❸

Closes the dialog ❹

Alters the position of the dialog ❺

Increments the step ❻

The core of this example is a single dialog with three instructional `<p>` tags in it, one for each step you want to walk the user through. With a little CSS, you configure the dialog to only show the paragraph that matches the value of the dialog's `data-step` attribute ❶. Because the dialog starts with a `data-step` of `"1"`, the `#dialog[data-step="1"] #step-1 { display: block; }` rule applies and shows the first message.

The rest of the code is responsible for managing the dialog's `position` option and `data-step` attribute. You start by defining a `positions` array containing the three locations you want the dialog to display: under the header, to the left of the aside, and above the footer ❷. When you initialize the dialog widget, you set its `position` option to `position[ 0 ]` so the dialog initially displays under the header. To let the user move through the walkthrough, you add a Next button with the `buttons` option. When it's clicked, you retrieve the current value of the `data-step` attribute ❸. If the attribute is 3, you're at the last step so you close the dialog ❹. If not, you move the dialog to the next position in the array ❺ and then increment the dialog's `data-step` attribute ❻. (Remember that because of your CSS, a new `data-step` value will show a new message that corresponds to the new position.)

The result of this code is a dialog that moves around the screen as the user progresses through the walkthrough. This is shown in figure 12.3.

> **NOTE** Please excuse the horrible "design" of the header, sidebar, and footer elements. The point here is you can easily position the dialog next to *any* element in your interface.

Although you can do plenty of things with positioning dialogs, the widget where custom positioning is most often used is the tooltip widget. We'll look at things you can do with tooltips, but first we have to discuss one last of piece of functionality the position utility provides: collision detection.

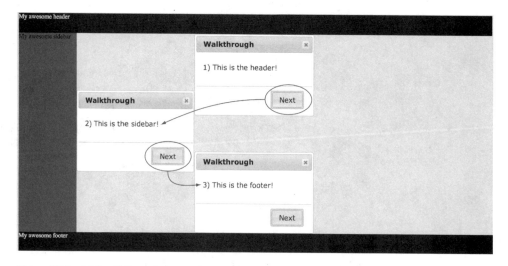

Figure 12.3   A UI walkthrough as a series of dialogs that explains parts of the interface to the user

12.1.2 *Handling collisions elegantly*

A common problem when positioning elements—and especially tooltip elements—is dealing with collisions. Let's say you want to globally show tooltips below elements, and you implement that with the following code:

```
$( document ).tooltip({
    position: {
        my: "center top",
        at: "center bottom+10"
    }
});
```

This shows a tooltip on all elements with a `title` attribute that appears 10 pixels below the element. This works great, except for one problem: what happens if the element is already at the bottom of the screen? With the preceding code you may expect the user to never see the tooltip, but instead, the tooltip displays 10 pixels *above* of the element. Why?

Built in to the position utility is the concept of collision detection. The utility automatically detects that the element it's positioning—in this case a tooltip—is outside the bounds of the window and, if so, attempts to reposition it in the window.

> **TIP** The position utility does collision detection against the window by default, but that can be configured using the `within` option. This is useful when you need to position elements within a scrollable container, and want to make sure they fit.

The position utility has two means of repositioning an element: flipping and fitting. Flipping is the default means of handling collisions, and what it does is straightforward: if the utility detects that the element doesn't fit in the window, it flips it to the opposite side of the element it's being positioned against. That's exactly what happened in the earlier example. Because the tooltip wouldn't fit below the elements on the bottom of the screen, the utility flipped it from the bottom to the top.

If flipping doesn't work, the other mechanism available is fitting, which moves the element in an attempt to get it on the screen. If you tried to display a tooltip and it was off the screen by a few pixels, fitting would move it back in the screen.

All this is configurable using the position utility's `collision` option, which has four values: `"flip"`, `"fit"`, `"flipfit"`, and `"none"`. Understanding these values is one of those situations where a picture is essential. Figure 12.4 shows a few `<input>` elements that have tooltips. The first input shows the default tooltip positioning, whereas the other four show the effect of applying the various `collision` values.

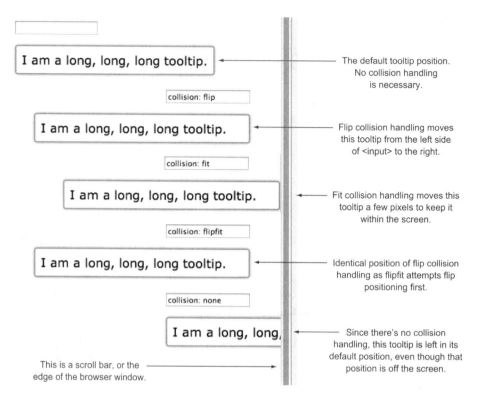

Figure 12.4 Values for the position utility's `collision` option and their effects

The top `<input>` here is the control; it shows where a tooltip appears when it's not near the screen's boundaries (left-aligned with the `<input>`). The next four apply the four available `collision` values:

- `flip`—This collision type flips the element to the opposite side of the element it's being positioned against. The name can be a bit confusing, as the tooltip isn't literally flipping vertically or horizontally on the x- or y-axis; instead, it's moving from one side of the element it's being positioned against to the other. In figure 12.4, because the second `<input>` element's tooltip does fit on the left-hand side of the `<input>`, it's moved to align on the right-hand side.

- `fit`—Rather than flipping, the fit collision type shifts the element in an attempt to keep it on the screen. Notice that the third `<input>` element's tooltip is shifted a few pixels from its default horizontal position (aligned with the left-hand side of the `<input>`).

- `flipfit`—This type is a combination of the previous two. First, the flip logic is applied, then—if the element still isn't within the screen—the fit logic is applied to show as much of the element as possible. In this example, because the flip logic is sufficient to place the tooltip on the screen, its behavior is identical to the flip `<input>`.

■ none—The final collision type tells the position utility to ignore collision detection altogether. The last `<input>` element's tooltip doesn't fit, but because its `collision` is set to `"none"`, it remains off the screen.

TIP You can specify different means of handling horizontal and vertical collisions by passing a pair of strings for the `collision` option. A `collision` of `"flip none"` tells the position utility to use flip collision handling for horizontal collisions, and no collision handling for vertical collisions.

Although these values give you flexibility in how you handle collisions, sometimes this isn't enough. Sometimes you need to know whether the element fits so you can take some custom action. To see what I mean, let's return to a tooltip example from chapter 7.

12.1.3 *Controlling the collision detection*

In chapter 7, you saw how to build tooltips with arrows that pointed at their corresponding element (which was an `<input>`). Also remember that, to ensure that the arrows always displayed on the correct side of the tooltip, you had to turn the position utility's collision detection off.

Although turning collision detection off does keep the arrow pointing at the element appropriately, it also means that the tooltip can potentially display outside of the screen. You know now that you can use the position utility's flip collision mechanism to move the arrow tooltip above or below the `<input>`. But that leaves a problem. You used CSS to draw the arrow, and you need to alter the CSS based on whether the tooltip is above or below the `<input>`. To make this possible, the position utility exposes this information to the `using` property. Before we show this in action, first remember that your example from chapter 7 used the following HTML:

```
<label for="amount">Amount:</label>
<input id="amount" title="Please use xx.xx format.">
```

You'll take this HTML and build an arrow tooltip that can display on either side of its `<input>`.

NOTE The full source of this example is available at http://jsfiddle.net/tj_vantoll/587n9/. Also, the result of this code is shown in figure 12.5. If you're having trouble understanding what this code is trying to accomplish, it may help to look at the picture first.

```
$( "#amount" ).tooltip({                         ❶ Configuration
    position: {                                     for the tooltip's
        my: "bottom",                               initial position
        at: "top-10",
        collision: "flip",
        using: function( position, feedback ) {   ❸ Adds a "top" or
            $( this ).addClass( feedback.vertical )   "bottom" class name
```

Uses flip collision detection ❷

```
            .css( position );
          }
        }
    });
```

◁——— **Performs the**
  ❹ positioning

You start by defaulting the tooltip to display above the `<input>` ❶. You subtract 10 pixels from the top of the tooltip (which moves the tooltip up 10 pixels) to make room for the pointer. Next, you set your `collision` to `"flip"` so the position utility automatically flips the tooltip below the `<input>` when it doesn't fit above ❷.

Next, you specify a `using` option. With a `using` option, the position utility continues to do its collision detection work, but it doesn't alter the position of the element; instead, you're responsible for that, and the `using` function is passed the information that you need to do it.

Specifically, the `using` function is passed two objects, named `position` and `feedback` by convention. The `position` parameter has the coordinates the position utility has calculated for the element as two properties: `top` and `left`. This format—an object with `top` and `left` properties—is designed to be passed directly into the jQuery Core `css()` method to do the positioning—which is exactly what you do here ❹.

The advantage of the `using` function is you can perform logic before the positioning takes place. And this is what the `feedback` argument is for. It's an object that contains a variety of data about the element being positioned and the element it's being positioned against. You can refer to http://api.jqueryui.com/position/ for a full list of the `feedback` argument's properties, but here you have a specific need: you need to know if the tooltip should display above or below the bottom of the `<input>`. This information is available in the `feedback` object's `vertical` property—which is set to `"top"` or `"bottom"` accordingly. You use this property to apply an appropriate CSS class name to the tooltip ❸.

Now that you have a `"top"` or `"bottom"` class name on the tooltip, you can add CSS to move the tooltip's pointer to the appropriate side of the `<input>`:

```
.bottom .ui-tooltip-content::before {
    bottom: -10px;
}
.bottom .ui-tooltip-content::after {
    bottom: -7px;
}
.top .ui-tooltip-content::before {
    top: -10px;
}
.top .ui-tooltip-content::after {
    top: -7px;
}
```

And with this you have a tooltip that not only points at an `<input>`, but also automatically adjusts to keep itself within the screen. This functionality is shown in figure 12.5.

For most of your positioning needs, the `my` and `at` properties are sufficient. When you need to keep elements within the screen at all times, you can configure the `collision` option to suit your needs. And in the case where you need fine-grained control

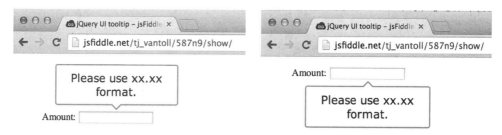

Figure 12.5 **The tooltip displays above the `<input>` by default (left picture), but if you scroll to move the `<input>` to the top of the window, the tooltip no longer fits within the viewport, so the tooltip flips to the bottom (right picture).**

over how the collision detection works, the `using` option gives you advanced control. The great thing about the position utility is that when you need these advanced configuration options, you're still spared the details of the mathematical computations and collision detection algorithms.

Let's move from the position utility to additional jQuery UI internals that can help you improve your own code, starting with a few utilities in jQuery UI Core.

12.2 Using the utility functionality in jQuery UI Core

When we looked at managing dependencies in chapter 10, we saw that almost every single file in jQuery UI depends on core.js, or jQuery UI Core (notable exceptions are the widget factory and the position utility, which are intended for easy use without any jQuery UI dependencies). jQuery UI Core is a collection of utilities that are used by the library internally, but because they're potentially useful outside the internal jQuery UI, the utilities are exposed and documented on the jQuery UI API site.

Let's look at some of the functionality that's available.

12.2.1 Generating unique ids

Sometimes when developing widgets you need elements to have an `id` attribute. Suppose you need to generate an `<input>` and a `<label>`, and you need their `id` and `for` attributes to match.

But generating your own `ids` is no easy task. By definition, `id` attributes must be unique, so you have to make sure you're not conflicting with any other `ids` already present. As a concrete example, recall the tooltips widgets you used to show validation messages in chapter 11. Following is a reduced version of that code:

```
<input name="to" required>
<script>
    $( "input" )
        .attr( "title", "You must provide an airport code." )
        .tooltip();
</script>
```

You used this approach because you wanted to make your form validation accessible, and the tooltip widget does this by associating the tooltip element with the `<input>` using an `aria-describedby` attribute.

NOTE Despite popular belief, screen readers don't read the HTML title attribute. For details, see http://blog.silktide.com/2013/01/i-thought-title-text-improved-accessibility-i-was-wrong/.

When the tooltip widget is active, the rendered markup is something like the following:

```
<input name="to" required aria-describedby="ui-id-1">
<div role="tooltip" class="ui-tooltip ..." id="ui-id-1">
    <div class="ui-tooltip-content">
        You must provide an airport code.
    </div>
</div>
```

The association between the `<input>` element's `aria-describedby` attribute and the tooltip element's `id` tells the screen reader to read the contents of the element with an id of `"ui-id-1"` (when the `<input>` receives focus).

The thing to note here is the `"ui-id-1"` value. It wasn't present in your initial markup, so the tooltip widget had to generate that value (and clean it up when the tooltip is no longer used). Internally, the tooltip widget uses jQuery UI Core's `uniqueId()` and `removeUniqueId()` methods to make this happen. Here's the code the widget uses to create the tooltip element:

```
var tooltip = $( "<div>" )
    .attr( "role", "tooltip" )
    .addClass( "ui-tooltip ui-widget ui-corner-all ui-widget-content " +
        ( this.options.tooltipClass || "" ) )
    .uniqueId();
```

The call to `uniqueId()` at the end is what adds the `"ui-id-1"` id attribute. jQuery UI Core adds the `uniqueId()` method to `$.fn` so it can be used on any jQuery object. For example, `$( "<div>" ).uniqueId()` creates a `<div>` that has a unique `id` attribute. The `uniqueId()` method is also smart enough to not add an `id` attribute if the element already has one. In the following code the `uniqueId()` call does nothing:

```
$( "<div id='foo'>" ).uniqueId();
```

The counterpart to `uniqueId()` is the `removeUniqueId()` method, which removes the id that `uniqueId()` added. The tooltip widget doesn't need `removeUniqueId()`—as the tooltip element is removed from the DOM when a tooltip is destroyed—but some jQuery UI widgets do.

The accordion widget, for example, adds an `aria-controls` attribute that associates its headers with its content panels. And like the `aria-describedby` attribute, the `aria-controls` association requires the headers and content panels to have unique `id` attributes. The accordion widget's `_destroy()` method includes the following code to remove the attributes when the accordion is destroyed (where `this.headers` is a reference to a jQuery object containing all the accordion's headers):

```
// clean up headers
this.headers.removeUniqueId();

// clean up content panels
this.headers.next().removeUniqueId();
```

The `removeUniqueId()` is smart enough to remove only the `id` attributes that the `uniqueId()` method generated; the following leaves the `"foo"` `id` attribute in place:

```
$( "<div id='foo'>" ).removeUniqueId();
```

In general, any time you have a need to generate an `id` attribute to associate elements, the `uniqueId()` and `removeUniqueId()` methods provide an elegant way to do so.

12.2.2 Using key code constants

jQuery UI Core provides a series of key code constants in the `$.ui.keyCode` object. If you want to detect Enter key presses in your code—and don't want to hardcode that the Enter key is equivalent to key code 13—you can use the following code:

```
$( document ).on( "keydown", function( event ) {
    if ( event.keyCode === $.ui.keyCode.ENTER ) {
        alert( "Enter was pressed!" );
    }
});
```

You can view a full list of the key codes jQuery UI provides at http://api.jqueryui.com/jQuery.ui.keyCode/.

The last piece of jQuery UI Core we need to discuss is the handy `:data` pseudo-selector, but to show what it's best used for, we'll include it in the broader context of dealing with widget instances.

What else is in jQuery UI Core?

If you dig into core.js, you'll see that there's far more to jQuery UI Core than ID and key code handling. So what's all that other stuff?

About half of the code in jQuery UI Core is code that manipulates logic in jQuery Core—either to add functionality or work around bugs in older versions. Remember that jQuery UI supports multiple versions of jQuery Core, so a user of jQuery UI 1.11 could be using any version of jQuery Core >= 1.6.

Before jQuery 1.8 you couldn't use the jQuery Core `outerHeight()` and `outerWidth()` functions as setters. jQuery UI needs this functionality, so it adds the functionality for users using jQuery Core < 1.8. Interestingly enough, jQuery UI Core uses the same duck-punching technique we discussed in chapter 9 to change the jQuery Core functionality.

In general, the hope is that in the near future jQuery UI Core will no longer exist as these workarounds become unnecessary. (The `outerHeight()` and `outerWidth()` workarounds will be removed when jQuery UI no longer supports jQuery Core versions < 1.8.) The utility functions—`uniqueId()`, `removeUniqueId()`, `keyCode`, and so on— in jQuery UI Core will be moved into their own files to make the library more modular.

As a final note, jQuery UI Core has some deprecated functions that I won't be discussing to discourage their use in new code. If you're curious, you can learn about these deprecated utilities at the jQuery UI Core documentation at http://api.jqueryui .com/category/ui-core/.

12.3 *Accessing and managing widget instances*

We've talked about widget instances on and off throughout the book, but now let's take an in-depth look at what they are and some of the things you can do with them. We'll start with a review before we get into the trickier stuff.

Every time you instantiate a widget on a DOM element, the widget factory creates an object—the instance—and associates it with the element using $.data(). The key used to store the instance on the element is the widget's full name—that is, the widget's namespace, plus a dash, plus the widget's name. The dialog widget is stored under a key of "ui-dialog" because its namespace is "ui" and its name is "dialog".

You can retrieve the instance a few ways. The first is to use $.data(), as shown in the following code, which assigns the instance of a newly created dialog to a variable (named instance):

```
var myDialog = $( "<div>" ).dialog(),
    instance = myDialog.data( "ui-dialog" );
```

As of jQuery UI 1.11, you can also retrieve the instance using the widget's instance() method. The following code assigns a newly created dialog instance to an instance variable:

```
var myDialog = $( "<div>" ).dialog(),
    instance = myDialog.dialog( "instance" );
```

The instance() method is the preferred means of accessing the instance as it doesn't rely on the jQuery UI internal implementation (storing the instance using $.data()). But regardless of how you access the instance, what might you want to do with it?

Unlike interacting with widgets through their plugins, instance references give you access to a number of things: all the widget's methods and properties, as well as the methods and properties on parent widgets' prototypes (more on additional things you can do with those references momentarily).

Furthermore, some developers prefer the instance-based method calls to plugin-based method calls. Consider the following example that creates a dialog with an OK button that closes it:

```
$( "<div>" ).dialog({
    buttons: {
        OK: function() {
            $( this ).dialog( "close" );
        }
    }
});
```

Some developers find the dialog("close") syntax awkward and prefer the following instanced-based approach:

```
var myDialog = $( "<div>" ).dialog({
    buttons: {
        OK: function() {
            myDialog.close();
```

```
        }
    }
}).dialog( "instance" );
```

You use the `instance()` method to store a reference to the instance in a `myDialog` variable. When the button is clicked, you use the instance reference to invoke the `close()` method with a more familiar JavaScript syntax. It's important to note that neither the instance-based nor plugin-based method invocation syntax is "correct"; it's a matter of personal preference.

Before we leave the topic of instances, there's one more technique we need to discuss.

> **TIP** Earlier you learned that trying to invoke widget methods through the widget's plugin throws an error if that element is not a widget, such as `$( "#not-a-dialog" ).dialog( "open" )`. The `instance()` method is the one exception to this rule. `$( "#not-a-dialog" ).dialog( "instance" )` returns `undefined` rather than throwing an error.

12.3.1 Detecting widget instances with :data()

Besides the syntax conveniences, instances are also the way that jQuery UI detects whether a given element has a widget initialized on it. Say you have the following element on the DOM:

```
<div id="foo"></div>
```

How do you know if the element is a dialog? As it turns out, internally jQuery UI has to ask this type of question a lot. When a dialog's `draggable` option is changed to `false`, the dialog's `_setOption()` method needs to know whether the dialog has a draggable instance on it to know if it's safe to call draggable's `destroy()` method. (Remember that calling widget methods before the widget is initialized—with the exception of `instance()`—throws an error.) As another example, when you drop a draggable on a droppable, the droppable widget needs to search for nested droppable widgets to fire events in the correct order. (It also affects the behavior of the `greedy` option. See http://api.jqueryui.com/droppable/#option-greedy.)

Because of this need, jQuery UI Core extends the jQuery Core selector engine (Sizzle) to add a custom `:data()` pseudo-selector.

It works by selecting elements that have data stored with a key that matches the value given to `:data()`. This is easier to see in an example.

> **TIP** jQuery UI adds the pseudo-selector with Sizzle's `createPseudo()` method. To learn more about Sizzle's APIs, including how to add your own pseudo-selectors, see its documentation at https://github.com/jquery/sizzle/wiki/Sizzle-Documentation.

```
<div id="one"></div>
<div id="two"></div>
<script>
```

**Stores a
string on the
first `<div>`** ➊

```
                    $( "#one" ).data( "foo", "bar" );
                    console.log( $( ":data(foo)" ) );      ⊲──┐  Logs all elements that
                </script>                                     ➋  have data stored with
                                                                 a key of foo
```

You use `$.data()` to store the key/value pair of `"foo"` and `"bar"` on the first `<div>` ➊. Then, you use the `:data()` pseudo-selector to select all elements that have data stored with a key of `"foo"` ➋. Because the first `<div>` has data stored with that key, it's selected and logged.

Because the jQuery UI widgets store their instances using `$.data()`, this same technique can be used to detect widgets. The following selects all dialog widgets:

```
$( ":data(ui-dialog)" );
```

Although finding all widgets can be handy for debugging, the more common scenario is determining whether a given element is a widget, and you can accomplish that by combining the `:data()` pseudo-selector with the jQuery Core `is()` method. Consider the following example:

```
            <div id="dialog"></div>
            <div id="not-dialog"></div>
            <script>
                $( "#dialog" ).dialog();
                $( "#dialog" ).is( ":data(ui-dialog)" );      ⊲── true
    false ──▷ $( "#not-dialog" ).is( ":data(ui-dialog)" );
            </script>
```

The first check returns `true` as the `<div id="dialog"></div>` has a dialog widget initialized on it, and the second check returns `false` as the `<div id="not-dialog"></div>` doesn't.

> **TIP** Because the mechanism of storing widget instances with `$.data()` is built in to the widget factory, the same `:data()` checks work with custom widgets. For example, `$( ":data(tj-todo)" )` finds all elements with your custom todo widget initialized on it.

We've now looked at things you can do with instances. Next, let's look at what the instance gives you access to: prototype objects.

12.4 *Advanced widget prototype methods and properties*

Although we've discussed most of what you can do with widgets built with the widget factory, we've glossed over the details of how the widget's methods are structured internally—such as how the widget factory automatically manages a prototype chain for you.

Having an understanding of a widget's prototype structure is important so you know all the things you can do with widget instances, and is vital for creating custom widgets, especially widgets that extend other widgets. You'll see how to use these methods and properties to streamline widget initialization, make widgets work in `<iframe>` elements, and make a `<div data-role="dialog"></div>` magically turn into a dialog widget.

But before we do that, we have to dig in deep to see how a widget's prototype chain works.

12.4.1 *A widget's prototype chain explained*

As with your instance discussion, let's begin with a quick review of what we've discussed on widget prototype objects. Suppose you create the following widget:

```
$.widget( "tj.custom", {
    _create: function() {}
});
```

Recall that the last argument to `$.widget()` is an object to use as the widget's prototype. You provide an object with a single _create() method. Because you didn't extend an existing widget, the widget factory uses `$.Widget` as a base widget by default. If you do specify a widget, that widget is extended. The following code extends the dialog widget:

```
$.widget( "tj.customDialog", $.ui.dialog, {} );
```

We've discussed all this before, but now let's get into more detail on what's happening behind the scenes. When you create widgets, the widget factory automatically structures the widget's prototype chain such that instances of the widget can access methods and properties on any parent widget's prototype objects. That sentence can be a mouthful, so let's break it down.

First, an explanation of prototype chains in JavaScript. Whenever you use the dot notation in JavaScript (as in `myObject.value`), the JavaScript interpreter looks for the subsequent string (`"value"`, in this case) as a property in the object itself. If it finds `myObject.value` it uses it, but if not, the interpreter then looks for the member (property or method) in the object's prototype object. And if it can't find the member there, it goes to the next prototype object and so on, until the interpreter reaches `Object.prototype`. This lookup chain is what gives the prototype chain its name.

As an example, consider the following:

```
"jQuery UI".trim();
"jQuery UI".hasOwnProperty( "whatever" );
```

Both lines of code invoke methods on `String` objects. On the first line, when the JavaScript interpreter sees `trim()`, it first looks for a `trim()` method on the `String` object's prototype (that is, `String.prototype.trim`). In this case, `String.prototype.trim` exists, so the interpreter invokes it.

On the second line, when the JavaScript interpreter sees `hasOwnProperty()`, it again looks for `String.prototype.hasOwnProperty`, but this time it doesn't find it, so it looks to the next object in the prototype chain: which in this case is `Object.prototype`. `Object.prototype.hasOwnProperty` exists, so the interpreter invokes it.

> **TIP** `Object.prototype.hasOwnProperty` returns whether the current object has the passed property defined. For more details, see https://developer.mozilla.org/en-US/docs/Web/JavaScript/Reference/Global_Objects/Object/hasOwnProperty).

NOTE   For a more thorough explanation of prototype chains in JavaScript, see http://yehudakatz.com/2011/08/12/understanding-prototypes-in-javascript/.

Having a complete understanding of prototype chains isn't necessary as the widget factory automatically builds the chain for you when you create widgets. Say I write the following code:

```
$.widget( "tj.customDialog", $.ui.dialog, {} );
var instance = $.tj.customDialog( {}, "<div>" );
```

This defines the same customDialog widget that inherits from the jQuery UI dialog. Then it creates an instance of the new customDialog and assigns it to an `instance` variable. After this code runs, suppose you want to add a new line that uses the instance:

```
instance.[?]
```

Because of the widget's prototype chain, when you use the dot notation here, the interpreter looks up members in the following order. Note that the order is extremely important as many of these objects contain methods and properties with the same names:

- *The instance object*—The instance object itself has data unique to the element it's instantiated on; it's not shared by other instances of the widget. The instance has an `options` object containing the current state of its options, for example, and an `element` property that refers to the DOM element the instance is associated with.

- `$.tj.customDialog.prototype`—If a member isn't found on the instance, the interpreter checks the customDialog widget's prototype object next. Because your code to create this widget specified an empty prototype object, this object contains only a few properties added by the widget factory (`widgetName`, `namespace`, and so on).

- `$.ui.dialog.prototype`—If a member isn't found on the customDialog's prototype, the interpreter consults its parent widget—in this case, dialog—next. The dialog widget's prototype has all the dialog widget's methods and properties.

- `$.Widget.prototype`—If a member isn't found on dialog's prototype, the interpreter moves on to the base widget prototype. The `$.Widget.prototype` methods and properties are documented at http://api.jqueryui.com/jquery.widget/.

- `Object.prototype`—This is the end of the line for all prototype chains. If the interpreter doesn't find a property here, it returns undefined. If you're invoking a method and the interpreter doesn't find it, the interpreter throws a `TypeError` (because `undefined` is not a function).

Figure 12.6 shows a visual representation of this lookup process.

Having an understanding of a widget's prototype chain is important when building custom widgets. When you extend a widget, you inherit members from parent widgets (and ultimately `$.Widget.prototype`), but you can override them by including a member on new widget's prototype object. Let's look at examples of that.

```
$.widget( "tj.customDialog", $.ui.dialog, {} );
var instance = $.tj.customDialog( {}, "<div>" );
```

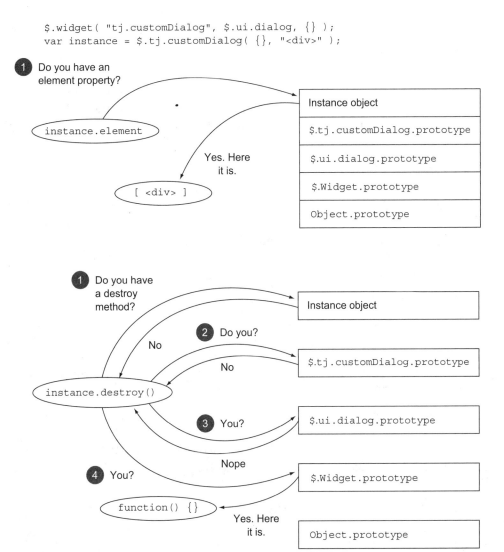

Figure 12.6 **Visualization of the JavaScript interpreter accessing a property or method on an instance. The first example looks for an element property and immediately finds it on the instance object. The second example looks for a destroy() method and has to go through the instance object, the custom widget's prototype, and the dialog widget's prototype, before finding the method on the base widget's prototype.**

12.4.2 *Using a widget's default element to streamline initialization*

One of the properties on $.Widget.prototype is defaultElement, which is an element to use when a widget instance is constructed without providing an element. How do you create a widget instance without providing an element?

Remember from chapter 8 that in addition to plugin-based initialization, all widgets created with the widget factory have constructor functions that can initialize widgets.

The following uses the dialog widget's constructor function to initialize a dialog widget on a newly created <div>:

```
$.ui.dialog( {}, "<div>" );
```

The first argument of each widget's constructor is an object containing the options to use, and the second argument is the element to create the widget on. What we haven't discussed is that you can omit the second argument, and this example does the same thing:

```
$.ui.dialog( {} );
```

This works because when only one argument is provided to the constructor function, the widget factory uses $.Widget.prototype.defaultElement, which is "<div>". Individual widgets can override the defaultElement on their prototype to specify more appropriate elements. For instance, because spinners need to be created on <input> elements, $.ui.spinner.prototype.defaultElement is set to "<input>". The following code creates a new spinner and appends it to the <body>:

```
$.ui.spinner( {} ).widget().appendTo( "body" );
```

> **NOTE** Remember that the widget() method returns the outer container of a widget. The preceding code needs this call because internally the spinner widget wraps the <input> element with additional markup. So $.ui.spinner({}).appendTo("body") alone would append the <input> but lose that additional markup.

When creating custom widgets, it's important to update this property if it's necessary for the widget you're creating. A <div> isn't appropriate for your todo widget from chapter 8 as it uses <ul> elements. To use a different defaultElement, you include the property on your widget's prototype object:

```
$.widget( "tj.todo", {
    defaultElement: "<ul>",
    options: { ... },
    ...
});
```

With this in place, you can use the constructor functions and omit the second argument. The following creates a new todo widget, adds two tasks, and appends it to the <body>:

```
var instance = $.tj.todo( {} );
instance.add( "Task One" );
instance.add( "Task Two" );
instance.element.appendTo( "body" );
```

Let's look at a few more properties on $.Widget.prototype.

12.4.3 *Supporting embedded-window use in widgets*

If you have perused the various widget properties, you may be surprised to see $.Widget .prototype.document and $.Widget.prototype.window. On the base widget's prototype, these properties are references to the browser's document and window objects. So why do these properties exist?

They exist for widgets used in <iframe> elements—which have their own document and window objects. Real-world uses of <iframe> elements are typically complex, and are frequently used to interact with third-party services, so you'll build a simple example to show the intention of these two properties.

Let's start with this:

```
<div>Parent</div>
<iframe src="child.html"></iframe>              ◁──┐  Embeds
                                                   │  child.html
<script>
    $.widget( "tj.blink", {
        _create: function() {
            this._on( window, {
                click: function() {
                    this.element.fadeOut( "fast" ).fadeIn( "fast" );
                }
            });
        }
    });                                    ❶ Initializes a blink widget
                                             on each <div>
    $( "div" ).blink();              ◁──┘
    var child = $( "iframe" ).load(function() {
        $( "div", child.contents() ).blink();   ◁──  Initializes a blink widget
    });                                              on each <div> in the
</script>                                         ❷  <iframe>
```

This code defines the extremely useful blink widget, which makes an element blink when the user clicks anywhere on the window. In this example, you initialize a blink widget on the page's <div> elements ❶, and, after the <iframe> loads, you initialize a blink widget on each of its <div> elements ❷.

> **TIP** jQuery UI supports creating widgets in multiple windows as is shown here. But it's a one-way street; after you create a widget in a window, you can't move it to another window and expect it to work. (Technically it *might* work in some cases, but moving widgets across windows in general isn't supported by jQuery UI.)

With this approach, any click on the window makes all blink widgets, well, blink. This includes elements on the main page, as well as elements in the <iframe>. To switch up this logic, let's return to the code that attaches the click event handler to the window:

```
this._on( window, {
    click: function() { ... }
});
```

For example's sake, let's change it to use the `window` property on the instance (which is set to `this`):

```
this._on( this.window, {
    click: function() { ... }
});
```

Whenever a widget is initialized, its instance object is given `window` and `document` properties that point to the `window` and `document` objects of the window it was created in. After making this change, blink widgets blink only on clicks of their respective windows.

When creating custom widgets, use of the instance `window` and `document` objects (as opposed to the `window` and `document` global objects) is recommended to support embedded-window use. Although in this example the code works in both cases (albeit with different behavior), many times this isn't the case, such as getting coordinates for positioning. jQuery UI uses the `window` and `document` instance properties internally.

12.4.4 *Displaying elements with _show() and _hide()*

Recall from chapter 6 that several of the jQuery UI widgets provide `show` and `hide` options that tie into the jQuery UI effects suite. Under the hood, all these widgets defer to `$.Widget._show()` and `$.Widget._hide()` to do the dirty work of processing the options.

To see how you can use these methods yourself, let's build a small example using a widget that adds a notification message to the bottom corner of the screen. The widget is shown in action in figure 12.7.

Figure 12.7 View of the notification widget you'll build

The code used to build this widget is shown in the following listing.

> **NOTE** Some code is omitted to focus on the effects integration. You can find the full code and see this widget live at http://jsfiddle.net/tj_vantoll/phkCB/.

Listing 12.1 A notification widget

```
$.widget( "tj.notification", {
    options: {
        show: true,
        hide: true
```
❶ Defaults the show and hide options to true

```
    },
    _create: function() {
        this.button = $( "<button>Close</button>" )
            .addClass( "tj-notification-button" )
            .button({
                text: false,
                icons: { primary: "ui-icon-closethick" }
            })
            .appendTo( this.element );
        this._on( this.button, {
            click: this.close
        });

        this.element
            .addClass( "ui-widget ui-widget-content tj-notification" )
            .position({
                my: "right-10 bottom-10",
                at: "right bottom",
                of: window
            });
    },
    open: function() {
        this._show( this.element, this.options.show );
    },
    close: function() {
        this._hide( this.element, this.options.hide );
    }
});
```

Calls the close() method when the close button is clicked

❷ Uses _show() to display the notification

Positions the notification at the bottom right of the screen

❸ Uses _hide() to hide the notification

The code in `_create()` performs the setup necessary—creating the close button and positioning the notification—but for the effects integration we're mostly interested in the two options, as well as the `open()` and `close()` methods.

The start of the code declares two options, `show` and `hide`, and defaults them to `true`, which—as you may recall from chapter 6—tells jQuery UI to use a fade in and fade out effect, respectively ❶.

The options are used in the `open()` and `close()` methods, which are wrappers of the `_show()` ❷ and `_hide()` ❸ methods. Both `_show()` and `_hide()` take three arguments: an element, an options argument, and an optional callback function (which we're not using here).

What's cool about this approach is that's all the code you need to tie into the jQuery UI effects suite. The following creates a notification that fades in over 300 milliseconds and hides with the jQuery UI blind effect:

```
$( "<div>Your account has been updated.</div>" )
    .appendTo( "body" )
    .notification({
        show: 300,
        hide: "blind"
    });
```

For a full listing of the types of data you can use for `show` and `hide`, either return to chapter 6 where we first discussed this, or check out the options' documentation at http://api.jqueryui.com/jquery.widget/#option-hide and http://api.jqueryui.com/ jquery.widget/#option-show.

12.4.5 *Customizing options on the fly*

The last widget method we're going to discuss is one of the more useful ones; it's the basis of how jQuery Mobile's autoinitialization works. The method is `_getCreateOptions()`, and it gives you the ability to define options during widget initialization. When you provide a `_getCreateOptions()` method, you can define options that override the widget's defaults. Consider the following code that creates a test widget:

```
$.widget( "tj.test", {                    Defaults the foo
    option: {                             option to "bar"
        foo: "bar"
Uses a foo  ❶ },
option of        _getCreateOptions: function() {
 "bang"              return { foo: "bang" };
            }
        });

        $.tj.test( {} ).options.foo;        ← ❷  "bang"
"biz" ❸ →  $.tj.test({ foo: "biz" }).options.foo;
```

Each time the test widget's constructor function is called, the `_getCreateOptions()` method is invoked ❶. Here the `_getCreateOptions()` method returns a hardcoded foo option, which overrides the widget's default value for this option (`"bar"`) with `"bang"`.

Because of this override, when you create an instance with no options, its foo option is set to `"bang"` ❷. Despite the override, user-supplied options still override the values given in `_getCreateOptions()`; therefore, your second instance maintains the `"biz"` option that was passed to its constructor ❸.

Now that you have an idea of how `_getCreateOptions()` works, let's see how this is useful, starting with a few ways that jQuery UI itself uses these methods. The jQuery UI selectmenu widget uses the following method:

```
_getCreateOptions: function() {
    return { disabled: this.element.prop( "disabled" ) };
}
```

The context of `_getCreateOptions()` (`this`) is set to the widget instance, which gives access to the element the widget is being created on. The selectmenu widget uses that reference to default its `disabled` option to whether the `<select>` it's initializing is disabled. Deriving widget options from element attributes like this is the most common use of `_getCreateOptions()`. The spinner widget does something similar.

You may remember from chapter 3 that the spinner widget has min, max, and step options, but you can also provide these values as HTML attributes. The following creates a spinner widget with a min option of 2, a max option of 20, and a step option of 2:

```
<input min="2" max="20" step="2">
<script>
    $( "input" ).spinner();
</script>
```

The spinner widget makes this possible with the following _getCreateOptions()
method:

```
_getCreateOptions: function() {
    var options = {},
        element = this.element;

    $.each([ "min", "max", "step" ], function( i, option ) {
        var value = element.attr( option );
        if ( value !== undefined && value.length ) {
            options[ option ] = value;
        }
    });

    return options;
}
```

Here the widget loops over an array of three strings—"min", "max", and "step"—and
checks whether each exists as an option. (The value.length check also makes sure
the attribute value has at least one character in it.) The attributes that do have values
are added to an options object that's returned at the end of the method.

The approach of initializing widgets based on their attributes is cool, and leads to
another question: why not allow any option to be specified as an attribute? Let's see
how to do that next.

12.5 *Using autoinitialization to remove boilerplate code*

If you work with jQuery UI long enough, you'll notice yourself writing a lot of code
that initializes widgets. Your flight search example from the previous chapter included
this block:

```
$( "#from-airport" ).autocomplete(...);
$( "#to-airport" ).autocomplete(...);
$( "#date" ).datepicker();
$( "#hops" ).buttonset();
$( "#order-by" ).selectmenu();
```

This code becomes tedious because you're doing the same task: selecting elements
and converting them to widgets. When the jQuery Mobile project—which uses the
widget factory for its widgets—came out, they provided a new technique for initializing widgets known as autoinitialization.

Autoinitialization works by configuring elements with a series of attributes, and
then letting jQuery Mobile turn those elements into widgets automatically. Consider
the following jQuery Mobile application:

```
<!doctype html>
<html lang="en">
<head>
    <meta charset="utf-8">
```

```
        <meta name="viewport" content="width=device-width, initial-scale=1">
        <title>jQuery Mobile</title>

        <link rel="stylesheet" href="//code.jquery.com/mobile/1.4.2/
          jquery.mobile-1.4.2.min.css">
        <script src="//code.jquery.com/jquery-1.11.1.min.js"></script>
        <script src="//code.jquery.com/mobile/1.4.2/jquery.mobile-
          1.4.2.min.js"></script>
    </head>
    <body>

    <div data-role="page">
        <div data-role="header">
            <h1>jQuery Mobile Rocks!</h1>
        </div>
        <div data-role="main" class="ui-content">
            <input type="button" data-icon="gear" value="Settings">
        </div>
    </div>

    </body>
    </html>
```

When this page loads, three widgets are created: a page, a header, and a button. The display of this page is shown in figure 12.8.

Notice that you didn't need to write a single line of JavaScript to create this UI and these widgets, which is cool, but how does this work? And more importantly, how can you get this behavior with jQuery UI? To answer, let's dig into jQuery Mobile's code.

12.5.1 How jQuery Mobile's autoinitialization works

The magic starts in a method that jQuery Mobile adds to `$.fn`: `enhanceWithin()`. The primary job of `enhanceWithin()` is detecting which elements should be enhanced in the given element. The following adds a new `<input type="button">` element to the page and converts it to a button widget:

```
$( ".ui-content" ).append( "<input type='button' value='New!'>" );
$( document ).enhanceWithin();
```

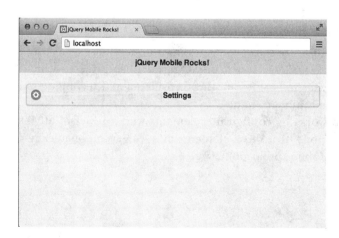

Figure 12.8   Display of a jQuery Mobile app with one button

To make this possible, each jQuery Mobile widget has an `initSelector` property that tells the `enhanceWithin()` method what elements should be enhanced. Because `$.mobile.button.prototype.initSelector` contains `"input[type='button']"`, jQuery Mobile knows to turn it into a button widget.

Internally, jQuery Mobile calls `enhanceWithin()` on each page to initialize widgets. For your purposes, what's interesting is what `enhanceWithin()` does under the hood, or rather, what it doesn't. The following is a condensed version of jQuery Mobile's `enhanceWithin()` method:

```
var index,
    widgetElements = {},
    that = this;

$.each( $.mobile.widgets, function( name, constructor ) {
    var elements = $.mobile.enhanceable(
        that.find( constructor.initSelector ) );

    if ( elements.length > 0 ) {
        widgetElements[ constructor.prototype.widgetName ] = elements;
    }
});

for ( index in widgetElements ) {
    widgetElements[ index ][ index ]();
}
```

① Loops over all widgets in jQuery Mobile

② Finds all elements that match the widget's initSelector

③ Loops over each widget with matches

④ Adds any matching element to a collection

⑤ Invokes the widget's plugin

This code starts by looping over all of jQuery Mobile's widgets **①**. `$.mobile.widgets` is an object where the key is the name of the widget and the value is the widget's constructor—which is how the name and constructor functions are assigned to the `name` and `constructor` variables in the `$.each()` callback. For the button widget, `name` and `constructor` are set to `"button"` and `$.mobile.button`, respectively.

For each widget, the code looks for any elements that match the widget's `initSelector` property and assigns the matches to an `elements` variable **②**. The context (`that`, in this case) is set to the jQuery object `enhanceWithin()` was invoked on. In a `$( document ).enhanceWithin()` call, `that` is set to a jQuery object containing the document. If there are elements that matched the widget's `initSelector`, they're added to the `widgetElements` object **③**.

After that, the code loops over each widget that has matches **④** and invokes those widgets' respective plugins **⑤**. The `widgetElements[ index ][ index ]()` line is a bit weird, because the `index` variable is the widget's name. So in your button example, you go into this loop with `index` set to `"button"`. `widgetElements[ "button" ]` resolves to a jQuery object with all matched elements, and `widgetElements[ "button" ][ "button" ]()` is a fancy way of writing `widgetElements.button.button()`, which invokes the plugin on all matched elements.

To take a step back, remember how I said the important part of this code is what isn't here? There's no code to handle options; the `enhanceWithin()` method invokes the plugin with no arguments. But your original jQuery Mobile example used `<input type="button" data-icon="gear" value="Settings">` (note the `data-icon="gear"` attribute), and figure 12.8 shows that a gear showed up. You can use your knowledge of the widget factory from earlier in this chapter to see that an `icon` option is indeed set on the element:

```
$( "input" ).button( "instance" ).options.icon      ⟵  "gear"
```

So…how did that happen?

12.5.2 jQuery Mobile's widget extension

The answer is the widget factory's `_getCreateOption()` method. jQuery Mobile takes the default `$.Widget.prototype._getCreateOptions()` method (which does nothing), and changes it to populate options based on the element's attributes. The following shows the complete code:

```
var rcapitals = /[A-Z]/g,
    replaceFunction = function( c ) {
        return "-" + c.toLowerCase();
    };

$.extend( $.Widget.prototype, {
    _getCreateOptions: function() {
        var option, value,
            elem = this.element[ 0 ],
            options = {};

        for ( option in this.options ) {
            value = $.mobile.getAttribute( elem,
                option.replace( rcapitals, replaceFunction ) );

            if ( value != null ) {
                options[ option ] = value;
            }
        }

        return options;
    }
});
```

Loops ❶ er each option ⟶ (for loop)

❷ **Retrieves the attribute's value**

❸ **Includes the option from the attribute if present**

This code starts by looping over each option ❶. (Remember the context of `_getCreateOptions()` is set to the instance object.) For each option, it calls a `$.mobile.getAttribute()` method ❷. Internally, `$.mobile.getAttribute()` gets an HTML5 data-* attribute off the element and does some data-type coercion (for instance, converting `"false"` to `false`, `"2"` to `2`, and so on). The name of the attribute `$.mobile.getAttribute()` retrieves is determined by this call:

```
option.replace( rcapitals, replaceFunction )
```

This takes the name of the option (the `option` variable) and replaces all capital letters in the name with a `"-"` and the letter lowercased. This code would convert the dialog widget's `"autoOpen"` option to `"auto-open"`. jQuery Mobile's `$.mobile.getAttribute()` would then look for a `"data-auto-open"` attribute on the element.

The rest of the code is straightforward. When a data-* attribute is found for the given option, it is added to the `options` object ❸, which becomes the instance's set of starting options.

This code explains why `<input type="button" data-icon="gear" value="Settings">` had its `icon` option automatically set to `"gear"`. When this widget is initialized, jQuery Mobile's `_getCreateOptions()` method loops over all the button widget's options, searches the element for data-* attributes that align with the options, finds one (`data-icon`), and initializes the widget with that option set.

This type of initialization is known as declarative initialization. As opposed to imperative initialization—where you need to list out option values explicitly in code—declarative initialization lets you associate a widget's options directly on the HTML elements. I personally find declarative initialization to be elegant as it removes boilerplate JavaScript code.

But this is jQuery Mobile code, not jQuery UI code. Because this code is so simple, you can port this to use with the jQuery UI widgets. Let's look at how to do that.

12.5.3 Autoinitializing jQuery UI widgets

If you look at the preceding jQuery Mobile code, the only jQuery Mobile–specific code was the `$.mobile.getAttribute()` method. Therefore, if you abstract that code from jQuery Mobile, you can bring the benefits of declarative initialization to jQuery UI. This approach is shown in the following listing.

Listing 12.2 Declarative initialization of jQuery UI widgets

```
$.extend( $.Widget.prototype, {
    _getCreateOptions: function() {
        var option,
            value,
            options = {};

        for ( option in this.options ) {
            value = this.element.data( option );    ◁——┐ ❶ Retrieves the data-*
            if ( value != null ) {                          attribute from the element
                options[ option ] = value;
            }
        }
    }
});
```

There's a lot of code here, but most of this you've seen before. The only real difference is the use of the jQuery Core `data()` method to retrieve the data-* attributes from the element ❶. To get a sense of what `data()` is doing for you, look at the following code:

```
<div data-one="false" data-two="2" data-foo-bar="foo"></div>
<script>
    $( "div" ).data( "one" ) === false;
    $( "div" ).data( "two" ) === 2;            true
    $( "div" ).data( "fooBar" ) === "foo";
</script>
```

As you can see, the data() method takes care of performing data type conversions, as well as converting multiword attributes into camel-case variables. Why doesn't jQuery Mobile use this? Its $.mobile.getAttribute() method has additional (jQuery Mobile specific) logic that forces it to replicate some of the functionality built in to data(), which you don't need here. With this setup in place, you can now write code like this:

```
<div id="dialog" data-height="200" data-width="500"></div>
<script>
    $( "#dialog" ).dialog();
</script>
```

This creates a dialog that's 200 pixels tall and 500 pixels wide, and you didn't have to specify any of those options in JavaScript. This approach handles reading attributes, but you're still not autoinitializing widgets. You still had to explicitly select an element and call the dialog plugin on it.

Remember that jQuery Mobile has a whole construct built around this with the initSelector properties. You can build something lightweight that works like that fairly easily. Consider the following approach:

```
$.extend( $.fn, {
    enhance: function() {
        this.find( "[data-role]" ).addBack( "[data-role]" )
            .each(function() {
                var element = $( this ),
                    role = element.attr( "data-role" );
                element[ role ]();
            });
        return this;
    }
});
```

This adds a new enhance() jQuery plugin that finds all elements with a data-role attribute and initializes a widget with that value on the element.

> **NOTE** Because the find() method selects only child elements, the addBack() call in the preceding code ensures that if a data-role attribute is applied to the element enhance() is invoked on, that element is also selected. For example, $("<ul data-role='todo'></ul>").find("[data-role]") doesn't select the newly created <ul>, but $("<ul data-role='todo'></ul>").find("[data-role]").addBack("[data-role]") does. For more information on addBack(), see http://api.jquery.com/addBack/.

This new plugin means you can rewrite your previous example as follows:

```
<div data-role="dialog" id="dialog" data-height="200"
    data-width="500"></div>
<script>
    $( document ).enhance();
</script>
```

Notice that to make this work, you had to add a `data-role="dialog"` attribute to the element. You still had to write some JavaScript here, but the great thing is it'll handle as many widgets as you need, including nested widgets. The following example creates a tabs widget, progressbar widget, and slider widget:

```
<div data-role="tabs">
    <ul>
        <li><a href="#one">One</a></li>
        <li><a href="#two">Two</a></li>
    </ul>
    <div id="one">
        <div data-role="progressbar" data-value="false"></div>
    </div>
    <div id="two">
        <div data-role="slider" data-min="0" data-max="50"
            data-step="10"></div>
    </div>
</div>
<script>
    $( document ).enhance();
</script>
```

Because the implementation is based on the widget factory, it also works with custom widgets—such as your to-do list:

```
<ul data-role="todo">
    <li>Clean dishes</li>
    <li>Walk dog</li>
    <li>Mop floor</li>
</ul>
<script>
    $( document ).enhance();
</script>
```

This approach also works well when you dynamically insert HTML chunks into an existing document. The technique is common with MVC frameworks like Backbone, so we'll have a more thorough discussion of that in appendix C (which is specifically about using jQuery UI with Backbone).

If you're interested, the code we discussed to use declarative widgets is available as a library on GitHub at https://github.com/tjvantoll/Declarative-Widgets. Its only dependencies are jQuery Core and the widget factory, and it supports the use of AMD.

The use of declarative widgets isn't right or wrong; it gives you flexibility in how you define widgets used in your applications. I personally find it elegant as it usually removes JavaScript boilerplate, but some prefer the explicitness of imperative JavaScript-based initialization. Declarative initialization does get verbose with more complex options—for example, `data-icons='{"primary":"ui-icon-heart"}'` to get a heart icon on a button widget—but for most options I find HTML-based initialization cleaner and easier to read.

12.6 Summary

The way we built the declarative widgets library shows that it's valuable to know what's going on under the hood. Often knowing the inner workings can lead to solutions you may not have thought existed. Who knew the widget factory's _getCreateOptions() method was one of the cornerstones of the jQuery Mobile project?

And it goes beyond the methods we discussed in this chapter, or in this book. Despite all that it does, the jQuery UI source code is surprisingly approachable. If you're stuck in a tricky situation, or are curious how the library works, digging into the source can be a valuable learning experience. It's how I got started on the journey that led to this book ☺.

appendix A
Learning jQuery

Because this is a book on jQuery UI and not jQuery Core, I assume the reader has *some* knowledge of the jQuery library before starting this book. Because I often get asked, "What's the best way to learn jQuery?" I thought I'd gather a few of the resources that have worked for me.

Experimentation

Different people learn in different ways, but what has helped me is digging right into code. The appeal of jQuery is that it makes difficult tasks extraordinarily easy (its motto is *write less, do more,* after all!), and seeing results visually provides amazing feedback. Here are some of my favorite ways to experiment.

Try jQuery (try.jquery.com)

My go-to starting point for learning jQuery is Try jQuery—which is available at http://try.jquery.com. The great thing about Try jQuery is that it's an interactive tutorial that you must actively participate in to advance. Figure A.1 shows an example exercise.

This example teaches how to select elements with jQuery; it specifically asks the user to select the <h2> element in the HTML provided. The user must type this in the console located at the bottom of the screen (which works the same as the browser's developer tools that we'll look at in a minute). In the screenshot, I have already typed the correct answer, $("h2"), and the UI responded with a success message and a Continue button that takes me to the next exercise.

I highly recommend going through the entire set of Try jQuery tutorials as a starting point to learning jQuery.

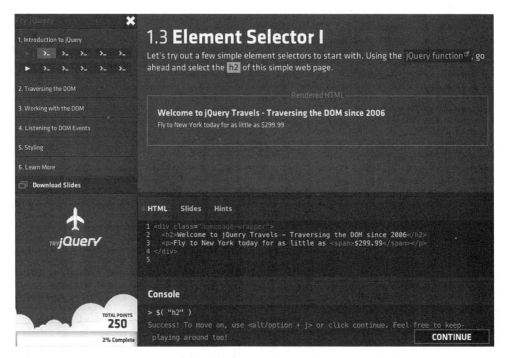

Figure A.1   An example exercise from Try jQuery about selecting elements

Online testing tools

Another set of learning tools I'm fond of are the online environments that let you run web code—such as HTML, CSS, and JavaScript—in the browser. You can easily experiment without worrying about the setup and boilerplate that typically goes into building a web page.

Each of these tools has different features, but they all function similarly. The next three figures show the same code—appending a new <h2> to the <body> and underlining its text—running in the three most popular of these tools: JS Bin (figure A.2), jsFiddle (figure A.3), and CodePen (figure A.4).

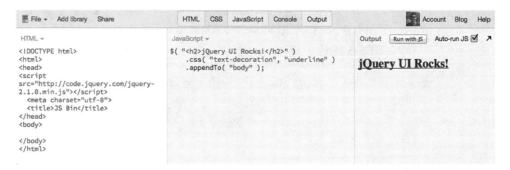

Figure A.2   Live coding in JS Bin

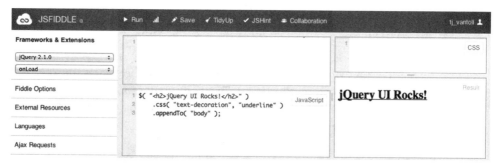

Figure A.3   Live coding in jsFiddle

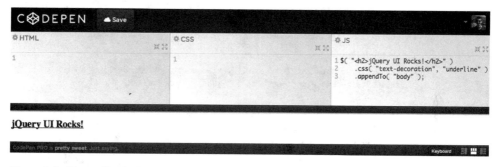

Figure A.4   Live coding in CodePen

Each tool gives you an area to write HTML, CSS, and JavaScript, and then shows you the result in another area. For the purposes of learning jQuery, each tool has a convenient way of adding jQuery to your example. In JS Bin, it's the Add library button; in jsFiddle, it's the Frameworks & Extensions section; and in CodePen, it's the cog or gear icon at the top of the JS panel.

Which of these tools to use is largely a matter of personal preference, and I encourage you to play with them all to decide which you like best. Personally, I'm a fan of jsFiddle because of its screen layout (I like the four panels in a grid) and how it handles URLs for sharing test cases with others. I'm such a fan of jsFiddle that I use it in numerous examples throughout this book. You can learn more about jsFiddle in chapter 1.

The browser's developer tools

One of the best ways to experiment with jQuery is to use the browser's built-in developer tools. I recommend learning the browser's developer tools early on because you'll acquire knowledge that extends far beyond learning jQuery. In my opinion, it's the single most valuable tool a web developer has, enabling you to inspect the DOM, alter CSS, profile your applications, and more.

Although all browsers' developer tools are different, they have consolidated around a few core pieces of functionality, including the keyboard shortcut needed to open them. You can use F12 on Windows and Cmd + Option + I on OS X.

TIP   For Safari on OS X, you first have to enable the developer tools by going to Preferences → Advanced and clicking the Show Develop Menu in Menu Bar check box.

The main task worth familiarizing yourself with is the browser's console, as it lets you execute JavaScript code and is great for experimentation. Figures A.5 and A.6 show the same example of adding an underlined <h2> to a page using the developer tools in Chrome and Internet Explorer.

Figure A.5   Adding an <h2> with Chrome's developer tools

Figure A.6   Adding an <h2> with Internet Explorer's developer tools

You can do a lot with the browsers' develop tools, and it's worth taking time to learn them. For a more detailed guide on these tools, you can use the following resources:

- *Chrome*—https://developers.google.com/chrome-developer-tools/
- *Internet Explorer*—http://msdn.microsoft.com/library/ie/bg182326(v=vs.85)
- *Firefox*—https://developer.mozilla.org/en-US/docs/Tools
- *Safari*—https://developer.apple.com/library/safari/documentation/AppleApplications/Conceptual/Safari_Developer_Guide/Introduction/Introduction.html

Chrome's documentation is particularly good, and it also has a free interactive course that works exactly like Try jQuery at http://discover-devtools.codeschool.com/. If you're a Chrome user, it's a great set of tutorials to go through; even seasoned developers can learn a thing or two.

Reading

After you've experimented with jQuery, a well-written resource can help you learn the finer points of the library, and to understand why the library works as it does. I'll give a few recommendations for reading material.

jQuery Learning Center (learn.jquery.com)

The jQuery Learning Center (http://learn.jquery.com) is a collection of articles and tutorials about all things jQuery. Here you can find everything from jQuery 101 to tutorials on advanced features of the library. You can even find material on jQuery UI (some authored by yours truly). Figure A.7 shows the site with a sampling of topics.

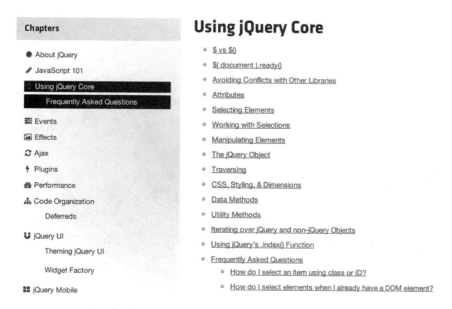

Figure A.7 Sampling of topics on the jQuery Learning Center. The screenshot is from http://learn.jquery.com/using-jquery-core/.

What's cool is that the Learning Center is an open source project that's officially maintained by the jQuery Foundation. The project is hosted on GitHub at https://github.com/jquery/learn.jquery.com, and there you can report issues with the site, contribute fixes, and even write your own articles!

Books

Although the Learning Center is great for reference material, it doesn't give you the thorough walkthrough of jQuery that you get from a whole book dedicated to it. There are a ton of books on jQuery out there, so to help you sift through the list, I'll make two recommendations for books I've personally read.

Although now slightly dated, *jQuery Enlightenment* by Cody Lindley (2009) is the best free book I know of on jQuery. The book is full of examples that link to live code on JS Bin (this book is where I got the inspiration to use jsFiddle examples throughout the book), which in my opinion significantly enhances the learning experience. *jQuery Enlightenment* is freely available as a PDF on http://jqueryenlightenment.com/.

About a year after I read *jQuery Enlightenment,* Bear Bibeault and Yehuda Katz released the second edition of *jQuery in Action* (Manning, 2010). This book fascinated me, as it explained not just how jQuery works, but also *why* it works the way that it does. It inspired me to mimic this approach and answer the whys behind jQuery UI in this book. The second edition of *jQuery in Action* is now a little dated. Aurelio De Rosa is completing a third edition to get the content up to speed. You can check out the third edition of *jQuery in Action* at http://manning.com/derosa/.

To verify that the various features of jQuery UI work as intended, the library has a series of unit tests that run in all the library's supported browsers. The tests themselves are written using the QUnit testing library. Because several excellent QUnit tutorials are online (http://qunitjs.com/cookbook/ is a particularly good one), I won't give one here. Instead, I'll show how jQuery UI tests its own widgets, using examples directly from the jQuery UI source code. Hopefully, looking at how jQuery UI tests its own widgets will help you approach testing yours.

Testing options

jQuery UI attempts to test every potential value of every option for every widget. Although the test coverage isn't perfect, the majority of options have tests to verify their behavior.

> **NOTE** The $("#spin") call selects an `<input id="spin">` element in the `<div id="qunit-fixture">`. If you're not familiar with QUnit, the fixture `<div>` is a place to put markup to use during the tests. QUnit resets the markup in the fixture to its initial state before each test—ensuring changes made in one test don't affect others.

Here's the spinner widget's tests for its max option:

```
test( "max", function() {
    expect( 3 );
    var element = $( "#spin" ).val( 1000 ).spinner({ max: 100 });
    equal( element.val(), 1000, "value not constrained on init" );

    element.spinner( "value", 1000 );
```

1 Declares the number of expected assertions

2 Asserts the value is preserved on init

```
    equal( element.val(), 100, "max constrained in value method" );    ◁——┐
                                                                            │
    element.val( 1000 ).blur();                                             │
┌─▷ equal( element.val(), 1000, "max not constrained if manual entry" );    │
│ });                                                                        │
                                                        **Asserts the value is**  │
                                                        **constrained in value()** ❸
**❹ Asserts the value is preserved**
**from manual entry**
```

The test starts by calling QUnit's expect() function, which tells QUnit how many assertions this test should perform ❶. If this test completes, and exactly three assertions
were *not* performed, QUnit will fail the test. Explicitly declaring the number of assertions acts as a safeguard; it ensures you don't include an assertion that QUnit can't
execute, which may happen during a refactor, or when dealing with asynchronous
code. The call to expect() is important enough that jQuery UI sets the QUnit
requireExpects configuration variable to true (QUnit.config.requireExpects =
true), which tells QUnit to require a call to expect() in each test. With require-
Expects set, QUnit fails any test without an expect() call automatically.

Next, this test does a few assertions to verify the max option's behavior. The code
starts by setting the <input> element's value to 1000, and then initializing a spinner
widget on it. The spinner's max option is set to 100. The first assertion ensures that the
<input> element's value wasn't constrained by the max option, specifically, that the
value remained 1000 despite the max of 100 ❷. This behavior is for consistency with
the native <input type="number"> control. If you create a <input type="number"
value="1000" max="100"> element, its starting value is 1000.

The next assertion checks the opposite behavior—that the value *is* constrained
when using the value() method. It does so by invoking the value() method with a
value of 1000, and asserting that the value was limited to the max (100) ❸.

The last assertion is another check to ensure consistent behavior with <input
type="number"> controls. If a user manually types a number greater than the <input>
element's max, the browser doesn't update the <input> element's value on blur. The
test makes sure the spinner adheres to this behavior by setting the <input> element's
value to 1000, explicitly triggering a blur event, and asserting that the value of 1000
wasn't altered ❹.

These tests ensure that the spinner's max option does what its documentation says
that it does. But this doesn't cover everything the max option does. When using the
spinner widget with Globalize, you can also pass formatted strings to use as the max
option (appendix D looks at this in detail); therefore, the spinner widget includes a
test for that as well:

```
test( "max, string", function() {
    expect( 3 );
    var element = $( "#spin" )
        .val( 1000 )
        .spinner({
            max: "$100.00",
            numberFormat: "C",
            culture: "en"
```

```
        });
    equal( element.val(), "$1,000.00", "value not constrained on init" );
    equal( element.spinner( "option", "max" ), 100, "option converted to
      number" );

    element.spinner( "value", 1000 );
    equal( element.val(), "$100.00", "max constrained in value method" );
});
```

This is more or less the same test as before; the only difference is the use of strings for the max option instead of numbers. jQuery UI attempts to write tests that cover every type documented in its API documentation. For instance, the autocomplete's source option has tests that cover the three data types it accepts (array, object, and function).

For your own widgets, testing each type of each option verifies that the widget works correctly—especially as the widget is worked on over time. Looking for tests is also a good criterion for judging third-party widgets. A third-party widget with thorough test coverage is more likely to work as advertised than one without tests.

Let's move from options to how jQuery UI tests its methods.

Testing methods

Like options, jQuery UI attempts to test every documented method for every widget. Importantly, though, jQuery UI doesn't test internal, undocumented methods. Here's the test for the spinner widget's isValid() method:

```
test( "isValid", function() {
    expect( 8 );
    var element = $( "#spin" ).spinner({
            min: 0,
            max: 10,
            step: 2
        }),
        spinner = element.spinner( "instance" );
    ok( !spinner.isValid(), "initial state is invalid" );         ❶ Ensures nonnumeric
                                                                     strings are invalid
    element.val( "this is not a number" );
    ok( !spinner.isValid(), "text string is not valid" );

    element.val( "0" );
    ok( spinner.isValid(), "min value is valid" );

    element.val( "10" );
    ok( spinner.isValid(), "max value is valid" );

    element.val( "4" );
    ok( spinner.isValid(), "inbetween step is valid" );           ❷ Ensures numbers below
                                                                     the min are invalid
    element.val( "-1" );
    ok( !spinner.isValid(), "below min is invalid" );

    element.val( "11" );
    ok( !spinner.isValid(), "above max is invalid" );             Ensures numbers
                                                                  above the max
    element.val( "1" );                                          ❸ are invalid
    ok( !spinner.isValid(), "step mismatch is invalid" );
});
```

The test makes a number of assertions to ensure the isValid() method correctly determines the validity of the spinner. It ensures that nonnumeric strings ❶, values below the min ❷, and values above the max ❸ are all invalid—among other checks for the strings users can potentially input.

What you don't see here is that internally isValid() uses an _adjustValue() method to do most of the dirty work of determining the validity of a user's input. But because jQuery UI tests only the public API, you won't find a single test that hits _adjustValue() directly. The _adjustValue() method gets indirectly tested when it's called from the public API methods.

Like options, jQuery UI also tests all method variations. The spinner widget's stepUp() method, for instance, can be called with no arguments—that is, spinner("stepUp")—or with a single argument indicating the number of steps to take—that is, spinner("stepUp", 5). Here's the test that jQuery UI uses to verify this method works as documented:

```
test( "stepUp", function() {
    expect( 4 );
    var element = $( "#spin" ).val( 0 ).spinner({
        step: 2,
        max: 16                                   ❶ Asserts stepUp()'s
    });                                             behavior with no
                                                    arguments
    element.spinner( "stepUp" );
    equal( element.val(), 2, "stepUp 1 step" );   ❷ Asserts stepUp()'s
                                                    behavior with an
                                                    argument
    element.spinner( "stepUp", 5 );
    equal( element.val(), 12, "stepUp 5 steps" );

    element.spinner( "stepUp", 4 );
    equal( element.val(), 16, "close to max and stepUp 4 steps" );

    element.spinner( "stepUp" );
    equal( element.val(), 16, "at max and stepUp 1 step" );
});
```

❸ Asserts stepUp() is constrained by the max

Asserts stepUp() is constrained while at the max ❹

The test starts by creating a spinner widget with a value of 0, a step of 2, and a max of 16. The first assertion calls the stepUp() method and ensures it increments the <input> element's value by a single step (from 0 to 2) ❶. The next assertion invokes the stepUp() method with 5 and ensures it increments the <input> element's value by 5 steps (from 2 to 12) ❷. The last two assertions ensure that the stepUp() method respects the spinner's max and stops the value at 16—both when the spinner's value starts below the max ❸ and when it starts at it ❹.

Let's move from options to how jQuery UI tests events.

Testing events

Like options and methods, jQuery UI attempts to test each documented event for each widget. But testing events has a few unique twists. For one, events are often asynchronous, which requires extra logic in the tests. Listing B.1 shows a test for the autocomplete widget's `focus` event.

NOTE A little background: the autocomplete widget's `focus` event is triggered every time an item in the autocomplete's menu is focused. By default, the widget replaces the text `<input>` element's `value` with the content of the focused menu item, but canceling the `focus` event prevents this behavior. The canceling behavior is what this test is concerned with.

Listing B.1 Testing canceling the autocomplete's `focus` event

```
var data = [ "Clojure", "COBOL", "ColdFusion", "Java",
    "JavaScript", "Scala", "Scheme" ];
asyncTest( "cancel focus", function() {                    ◁── Declares the test as
    expect( 1 );                                           ❶   an asynchronous test
    var customVal = "custom value",
        element = $( "#autocomplete" ).autocomplete({
            delay: 0,
            source: data,                       Sets the ❷
            focus: function() {               <input> to
                $( this ).val( customVal );  "custom value"   ❸ Cancels
                return false;                            ◁──    the event
            }
        });                                               ❺ Delays execution by
    element.val( "ja" ).keydown();          Displays ❹        50 milliseconds
    setTimeout(function() {                  the menu    ◁──
        element.simulate( "keydown", { keyCode: $.ui.keyCode.DOWN } );
        equal( element.val(), customVal );  Simulates ◁──
        start();                    ◁──      a down
    }, 50 );                                 arrow key ❻        Asserts the
});                                     ❼ Restarts the           custom value is
                                           test runner   ❽ in the <input>
```

To start, you declare this test as an `asyncTest()` instead of a `test()` ❶. (You'll see why momentarily.) With a synchronous test, QUnit executes each line of code in the `test()` and then moves on to the next `test()`. With an asynchronous test, QUnit doesn't continue when it reaches the end of an `asyncTest()`; instead, it waits for a call to `start()` before continuing.

Within the test, the first thing you do is instantiate an autocomplete widget with a `focus` event callback. The callback sets the autocomplete's `<input>` to a static string ❷, and then returns `false` to cancel the event ❸. (Remember that you can return `false` or call `preventDefault()` on the event argument—which isn't used here—to cancel an event.)

Now, you need to trigger a `focus` event to get this callback to run. To make this happen, you do two things. First, you need to show the menu. You do this by setting the `<input>` element's `value` to the first two characters of a match (`"ja"`) and triggering a `keydown` event ❹. The next step is to simulate a down-arrow-key press (which moves focus to the first option), but you can't do that quite yet.

How jQuery UI automates its tests

We discussed all that jQuery UI does to write its tests, but we haven't touched on how jQuery UI runs them. To start, because QUnit runs in a browser, you can run the library's test suite yourself by downloading jQuery UI from https://github.com/jquery/jquery-ui/ and opening tests/unit/all.html in your browser of choice.

But that's a manual process; to automate this, jQuery UI does a couple of things. First, every time code is committed to the master branch in the project's git repository, a Travis CI (Continuous Integration) server runs checks on the project—including linting the project's HTML, CSS, and JavaScript, as well as running all the unit tests. The committer of the code is notified if any problems are found. You can view the project's Travis builds at https://travis-ci.org/jquery/jquery-ui.

Every commit also triggers a run on another CI server—TestSwarm. Unlike a more fully featured CI server, TestSwarm serves a single purpose: executing HTML-based tests across multiple browsers. Instead of opening an HTML page in dozens of browser + OS combinations, the jQuery UI team can test in their local browser and let TestSwarm handle the full suite of browsers that the library supports. You can learn more about TestSwarm, including how to set up your own TestSwarm infrastructure, at https://github.com/jquery/testswarm. You can view the results of the jQuery UI test runs at http://swarm.jquery.org/project/jqueryui.

Internally, jQuery UI displays the autocomplete menu asynchronously, with a delay that's configurable by the `delay` option. Your code needs to wait for the menu to display before it can continue. To do that, you wrap the rest of the test's code in a `setTimeout()` call that delays its execution by 50 milliseconds ❺. Remember that because this is an `asyncTest()`, QUnit won't move on to the next test automatically. Instead, it idles until `start()` is called.

After the delay, the menu has now been displayed, so you can continue. You simulate a down-arrow key being pressed ❻, which moves focus to the first menu item and triggers your `focus` event callback. You ensure that the `focus` event was triggered, and that the `<input>` has the custom value (as opposed to "Java") ❼. Then you invoke `start()` to tell QUnit to continue with normal execution ❽.

There are other tests for the `focus` event when it's not canceled, and tests to make sure `focus` event callbacks are triggered with the documented arguments (`ui` and `event`). As you can see, testing events is a little more work, but the same premise applies: jQuery UI attempts to test all its behavior that's publicly documented.

And this premise extends beyond options, methods, and events. Each widget has tests to verify that the documented markup structures are parsed correctly, that the appropriate ARIA attributes are added, that the documented class names are added to the correct elements, and more. Writing and maintaining all these tests is no small task, but it helps make jQuery UI the stable library that it is.

jQuery simulate

In listing B.1 you may have noticed the call to `simulate()`—which isn't a part of jQuery Core or jQuery UI. This works because jQuery UI includes the jQuery simulate plugin as part of its test suite. The simulate plugin is a small library specifically intended for simulating browser mouse and keyboard events.

The plugin works much like the jQuery Core `trigger()` method, except it has a convenient API to set properties on the event object passed to callbacks. Consider the call to simulate in listing B.1:

```
element.simulate( "keydown", { keyCode: $.ui.keyCode.DOWN });
```

If you were to call `trigger( "keydown" )` instead, `keydown` event handlers wouldn't know what key was pressed—and you can't include properties in the `Event` object through the `trigger()` API. (Although you can explicitly create a `jQuery.Event` object and pass it to `trigger()`. For more, see http://api.jquery.com/category/events/event-object/.)

With `simulate()`, you have the convenience of quickly including properties on the `Event` object. The plugin intelligently merges properties passed to its second argument with properties on an `Event` object that it creates internally.

In addition to the `Event` object niceties, the simulate plugin also provides a convenient means of simulating the user dragging something across the screen. The following simulates the user moving an element 10 pixels left and 10 pixels down:

```
element.simulate( "drag", {
    dx: 10,
    dy: 10
});
```

The draggable and sortable widgets use this abstraction heavily in their test suites. For more on what the simulate plugin can do, and to download it for use in your own test suites, check out its GitHub repository at https://github.com/jquery/jquery-simulate.

appendix C
Using jQuery
UI with Backbone

One question I frequently am asked is how jQuery UI works with MVC frameworks like Backbone. This definitely is a topic worth discussing, because jQuery UI compliments Backbone quite nicely. The best way to use the libraries is to let Backbone do what it does best—manage an application's data and views—and let jQuery UI do what it does best—the UI. Let's look at how to do that.

> **NOTE** This guide is intended for readers who have some familiarly with the Backbone library, although I'll try to provide enough context so that everyone can follow. To learn more about Backbone, you can refer to its documentation at http://backbonejs.org/, or Addy Osmani's excellent (and free!) book on writing Backbone applications, available at http://addyosmani.github.io/backbone-fundamentals/.

Building a Backbone view

To show the integration in action, you'll build a small sample app to manage a grocery list. Your grocery list will have a single piece of functionality: a button that removes individual groceries from the list. The HTML you'll use to build this is shown here

```
<ul id="grocery-list"></ul>
<script type="text/template" id="grocery-template">
    <% _.each( groceries, function( grocery ) { %>
        <li>
            <%= grocery.name %>
            <button data-id="<%= grocery.id %>">Remove</button>
        </li>
    <% }); %>
</script>
```

and here's the JavaScript you need:

```
var Grocery = Backbone.Model.extend({}),
    GroceryList = Backbone.Collection.extend({
        model: Grocery
    }),
    GroceryView = Backbone.View.extend({
        template: _.template( $( "#grocery-template" ).html() ),
        el: "#grocery-list",
        events: {
            "click button": "remove"
        }
        render: function() {
            this.$el.html(
                this.template({ groceries: this.model.toJSON() }));
        },
        remove: function( event ) {
            var grocery = this.model.get(
                $( event.currentTarget ).attr( "data-id" ) );
            this.model.remove( grocery );
            this.render();                    ◁
        }
    });
new GroceryView({
    model: new GroceryList([
        new Grocery({ id: 1, name: "Apples" }),
        new Grocery({ id: 2, name: "Bananas" }),
        new Grocery({ id: 3, name: "Peanut Butter" }),
        new Grocery({ id: 4, name: "Bread" }),
        new Grocery({ id: 5, name: "Milk" })
    ])
}).render();                    ◁
```

❶ Renders the list to reflect the grocery removal

❷ Renders the initial grocery list

NOTE You can play with this example at http://jsfiddle.net/tj_vantoll/H3fHr/.

If you're not familiar with Backbone, don't worry too much about the specific syntax used here. Backbone works by separating the model data (in this case, `Grocery` and `GroceryList`) from the view logic (in this case, `GroceryView`). But because we're concerned about jQuery UI integration, the main thing to focus on is the `render()` method. Here, `render()` takes the data in the View's model (`GroceryList`) and uses a template to inject the data into the `<ul id="grocery-list"></ul>`.

TIP If you don't understand what the template is doing here, refer to chapter 11 where we discuss templating in more detail.

Because `render()` is what updates the HTML, it must be explicitly called every time the view's data changes. In this example, it's called twice, once after the initial `GroceryList` is created ❷ and again in the `remove()` method, which is invoked after the user clicks the Remove buttons in the UI ❶. Now that you have an example in place, let's see how you can add in jQuery UI widgets.

Adding jQuery UI to the view

Let's suppose that you want to change your example's remove buttons to use a jQuery UI button widget with an icon. You could start by selecting elements and invoking the button widget's plugin:

```
$( "button" ).button({
    icons: { primary: "ui-icon-closethick" },
    text: false
});
```

This works initially, but as soon as you remove a grocery item from the list, the buttons are no longer button widgets. Why? Every time you call render(), the entire view is rerendered from scratch; the buttons you initially created are removed as soon as render() is reinvoked.

Because of this, you must put the widget instantiation in the render() method itself. The following initializes button widgets on each of the remove buttons:

```
render: function() {
    this.$el.html(
        this.template({ groceries: this.model.toJSON() }));

    this.$el.find( "button" ).button({
        icons: { primary: "ui-icon-closethick" },
        text: false
    });
}
```

> **TIP** All Backbone views have el and $el properties. el is a reference to the view element's DOM node (as an HTMLElement), and $el is that same element wrapped in a jQuery object. Because it is a jQuery object, the $el property gives you direct access to all methods on $.fn—show(), hide(), find(), html(), and so forth.

Now, each time this view is rendered, its HTML is replaced and button widgets are instantiated on each of the newly created <button> elements. This approach works, but it can be a bit verbose to manually instantiate widgets in render()—especially in complex views with a lot of widgets. Let's see how a library we built in chapter 12 can help out with this.

Using declarative widgets

In chapter 12 you built the declarative widgets library, a simple means of creating widgets through HTML attributes—rather than explicit JavaScript-based instantiation. Moving the configuration to HTML from JavaScript can be elegant, and in my opinion, it works well in MVC frameworks like Backbone.

To see what I'm talking about, let's add the declarative widgets library to your example. Currently your template is using the following code to create <button> elements:

```
<% _.each( groceries, function( grocery ) { %>
    ...
    <button>Remove</button>
    ...
<% }); %>
```

To switch to using declarative widgets, you have to move the option configuration currently in JavaScript into HTML5 data-* attributes on the <button>:

```
<% _.each( groceries, function( grocery ) { %>
    ...
    <button data-role="button" data-text="false"
        data-icons='{"primary":"ui-icon-closethick"}'>
        Remove
    </button>
    ...
<% }); %>
```

Here, the data-role attribute tells declarative widgets which widget the markup should become, and the other data-* attributes correspond to button widget options. So data-role="button" tells declarative widgets this should become a button widget, data-text="false" says to set the button widget's text option to false, and data-icons='{"primary":"ui-icon-closethick"} says to set the button widget's icons option to {"primary":"ui-icon-closethick"}.

Notice that for options that are objects—in this case, the icons option—the declarative widgets library requires the corresponding HTML attribute be valid JSON. Both the keys of the object must be enclosed in double quotes. So both data-icons="{'primary':'ui-icon-closethick'}" (single quotes around the key) and data-icons="{primary:'ui-icon-closethick'}" (no quotes around the key) aren't valid options when using declarative widgets.

Now that you have the HTML attributes in place, you need to use it. The declarative widgets library exposes a single enhance() jQuery plugin method, and all you need to do is call it in render():

```
render: function() {
    this.$el
        .html(this.template({ groceries: this.model.toJSON() }))
        .enhance();
}
```

> **NOTE** You can view the declarative approach to this example at http://
> jsfiddle.net/tj_vantoll/Y5BRP/.

Notice that you're not explicitly instantiating any widgets here. The single call to enhance() finds all elements with a data-role attribute—specifically, itself and each of its children—and initializes the appropriate widgets on those elements. Although I personally find this approach elegant, it's worth noting that neither the JavaScript-based initialization nor the declarative initialization approaches are correct; it's a matter of personal preference.

Regardless of how you choose to initialize widgets, Backbone's `render()` method is the ideal place to do so, as it's typically the place that HTML is injected into the DOM. With this approach jQuery UI is a nice compliment to Backbone. You can let Backbone handle your data, routing, and views—and let jQuery UI handle the widgets that you need to build your UI.

appendix D
Creating decimal, currency,
and time pickers with Globalize

In chapter 3 we discussed how to use the jQuery UI spinner widget to transform `<input>` elements into basic number pickers. Here, we'll look at more complex usage scenarios of the spinner widget, including how to create decimal, currency, and time pickers.

To make this possible, the spinner widget uses another jQuery project known as Globalize. *Globalize* is a library that handles the formatting and parsing of various data types—strings, dates, numbers, and the like—in numerous cultures around the world. The spinner widget integrates with Globalize's formatting and parsing to make these complex widgets possible. Let's look at how, starting with decimal pickers.

Building decimal pickers

Keeping track of how various cultures handle something as simple as decimals is tricky because you have to know whether the culture use a period (1.23) or a comma (1,23) to delimit whole numbers from fractional numbers. Let's assume you want to get a numeric value from a user that has two digits after the decimal mark. You could start with the following approach:

```
<input id="spinner">
<script>
    $( "#spinner" ).spinner({
        step: 0.01,
        page: 100
    });
</script>
```

This mostly works, but it has two problems. First, the spinner shortens trailing zeros. For instance, the whole number 1 displays as `"1"` rather than `"1.00"`. Second, the spinner doesn't use the correct delimiter based on the user's culture. U.S. users expect to see a value of `"0.25"` to represent one quarter, but most European users expect to see `"0,25"`.

The solutions to these problems lie in two of the spinner widget's options—`cul-ture` and `numberFormat`—which are used in tandem. The `culture` option accepts a Globalize culture. In general, culture codes are shorthand language codes—`"en"` = English, `"es"` = Spanish, `"fr"` = French, and `"de"` = German. The `numberFormat` option controls the format of the data that the spinner should use. The two most common formats are `"n"` for decimal numbers and `"C"` for currency values.

With this in mind, let's see how you can alter your spinner to use these options. Before we look at the code, there's one important thing to note: for space considerations, Globalize and its culture information aren't stored on jQuery's CDN. Therefore, you must download Globalize from https://github.com/jquery/globalize/releases (get version 0.1.1, as that's the version this appendix uses), or from another CDN. Microsoft's CDN has Globalize, and that's what we use in the following listing.

Listing D.1   Creating spinners with decimal values

```
<script src="http://ajax.aspnetcdn.com/ajax/globalize/0.1.1/          Imports Globalize from
    globalize.min.js">                                                 Microsoft's CDN
</script>
<script src="http://ajax.aspnetcdn.com/ajax/globalize/0.1.1/cultures/
    globalize.cultures.js">
</script>                                              Imports Globalize's culture
                                                       data from Microsoft's CDN
<input id="spinner">
<script>
    $( "#spinner" ).spinner({
        step: 0.01,                            ❶ Sets the numberFormat
        page: 100,                                to "n" for a decimal
        numberFormat: "n",                        spinner
        culture: "de"
    });
</script>
```

Sets the ❷ culture to "de" (German)

❶ Sets the numberFormat to "n" for a decimal spinner

This example solves both of your previous issues. Because you set `numberFormat` to `"n"` ❶, the spinner control knows you want to display a decimal value and always displays two decimal digits regardless of the number. You no longer see whole numbers such as `"1"`. Second, because the culture is set to `"de"` (German) ❷, the spinner uses a comma instead of a period to separate whole numbers from fractional numbers.

NOTE Globalize has multiple number formats to handle values with different numbers of decimal digits. For example, `n0`, `n1`, `n2`, and `n3` handle numbers with 0, 1, 2, and 3 decimal digits, respectively. For a full list of the formats Globalize can handle, refer to its documentation.

TIP Don't know the language the user speaks? You can grab that value from `navigator.language` and pass it to the `culture` option.

This updated spinner functionality is shown in figure D.1.

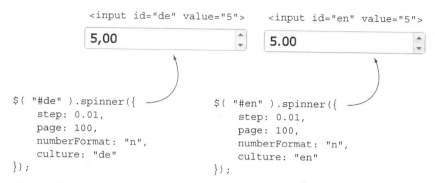

Figure D.1 Display of a decimal picker in the English and German cultures

The cool thing about using Globalize is that you don't have to know which cultures use which conventions for handling decimal numbers—you just need to tell the widget which culture to use and let it handle the rest. The story is similar with another tricky data type: currency.

Building currency pickers

Currency has the same challenges decimal pickers have and more. In addition to knowing the period-versus-comma rules, you also need to know the appropriate currency symbol to use: the United States uses the dollar sign ($), much of Europe uses the Euro (€), Japan uses the Yen (¥), and so forth. In addition, some currencies have niche rules. For instance, the Yen can't have fractional values. (There's no such thing as half a Yen.)

To create a currency spinner, set the spinner's `culture` option to the user's culture and its `numberFormat` option to `"C"`—which stands for currency. The following listing shows a currency spinner that steps by a value of 25.

NOTE You can play with this example live at http://jsfiddle.net/tj_vantoll/ fC5j8/.

Listing D.2 A currency spinner

```
<script src="http://ajax.aspnetcdn.com/ajax/globalize/0.1.1/
    globalize.min.js"></script>
<script src="http://ajax.aspnetcdn.com/ajax/globalize/0.1.1/cultures/
    globalize.cultures.js">
</script>

<input id="spinner" value="1025">
<script>
    $( "#spinner" ).spinner({
        step: 25,
        numberFormat: "C",
        culture: "de"
    });
</script>
```

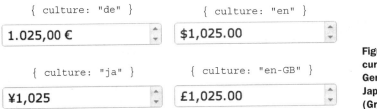

{ culture: "de" }

1.025,00 €

{ culture: "en" }

$1,025.00

{ culture: "ja" }

¥1,025

{ culture: "en-GB" }

£1,025.00

Figure D.2 Display of currency spinners in German, English (U.S.), Japanese, and English (Great Britain)

Figure D.2 shows the display of the spinner in a variety of cultures.

That's really all there is to it. Globalize ensured that the correct delimiters (decimal points vs. commas) were used, as well as the correct currency symbols. It even ensured that the Yen picker didn't display fractional values automatically. If you want to get a consistent value, you call the spinner's value() method. The following code returns 1025 for all the examples in figure D.2:

```
$( "#spinner" ).spinner( "value" );
```

Before leaving the topic of globalization, let's look at another complex data type that Globalize can help with: times.

Building time pickers

Different cultures also have different ways of storing times. Unlike currencies, times are typically displayed in only two ways across cultures: with a 12-hour clock or a 24-hour clock. But even handling these two options can be tricky. The same time could display as 5:00 PM or 17:00 depending on where the user is located, and you don't want to worry about which culture uses which format.

Unlike the earlier examples, the spinner widget doesn't directly integrate time support. But you can add support to the widget with a little extra code. The following listing shows an approach that's used on the jQuery UI demo site. (You can view the demo at http://jqueryui.com/spinner/#time.)

Listing D.3   A timespinner widget

```
$.widget( "ui.timespinner", $.ui.spinner, {          ◁────   ❶ Creates an extension
    options: {                                               of the spinner widget
        step: 60 * 1000,
        page: 60
    },                                                ❷ Defaults the step
    _parse: function( value ) {                          and page options
        if ( typeof value === "string" ) {
            if ( Number( value ) == value ) {        ❸ Converts a
                return Number( value );                  formatted string to
            }                                            a millisecond value
            return +Globalize.parseDate( value );
        }
        return value;
    },
    _format: function( value ) {
```

```
            return Globalize.format( new Date( value ), "t" );
    }
});
```

Converts a
millisecond value to
❹ a formatted string

This code creates a timespinner extension of the spinner widget ❶. (You can read more about widget extensions in chapter 9.) To keep the timespinner's value culture-independent, it's stored as a millisecond value. You'll see how to use the value momentarily, but knowing that the value is millisecond-based explains why you default the step and page options ❷. You set step to 60000 because 60,000 milliseconds is 60 seconds, or one minute. You set page to 60 because there are 60 minutes (or steps) in an hour. This lets the user step the timespinner in one-minute increments (for example, 5:00 → 5:01 or 5:00 → 4:59) and one-hour increments (for example, 5:00 → 6:00 or 5:00 → 4:00).

The rest of the code converts between the millisecond value of the date and the formatted string that displays. The _format() method converts a millisecond value (passed in via the value argument) and converts it to a formatted string using Globalize's format() method ❹. The "t" argument you pass to format() tells Globalize to format the string as a time. The _parse() method does the opposite. It takes a formatted value (for example, "19:00" or "7:00 PM") and returns the millisecond value it represents ❸. It calls Globalize's parseDate() method to normalize the cultural difference.

With this in place, you can create a spinner using the following code:

```
<input id="spinner">
<script>
    Globalize.culture( "en" );
    $( "#spinner" ).timespinner();
</script>
```

Globalize.culture() sets the default culture so you don't have to continuously tell Globalize which culture to use. By setting the culture to "en" (which defaults to U.S. English), you get a spinner that displays a 12-hour clock. Because the timespinner widget uses a millisecond representation under the hood, you can get the value to determine the user-selected time in a culture-agnostic way.

The following logs the spinner's current hour:

```
var spinner = $( "#spinner" ),
date = new Date( spinner.timespinner( "value" ) );
console.log( date.getHours() );
```

This code logs 19, regardless of whether a spinner displays 7:00 PM (in the case of a culture with a 12-hour clock) or 19:00 (in the case of a culture with a 24-hour clock). The most common way of handling this situation is storing the timestamp in a server-side database. Figure D.3 shows the display of a few timespinner widgets. As you can see, the spinner can be initialized with a culture-specific string or a culture-agnostic timestamp.

Although we've focused on spinner integrations, these examples have showcased only some of what Globalize can do. Globalize handles number, decimal, percentage, currency, time, and date formatting in numerous cultures. And Globalize has no

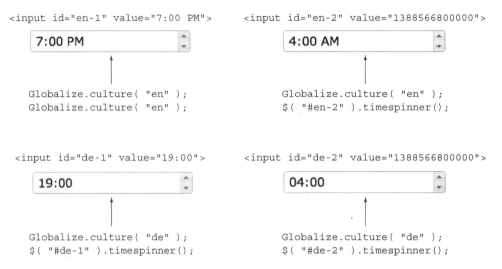

```
<input id="en-1" value="7:00 PM">          <input id="en-2" value="1388566800000">

    7:00 PM                        ▲            4:00 AM                        ▲
                                   ▼                                           ▼

    Globalize.culture( "en" );                 Globalize.culture( "en" );
    Globalize.culture( "en" );                 $( "#en-2" ).timespinner();


<input id="de-1" value="19:00">            <input id="de-2" value="1388566800000">

    19:00                          ▲            04:00                          ▲
                                   ▼                                           ▼

    Globalize.culture( "de" );                 Globalize.culture( "de" );
    $( "#de-1" ).timespinner();                $( "#de-2" ).timespinner();
```

Figure D.3   Display of four timespinner widgets. The top two use the U.S. English culture (which uses a 12-hour clock), and the bottom two use the German culture (which uses a 24-hour clock). The spinners can be initialized with a formatted string—7:00 PM or 19:00—or with a timestamp. In this example, the 1388566800000 timestamp represents a date with its hour set to 4 and its minutes set to 0.

dependencies. You can use it with the jQuery UI widgets if you'd like, but you can use it to parse and format data in an application that doesn't use jQuery at all. If your application is used by multiple cultures, it's worth taking a look at Globalize's documentation at https://github.com/jquery/globalize to see all you can do with it.

Why doesn't datepicker use Globalize?

Unfortunately, datepicker and spinner use different globalization approaches; to use both, you have to import Globalize and its data, as well as datepicker's locale scripts.

Datepicker is some of the oldest code in jQuery UI and therefore hasn't been updated to modern conventions the library is using, such as Globalize. A rewrite of datepicker to use Globalize is in the works; you can monitor the progress at http://wiki.jqueryui.com/w/page/12137778/Datepicker.

appendix E
Contributing to jQuery UI

Believe it or not, the vast majority of work done on jQuery UI (and all other jQuery projects, for that matter) is a volunteer effort. Because of this, and because of the ever-increasing amount of work to do, the jQuery UI project is constantly looking for help from the community.

For whatever reason, when most people decide they want to contribute, they start by heading to the jQuery UI bug tracker and trying to fix bugs. The problem with this is that the vast majority of outstanding bugs aren't easy to fix. When simple bugs come in, we (the jQuery UI team) fix them immediately. It's the tricky ones or the ones that have no clear solution that stick around. And as an aspiring contributor, trying to tackle these problems when you're just getting started is almost always a frustrating experience.

Unless you have a lot of jQuery UI and open source experience, you're better off contributing in another way in the beginning. But don't worry; there's plenty to do! What follows is a list of ways you can help jQuery UI.

> **TIP** The first place to head when you're considering contributing to any jQuery project is http://contribute.jquery.org/. The site goes into explicit detail on how to contribute to all aspects of jQuery. The information in this appendix summarizes these guides specifically for the jQuery UI project.

Help others on the forums, Stack Overflow, and IRC

In my opinion, the best way to start giving back to jQuery UI is by helping others with the library. You can provide support on many venues:

- *jQuery Forum (http://forum.jquery.com/)*—jQuery hosts a forum where users can submit questions and provide feedback on all jQuery projects, including jQuery UI. The jQuery UI–specific forum is located at http://forum.jquery.com/using-jquery-ui.

- *Stack Overflow (http://stackoverflow.com/)*—Stack Overflow is an extremely popular question-and-answer site that you have likely heard of and used. For questions specifically about jQuery UI, see http://stackoverflow.com/questions/tagged/jquery-ui.
- *#jquery on IRC*—jQuery hosts a series of IRC channels on Freenode. The #jquery channel is specifically dedicated for support, aiding people who come to the channel looking for help on using the various jQuery projects. For more information on what IRC and Freenode are, how to join, and how to help, see http://irc.jquery.org/.

These three locations have a lot of people with a lot of questions about jQuery and jQuery UI. The jQuery UI team itself simply can't deal with this quantity. We need people to step in and help.

Besides the altruistic aspect of helping others, answering questions is a spectacular way to learn and get started contributing to the project. You learn about the problems people are having, and by helping to solve them, you learn a lot about the project.

Triage bugs

Bug triage refers to the process of reviewing existing and incoming bug tickets and processing them. This means doing a number of things:

- *Making sure the ticket is valid*—Lots of people submit jQuery UI bugs, but not all the issues are bugs. Oftentimes people come to the bug tracker when they should be going to support venues such as the forums, Stack Overflow, or #jquery on IRC.
- *Checking for duplicates*—When jQuery UI has a bug, it's not uncommon for multiple people to report it. Detecting duplicate bugs can be a tricky and time-consuming task, but finding duplicates is valuable, as an existing ticket may have a long conversation associated with it, or the project may have already decided not to support a given use case. It's even possible that the issue has already been fixed, but has yet to make it into a stable release.
- *Creating a reduced test case*—People sometimes submit issues with a substantial amount of code, which makes it difficult to track down the underlying problem. Reducing the amount of code needed to reproduce an issue—even by a few lines—can be invaluable for debugging. Oftentimes reducing test cases reveals issues that are unrelated to jQuery UI, such as bugs in the browser or jQuery Core.

As with support, triaging bugs takes time and effort, and is a great way to assist the jQuery UI team. The jQuery UI bug tracker is located at http://bugs.jqueryui.com/. You can create an account and comment on any existing issue. If you find duplicate issues, comment about it. If you can create a better test case, comment with the new test case. If you find an old issue that's no longer relevant, comment and let us know.

If you create an account on http://bugs.jqueryui.com/, you can also set up email notifications for new tickets and new comments. With the notifications, you can help the project by responding to tickets and questions as they come in—which lessens the load on the core team.

The same as contributing to the jQuery UI support efforts, it can be tremendously valuable to contribute to the jQuery UI triage effort. Triaging is the easiest way to keep track of the day-to-day activities on the project. In the bug tracker you'll work side by side with the team, because we're also in there managing tickets. And if you're looking to eventually contribute code, the bug tracker can teach you how the team's processes work, and how we address issues as they come in. Over time, you'll learn how to tackle the issues yourself.

Write documentation and maintain the websites

Another great way to get involved with jQuery UI is with its documentation. jQuery UI has a lot of code, and it's important to the project to have comprehensive guides on how to use it. Many people don't realize that all the jQuery UI documentation is open source and available on GitHub (https://github.com/jquery/api.jqueryui.com). So if you notice a problem with the documentation, you can fix it!

And it's not just the documentation source code that's online. All jQuery's websites are open source and available on GitHub as well. For instance, the code behind http: //jqueryui.com is available at https://github.com/jquery/jqueryui.com.

If you'd like to contribute to this process, there's plenty you can do. To start, you can write new documentation for the API site or fix existing API issues (which you can view at https://github.com/jquery/api.jqueryui.com/issues). If you're interested in writing, you can author new articles for the jQuery Learning Center (learn.jquery.com). If you're interested in design, you can help us improve the look of our sites. If you're interested in UX, we'd love help improving the user experience on http://jqueryui.com and http://api.jqueryui.com. For more details on the specifics, see http://contribute.jquery.org/web-sites/.

Write code

Last but not least, you can always contribute code to jQuery UI, but I'll offer one word of warning: if you find an issue with the library, don't jump directly to submitting a pull request with a fix on GitHub. jQuery UI has a number of processes in place to assure consistency and improve the long-term maintainability of the project. We require the following things:

- The issue must have a ticket created on http://bugs.jqueryui.com and a team member must mark the ticket as valid.
- There must be a unit test that verifies the fix being offered works as expected. This is to prevent regressions, where the original issue comes back after some unrelated change.

- Code must adhere to jQuery's JavaScript style guide (http://contribute.jquery .org/style-guide/js/).
- Commit messages must adhere to our guidelines (http://contribute.jquery.org/ commits-and-pull-requests/).

Don't let this discourage you. These best practices help maintain the high quality of the jQuery UI codebase, and adhering to them doesn't require much more effort. Sometimes it's helpful to look at a list of previous commits to get an idea of how the team does it. You can see the latest commits to jQuery UI at https://github.com/ jquery/jquery-ui/commits/master.

If you're completely unfamiliar with GitHub, http://contribute.jquery.org/ commits-and-pull-requests/ is a great place to start as it walks you through all the processes necessary to contribute code to any jQuery project. For more specific information on jQuery UI, such as how to run the unit tests, see its GitHub repository at https://github.com/jquery/jquery-ui.

Ask for help

If all else fails, feel free to join #jqueryui-dev on IRC and say that you want to help. The jQuery UI team hangs out in that channel, and we can help point you in the right direction. The team also has a weekly meeting in #jquery-meeting if you want to find us all in one place. The meeting is open to anyone, so feel free to lurk in the channel or introduce yourself. For meeting times, as well as meeting notes from previous meetings, see http://meetings.jquery.org.

My own journey with jQuery UI

I started in jQuery UI when a previous employer switched to using jQuery UI from a another UI library (which I won't name), and I instantly fell in love. The ease of performing complex tasks made the library a joy to work with.

Eventually, I wanted to do more. Learning and playing with jQuery and jQuery UI became my fun side project I worked on at home. I created a Stack Overflow account and started answering jQuery UI questions. (My username is tj-vantoll, if you're curious.) As I learned more about the library, I decided I wanted to try to contribute code.

I found the bug tracker and tried to fix a few bugs, but I mostly failed. But I did start commenting on the tickets. Even if I couldn't fix the bug, I'd comment on what I thought the problem was. I'd reduce the test case to show the least amount of code needed to recreate the problem. I did this a lot. And as I gained confidence and experience, I started to do more. Along with some other team members, we methodically went through each ticket open in the bug tracker. We found hundreds of bugs that were either duplicates or no longer relevant.

(continued)

In the process, I found bugs that I could fix. I had learned the processes and had met a few of the team members. My first code contribution to jQuery UI was a patch to fix resizable dialogs in Opera 11; it was included in version 1.8.18. As I learned more about the code, I could tackle harder problems, such as complex bugs and new features.

My experience with jQuery UI has been invaluable. I've met many awesome people and traveled to amazing places. Seeing how the jQuery UI team works, and coding alongside them, made me a far better developer. Doors that were previously closed have opened. I've even had the opportunity to write a book!

appendix F
Polyfilling HTML5
with jQuery UI

In chapter 3 we discussed a number of new HTML5 elements and compared them to jQuery UI widgets. In summary, we concluded that the major advantages of the HTML5 controls are

- Ease of use.
- Dependency-free.
- The browser controls how data is inputted. (For instance, you get optimized mobile keyboards.)

The main detriments are

- You have little control over the display.
- They handle only trivial use cases.
- Only some browsers support the controls.

In chapter 3 we also had a brief discussion of which control you should use. To start, if you have a nontrivial usage scenario, you have no choice but to use JavaScript-based widgets like those of jQuery UI. If you want to build a calendar where the user can't select weekends, you have to use a JavaScript-based datepicker—as that's impossible to build with an `<input type="date">`. Conversely, if you have a trivial use case, using the HTML5 controls makes sense. You get mobile-optimized keyboards without the need to introduce a JavaScript-based control.

No matter how simple the use case, the native controls still have one big problem: browser support. Although some HTML5 elements are now widely implemented, others—like `<input type="date">`—are only present in a handful of browsers. But you have another option. If you want to use HTML5 controls today, and you don't want to worry about browser support, you can use jQuery UI to polyfill the native functionality.

Using polyfills

A polyfill is a piece of code that adds a feature when it's not natively available on the platform. In our case, the native features we're interested in are the new HTML5 elements and input types. To use a polyfill, first you need to detect whether the feature is supported on the platform the code is running on. The following shows a function that does a feature detect for native date support and uses the jQuery UI datepicker if native support isn't available:

```
<input type="date">
<script>
    function dateSupport() {                              ❶ Detects and
        var input = document.createElement( "input" );     returns whether
        input.setAttribute( "type", "date" );              the browser
        return input.type == "date";                       supports a date
    };                                                     <input>

    if ( !dateSupport() ) {
        $( "input[type=date]" ).datepicker({             ◁─── Converts all
            dateFormat: "yy-mm-dd"   ◁────                     date inputs to
        });                                               ❷ datepickers
    }
</script>                                    Uses the HTML5-
                                          ❸ specified format
```

Here you first test whether the browser natively supports `<input type="date">` ❶. The check creates an `<input>` element and changes its `type` to `"date"`. If the browser recognizes the `type`, it remains `"date"`; otherwise, the browser uses `"text"`.

If the browser supports the native picker, you're done. If not, you convert all date inputs to datepicker widgets ❷. The default date format of HTML5's date input differs from datepicker's default. The final step is to set the datepicker's `dateFormat` option equal to the specification's format (`"yy-mm-dd"`) ❸; that way, you get a consistently formatted date server-side, regardless of whether the browser natively supports the control.

If you run this code in a browser that supports `<input type="date">`, such as Chrome, you'll see no visual change. In browsers with no support, such as Internet Explorer or Safari, you'll see a jQuery UI datepicker control being used. The cool thing with polyfills is you don't have to care about which browsers support the element and which don't. You can rest assured that all users can use a calendar to enter a date.

To make all this possible, though, you need to accurately detect whether the user's platform supports a given feature. And doing that can be hard; how would you know that dynamically creating an `<input>`, changing its `type` to `"date"`, and seeing if the change took would be an accurate test for `<input type="date">` support? Luckily, there's a library that aggregates these tests for us.

Using Modernizr

Modernizr is a library that does exactly what we're looking for: it detects HTML5 and CSS3 features in the user's browser. It takes the guesswork out of testing for features. With Modernizr, instead of writing your own test for `<input type="date">` support, you can check the `Modernizr.inputtypes.date` property.

You can download either a development or production version of Modernizr from http://modernizr.com/. The development version is perfect for development, as it has every check that Modernizr uses. But each of those checks takes time, and doing every check has the potential to take a long time—especially for users with slower browsers. Before using Modernizr in production, it's a best practice to create a production build with only the checks that you need. For your purpose, you need two checks: Input Attributes and Input Types. Figure F.1 shows Modernizr's download builder with these two checks selected.

Select additional check boxes if you need them in your application, but the input attributes and types are all you need to polyfill HTML5 elements using jQuery UI. Now that we have Modernizr in place, let's look at the polyfills jQuery UI makes possible.

NOTE You can view all these polyfills in action at http://jsfiddle.net/tj_vantoll/A62Jt/. If you view this in Chrome you'll see all native controls—as it supports all the controls we'll discuss—but if you open it in an older browser, such as Internet Explorer 8, you'll see jQuery UI widgets used in place of the native controls.

TIP There's more to Modernizr than the handful of feature detects we need here. To learn more, check out Modernizr's documentation at http://modernizr.com/docs/.

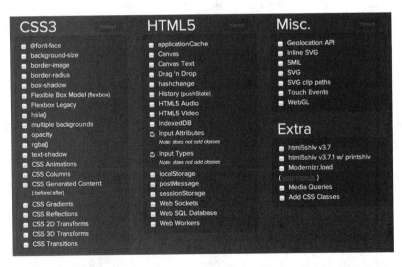

Figure F.1   Modernizr's production build tool at http://modernizr.com/download/. The two checks we need for polyfilling HTML5 elements are Input Attributes and Input Types.

> ### How to know which browser supports what
>
> Polyfills remove the need to keep a mental list of which browsers support which features, but sometimes it's nice to see a list. If all the browsers you support already have the native control, you have no need to use a polyfill. In my experience, the best resource for up-to-date browser feature support documentation is http://caniuse.com/, which lists support by feature in a number of tables. Support documentation on the features we'll discuss in this appendix is at the following URLs:
>
> - `<input type="date">`—http://caniuse.com/#search=input-date
> - `<input type="number">`—http://caniuse.com/#feat=input-number
> - `<input type="range">`—http://caniuse.com/#feat=input-range
> - `<progress>`—http://caniuse.com/#feat=progressmeter
> - `<datalist>`—http://caniuse.com/#feat=datalist

Polyfilling `<input type="date">` with datepicker

The first polyfill you'll use is also the easiest, because you've written it before. In the following code, the only difference is your feature check for `<input type="date">` support, which is now a check of `Modernizr.inputtypes.date`.

```
if ( !Modernizr.inputtypes.date ) {
    $( "input[type=date]" ).datepicker({ dateFormat: "yy-mm-dd" });
}
```

Polyfilling `<input type="number">` with spinner

The code to polyfill native number `<input>` elements is similarly simple:

```
if ( !Modernizr.inputtypes.number ) {
    $( "input[type=number]" ).spinner();
}
```

Like the spinner widget, native `<input type="number">` elements support the `min`, `max`, and `step` attributes to customize their behavior. But because the spinner widget automatically reads those attributes, they're supported here without any extra work.

Polyfilling `<input type="range">` with slider

The range polyfill is a bit more complex, because—unlike datepicker and spinner—a slider must be created on a `<div>` rather than an `<input>`. You need to create an extra element for each `<input>` you need to polyfill. The approach you'll take is shown here:

```
if ( !Modernizr.inputtypes.range ) {
    $( "input[type=range]" ).each(function( index, input ) {    ❶ Creates a new
        var input = $( input ),                                     <div> to use
        slider = $( "<div>" ).slider({                              as the slider
            min: parseInt( input.attr( "min" ), 10 ) || 0,
            max: parseInt( input.attr( "max" ), 10 ) || 100,
            value: parseInt( input.attr( "value" ), 10 ) || 50,
            step: parseInt( input.attr( "step" ), 10 ) || 1,
```

Transfers the `<input>` element's attributes ❷

```
        change: function( event, ui ) {
            $( this ).prev( "input" ).val( ui.value );      ⟵┐   Keeps the
        }                                                         <input>
    });                                                           in sync with
    slider.insertAfter( input );    ⟵┐                      ❸   the slider
    input.hide();    ⟵┐           Appends the
});                  Hides the   slider after
}              ❺   <input>    ❹  the <input>
```

In browsers without `<input type="range">` support, you loop over each `<input
type="range">`. For each one, you create a new `<div>` and initialize a slider widget on
it ❶. (Remember that you can't initialize a slider widget on the `<input>` itself.)

To ensure the `min`, `max`, `step`, and `value` attributes on the `<input type="range">`
are reflected on the `<div>` you create, you must explicitly read each attribute from the
`<input>` and set them as an option of the slider ❷. If the attribute isn't present on the
`<input>`, you pass the HTML5 range input's default (`0` for `min`, `100` for `max`, `50` for
`value`, and `1` for `step`).

At the end of the loop, you append the newly created `<div>`—which is now a
slider—directly after the `<input>` ❹, and then hide the `<input>` itself ❺. You leave
the `<input>` around so that it's included in form submissions, but you hide it so the
user sees only the slider. To make sure the hidden `<input>` maintains the correct
value, the last thing you do is add a `change` event callback that keeps the `<input>` element's `value` and slider's `value` in sync ❸.

Polyfilling <progress> with progressbar

Next, we'll look at the `<progress>` element, which is an element that displays the
progress of a task, much like the progressbar widget. The `<progress>` element has two
custom attributes—`max` and `value`—that work exactly like the progressbar's `max` and
`value` options.

> **TIP** You can learn more about the `<progress>` element at http://css-
> tricks.com/html5-progress-element/.

Modernizr core doesn't have a check for the `<progress>` element. Modernizr's download site has a noncore (Modernizr's wording) set of checks—which includes a `<prog-
ress>` test—but because the check is a single line we'll just include it inline:

                                    Checks for <progress> support ❶

```
if ( document.createElement( "progress" ).max === undefined ) {      ⟵┐
    $( "progress" ).each(function() {
        var progress = $( this ),              Transfers the <progress>  element's  ❸
        div = $( "<div>" ).progressbar({           attributes to the progressbar
            max: parseInt( progress.attr( "max" ), 10 ) || 100,
            value: parseInt( progress.attr( "value" ), 10 ) || false
        });
      progress.replaceWith( div );      ⟵┐
    });                                 Replaces the <progress>
}                                    ❹  with the <div>
```

Creates a new
`<div>`, and
initializes a
progressbar
widget ❷

To check for native <progress> support, you create a new <progress> element, and see if it has a max property defined **❶**. For browsers with support, you're done, but for browsers without support, you then loop over each <progress> element. Like the previous slider example, you then create a new <div>. This time you initialize the new <div> with a progressbar widget **❷**—using the custom max and value attributes from the original <progress> element **❸**. For consistency with the HTML5 specification, if the user doesn't provide a value attribute, you default the value option to false, which creates an indeterminate progressbar. Finally, you replace the initial <progress> element with the progressbar <div> **❹**.

Polyfilling <datalist> with autocomplete

The last polyfill we'll look at is one for the <datalist> element. If you haven't seen a <datalist> before, it's a quick way of building an autocomplete that's native to the browser. You can associate a <datalist> with an <input> by having the <input> element's list attribute match the <datalist> element's id attribute. The following builds a basic autocomplete:

```
<input type="text" list="projects">
<datalist id="projects">
    <option>jQuery</option>
    <option>jQuery UI</option>
    <option>jQuery Mobile</option>
</datalist>
```

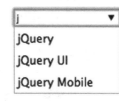

Figure F.2 shows the display of this <input> after the user types a "j".

Figure F.2 Display of a <datalist> element in Chrome on OS X

> **TIP** You can learn more about what <datalist> elements are and when to use them at http://msdn.microsoft.com/en-us/magazine/dn133614.aspx.

For browsers that don't support the <datalist> element, you'll use the following code to polyfill with an autocomplete widget:

```
if ( !Modernizr.input.list ) {                               ❶ Loops over all text inputs
    $( "input[type=text][list]" ).each(function() {               with a list attribute
        var options,
            listAttribute = $( this ).attr( "list" ),
            datalist = $( "#" + listAttribute );            ❷ Finds the <input>
        if ( datalist.length > 0 ) {                           element's associated
            options = [];                                       <datalist>
            datalist.find( "option" ).each(function() {
                options.push({ label: this.innerHTML, value: this.value });
            });
            $( this ).autocomplete({ source: options });   ❹ Builds the
        }                                                       autocomplete
    });                                                         widget
    $( "datalist" ).remove();              ❺ Removes all
}                                             <datalist> elements
                                              from the DOM
```

❸ Loops over each <option>

You loop over each text <input> that has a `list` attribute—which indicates that it's associated with a <datalist> **❶**. For each one, you find the <input> element's <datalist> by searching for an element that matches the <input> element's `list` attribute **❷**.

> **NOTE** You can associate <datalist> elements with other types of <input> elements such as date <input>s, and even color <input>s. To see some in action, visit http://demo.agektmr.com/datalist/. For our purposes, we'll only polyfill the text-based version.

Assuming you find a <datalist> (that's what the `datalist.length > 0` check is for), you loop over each of its <option> elements and add them to an array of options **❸**. You then initialize an autocomplete widget on the <input> **❹** and use that option's array as the autocomplete's `source` option. Because you don't need the <datalist> elements to stick around in browsers that don't support them, you remove all of them from the DOM **❺**.

With this code in place, you can use <datalist> elements and rest assured that the user receives an autocomplete control in all browsers. There's one last quirk to be aware of, though. Internet Explorer versions < 10 don't recognize <option> elements unless they're in <select> elements, meaning, this polyfill doesn't work in those versions. Specifically, the `datalist.find( "option" )` check returns nothing. The workaround for this is a bit convoluted, but it works. The fix is using Internet Explorer conditional comments to add <select> elements in the <datalist> element:

```
<datalist id="projects">
    <!--[if IE]><select><!--<![endif]-->
    <option>jQuery</option>
    <option>jQuery UI</option>
    <option>jQuery Mobile</option>
    <!--[if IE]><select><!--<![endif]-->
</datalist>
```

All browsers other than Internet Explorer versions < 10 completely ignore the conditional comments, including versions 10 and above. (Conditional comment support was removed from Internet Explorer in version 10.) But in versions before 10, the comments are interpreted, and a <select> is created. Having a <select> present temporarily is all you need for your polyfill to read the <option> elements. The polyfill removes the <datalist> elements entirely at the end anyway.

So unfortunately, if you need to support Internet Explorer < 10 and you want to use <datalist> elements, you must use conditional comments that insert a <select> around <option> elements for these older browsers. With this in place, the polyfill works as expected.

index

RELATED MANNING TITLES

JQuery in Action, Third Edition
by Bear Bibeault, Yehuda Katz,
   Aurelio De Rosa

   ISBN: 9781617292071
   475 pages, $44.99
   January 2015

Extending jQuery
by Keith Wood

   ISBN: 9781617291036
   312 pages, $44.99
   August 2013

Single Page Web Applications
JavaScript end-to-end

by Michael S. Mikowski, Josh C. Powell

   ISBN: 9781617290756
   432 pages, $44.99
   September 2013

Secrets of the JavaScript Ninja
by John Resig, Bear Bibeault

   ISBN: 9781933988696
   392 pages, $39.99
   December 2012

For ordering information go to www.manning.com